contemporary
museums

architecture
history
collections

Imprint

The Deutsche Bibliothek lists this publication in the Deutsche Nationalbibli-
ographie; detailed bibliographical information can be found on the internet at
http://dnb.ddb.de

ISBN 978-3-03768-067-4
Copyright 2011 by Braun Publishing AG
www.braun-publishing.ch

1st edition 2011

Editorial coordination:
Editorial office van Uffelen
Editorial staff:
Jennifer Kozak, Lisa Rogers, Sarah Schkölziger
Translations:
Cosima Talhouni

Graphic design:
Michaela Prinz
Layout:
Christine Maier, Sarah Schkölziger, Georgia van Uffelen

contemporary museums

Chris van Uffelen

architecture
history
collections

CONTENTS

CONTEMPORARY MUSEUMS **PREFACE**

Contemporary Museums presents the sanctuaries of museums, according to the meaning of the Greek word Museion, the origin of the word museum. Just like the magnificent temples erected in antiquity, today's museum buildings are temples of our bourgeois enlightened cultural ideals — temples of art, language, technology, seafaring, literature, history, nature, but also memorials for less pleasurable memories. This is because museums usually deal scientifically with the past and prepare it for presentation to contemporary audiences. However, by archiving, documenting, analyzing and presenting, they also create a track from the past to the future and have to already select today the future presentation of the past according to criteria that cannot be objectively finally established.

The most elaborate "exhibit" into which museums today invest for their future is their own museum building, whether a new building, or the extension or renovation of existing buildings. It expresses a great deal about the self-image of the institution and its respective scientific discipline and can come across as self-confident, elegant, casual, experimental, spectacular, introverted or extroverted. In addition, there can be a focus on its role in the urban setting or on the collection, while the layout can favor scientific research, presentation of canonized cultural assets, or the discovery of new topics. Following the example of Gehry's Guggenheim Museum in Bilbao, today's museums are also tourist attractions. While this tendency started to emerge in the 1970s already, the "Bilbao effect" was nevertheless a turning point of modern museum construction. In line with the different self definitions and the multitude of collections, the design styles are equally versatile. Every current stylistic variation is also found in museum buildings, as the construction of these temples of enlightened societies is one of the most popular genres among architects. There are several reasons for that. The responsible bodies, whether public or private, want to appear interested in culture and subsequently invest in a prestigious building. For architects, a museum building offers a much larger scope of free design and interpretation than, for example, an office building built with the same budget. Even though the actual staging of the exhibition is often the responsibility of specialists, the architects determine the general setting and the outward appearance of the collection.

In this aspect, museum buildings resemble medieval reliquaries — no matter how objectively unimpressive the relic, the precious reliquary surrounding it determines its image. This is because an unimpressive appearance does not mean that the relic was unimportant, but its importance could only be made visible by the elaborate reliquary that contained it. Similarly, in the urban context, a museum building points out a collection well worth seeing, separates it from its trivial surrounding, since art museums are often located in the historic district or the periphery of the 19th century city center. This is why the renovation and restructuring measures of these museums often have to cope with limited building plots. At the same time, new museum buildings are also preferably built in inner cities where they have to fit in and find their place in a frequently heterogonous setting.

The many examples in *Contemporary Museums* of renovated and expanded older buildings are an indication that museum buildings have always been given great importance. As the collection rooms of churches or secular dignitaries, early museums can be considered the successors of treasure rooms, but also of the less magnificent study rooms of the private collections of scholars. More accessible to the general public were the galleries of castles that initially were colonnades with their own iconography and later also contained collections of busts or sculptures or paintings, often portraits.

For example, the Uffizi in Florence (1559 until approx. 1581, Giorgio Vasaris), which was still an administration building at the time, already contained a gallery in the 16th century for exhibiting paintings and the Medici also brought some sculptures to this location. The most famous of these galleries that was turned into a museum is certainly the Grande Galerie des Louvre (1595–1608, by Jacques Androuet de Cerceau and Louis Métezeau). It once extended 420 meters to connect the castles of Louvre and Tuileries, and its redesign into a museum was being considered since 1776. However, the first public new museum building was the Ashmolean Museum built 1678–1683 possibly by Christopher Wren, which contained the collection of curiosities bequeathed by Elias Ashmole to the University of Oxford in 1677. Born out of the Renaissance-era encyclopedic view of the world, curiosity cabinets included everything from art to natural objects, ethnography and history — anything that seemed wondrous and noteworthy at the time. The house of Sir John Soane in London gives an indication of such collections today. They are at the core of the great variety of museum genres known at present. The chambers filled with wonders in which the collectors gathered all these objects were usually packed right up to the ceiling and not very well organized. Anything curious seemed worthy of collecting — little thought was given whether genuine or fake. The scholar, physician, and Catholic bishop Paolo Giovio (approx. 1483–1552) was the first to use the word museum in the title of his collection of portraits of statesmen and war heroes in Como. In addition, even before the Ashmolean there were publicly accessible collections, such as the private collection of the Amerbach cabinet including the legacy of Erasmus von Rotterdam containing 100 paintings by Hans Holbein the Younger alone, which was purchased by the city of Basel in 1661 and made publicly accessible in 1671. This collection constitutes the core of the public museums of the Basel-Stadt canton. However, the majority of museums were established in the 18th and 19th centuries when private collections were made accessible to a wider audience. In 1734, the Uffizi were also finally converted into a museum and in 1753 the British Museum in London was established as the first public museum based on the collection of the physician Sloane. After Louis-Etienne Boullée already created his famous plans for a "Museum of France" in 1783, the Louvre was converted into a museum in the course of the French Revolution, an approach followed by several other countries. For example, the Prado in Madrid (1819) adopted the structure of a palace. The building of the British Museum by Robert and Sydney Smirke (1847) is placed as a four-wing complex around an open courtyard. Friedrich Schinkel's Altes Museum in Berlin, consisting of two courtyards flanking a domed hall, became the model for many museum buildings. In the post-modern era, this design was again adopted by James Stirling with now opened rotundas. During the Historicism era, large stairways became as crucial as the courtyards and many museum sought to revive a style in line with their exhibits that they considered national. At the turn of the 19th to the 20th century, many special museums or collections dedicated to a single artist emerged. In the early 20th century, art galleries were a new type of museum buildings derived from the exhibition buildings developed by the emerging industrial society. Large halls were created in the late 18th and early 19th century, the most famous of which is certainly Joseph Paxton's Crystal Palace in London of 1851 and in contrast the 1900 Grand Palais in Paris for commercial and industrial exhibitions. Starting in the 17th century, similar art exhibitions became common (Salon de Paris) and many counter-movements emerged in opposition to the official art shows (Impressionism, Secession). In 1863, the first Salon des Refusés, the salon of the rejected artists, was held in the rather grand Palais de l'Industrie of 1855, similar to the official Salon de Paris. While the established art scene was always aimed at conventional museum buildings, until the first third of the 20th century, the Avant-garde increasingly liked the simple constructional setting of a hall, with partitions where required. Of course, the general change in preference towards the sobriety of the International Style contributed to this. This tradition culminated in Ludwig Mies van der Rohe's Neue Nationalgalerie in Berlin (1968). Its exterior is a temple with (not quite) antique proportions of eight cross-shaped steel pillars and a flat roof (with metope sections and coffers) on a stepped substructure (stereobate), behind the wide tower gallery, the cella is entirely made of glass and contains 4,900 square meters of undivided exhibition space. In the late 20th century, due to lack of space or for the protection of buildings, witnessed an increase in underground exhibition buildings (I.M. Pei's Louvre extension) and museums increasingly turned into exhibition objects or cultural signposts of the city (Museum Embankment in Frankfurt/Main). The present highlight of this trend was the erection of the Guggenheim museum in Bilbao by Frank O. Gehry, where the objective for the museum was to render the city quarter, the city, and even the entire region ready for the future. *Contemporary Museums* also begins with this building, which additionally stands for the emerging trend of museum chains. The book features new museum construction since Bilbao. In addition, it also tells the history of the collections, explains the origin of the collection core and points out key exhibits. It presents the background of the museum, also including collections of natural and cultural history, as well as its educational or conservational aims.

Thus, *Contemporary Museums* not only presents master works of modern architecture by many famous architects along with lesser known buildings that are distinguished by extraordinary solutions. The 170 unique buildings of the book reflect the possibly most interesting and diverse architectural assignments of our times along with the social relevance of the collections containing the cultural heritage of humanity along with the geological and biological heritage of our planet.

americas

ALERIA ADRIANA VAREJÃO_BRAZIL_BRUMADINHO_MUSEU DO PÃO_BRA
IL_ILÓPOLIS_FUNDAÇÃO IBERÊ CAMARGO_BRAZIL_PORTO ALEGRE
USEÉ RODIN_BRAZIL_SALVADOR_ESTAÇÃO DA LUZ: MUSEU DA LÍNGU
ORTUGUESA_BRAZIL_SÃO PAULO_MUSEU EXPLORATÓRIO DE CIÊNCIAS D
NICAMP_BRAZIL_SÃO PAULO_ART GALLERY OF ALBERTA _CANADA_EDMON
ON_CANADIAN MUSEUM OF NATURE_CANADA_OTTAWA_MUSÉE NATIONAL DE
EAUX-ARTS IN QUEBEC_CANADA_QUÉBEC_GARDINER MUSEUM_CANADA_TO
ONTO_MUSEO DE LA MEMORIA Y LOS DERECHOS HUMANOS_CHILE_SANTIAGO
USEO DEL CHOCOLATE NESTLÉ_MEXICO_MEXICO CITY_MUSEO TAMAYO_MEX
CO_MEXICO CITY_HORNO3: MUSEO DEL ACERO_MEXICO_MONTERREY_MU
EO CAO _PERU_EL BRUJO_AKRON ART MUSEUM_USA_AKRON (OH)_LIGHT
ATCHER AT THE WHATCOM MUSEUM _USA_BELLINGHAM (WA) _MUSEUM O
INE ARTS_USA_BOSTON (MA)_BOSTON CHILDREN'S MUSEUM_USA_BOS
ON (MA) ELEANOR AND WILSON GREATBATCH PAVILION USA BUFFALO (NY)

BRAZIL_BRUMADINHO **GALERIA ADRIANA VAREJÃO**

ARCHITECTS: RODRIGO CERVIÑO LOPEZ_**COMPLETION:** 2008 **TYPE:** ART AND NATURE MUSEUM_**GROSS FLOOR AREA:** 558 M² **PHOTOS:** LEONARDO FINOTTI

THE ARCHITECTURE

This project aimed to recompose the site's topography and insert an artificial element: a regular block of reinforced concrete. The building structure consists of an irregular retaining wall that defines the space on the ground floor and bears the weight of the block through two beams at its deepest part and through four columns integrated into the wall at the center. The building was also conceived as a spiral path that connects two different levels of the park, alternating moments of contraction/passage and expansion/exhibition: a narrow promenade in the water pond; the small square plaza; the ground floor; the stairs; the first pavement; the ramp; the terrace; the bridge, and vice versa.

THE COLLECTION

The Galeria Adriana Varejão was commissioned to host a sculpture and a polyptych by Brazilian artist Adriana Varejão. Visitors move through the building, following a spiral path that leads them between two levels of the park in which it is situated. Adriana Varejão is a Brazilian artist who works in various disciplines including painting, sculpture, installation and photography. Born in 1964, Varejão is one of Brazil's leading contemporary artists. Much of her artwork considers the effects of colonialism and art history and illusion are themes she also often represents. Varejão's work is featured in exhibitions and collections worldwide, including the Guggenheim Museum in New York, The Tate Modern in London and the Museum of Contemporary Art, San Diego. She aims to address ideas of cultural identity, inherited culture and the many complex constructions that create individual identity. The fundamental chords of Varejão's artistic work range from the deeply private and personal to the historically universal, from reflections on the body and the blood to critical examinations of archeology and race. The famous work "Azul Branca em Carne Viva" (Blue, White, and Living Flesh) depicts a torn and cracked section of a wall. It also contains a mixture of the two surfaces the artist most often makes use of: tile and flesh.

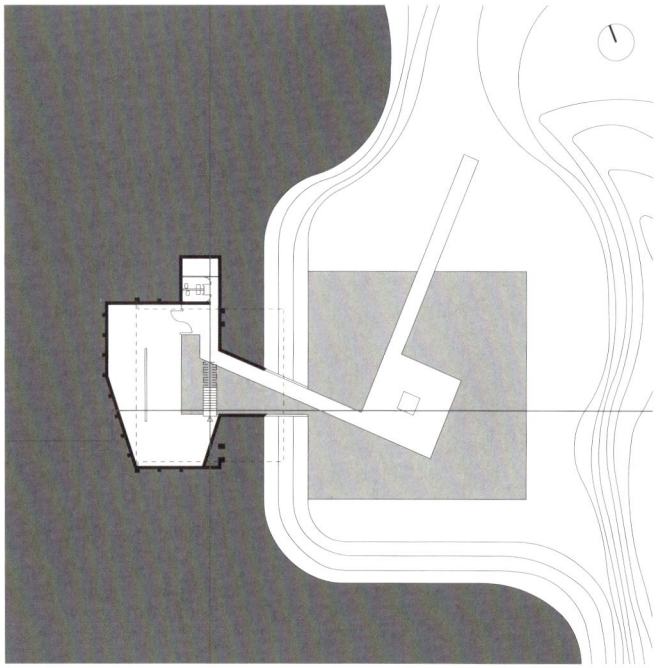

left: Ground floor plan_Bench on roof terrace_Concrete ramp_Exhibition hall ground floor. right: Façade_Exhibition hall first floor_Staircase in glass box.

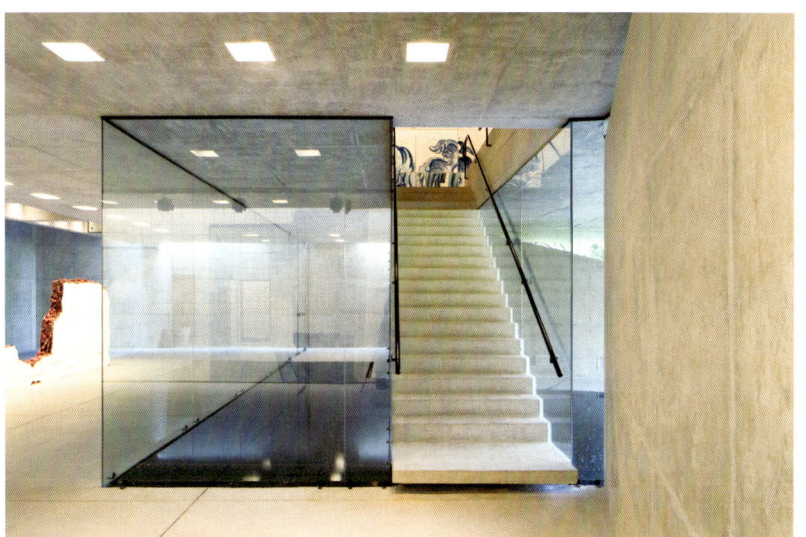

BRAZIL_ILÓPOLIS **MUSEU DO PÃO**

ARCHITECTS: BRASIL ARQUITETURA STUDIO WITH ANSELMO TURAZZI_**COMPLETION:** 2007_**ORIGINAL BUILDING:** 1910 **TYPE:** CULTURE MUSEUM_**GROSS FLOOR AREA:** NEW BUILDINGS 320 M²; OLD MILL 340 M²_**PHOTOS:** NELSON KON, SÃO PAULO

THE ARCHITECTURE

The Bread Museum constitutes the foundation of the "Route of the Taquari Valley Mills". The 100-year-old Ilópolis Mill was intended for demolition after the miller's death, but was revived as the venue of the Bread Museum and bakery workshop. The new constructions were inspired by the old ones with the raw pine boards used as formwork for the exposed concrete, irreversibly leaving their marks upon the new buildings. Museography and architecture are in sync in this project. The first exhibits consist of the old mill itself, the structure of the new volumes, their urban scale, the way the light enters, the materials, the timber walkways, the supports for the exhibits, and the exhibited pieces themselves, have been collected from the region.

THE COLLECTION

The idea for this museum was first conceived in 1996, when a group of entrepreneurs and scholars had the idea of establishing a Bread Museum in Serra da Estrela, Portugal. Time was then taken to construct a suitable building for the Museu do pão and to collect objects and artifacts for the exhibitions. The museum finally opened its doors in September 2002. The main goal of the museum is to preserve and display to the public the traditions, history and art of Portuguese bread making. For this purpose, the museum has four rooms. The first introduces "The Cycle of Bread" and shows the traditions of the ancient land and the traditional ways of bread making. The second exhibition space displays: "Political, Social and Religious Bread", cataloguing the history of Portuguese bread through the centuries. The third area, "The Art of Bread", shows several forms of art, inspired by bread and bread making, and the fourth, "The Pedagogical Room", is a room for children, where the cycle of bread is explained with light effects, music and animation. This space also contains an area where children can bake their own bread. Bread and other gastronomic products are sold in the Old Village Shop, and the library offers a wealth of bread-baking knowledge. In addition to its permanent collection, the museum hosts temporary exhibitions, literary meetings and cultural meetings.

left: Sketch_Interior of old mill_New bar in the old grain store_Garden with mill stones. right: Concrete and timber columns in the museum_Passageway outside of bakery workshop_Entrance_New and old building side by side.

BRAZIL_PORTO ALEGRE **FUNDAÇÃO IBERÊ CAMARGO**

ARCHITECTS: ÁLVARO SIZA VIEIRA_**COMPLETION:** 2008_**TYPE:** ART MUSEUM_**GROSS FLOOR AREA:** 11,834 M²_**PHOTOS:** LEONARDO FINOTTI

THE ARCHITECTURE

The first building by Álvaro Siza in Brazil, the museum rises as a four-floor white concrete structure above the quayside with a single-floor wing extending along it. The high building section is structured by ramps that increasingly separate from the basic building as they grow in height. They continue on the inside, developing the galleries as exhibition spaces. Elevator shafts are located on the narrow sides where the ramps separate from the basic structure. This way, the ramps enclose an internal as well as an external atrium. The low wing includes the reception, museum shop, and service facilities.

THE COLLECTION

The Iberê Camargo Foundation was opened in 1995, with the vision of conserving and sharing the work of Iberê Camargo, one of Brazil's best-known artists. The museum hosts exhibitions, workshops and seminars, aiming to encourage reflection upon contemporary art practices. Iberê Camargo was born in Restigna Seca and spent much of his life in Rio de Janeiro. He created an extensive body of work during his lifetime, which includes paintings, drawings and prints. Camargo never allowed himself to be connected with specific groups or cultural movements. Camargo passed away in 1994, leaving a collection of around 7,000 works. His artwork was bequeathed to his wife Maria Coussirat Camargo, but is now part of the foundation's collection. One of the museum's temporary exhibitions features work by prominent Latin American artist, León Ferrari. His work includes art of many different forms as he created ceramics, sculptures, collages and paintings. The museum also recently celebrated the 50th anniversary of the founding of Brasilia with several exhibitions illustrating different approaches to the city as well as contemporary artwork of local artists.

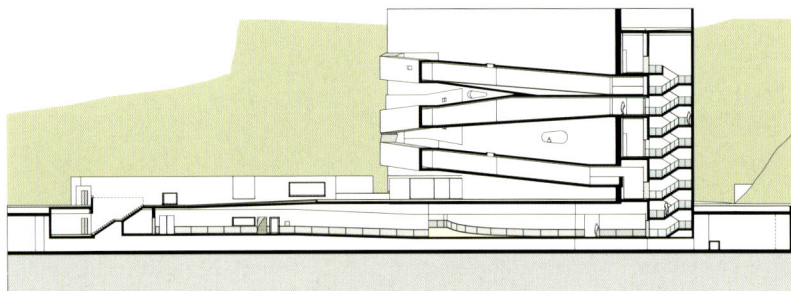

left: Section_Exterior_Inner Atrium. right: Galleries_Outside atrium_Sculptural form.

BRAZIL_SALVADOR **MUSÉE RODIN**

ARCHITECTS: BRASIL ARQUITETURA STUDIO_**COMPLETION:** 2006
ORIGINAL BUILDING: BAPTISTA ROSSI, 1912_**TYPE:** ART MUSEUM
GROSS FLOOR AREA: 3,055 M²_**PHOTOS:** NELSON KON, SÃO PAULO

THE ARCHITECTURE

This museum is the only branch of the Rodin Museum in Paris. It consists of an old manor and a contemporary section, made of concrete, glass, and timber elements. This section is used for travelling exhibitions, while the palace halls and the garden with its rich tropical vegetation, feature the work of the famous French sculptor. Built in 1912, the former residence was renovated and adjusted to its new function, and a small auditorium was added to the top floor. The new back section, made of concrete, serves as a vertical circulation shaft, while concrete also links the two buildings. Neither oppressive nor submissive, the new volume creates a subtle dialogue with the old, the two separated by a time span of 100 years.

THE COLLECTION

Auguste Rodin was a French sculptor and painter who was a pioneer of modern sculptures. He was born on November 12, 1940 in Paris. From 1870 he received his first public assignments. In the years 1875 and 1876 he went on a study trip to Italy where he saw the works of Michelangelo. He subsequently returned to Paris where he dedicated his time increasingly to the study of Gothic cathedrals. In 1889, he was commissioned to create a statue of the French writer Victor Hugo. Rodin depicted him naked and surrounded by muses. However, his model was rejected and the statue remained thus uncompleted. In the following years he always gathered young writers and artists around him. For example, in 1905/1906 Rainer Maria Rilke became his secretary. At the World Fair in Paris in 1900, a total of 171 of his works were presented. In 1907, Rodin set up his studio at the Hôtel Biron, which today contains France's Musée Rodin. The sculptor died in Paris on November 17, 1917. His most prominent works include "The Thinker," "The Burghers of Calais" and "The Kiss." Some of his key works were repeatedly presented in individual exhibitions in Brazil. Their success led to the idea of creating an extensive project about the artist. This resulted in today's Rodin Museum in Salvador.

left: Sketch of the new staircase and lift shaft_New Access into old building_New access lift shaft by night_Concrete bridge connecting old and new. right: New building_Sculpture garden_Main exhibition room.

BRAZIL_SÃO PAULO

ESTAÇÃO DA LUZ: MUSEU DA LÍNGUA PORTÚGUESA

ARCHITECTS: PAULO A. MENDES DA ROCHA ARQUITETOS ASSOCIADOS, PEDRO MENDES DA ROCHA ARQUITETOS ASSOCIADOS_**COMPLETION:** 2005_**TYPE:** LANGUAGE MUSEUM_**GROSS FLOOR AREA:** 7,088 M²
PHOTOS: LEONARDO FINOTTI

THE ARCHITECTURE

From the start, the intervention over this peculiar building aimed at organizing a large-scale visiting route, separated from the preexisting metropolitan transportation system access, which occupies the main central lobby. Two symmetrical patios on the western and eastern sides were designed as sheltered lobbies, providing the main access to the museum. New elevators were located inside the decorative towers at the building's four corners. These take groups of visitors to the third floor to the start of the tour (auditorium, language plaza, terrace), the second floor (grand gallery, influences gallery, timeline), and finally down to the first floor (temporary exhibitions, research, administration).

THE COLLECTION

The Museum of Portuguese Language is an interactive Portuguese language and linguistics development center, situated in São Paulo, Brazil. The project was conceived in 2001 and the city of São Paulo was chosen as the site for this museum because of its status as the largest Portuguese-speaking city in the world. The museum is housed in the Estação da Luz railway station, which was selected because it is a place where thousands of non-Portuguese–speaking immigrants arrived into the city and were introduced to the language for the first time. The museum's objective is to create a living representation of the Portuguese language, aimed both at native speakers and at language students, as its interactive displays aid non-native speakers to discover more about the language they are learning. Visitors can discover more about the origins of the Portuguese language, as Italian, French, German and Spanish all had a strong influence on its development. The museum also targets the Portuguese speaking population, made up of peoples from many regions and social backgrounds, but who still have not had the opportunity to gain a broader understanding of the origins, the history and the continuous evolution of their language.

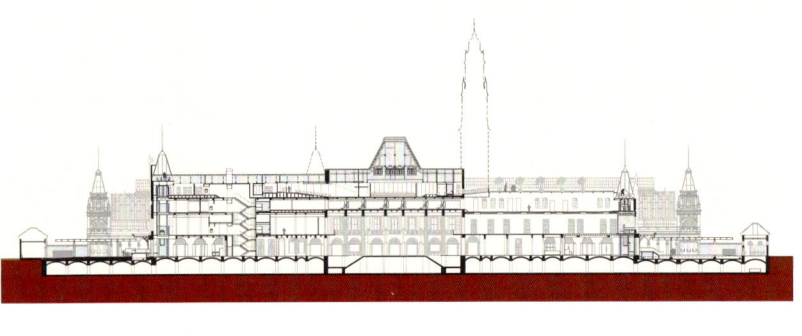
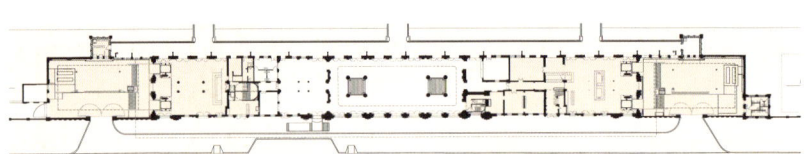

left: Section and ground floor plan_Tower seen through new roof_Court_Entrance. right: Exhibition_Mediawall_Interactive exhibition.

BRAZIL_SÃO PAULO **MUSEU EXPLORATÓRIO DE CIÊNCIAS DA UNICAMP**

ARCHITECTS: CORSI HIRANO ARQUITETOS_**COMPLETION:** ONGOING
TYPE: SCIENCE MUSEUM_**GROSS FLOOR AREA:** 5,370 M²
PHOTOS: COURTESY OF THE ARCHITECTS

THE ARCHITECTURE

As science is the basis and main purpose of this museum project, it was appropriate for the design to reveal the relation between mankind and nature. While, in that respect, science is concerned with understanding what exists, architecture deals with what still does not exist — presenting itself as an opportunity of expression of mankind and its creation, constituting a phenomenon of its own. Based on this, two absolute conditions are presented: the singular location where the project will be placed and the universal institution to be manifested. A relationship needs to be established between the new museum and the landscape to provide the project with a territorial aspect. It is a museum that observes and is observed.

THE COLLECTION

The Exploratory Science Museum opened in 2006 as part of the State University of Campinas, one of the most important universities in Brazil. The Mission of the Exploratory Science Museum is to promote scientific discovery, in a space that values learning, companionship and social interaction. In general terms, the museum aspires to showcase and promote the most recent scientific trends and aims to become a center of excellence, recognized throughout the world. The institution's main focus is on educating students and school children but curators also try to address adults and those who are no longer within the formal education system. The museum's exhibitions are centered round integrative themes, encouraging discussion of issues related to technology, social topics, the environment and the ethical impacts of scientific development. Visitors are encouraged to actively take part in hands-on exhibitions and experiments. As a cultural center, open to all educational institutions and beyond, the museum seeks to create a forum for debates on issues involving the relationship of the region to the broader cultural, technological and scientific panorama.

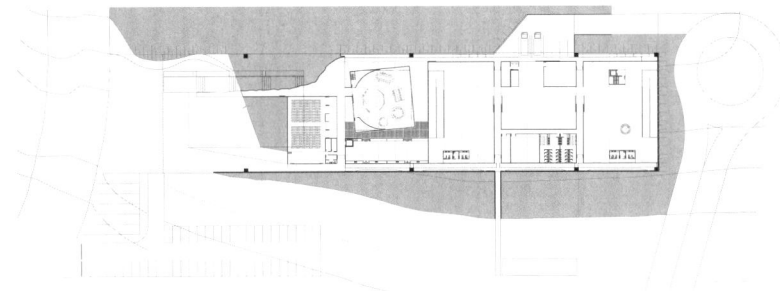

left: Ground floor plan_Museum access. right: Reception area_Time space square.

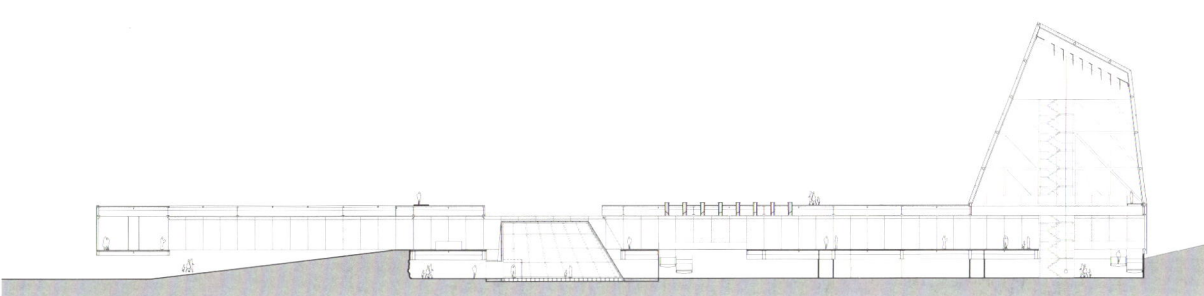

left: Permanent exhibition. right: Section_Temporary exhibition_Night air view.

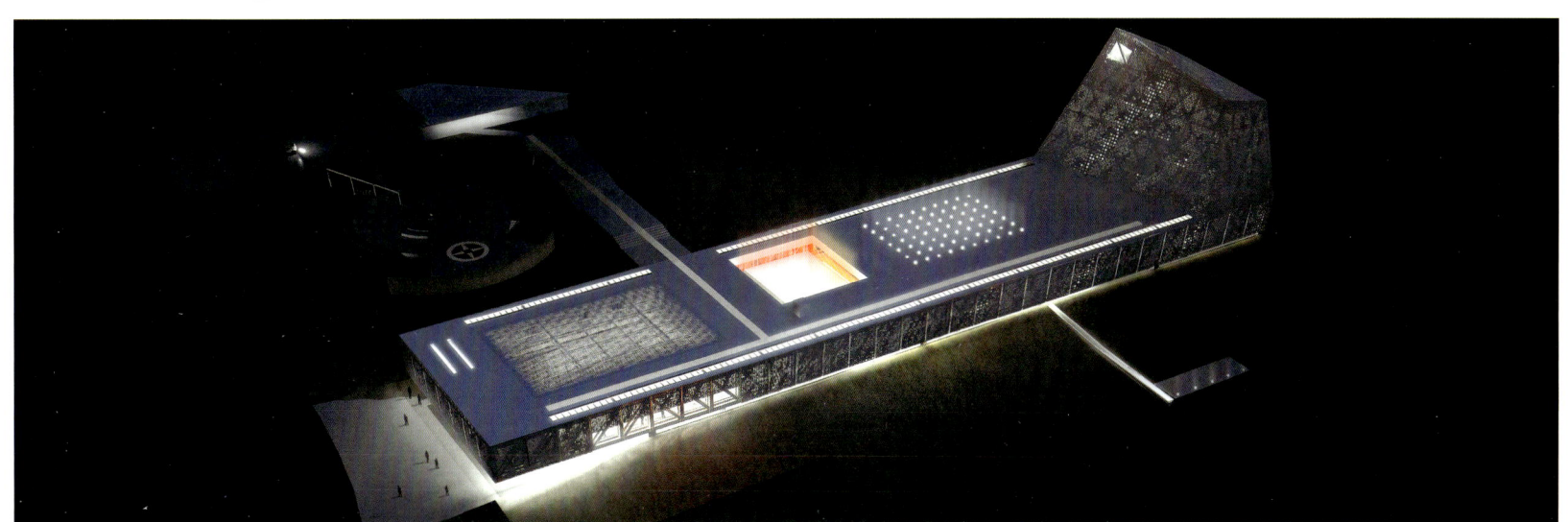

CANADA_EDMONTON **ART GALLERY OF ALBERTA**

ARCHITECTS: RANDALL STOUT ARCHITECTS, INC_**COMPLETION:** 2010_**ORIGINAL BUILDING:** DON BITTORF, 1968_**TYPE:** ART MUSEUM_**GROSS FLOOR AREA:** 7,800 M²_**PHOTOS:** RANDALL STOUT, LOS ANGELES (26 B. L., B. R.), ROBERT LEMERMEYER, CALGARY (27, 28, 29)

THE ARCHITECTURE

The new Art Gallery of Alberta celebrates its culturally prominent location on Sir Winston Churchill Square. The original 1960s structure is transformed by the addition of new public spaces and galleries, a unified education wing, café, and offices. The plan and vertical organization of the five-level design resolves the distinct areas dedicated to art, food service, staff, and visitors with great clarity, while connections to underground train lines and pedestrian paths improve urban connectivity. Crafted of painted zinc, high performance glazing, and stainless steel, the building is extraordinarily durable in the northern climate. Sinuous forms are used for intuitive orientation to galleries and public spaces as well as dramatic lighting.

THE COLLECTION

Founded in 1924, under the name The Edmonton Museum of the Arts, the Art Gallery of Alberta is the oldest cultural institution in Alberta and has a collection of over 6,000 works of art. The collection includes both historical and contemporary paintings, as well as sculptures and photographs by Canadian and international artists. The gallery underwent major changes in 2005, when, after an international architectural competition, Randall Stout Architects Inc was selected to design a new building for the museum. The new facility opened in 2010, providing new amenities and vastly increased exhibition space. The most important donation bequeathed to the museum to date, was the gift of 100 major Canadian paintings and sculptures donated by the Poole Foundation. The artworks included pieces by Emily Carr and Maurice Cullen. The museum's temporary exhibitions cover a range of current and relevant themes.

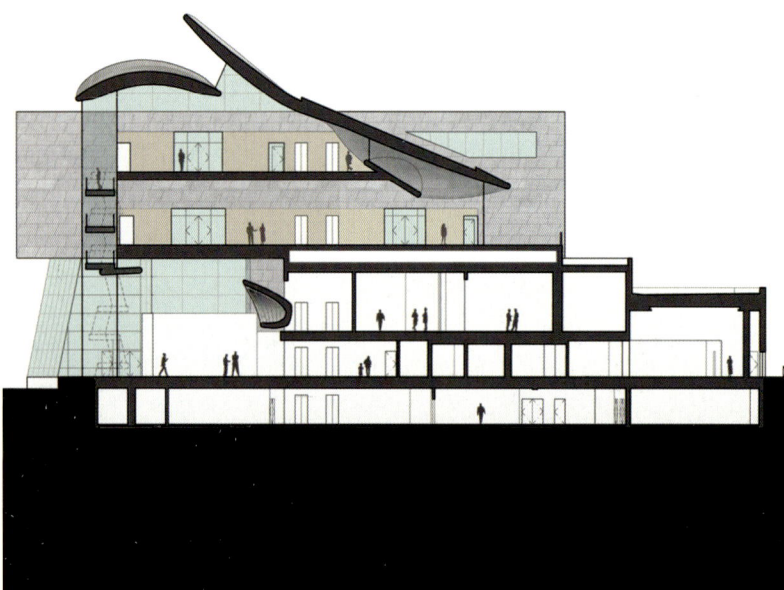

left: Section_Main atrium_Main atrium. right: View from Sir Winston Churchill Square.

left: Interior detail. right: Sketch_Gallery great hall_Third floor atrium.

CANADA_OTTAWA **CANADIAN MUSEUM OF NATURE**

ARCHITECTS: PADOLSKY, KUWABARA, GAGNON JOINT VENTURE ARCHITECTS_**COMPLETION:** 2010_**ORIGINAL BUILDING:** DAVID EWART, 1912_**TYPE:** NATURE MUSEUM_**GROSS FLOOR AREA:** 23,225 M² _**PHOTOS:** TOM ARBAN PHOTOGRAPHY, TORONTO

THE ARCHITECTURE

This museum was the first purpose-built museum in the country. The revitalization project showcases the original heritage building, using contemporary architecture to generate a dialogue between the past and the present. The glazed lantern element restores the original proportion of the main entrance and creates a super-sized display unit. Inside the lantern, a new butterfly stair initiates a continuous loop of movement around the atrium and through all four levels of the museum. Gallery spaces were reconfigured to offer a balance of black boxes and day-lit galleries. The southern terrace creates an indoor/outdoor venue for casual and formal gatherings.

THE COLLECTION

Housed in Ottawa's Victorian Memorial Museum, the Canadian Museum of Nature is a natural history museum dedicated to exploring all aspects of the relationship between human society and nature, from gardening to genetic engineering. The museum was built in the early 1900s, but its foundations were unfortunately laid on unstable clay. This eventually resulted in the demolition of a tall tower at the front of the building due to its ever-increasing instability and the prediction that the foundations would not support the weight of the museum. The structure became more instable when work on it began. Shifting foundations resulted in rocks falling on some members of the construction crew, forcing a temporary halt in the work. In 1916, a fire destroyed the majority of the central buildings on Parliament Hill. Following this disaster, the Victoria Museum building became the temporary home to the House of Commons. In 1968, the National Museum, as it was then called, was split into the National Museum of Nature and the National Museum of Civilization. In 1989, the Museum of Civilization moved location and the Nature Museum was able to occupy the whole of the Victoria Museum building.

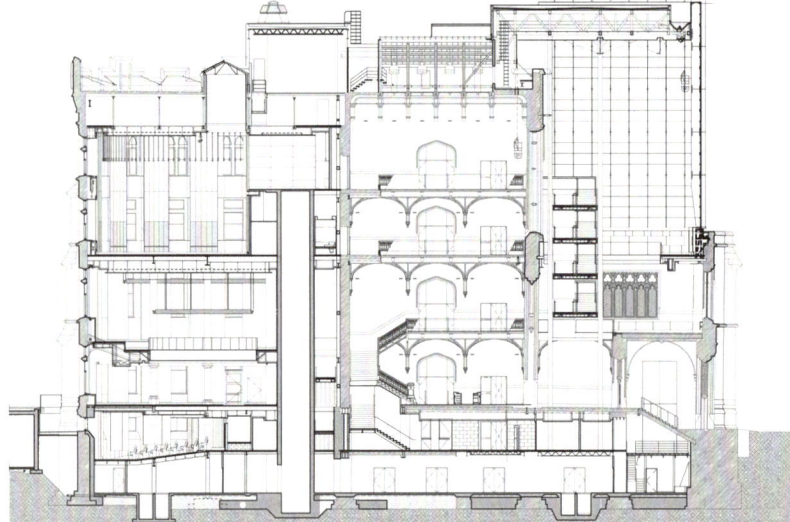

left: Section_View down Metcalfe Street_Ceiling of the lantern. right: Main entrance.

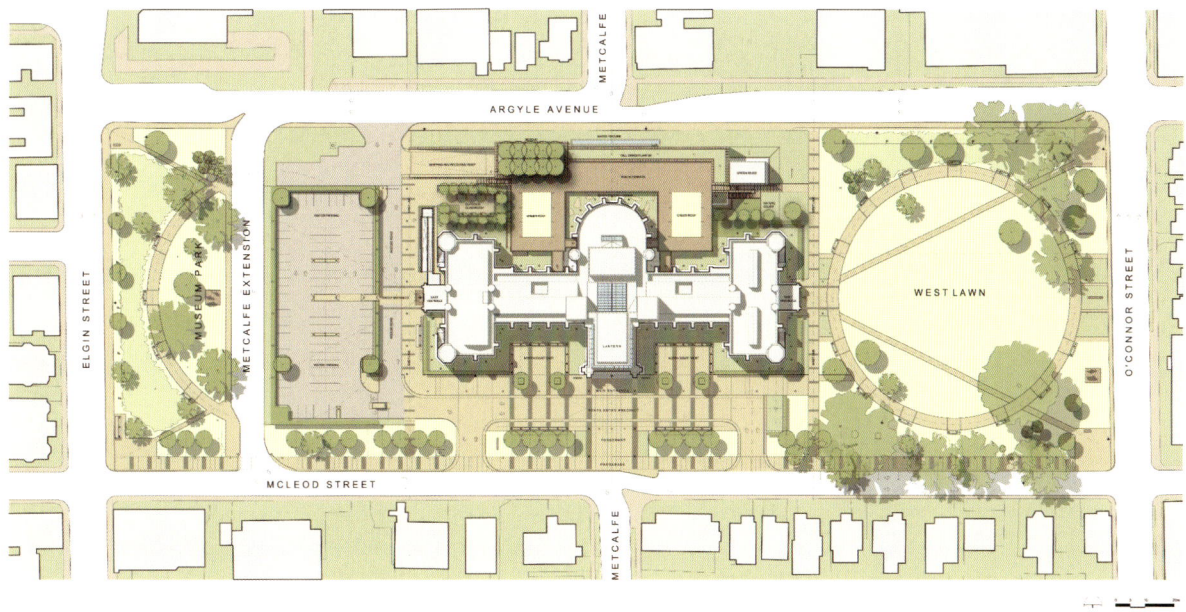

left: Butterfly stair. right: Site plan_Lantern and the butterfly stair_Atrium with heritage window
Atrium ceiling and butterfly stair.

CANADA_QUEBEC **MUSÉE NATIONAL DES BEAUX-ARTS DU QUÉBEC**

ARCHITECTS: OFFICE FOR METROPOLITAN ARCHITECTURE (OMA)
COMPLETION: 2013_**ORIGINAL BUILDING:** WILFRID LACROIX, 1933
(GÉRARD-MORISSET BUILDING), CHARLES BAILLAIRGÉ, 1867
(CHARLES-BAILLAIRGÉ BUILDING), 1991 (GRAND HALL)_**TYPE:**
ART MUSEUM_**GROSS FLOOR AREA:** 15,000 M²_**PHOTOS:** OFFICE
FOR METROPOLITAN ARCHITECTURE (OMA) (34 B. L.),
COPYRIGHT OMA; IMAGE BY LUXIGON (34 B. R., 35 A., B.)

THE ARCHITECTURE

The architects stacked the required new galleries into three volumes of decreasing size to create a cascade ascending from the park towards the city. The proposal aims to weave together the city, park and museum. The stacking creates a 14 meter high Grand Hall, sheltered under a dramatic cantilever. The Grand Hall serves as an interface to the Grande-allée, an urban plaza for the museum's public functions, and a series of gateways into the galleries, courtyard and auditorium. The new building is connected to the Pavilion Charles-Baillairge (1867), a former prison, by a tunnel. The building offers a mixture of gallery spaces that lead the visitor, as if by chance, to the rest of the museum complex.

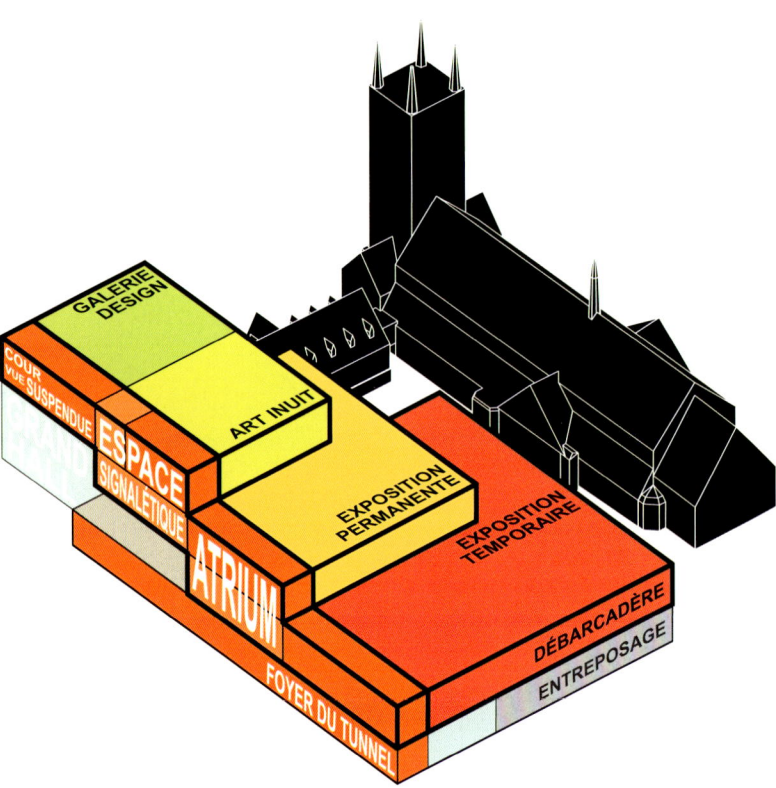

THE COLLECTION

The three separate galleries, consisting of the Gérard-Morisset Pavilion, Charles-Baillairge Building, and the Grand Hall, make up the body of this museum, accommodating a wide variety of exhibitions. The original museum building, the 1933 Gérard-Morisset Pavilion, houses much of the museum's permanent collection. The largest exhibition of Québec art in existence fills eight galleries of this building, including works produced from the beginning of the colony to the present. The museum also houses a permanent exhibition of works by famed Québec abstract expressionist and surrealist Jean-Paul Riopelle, such as his L'Hommage à Rosa Luxemburg, made up of 30 individual paintings that include spray-painted outlines of birds and tools. The second exhibition space, the Charles-Baillairge Building, was for more than a century the City Prison and one cellblock has been left intact to show visitors the nature of prison life in the 1900s. The museum also hosts a collection of Inuit art, collected by Raymond Brousseau, whose major collection was acquired by the museum in 2005. Much of the collection has been produced in the last 20 years, and 285 works from the 2,635-piece collection are on display.

left: Programmatic axonometry_Translucent model_Night exterior. right: Bird's eye view_Atrium.

CANADA_TORONTO **GARDINER MUSEUM**

ARCHITECTS: KUWABARA PAYNE MCKENNA BLUMBERG
ARCHITECTS_**SCENOGRAPHY:** PS DESIGN_**COMPLETION:** 2006
ORIGINAL BUILDING: KEITH WAGLAND, 1984_**TYPE:** ART MUSEUM
GROSS FLOOR AREA: 4,300 M² _**PHOTOS:** EDUARD HUEBER /
ARCHPHOTO INC., NEW YORK (36 B.L., B. R., 37 B. L.), SHAI GIL
PHOTOGRAPHY, TORONTO (37 A.), TOM ARBAN PHOTOGRAPHY,
TORONTO (37 B. R.)

THE ARCHITECTURE

This museum is Canada's only museum dedicated to ceramic arts. The renewal is one of the projects of Toronto's Cultural Renaissance that corresponds directly to the client's brief of accommodating growing collections and educational and research programs. It involved the complete reorganization of the entrance and vertical circulation and the addition of a third floor to provide a column-free temporary exhibit space as well as a restaurant and multi-purpose space with access to the southern-facing terraces. The former pink granite cladding was stripped and the structure was re-wrapped in polished buff Indiana limestone and black granite.

THE COLLECTION

The Gardiner Museum offers visitors an intimate look at ceramics, one of the world's most universal forms of art and material culture. It is also one of the world's oldest forms of culture that can be traced back more than 11,000 years to Asia and the Middle East. Because of the long-lasting nature of fired clay, pottery keeps a detailed record of the development of civilization. In most cultures ceramics were used at different social levels and served many different purposes; such as eating and drinking, religious practice, and household decoration. Even today, practically every home contains ceramic objects. The museum's collection, donated in 1984 by the museum founders George and Helen Gardiner, has since been enhanced by other major gifts. As a result, the collection now consists of more than 3,000 pieces, ranging from ancient American vessels to the fine porcelains of Asia and Europe and further, to dynamic contemporary pieces. The breadth of the collection provides a glimpse into the development of the ceramic process, decoration and shape. The museum's permanent collection is often complimented by special exhibitions, which focus on specific themes within ceramic works, such as Chinese blue and white pottery and its impact on the world.

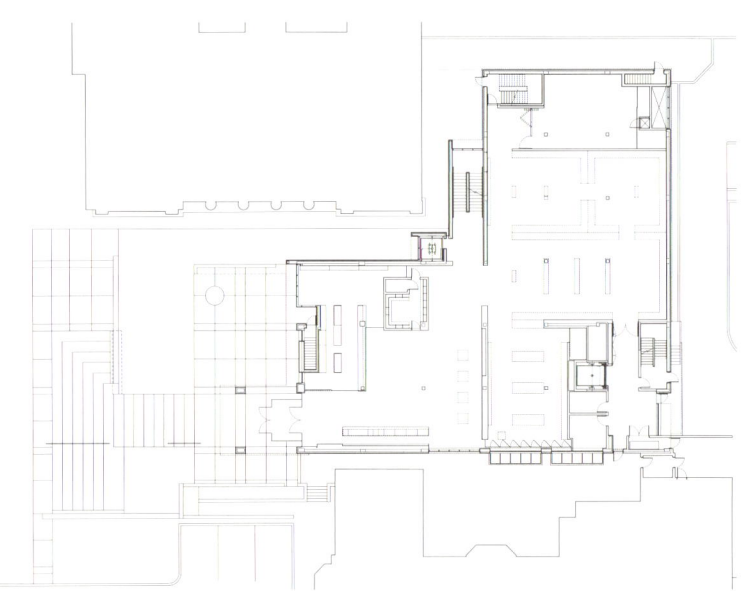

left: Ground floor plan_Main lobby and gift shop_Third floor flexible space. right: Front façade_Permanent collections gallery_Clay studio.

CHILE_SANTIAGO **MUSEO DE LA MEMORIA Y LOS DERECHOS HUMANOS**

ARCHITECTS: ESTUDIO AMERICA DE ARQUITETURA – CARLOS DIAS, LUCAS FEHR AND MARIO FIGUEROA_**COMPLETION:** 2010_**TYPE:** HISTORY MUSEUM_**GROSS FLOOR AREA:** 10,900 M²
PHOTOS: CRISTÓBAL PALMA, SANTIAGO

THE ARCHITECTURE

Taking downtown Santiago's tradition into account, the project proposed the construction of a new area incorporating the city's residents' diversity and democracy. The result is a generous space, full of possibilities and pathways. There are two conceptual areas: the Exposition Beam and the Base. The first is elevated and open at both ends — representing history, information, and the act of living memory. The Base, at first deep as a mine, is the place where research, production, and knowledge are placed. Inside, glass boxes create a necessary transparency, vivacity; and fragmentary memory, all coming together to create the repertory of a nation's idiosyncrasies.

THE COLLECTION

The Museo de La Memoria Y Los Derechos Humanos, (Museum of Memory and Human Rights), was officially opened in January 2010 by President Michelle Bachelet. This museum is a memorial to the violations and atrocities committed against the people of Chile between 1973 and 1990, when the country was controlled by General Pinochet. The museum aims to keep the atrocities committed during Pinochet's dictatorship very much in the public consciousness, therefore preventing the horrific events from being forgotten. The institution aspires to promote tolerance, solidarity, and diversity. It does so, in part, by promoting educational programs, designed to encourage knowledge and reflection. The story of the country's history is told through objects, documents and files together with audio and visual displays. Oral and written testimonies are also exhibited within the museum, including wrenching testimonies, documents, letters, personal objects and art by prisoners, as well as the photos of the 1,197 people who disappeared during the crackdown by security forces on Pinochet's opponents. The exhibits include a small metal bed that victims were tied to before receiving electrical shocks.

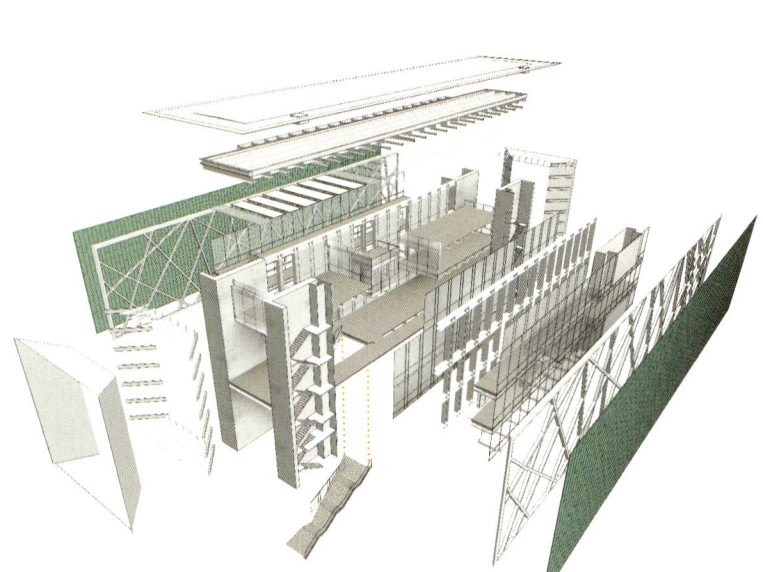

left: Exploded view_Free span of the exposition beam_The city viewed from the inside. right: Access ramp_Plaza de la Memoria.

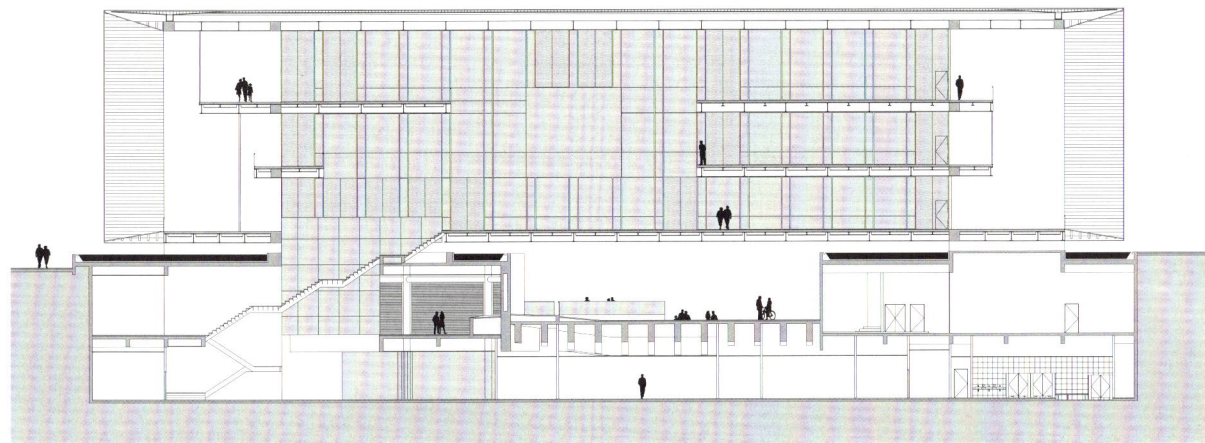

left: Exposition beam and Plaza de la Memoria. right: Section_Access to the exposition_Main exposition room.

MEXICO_MEXICO CITY **MUSEO DEL CHOCOLATE NESTLÉ**

ARCHITECTS: ROJKIND ARQUITECTOS_**COMPLETION:** 2007
TYPE: COMPANY MUSEUM_**GROSS FLOOR AREA:** 634 M²
PHOTOS: © PAÚL RIVERA / ARCHPHOTO.COM

THE ARCHITECTURE

Nestlé's chocolate factory in Mexico City near Toluca was in need of an inner tour path for visitors to witness the production of chocolates. The architects created the first chocolate museum in Mexico, along with a 300 meter long façade along the motorway as the new image of the factory. The first phase involved a space that would serve as the main entrance for children to offer them the most pleasant experience and to start their voyage into the choco-late factory as soon as they enter this playful yet striking space. From there they can proceed to the reception area, the theater that serves as preparation for the Nestlé experience, the store or museum shop, and the passage to the tunnel inside the old existing factory.

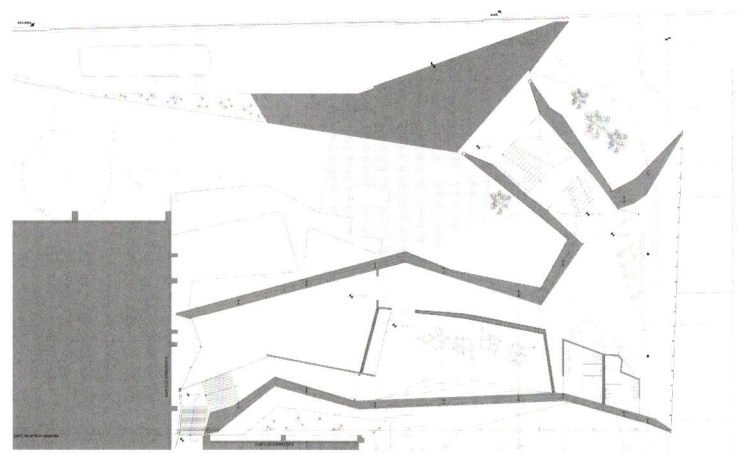

THE COLLECTION

The success of the corporation is based on the efforts of the Frankfurt native Henri Nestlé (1814-1890). After completing his professional training in pharmacy, he moved to Switzerland where he gained professional experience and passed the exam as a pharmaceutical assistant in 1839. From 1843 he produced and sold alcoholics and oils, later on also carbonated mineral water and various lemonades. In the fall of 1867, he achieved a break-through in the food industry with his invention of infant formula. The manufacturing of infant formula revolutionized the market of child nutrition and established the global success of Nestlé that still lasts to this day. Nestlé switched his company's focus to the production of the infant formula, which saved the lives of many infants that could not be breast-fed and could not digest other nutrition substitutes. In the course of seven years, he sold 1.6 million cans of infant formula in 18 countries across all continents. In addition to powdered milk, Nestlé also produced condensed milk, which became the basis of the first (Swiss) milk chocolate produced by Daniel Peter. In 1875, Nestlé sold his company to his flour supplier Pierre Sanual Roussy, who took over the "Farine Lactineé Henri Nestlé" name. At age 60, Henri Nestlé retired from public life and settled into his house in Glion, which is today known as "Villa Nestlé."

left: Ground floor plan_Exterior view. right: Entrance_Exterior view_Stairs.

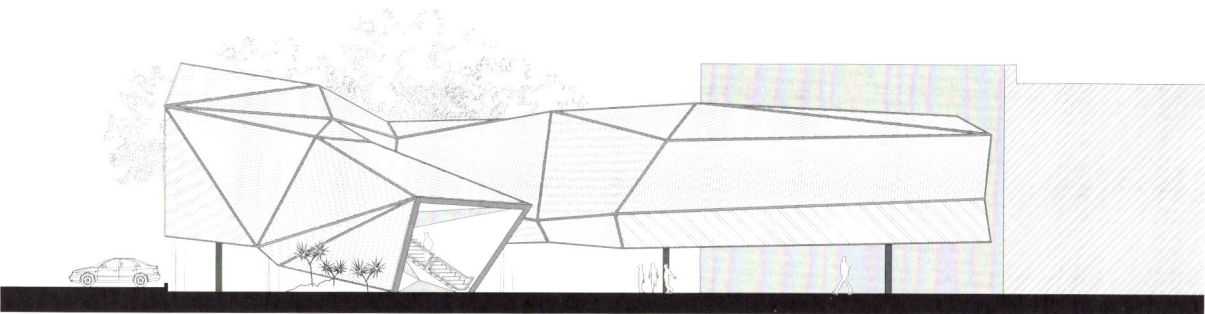

left: Stairs. right: East elevation_Exterior view, detail_Interior_Seating.

MEXICO_MEXICO CITY **MUSEO TAMAYO**

ARCHITECTS: BIG AND MICHEL ROJKIND_**COMPLETION:** ONGOING_**TYPE:** ART AND CULTURE MUSEUM_**GROSS FLOOR AREA:** 2,250 M² _**PHOTOS:** COURTESY OF THE ARCHITECTS

THE ARCHITECTURE

This museum, situated upon a steep hillside in Atizapan, will serve as a nucleus of local, regional, and international education and culture. Named after the Oaxacan-born artist Rufino Tamayo, the very strong and symbolic shape of the cross is a direct interpretation of the client's preliminary program studies that defined the museum's optimal functionality. The main concept is an "opened box" that unfolds, opens and invites the visitors inside. Exterior and interior spaces overlap to provide the best environment possible for each function, and optimal climatic performance. The permeable brick, shading façade combines good daylight penetration with sun protection and plenty of natural ventilation.

THE COLLECTION

The Museo Tamayo presents exhibitions of the work of contemporary international artists, as well as exhibitions of the works of Rufino Tamayo and collections of Columbian art, previously owned by Tamayo himself. Rufino Tamayo is an artist of great importance to the Mexican culture. One of the main goals of the museum is to collect and preserve pieces by Tamayo and prevent them from falling into the hands of illegal artifact traders. Tamayo believed that his work expressed the traditional Mexico, and because of this belief he refused to portray or follow the changing political trends that many of his contemporaries did. Many interesting stories surround Tamayo and his works, one of which involves the purchase of his 1970 painting, "Tres Personajes", which was bought in 1997 by a Texan as a gift to his wife. This painting was then stolen from a storage locker in 2003 and found by Elizabeth Gibson mixed in with the trash in a New York City suburb. Gibson was not aware of the painting's creator or its market value until she saw the artwork featured on Antique Road Show, as part of a "Missing Masterpieces" episode. After locating the original owners, in November 2007 Gibson received a $15,000 reward plus a portion of the USD $1,049,000 auction sales price.

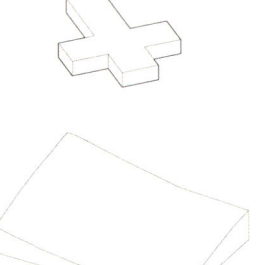

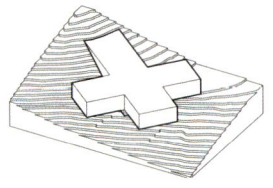

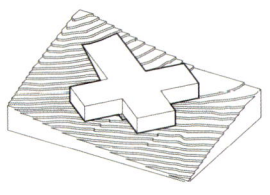

left: Situation on site_Cantilever_Exhibition space. right: Staircase and façades_Observation deck on the roof.

MEXICO_MONTERREY **HORNO 3: MUSEO DEL ACERO**

ARCHITECTS: GRIMSHAW WITH OFICINA DE ARQUITECTURA
STRUCTURAL ENGINEERS: WERNER SOBEK_**SCENOGRAPHY:**
ALDRICH PEARS_**LANDSCAPE ARCHITECT:** CLAUDIA HARARI
COMPLETION: 2007_**TYPE:** INDUSTRY MUSEUM
GROSS FLOOR AREA: 9,000 M²_**PHOTOS:** CHRISTIAN
HOENIGSCHMID-GROSSICH / GRIMSHAW (48 L.),
PAÚL RIVERA / ARCHPHOTO (48 R., 49)

THE ARCHITECTURE

Horno 3: Museo Del Acero comprises a full restoration of the once derelict 1960's blast furnace structure, including the conversion of the 70 meter high furnace into a series of habitable volumes, adding 9,000 square meters of indoor and outdoor museum space. Intended to host an exhibition of steel, the museum was created partially from the adaptive re-use of the furnace, its platforms, tanks and control rooms, and partially as a new extension adjacent to the existing complex. The abandoned blast furnace structure and cast hall are the center pieces of the museum, housing an interactive exhibit that brings the old furnace to life, allowing visitors the unique experience of touring inside this piece of industrial history.

THE COLLECTION

HORNO 3 is a non-profit science and technology center. The building provides multiple interactive areas that enforce scientific and technological education, commemorating the history of steel and its industrial development. The "History Gallery" also honors the workers that contributed to it. The 44 enthralling exhibitions take visitors back in time — Birth of a Steel Nation, Revolution to Recovery, Industrial Renaissance, Golden Era of Expansion, Facing New Challenges, History Gallery, and current Layout. The abandoned blast furnace structure and cast hall are the centerpieces of the museum. They house an interactive exhibit which brings the old furnace to simulated life, allowing visitors the unique experience of touring inside this piece of industrial history. Due to its location, the furnace also acts as the central organizing hub for the rest of the museum. The elevator climbs 42 meters into the sky, allowing visitors to stroll around the original exterior catwalks that stretch around the furnace, its pipes and stoves. Next to the restored blast furnace, a new addition houses an entry wing and the striking Steel Gallery, which acts as an architectural focal point and a counterpoint to the existing industrial complex. This new gallery is largely subterranean, allowing it to work discreetly within the context of the blast furnace.

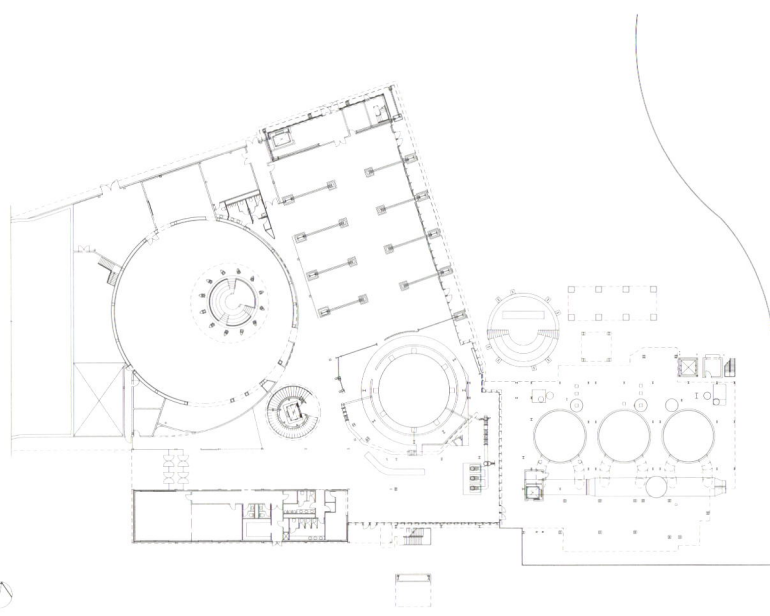

left: Ground floor plan_Helical stair_Elevator in framework_Cantilevering stairs. right: Blast Furnace inside the pipework and the newly-clad Cast Hall_Landscaped roof_Exterior.

PERU_EL BRUJO **MUSEO CAO**

ARCHITECTS: CLAUDIA UCCELLI_**COMPLETION:** 2008_**TYPE:**
ARCHEOLOGY MUSEUM_**GROSS FLOOR AREA:** 1,420 M²
PHOTOS: EDUARDO HIROSE

THE ARCHITECTURE

The Cao Museum is located inside the "El Brujo Archeological Site" on the northern Peruvian pacific coast, 70 kilometers north of the city of Trujillo. Spanning an area of 100 hectares, this archeological site has been occupied for more than 5000 years. There are three Huacas, sacred pyramids, to be found here, including Huaca Prieta, one of the oldest in South America. The Museo Cao was built next to an imaginary triangle joining these three adobe structures. The visual perspectives, the wind direction and the sea were important factors determining the aesthetics and formal characteristics of the museum. Its architecture pretends to be almost topographic, adapting itself to its surroundings.

THE COLLECTION

The main exhibit of the Cao Museum is the mummy of the Señora de Cao, covered in tattooed snakes and spiders. The Señora de Cao was young female ruler who ruled the Mochica warrior people around 1700 years ago and who was buried in the clay pyramid of El Brujo north of Trujillo, which was especially erected for her and decorated with magnificent frescoes. The mummy finding is considered to be very exceptional, as it provides evidence for the first time of a woman with significant religious and/or political power in the pre-Inca culture. In addition to the perfectly preserved mummy, the museum also presents many of the grave goods found alongside the it in the stepped pyramid, including a golden mask that covered the face of the ruler, precious jewelry, ceramics, two ceremonial war clubs, and 28 atlatls. In addition to exhibits from the Mochica culture, ranging from the year 100 BC to 700 AD, the museum also displays exhibits from other eras. They were all found in the excavation complex Huaca El Brujo, which had been constantly settled for more than 5000 years, providing evidence of the cultural development of the region.

left: Floor plan_Panoramic view including Huaca Cao and tensile structure. right: Entrance_Museum Cao and Huaca Cao in the background.

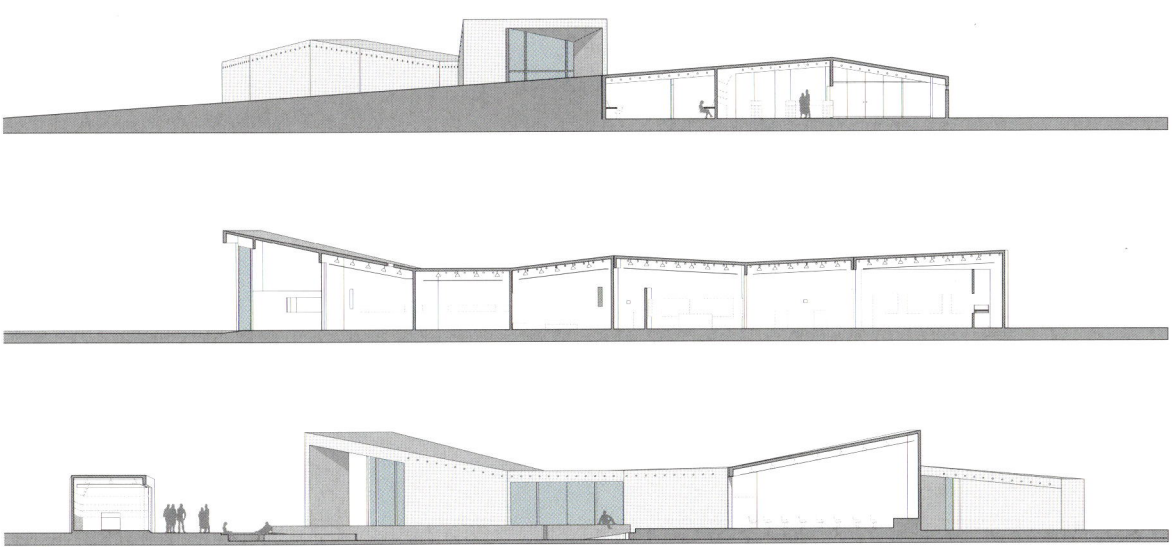

left: Room 5 Funeral Rituals. right: Sections_Room 3 Moche's idole_Room 4 Death Rituals_Interior.

USA_AKRON (OH) **AKRON ART MUSEUM**

ARCHITECTS: COOP HIMMELB(L)AU_**COMPLETION:** 2007_**TYPE:** ART MUSEUM_**GROSS FLOOR AREA:** 8,370 M²_**PHOTOS:** ROLAND HALBE / ARTURIMAGES

THE ARCHITECTURE

The museum of today is no longer only a place of knowledge or an exhibition space, but rather an urban arena offering various experiences as well as a three-dimensional urban signal communicating the contents of our world of images. Therefore, art must be allowed to flow outside of the building and the city allowed to flow inside it, within a hybrid space. The building consists of three parts — the crystal orientation and access area, the flexible gallery box, and the suspended roof cloud, which encloses the interior area, provides shading to various external space, and creates a horizontal landmark in the urban setting. The volumes and materials of the individual elements interact within a sophisticated room climate and illumination concept.

THE COLLECTION

The Akron Art Museum began in 1922 as a small project located in two basement rooms borrowed from the public library offering classes in arts appreciation. The museum, which has grown considerably since its humble beginnings, was initially run entirely by volunteer efforts until 1924, when it briefly gained funding from the city. Shortly afterwards, the Great Depression hit the US and funding was cut, forcing the museum to rely once again on volunteers. In 1937, with a collection comprised entirely of donations, the institution moved to its first permanent home. Four years later, the museum suffered a setback as a disastrous fire destroyed the building and much of the collection. New life was breathed into the museum after World War II, when it was re-born with a professional staff and a new focus on fine art and design. In 1950, the museum returned to its original residence in the public library, although this time renovating and occupying the entire building. Alongside its permanent collection, the museum hosts temporary exhibitions, including traveling shows and photographic media, and provides space for exhibitions by emerging and mid-career artists.

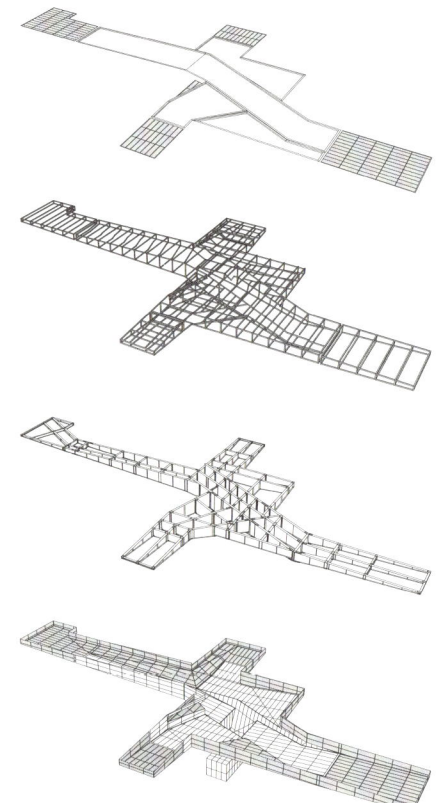

left: Roof cloud exploded elements_Entrance hall_View outside_Glass wall. right: Main entrance Exterior_Exterior from the other side.

USA_BELLINGHAM (WA) **LIGHTCATCHER AT THE WHATCOM MUSEUM**

ARCHITECTS: OLSON KUNDIG ARCHITECTS_**COMPLETION:** 2009
TYPE: ART MUSEUM_**GROSS FLOOR AREA:** 3,902 M²
PHOTOS: BENJAMIN BENSCHNEIDER (56 B. R., 57, 58, 59 B. R.),
TIM BIES / OLSON KUNDIG ARCHITECTS (56 B. L., 59 B. L.)

THE ARCHITECTURE

The Lightcatcher is a regional art and children's museum. It takes its name from its most visible feature — the lightcatcher, an eleven meter high and 55 meter long structure that curves gently, to form a 2,200 square meter courtyard. In daylight hours, the light-porous wall fills the inside with light and becomes an energy-saving light fixture; at night it becomes a beacon. The lightcatcher's double-walled construction helps ventilate the building, expelling hot air in summer and insulating the building in winter. The building program includes a mix of galleries, classrooms, offices, and amenity spaces. The single-story lobby is topped by a 915 square meter green roof. The building is designed in accordance with LEED Silver standards.

THE COLLECTION

The Whatcom Museum, formerly known as the Bellingham Public Museum, was first established in 1944. In 1962, a fire destroyed the roof of the museum. To prevent the building from being demolished, a group of Bellingham citizens raised funds to save the museum and also campaigned to get the building listed on the National Register of Historic Places. They were successful and the building became listed in 1970. The museum of History and Art is housed in the old City Hall building, which serves as the main building for the expanding museum campus. The building was renovated in 1999 and the first floor houses changing local natural-history exhibits; the second floor hosts displays of contemporary art; and the third retains a permanent display of Victorian clothing, woodworking and toys. Recent special exhibitions include the "Show of Hands" display, which takes an in-depth look at Northwest women artists. Programmed to coincide with the 100th anniversary of Women's suffrage in Washington State, the display features more than 90 works of art by 63 women artists from Washington, Oregon and British Columbia. With the addition of the Lightcatcher building to the museum campus, the Whatcom Museum maintains its status as a local and regional landmark, garnering national attention.

left: Main floor plan_Courtyard_Lightcatcher. right: Side view.

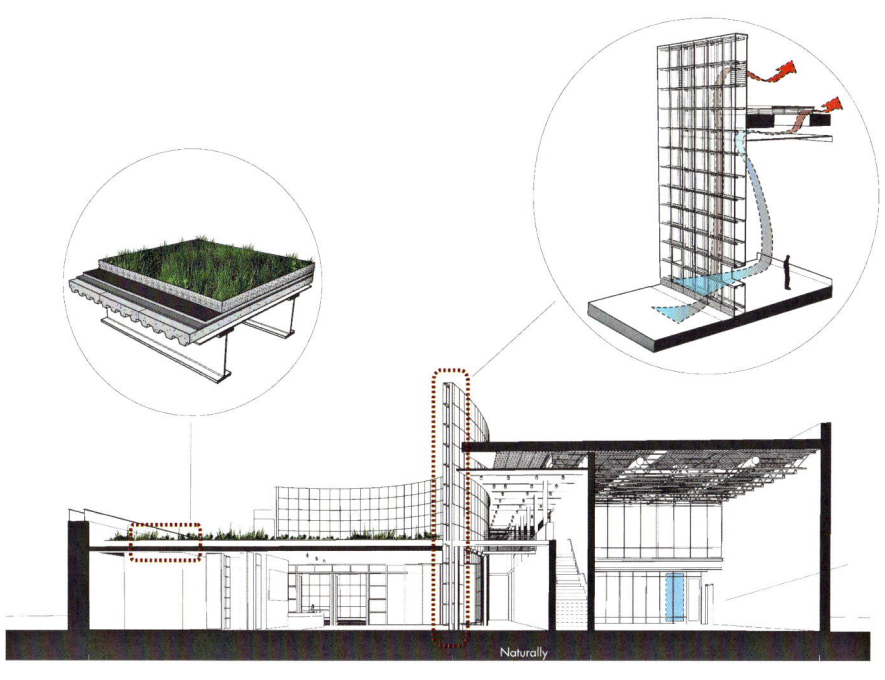

Naturally

left: Exhibition hall. right: Section_Lightcatcher, detail_Circulation.

OUT OI
Art from the Collectio

USA_BOSTON (MA) **MUSEUM OF FINE ARTS**

ARCHITECTS: FOSTER + PARTNERS WITH CHILDS BERTMAN TSECKARES INC_**COMPLETION:** 2010_**ORIGINAL BUILDING:** STURGIS AND BRIGHAM, 1876, GUY LOWELL, 1909_**TYPE:** ART MUSEUM_**GROSS FLOOR AREA:** 12,415 M² **PHOTOS:** FOSTER + PARTNERS

THE ARCHITECTURE

This museum stages a program of exhibitions, lectures, films and educational events. At the core of the scheme is the restoration of the symmetry and logic of the museum's original Beaux-Arts plan. The central axis of the main building, situated on Huntington Avenue, is reasserted by the reintroduction of the main entrance to the south and the reopening of the northern entrance. At the heart of this axis is a new information center. A glazed structure — "a crystal spine" — provides new accommodation and partly encloses the two grand courtyards at the center of the museum, in a glass "jewel box". Surrounding the museum, extensive new landscaping is designed to strengthen links with the adjacent Back Bay Fens.

THE COLLECTION

The Museum of Fine Arts first opened its doors in 1876 and initially housed 5,600 works of art. Since that time, the museum's collection has grown to a vast 450,000 pieces, making it one of the most comprehensive art collections in the world. It is also one of the largest in the United States, attracting over 1 million visitors each year. The extensive collection includes artwork from both the ancient and modern worlds, from places as far flung as Egypt, the Americas, Asia and Europe and featuring topics as diverse as Egyptian mummies, musical instruments and impressionist art work. The museum also houses the department of Prints, Drawings and Photographs. This encyclopedic collection of works on paper dates from the 15th century to the present. Sections of the collection are presented on a rotating basis, to prevent sensitive paper materials from being damaged due to prolonged exposure to sunlight. The museum gives the option of interactive online tours and has an extensive online catalogue. In the mid-2000s the museum began an ambitious renovation project. The new MFA building will add a new wing for the Art of the Americas collection, improved education facilities and a larger public space.

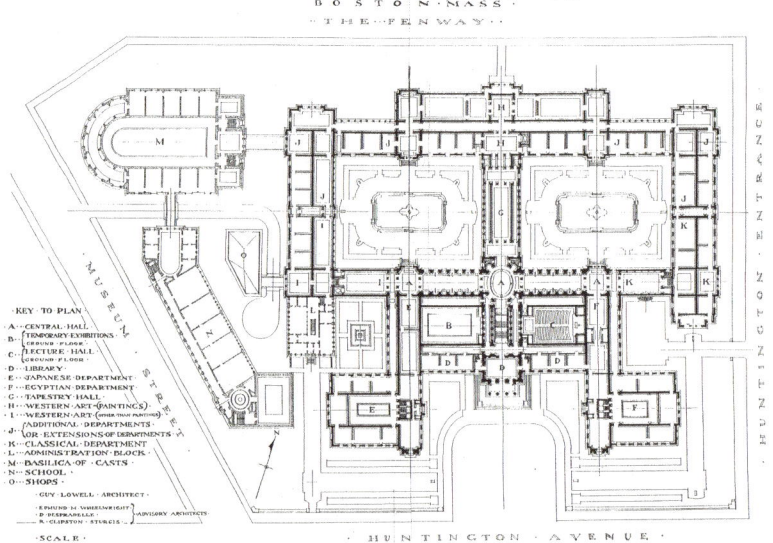

left: Ground floor plan_Extension exterior by day_Extension exterior at night. right: Existence main entrance_Existence façade.

The crystal spine...

and the extended landscape...

MFA   MF

left: Café. right: Sketch by Norman Foster_Visualization of the Gallery_Visualization of new connecting building_Visualization of the atrium.

USA_BOSTON (MA) **BOSTON CHILDREN'S MUSEUM**

ARCHITECTS: CAMBRIDGE SEVEN ASSOCIATES, INC.
COMPLETION: 2007_**ORIGINAL BUILDING:** 1889_**TYPE:** CHILDREN
MUSEUM_**GROSS FLOOR AREA:** 2,137 M² _**PHOTOS:** © ROBERT
BENSON PHOTOGRAPHY

THE ARCHITECTURE

This 2,137 square meter metal and glass enclosed addition was conceived as a straightforward, geometric armature connected to the existing building on three levels via glass bridges. The exterior protrusions are made of wood and accentuated with bright green splashes of color. The glass also activates the lobby by means of circular perforations in the metal façade that reveal slivers of green and yellow color. Looking out from each level within the new addition, visitors glimpse the waterfront and Fort Point Channel through the ample glass façade. The museum's front door was moved to a new location facing Fort Point Channel. This provides views of the channel and out across Boston Harbor.

THE COLLECTION

First founded in 1913 by a group of teachers, the Boston's Children's Museum developed a "hands-on" approach to education and interactive learning. The museum developed various projects aimed at engaging children in different activities. As early as 1913, these included identifying and marking nature walks, as well as creating models made from clay and wax. In the 1960s, museum director Michael Spock revolutionized the typical museum experience. He worked to provide an environment where exhibits were not merely displayed in cases to be looked at, but were made part of an interactive experience where children could touch and explore different objects. After 90 years of operation, the museum today aims to help children investigate and enjoy the world they live in, and to experiment and follow their own ideas instead of being directed. The museum also has its own permanent collections, including "Arthur and Friends," which exhibits characters from Marc Brown's books and television series. The exhibition features areas recognizable from the TV program, where children can play, such as the Read Family Kitchen and Mr. Ratburn's Classroom. The museum also educates its visitors about environmental issues and has a recycle shop, where customers can buy re-useable items for crafts projects.

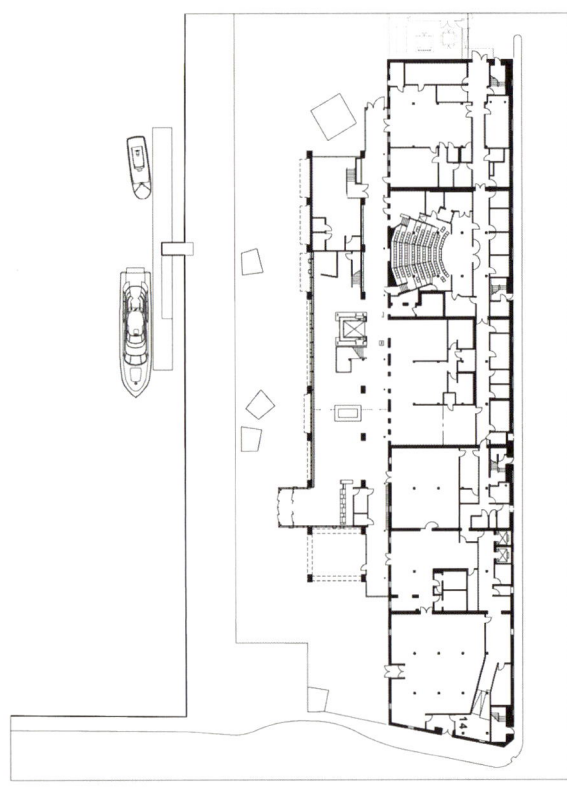

left: Ground floor plan_Curtain wall with perforated panels and color-tinted glass_Main lobby with climbing structure. right: Lobby and hangar doors_Evening view from the Congress Street bridge.

USA_BUFFALO (NY) **ELEANOR AND WILSON GREATBATCH PAVILION**

ARCHITECTS: TOSHIKO MORI ARCHITECT PLLC_**STRUCTURAL ENGINEERS:** SOM_**LANDSCAPE ARCHITECTS:** QRP_**COMPLETION:** 2009_**TYPE:** ARCHITECTURE MUSEUM_**GROSS FLOOR AREA:** 530 M² **PHOTOS:** PAUL WARCHOL PHOTOGRAPHY, NEW YORK

THE ARCHITECTURE

This visitor center provides media exhibition and orientation spaces for Frank Lloyd Wright's Darwin D. Martin House residential complex. The design fosters a dialogue with the Martin House by creating a contrast. The inverted roof references Wright's hip roof and the transparent façade and open plan design are filled with daylight, in contrast to the Martin House's introverted interior. The stainless steel columns along the perimeter are directly projected from the brick piers of the Martin House pergola. The pavilion reinterprets Wright's concept of "organic architecture," reflecting innovation and integration of structure, infrastructure and programmatic relationships.

THE COLLECTION

Built based on a design that won a competition organized by the Martin House Restoration Corporation, the Eleanor and Wilson Greatbatch Pavilion serves as the visitors' center for the Darwin D. Martin House complex. The group selected five emerging architects for the competition, mirroring the way in which Darwin D. Martin selected the previously untried architect Frank Lloyd Wright, to build what later became the Darwin D. Martin house back in the early 20th century. Because of the deliberate linkage between the modern building and the origins of the Martin House, it was important that the two buildings were linked together visually. Architect, Toshiko Mori states that the aim of his design was to "restate the significance of Wright's contributions to the legacy of modern architecture and to express a 'higher ideal of unity'." The building was named the Eleanor and Wilson Greatbatch Pavillion, after the inventors of a highly successful cardiac pacemaker. The donation given by the family to the visitor's center illustrated their wish to pay homage to the spirit of invention.

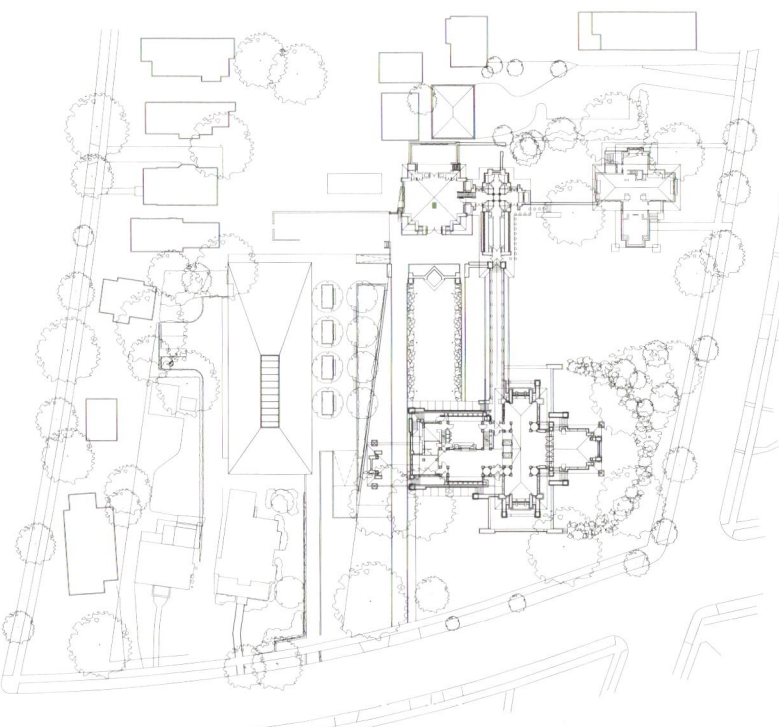

left: Site plan_East façade. right: Transparent holographic projection wall for animated presentations.

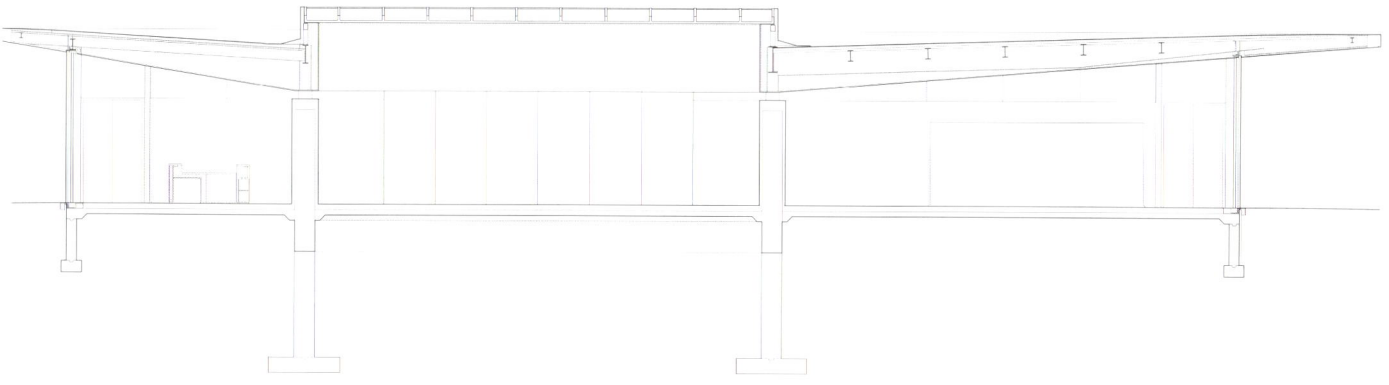

left: South façade. right: Longitudinal section_Entry to pavilion_Interpretive exhibition displays.

USA_CHATTANOOGA (TN) **HUNTER MUSEUM OF AMERICAN ART**

ARCHITECTS: RANDALL STOUT ARCHITECTS, INC
COMPLETION: 2005_**ORIGINAL BUILDING:** MEAD AND GARFIELD, 1904 (FAXON-THOMAS MANSION), DERTHICK, HENLEY AND WILKERSON, 1975_**TYPE:** ART MUSEUM_**GROSS FLOOR AREA:** 6,290 M² _**PHOTOS:** TIM GRIFFITH, SAN FRANCISCO

THE ARCHITECTURE

This project transforms a previously isolated site into an easily accessible and prominent public space by creating a "museum in a garden." Flowing geometries direct the visitor to the multifunctional lobby and its riverfront views, to galleries, and up to the special exhibitions and sculpture terraces. The design consolidates the permanent collection onto a single floor, together with the lobby, auditorium, education studios, café, and gift shop. The new design creates a state-of-the-art underground loading dock, along with storage and work areas, security, and oversized art freight elevators. Bold exterior materials include glass, an aluminum curtain wall, oxidized zinc cladding, and a stainless steel roof.

THE COLLECTION

Perched above the Tennessee River, the Hunter Museum of American Art offers visitors views of both the river and the surrounding mountains. The museum takes its name from local philanthropist and business man, George Hunter, who inherited the infamous Coca Cola Bottling company from his uncle. After his death, much of Hunter's estate was left to charity and The Hunter Museum of American Art, which opened in 1952, has become his lasting legacy in the Chattanooga region of Tennessee, where the museum is situated. The museum focuses on American art, ranging from the colonial period to present day, inviting the visitor to consider the evolution of American society. The museum houses both temporary and permanent collections, including works representing the Hudson River School, American Impressionism, the renowned Ashcan School, and post World War II modern and contemporary art. The museum's permanent collection includes the well-known painting, "The Seaside House" by influential American Modernist, Edward Hopper. A recent temporary exhibition saw the museum collaborating with the Tennessee Aquarium, to produce an unusual display entitled, "Jellies: Live Art", featuring jellyfish, some of nature's most ethereal creatures, alongside glass sculptures.

left: Roof forms_View from Tennessee River_Entry view from sculpture garden. right: View from Walnut Street pedestrian bridge.

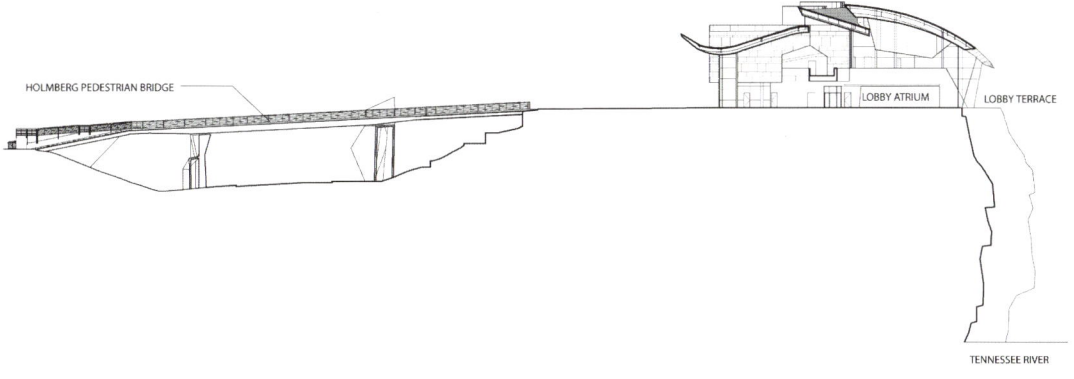

HOLMBERG PEDESTRIAN BRIDGE

LOBBY ATRIUM   LOBBY TERRACE

TENNESSEE RIVER

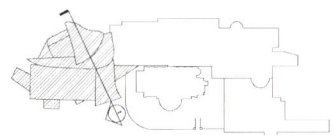

left: Lobby. right: Section_Reception desk_Permanent collection gallery_Holmberg pedestrian bridge.

VISITOR SERVICES

USA_CHICAGO (IL) **CHICAGO ART INSTITUTE**

ARCHITECTS: RENZO PIANO BUILDING WORKSHOP, ARCHITECT WITH INTERACTIVE DESIGN INC., ARCHITECTS_**COMPLETION:** 2009_**TYPE:** ART MUSEUM_**GROSS FLOOR AREA:** 264,000 M² **PHOTOS:** NIC LEHOUX / RPBW

THE ARCHITECTURE

This new wing, at the northeastern corner of the Art Institute of Chicago's block connects the Millennium Park to the heart of the existing museum, through the new Griffin Court. On the first floor, this day-lit court is flanked by new educational facilities, public amenities, galleries and a garden. The second and third floors are dedicated to art. The shelter above the art pavilion is a kind of flying carpet made of aluminum. Limestone is used for the entire museum, from its original Beaux Arts palace to recent additions. Above this structure, the building stands light, transparent, and permeable in steel and glass — solid and robust, yet at the same time light and crisp.

THE COLLECTION

The Art Institute of Chicago, founded in 1879 as both a museum and school, was built on rubble from the 1871 Chicago fire. The collection has grown from its humble beginnings, when it housed a collection of plaster casts, to exhibiting art of all kinds. It now encompasses more than 5,000 years of human expression from cultures around the world and contains more than 260,000 exhibits, encompassing everything from early Japanese prints to modern American art. Today, the museum is most famous for its collections of Impressionist, Post-Impressionist and American paintings. The Impressionist and Post-Impressionist collection includes more than 30 paintings by Claude Monet, including six of his Haystacks and a number of Water Lilies. The museum also houses several influential American works, including Grant Wood's American Gothic and Edward Hopper's Nighthawks. In addition to paintings, the Art Institute offers a number of other works, including European and Asian architectural and furniture styles from the Middle Ages to the 1930s. A special feature of the museum is the Touch Gallery, which is specially designed for the visually impaired. It features several works that museum guests are encouraged to experience through the sense of touch instead of sight, as well as specially-designed description plates written in Braille.

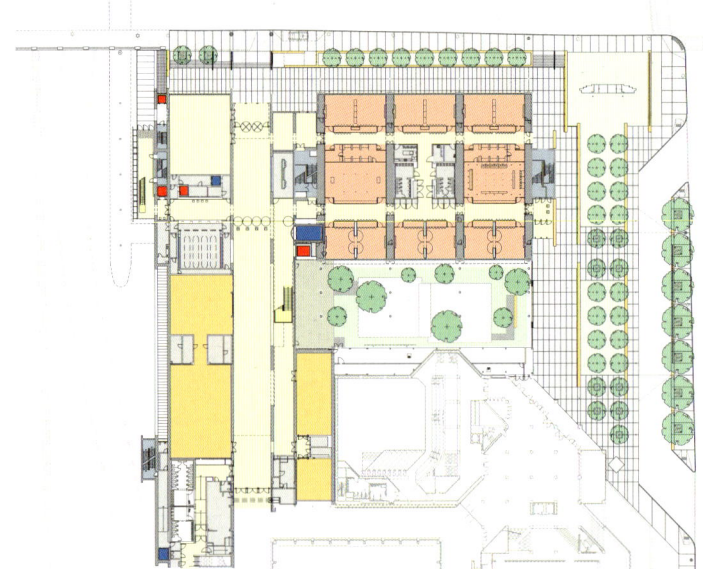

left: Ground floor plan_Exterior_Top level with skyline. right: Façade.

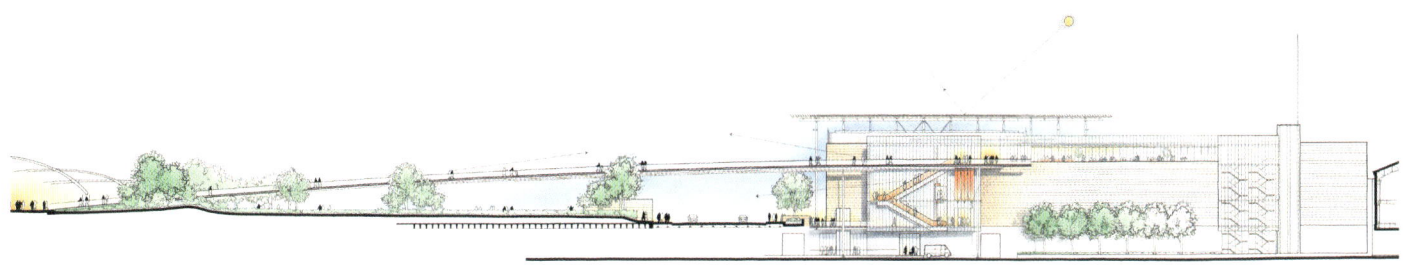

left: Foyer. right: Elevation_Staircase_Exhibition rooms.

USA_CINCINNATI (OH) **ROSENTHAL CENTER FOR CONTEMPORARY ART**

ARCHITECTS: ZAHA HADID ARCHITECTS_**COMPLETION:** 2003
TYPE: ART MUSEUM_**GROSS FLOOR AREA:** 8,500 M² _**PHOTOS:**
ROLAND HALBE / ARTURIMAGES

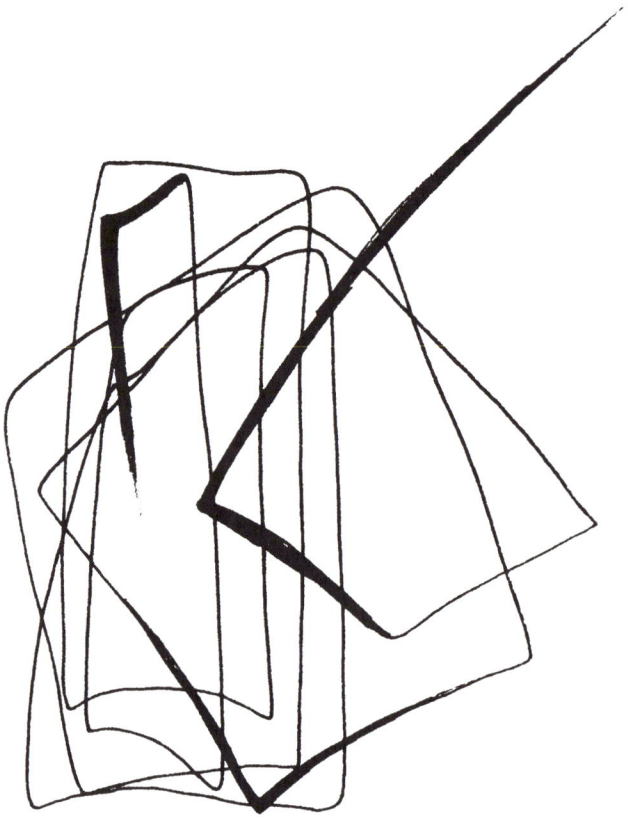

THE ARCHITECTURE

To draw pedestrians into the temporary exhibitions and create a sense of dynamic public space, the entrance, lobby and lead-in to the circulation system are organized as an "Urban Carpet." As it rises and turns, this Urban Carpet leads up a suspended mezzanine ramp through the full length of the lobby, which during the day functions as an open, day-lit, "landscaped" expanse that resembles an artificial park. In contrast to these polished, undulating surfaces, the galleries are styled as if carved from a single block of concrete and float over the lobby space. Carpet, ramps and galleries interlock like a three-dimensional jigsaw puzzle, made up of solids and voids.

THE COLLECTION

The new Lois & Richard Rosenthal Center for Contemporary Art is a freestanding building housing the Contemporary Arts Center. Founded in Cincinnati in 1939, the CAC is one of the first institutions in the United States dedicated to the exhibition of contemporary visual arts. The museum does not contain a permanent collection, but provides space for temporary exhibitions, site-specific installations, and performances instead. Due to its status as promoter of daring and farsighted artistic strategies, the CAC can adapt to changes in artistic trends and always display the most provocative and daring artwork. Following this theme, the museum was the first major American museum designed by a woman, London-based architect Zaha Hadid, who won a competition to design the new premises for the CAC in 1997. The CAC aims to provide a cultural forum, and to encourage visitors to explore the displayed artwork and the themes therein. By exhibiting the most daring and controversial projects, the CAC exposes visitors to new ideas and encourages them to connect both with each other and to the world outside.

left: Sketch_Mezzanine ramp in the lobby_Staircase_Façade. right: Exterior.

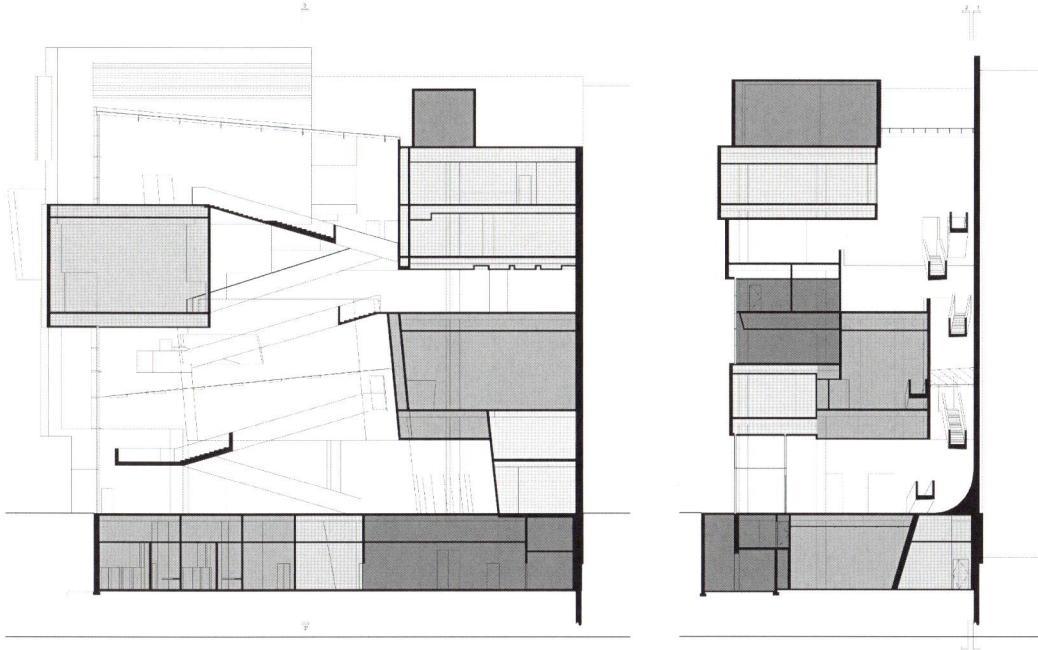

left: Staircases top view. right: Sections_Staircase_Exhibition space_Café.

USA_CULVER CITY (CA) **SPF:A HEADQUARTERS**

ARCHITECTS: SPF:A_**COMPLETION:** 2006_**TYPE:** DESIGN, ART AND ARCHITECTURE MUSEUM_**GROSS FLOOR AREA:** 2,604 M² _**PHOTOS:** JOHN EDWARD LINDEN

THE ARCHITECTURE

This building consists of an architecture studio, a restaurant and a public gallery on the ground floor, plus seven lofts on the second floor. Populated by a variety of artists and creative businesses, the gallery explores the relationship between design, art and architecture, animated through a series of exhibitions, lectures and cultural events. Concrete fiber panel boards on the exterior, break up the street noise of the busy Washington Boulevard below and insulate the building from constant exposure to sunshine. The variation of the width and depth of the panels is intended as visual "music," playing changes in variations of 20, 40, and 80 centimeters panel widths and three different colors that randomly alternate on the surface of the building.

THE COLLECTION

The building of the SPF:a Headquarters, with its dynamic façade and mixed-use program, amplifies the enthusiasm and motion of the city's growth and serves as a visual bridge between the city's downtown art deco theater district and the world-class art gallery district emerging directly to the east. Studio Pali Fekete architects established the SPF:a gallery with a mission "to publicly explore the synergistic relationship between design, art, and architecture." The building explores such relationships in the gallery-specific space, but also in the synergy of disciplines that occupy the entire building. The 200 square meter gallery space is sandwiched between the studio SPF offices and a gourmet café wine bar. The gallery is open on both sides, allowing continuous flow of visitors to every portion of the building's ground floor. The architecture studio and the gallery space are both open for exploration and feature contemporary art, design, and architecture exhibitions that change throughout the year. The upper level of the building includes seven live/work artist residences, enhancing the company's design synergy "experiment." These house the two principal architects of SPF and six independent design-related enterprises.

left: Cross section_Building by night_Detail of the façade. right: Façade_Exhibition hall_View into studio.

USA_DENVER (CO) **DENVER ART MUSEUM**

ARCHITECTS: STUDIO DANIEL LIBESKIND WITH DAVIS PARTNERSHIP_**COMPLETION:** 2006_**ORIGINAL BUILDING:** GIO PONTI, 1971_**TYPE:** ART MUSEUM_**GROSS FLOOR AREA:** 13,560 M² _**PHOTOS:** BITTER BREDT FOTOGRAFIE, BERLIN

THE ARCHITECTURE

The 13,560 square meter extension, which opened in October 2006, currently houses modern and contemporary art collections, as well as collections of Oceanic and African Art. The Hamilton Building's design recalls the peaks of the Rocky Mountains and geometric rock crystals found in the foothills near Denver. The materials of the building are closely related to the existing context, while introducing innovative new materials, such as the 9,000 titanium panels, which cover the building's surface and reflect the brilliant Colorado sunlight. The project is designed as a part of a composition of public spaces, monuments and gateways in this developing part of the city.

THE COLLECTION

The Denver Art Museum is a private, non-profit, educational resource for Colorado. Since its beginnings in the 1890s as the Denver Artists' Club, the Denver Art Museum has had a number of temporary homes, from the public library and a downtown mansion to a portion of the Denver City and County Building. The museum opened its own galleries on 14th Avenue Parkway in 1949, and a center for children's art activities was added in the early 1950s. In 1971, the museum expanded and opened the North Building. In 2006 the Frederic C. Hamilton Building was added. Today, the 33,000 square meter museum complex includes collection gallery space, three temporary exhibition venues, and the Lewis I. Sharp Auditorium. In addition to art collections, the Denver Art Museum has received critical acclaim for encouraging art appreciation through interactive activities. The DAM is also gradually conserving and restoring the Old Master paintings in its collection. For example, Bernardo Zenale's, "Madonna and Child with Saints" has been a recent restoration project undertaken by the museum that can now be viewed on level six of the North Building.

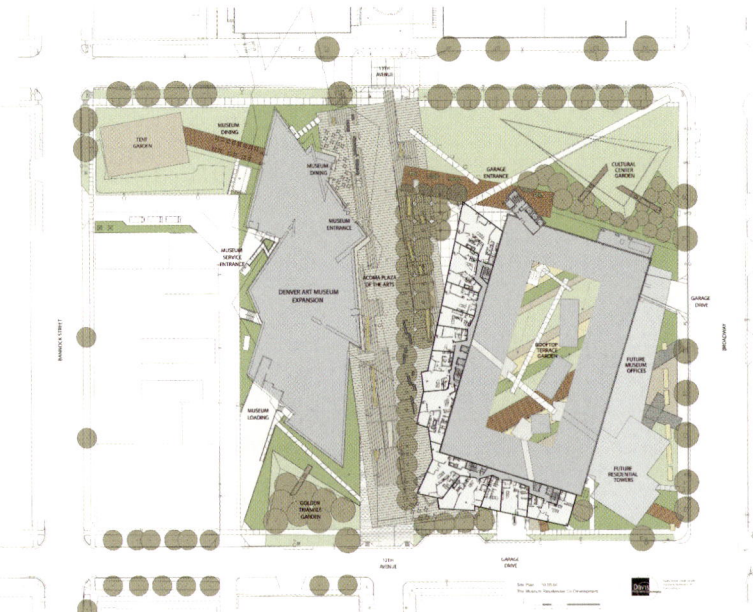

left: Site plan_The cantilever hovers over the street_Titanium clad entryway. right: Detail_Aerial view.

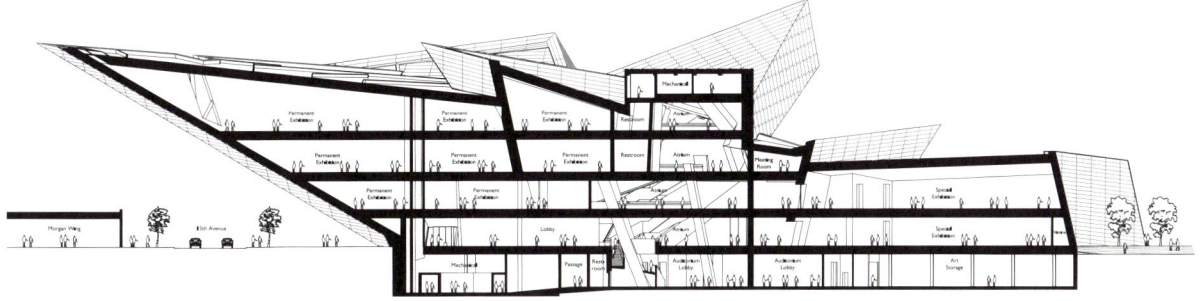

left: Atrium stair showing digital Engi installation. right: Section looking east_View of atrium stair from ground floor_Contemporary art gallery_Contemporary art gallery with stairs.

USA_FORT WORTH (TX) **MODERN ART MUSEUM OF FORT WORTH**

ARCHITECTS: TADAO ANDO ARCHITECT & ASSOCIATES
COMPLETION: 2002_**TYPE:** ART MUSEUM_**GROSS FLOOR AREA:**
14,820 M² _**PHOTOS:** MITSUO MATSUOKA

THE ARCHITECTURE

The architect created spatial essence comprising of a strong simplicity and clarity in the concept of an "art forest." With no distinction between interior and exterior, this project consists of a composition of five rectangular solids in a row, each with a double-layer structure of a bare concrete box enclosed by glass, within a forest surrounded by water and greenery. Nature and light are taken inside, while the appearance of the exhibition rooms is visible from the outside through the glass. With constant awareness of the artworks that dot the site, concerts, outdoor parties, or similar events may be enjoyed in the outdoor lawn plaza and water garden.

THE COLLECTION

The Modern Art Museum of Fort Worth is dedicated to collecting, presenting, and interpreting international developments in post–World War II art. The museum promotes understanding and interest in art and artists through curatorial research and publications, and has developed a variety of educational programs, including lectures, guided tours, classes, and workshops. The Modern maintains one of the foremost collections of modern and contemporary art in the central United States, consisting of more than 2,600 works of international art. The museum features 4,900 square meter of gallery space and also hosts major traveling exhibitions. Various movements, themes, and styles are on display, including Abstract Expressionism, Color Field painting, Pop art, and Minimalism, as well as aspects of New Image Painting from the 1970s and beyond. Recent developments in abstraction and figurative sculpture, and contemporary movements in photography, video, and digital imagery are also represented. The Permanent Collection includes pieces by Anselm Kiefer, Robert Motherwell, Pablo Picasso, Jackson Pollock, and Andy Warhol. A variety of gallery spaces are accommodated throughout the two levels of the museum. The building's two levels permit the museum's curatorial staff to display works from the permanent collection on one floor, while hosting a major traveling exhibition on another.

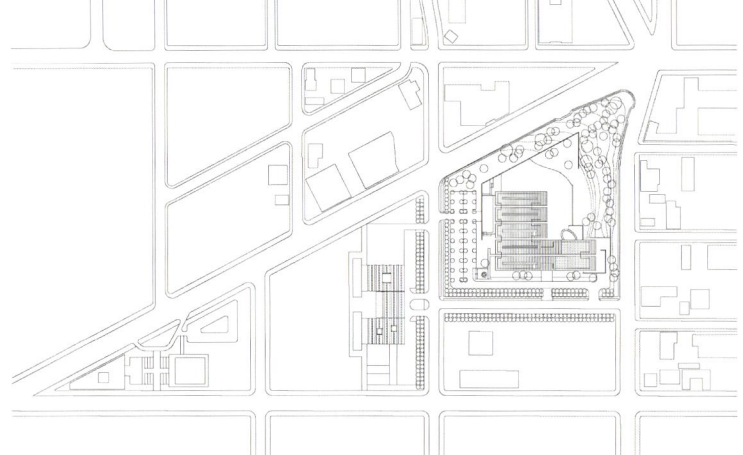

left: Site plan_Roofs shade the building's exterior_Exterior view. right: Exhibition area_Large reflecting pond.

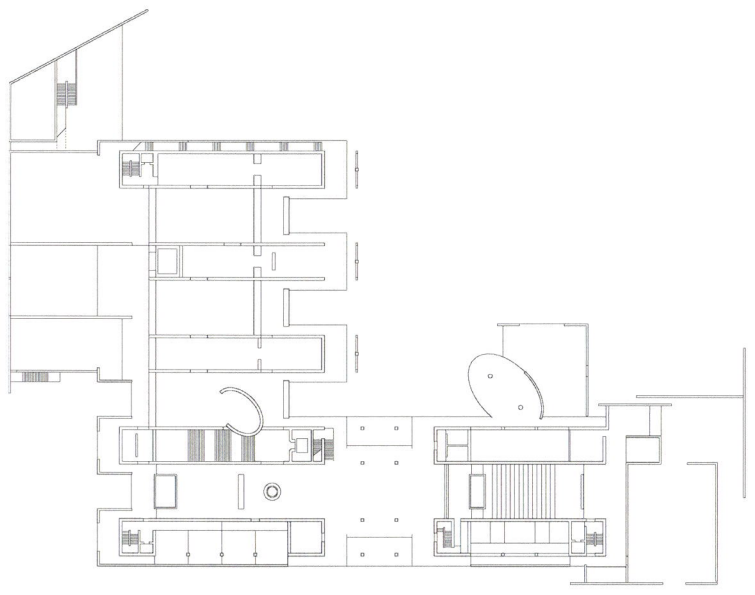

left: Staircase. right: First floor plan_Concrete y-shaped column_Cabinet for Anselm Kiefers "Book with wings"_Shop.

USA_GRAND RAPIDS (MI) **GRAND RAPIDS ART MUSEUM**

ARCHITECTS: WHY ARCHITECTURE WITH DESIGN PLUS, INC.
COMPLETION: 2007_**TYPE:** ART MUSEUM_**GROSS FLOOR AREA:**
11,600 M² _**PHOTOS:** STEVE HALL (92, 93 A., 94), COURTESY OF THE
ARCHITECTS (93 B.), SCOTT MCDONALD (95)

THE ARCHITECTURE

This new building is located next to the park, forming an urban oasis surrounded by tall buildings. The projecting canopies, resembling large canopies of trees extend up and reach out to frame the park and the city, similar to the Japanese concept of "borrowed scenery." Museum lobby, restaurant, and education center are located in pavilions projecting towards the park, with pockets of nature in between. The inner sanctuary is the 3-level gallery tower in which top floor galleries are lit with lantern skylights. As the first new art museum in the world designed with LEED Gold certification, natural light is planned to be used throughout the building.

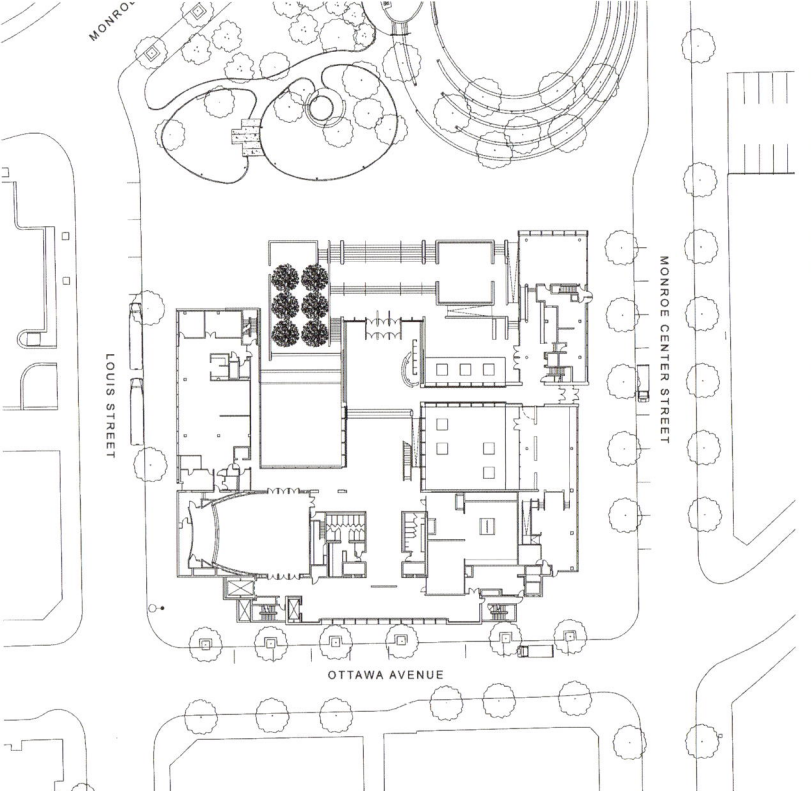

THE COLLECTION

In 1910, when the Grand Rapids Art Museum first opened, Grand Rapids was a city of furniture companies employing thousands of workers who walked or rode streetcars downtown to the factories lining the banks of the city's Grand River. The beginning of a new century brought with it new ideas and a new era of urban development known as the "City Beautiful Movement." This movement influenced the founding of the Grand Rapids Art Museum. In 1912, the Grand Rapids Art Association played a leading role in forming the Michigan Federation of the Arts. For the next twelve years, the Association held exhibitions in a variety of downtown locations, including St. Cecilia Music Society and the Ryerson Public Library. The museum's collection has grown considerably since its beginnings and now houses 5,000 works of art, ranging from Renaissance to Modern Art, with special collections of 19th and 20th century European and American art. The museum celebrated its centennial anniversary in May 2010, with a collaboration to mark the joint centennials of Ox-Bow school of art and the Grand Rapids Art Museum. The two oldest art organizations in West Michigan were both founded in 1910.

left: Ground floor plan_Main entrance_Entrance Monroe Avenue. right: Façade at night_Lobby Exterior.

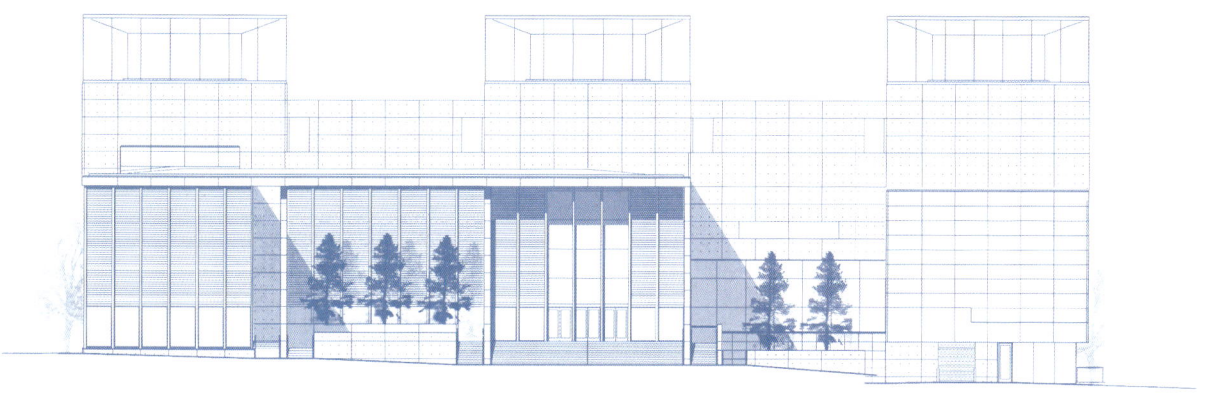

left: Façade Pocket Park. right: Main façade_Gallery_East building.

USA_KANSAS CITY (MO) **NELSON-ATKINS MUSEUM OF ART**

ARCHITECTS: STEVEN HOLL ARCHITECTS_**COMPLETION:** 2007
ORIGINAL BUILDING: WIGHT AND WIGHT, 1933_**TYPE:** ART
MUSEUM_**GROSS FLOOR AREA:** 15,300 M²
PHOTOS: ANDY RYAN

THE ARCHITECTURE

The concept was to build five glass galleries, called "lenses", along the eastern edge of the campus. They sit atop the Bloch Building, a 15,300 square meters structure, all of which is underground, except for the "lenses." This new addition engages the existing sculpture garden, transforming the entire museum site into the precinct of the visitor's experience. There are seven entrances to the building. The first of the five "lenses" forms a bright and transparent lobby, inviting visitors into the museum and encouraging movement via ramps toward the galleries as they progress downward into the garden. The collaboration with curators and artists allows a merging of landscape, architecture and art.

THE COLLECTION

Recognized internationally as one of the finest general art museums in the United States, the Nelson-Atkins Museum of Art currently maintains collections of more than 33,500 works of art. The museum's permanent collection of European painting and sculpture ranges from medieval to late 19th century and contains approximately 900 works of art. Among the best known examples, are the Italian, German and Netherlandish paintings. The Italian paintings collection includes one of the museum's greatest treasures, "Saint John the Baptist in the Wilderness" by Caravaggio. This masterpiece is one of only a few original works by Caravaggio in American collections, while other important Italian works from the 16th to the 18th centuries are also displayed. Examples of Dutch and German paintings include "Virgin and Child" in a Gothic Interior by Petrus Christus, Cranach the Elder's "Three Graces", Wtewael's "Martyrdom of Saint Sebastian," portraits by Rembrandt and Frans Hals, and an interior scene by Jan Steen. The extensive collection also includes works on paper, pastels by Degas and Berthe Morisot, and drawings by Tiepolo and Ingres. American art at the museum features painting, sculpture and works on paper created in the United States from the 18th century through World War II.

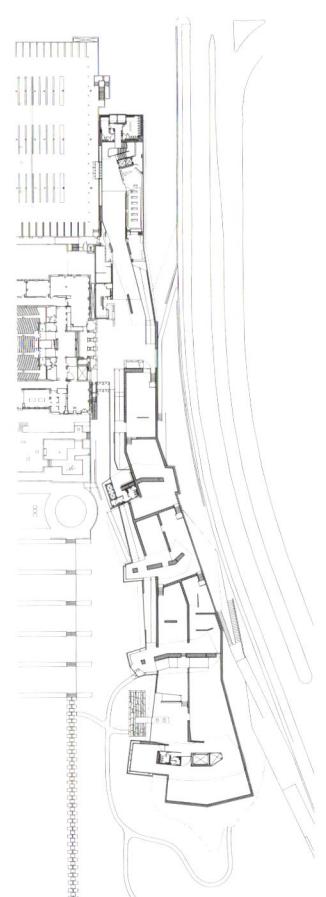

left: Ground floor plan_Exterior by night_Panorama view. right: Exterior_Detail of the wall_Staircase_Stairs and gallery.

USA_MANCHESTER (NH) **CURRIER MUSEUM OF ART**

ARCHITECTS: ANN BEHA ARCHITECTS_**COMPLETION:** 2008
ORIGINAL BUILDING: TILTON & GITHENS, 1929; HARDY
HOLZMAN PFEIFFER, 1982_**TYPE:** ART MUSEUM_**GROSS FLOOR
AREA:** 6,781 M² _**PHOTOS:** JONATHAN HILLYER,
ATLANTA (98, 99 B.), BRUCE T. MARTIN, NATICK (99 A.)

THE ARCHITECTURE

The renovation and expansion of this historic museum doubled the amount of space for exhibits, programs and visitor services. Two additions offer a fresh interpretation of the building's retrained classicism. A north addition features a new lobby and expanded visitor services. On the south, three new galleries surround an enclosed winter garden, creating a year-round space for a café, receptions and performances. Stairs from the winter garden lead to a new auditorium, classrooms and administrative offices. The placement of new spaces and reutilization of existing ones establishes a path through the galleries, building on the Beaux Arts symmetry of the original plan.

THE COLLECTION

Founded in 1929 at the bequest of New Hampshire Governor Moody Currier and his wife Hannah Currier, the Currier Museum of Art is an internationally renowned museum situated in the state of New Hampshire. After Hannah's death in 1915, a board of trustees was appointed to carry out the Currier's wishes. The museum's diverse collection includes items from European to American artworks, decorative arts, sculpture and photographs. Works by famous artists such as Picasso, Monet, and O'Keefe are featured, as well as traveling and temporary exhibitions. The museum also owns the nearby Zimmerman House, designed by one of the world most renowned modern architects, Frank Lloyd Wright. The house was opened to the public in 1990 and visitors today can view the house itself and the private art collection of the house's previous owners, Lucille and Isadore Zimmerman. The display includes modern art, pottery and sculpture, donated by the Zimmermanns. The museum offers tours of the house, one of only a few Wright buildings owned by an art museum. Previous exhibitions include "From Homer to Hopper," a display of 75 works that traced the history of watercolor art over the last 175 years, featuring American greats, such as Winslow Homer and Edward Hopper.

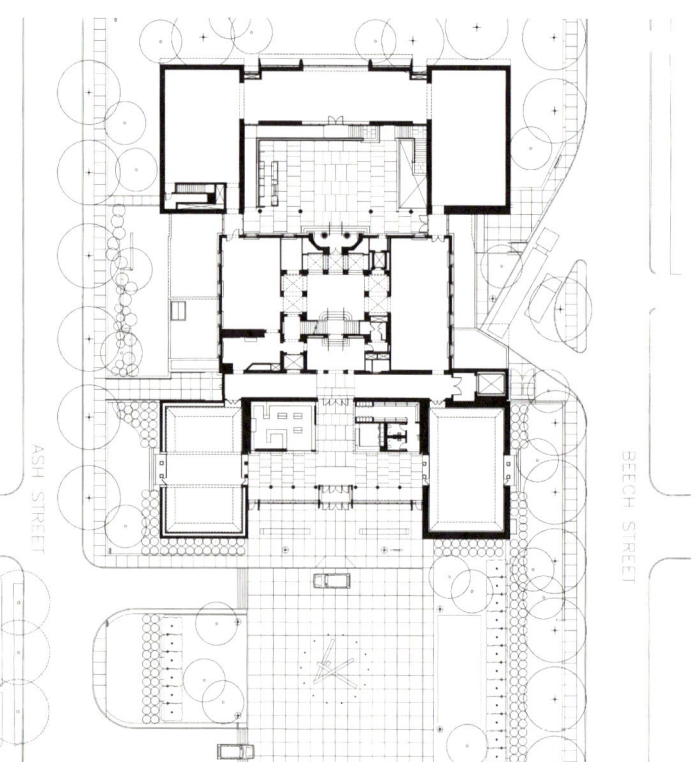

left: Main level floor plan_New museum entrance_New south addition. right: Connection between new and existing_South gallery looking into enclosed winter garden_New main lobby.

USA_MILWAUKEE (WI) **MILWAUKEE ART MUSEUM**

ARCHITECTS: SANTIAGO CALATRAVA ARCHITECT & ENGINEER
COMPLETION: 2001_**TYPE:** ART MUSEUM_**GROSS FLOOR AREA:**
13,200 M² _**PHOTOS:** ALAN KARCHMER

THE ARCHITECTURE

This museum was partially housed in a building designed in 1957 by Eero Saarinen as a war memorial. Calatrava proposed a pavilion-like construction on the same axis as Wisconsin Avenue. Conceived as an independent entity, the pavilion contrasts with the existing ensemble in both geometry and materials, with its white steel-and-concrete form reminiscent of a ship. The design adds 13,200 square meters, including a linear wing (made of glass and stainless steel, with lamella roof) that is set at a right angle to Saarinen's structure, allowings for future expansion. The pavilion features a kinetic structure: a bris-soleil with louvers that open and close like the wings of a great bird.

THE COLLECTION

With a history dating back to 1888, the Milwaukee Art Museum's far-reaching collection includes nearly 20,000 works from antiquity to the present. The museum's permanent holdings include important collections of Old Masters and 19th and 20th century art. Central to the museum's mission is its role as a premier educational resource, with educational programs that are among the largest in the USA, involving classes, tours, and a full calendar of events. The Research Library houses an extensive collection of materials on fine art and architecture, including painting, graphic arts, sculpture, drawing, design, and photography. Library resources include national and international museum and gallery publications. The museum's collection is exhibited across 40 galleries and is regularly rotated to fully represent its varying themes. The exhibitions of American decorative arts, German Expressionism, Folk and Haitian art, and American art after 1960, are recognized as being amongst the best in the nation and the museum also holds one of the largest collections of works by world-renowned Wisconsin native Georgia O'Keeffe. In addition to the works in the collection galleries, the museum also hosts a variety of temporary exhibitions throughout the year.

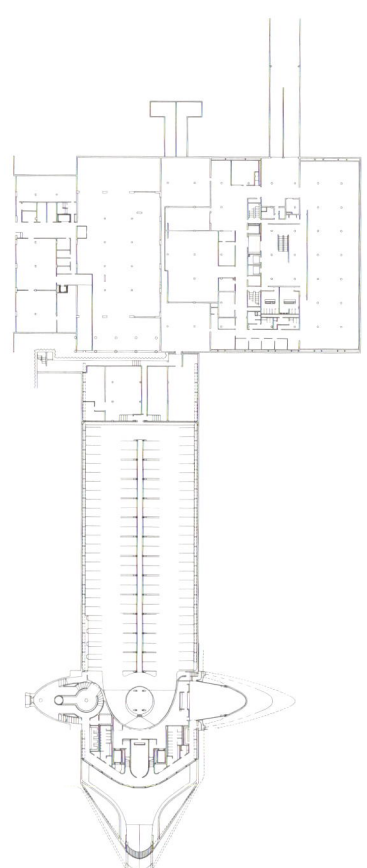

left: Floor plan_Sequence opening. right: Elevation dusk_Elevation context.

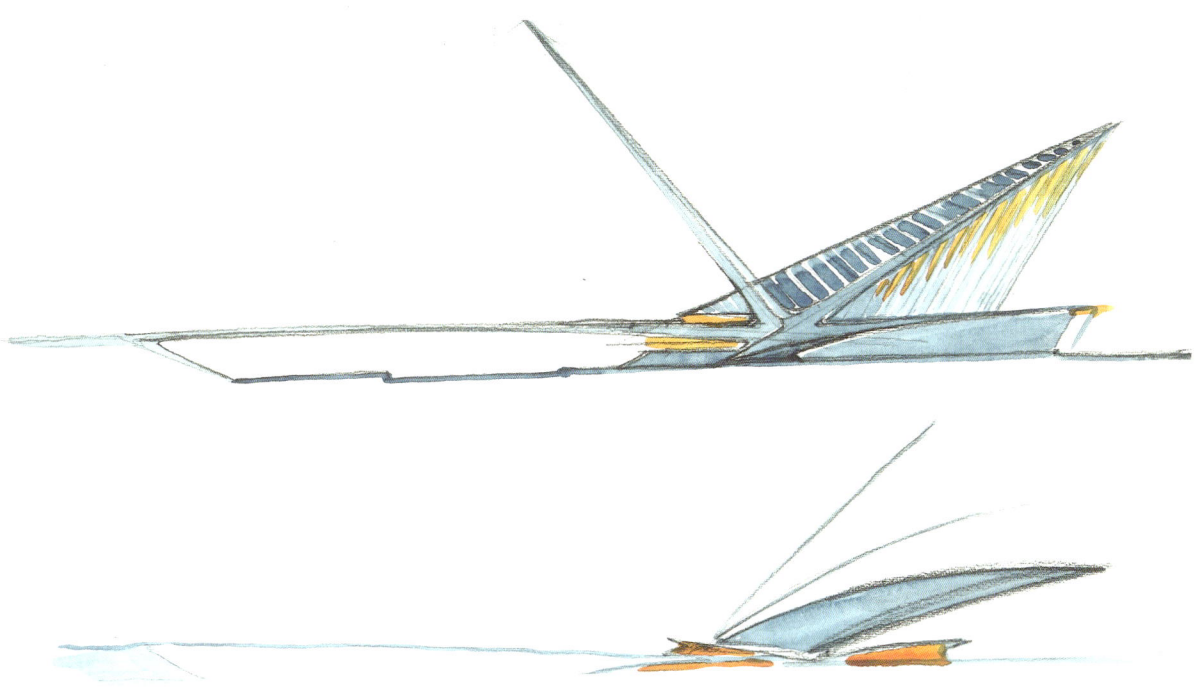

left: Detail exterior. right: Sketch_Skylight and view_Museum's interior_Interior.

USA_NATCHITOCHES (LA) **LOUISIANA STATE SPORTS HALL OF FAME AND REGIONAL HISTORY MUSEUM**

ARCHITECTS: TRAHAN ARCHITECTS_**COMPLETION:** 2011
TYPE: SPORTS AND HISTORY MUSEUM_**GROSS FLOOR AREA:**
2,600 M² _**PHOTOS:** COURTESY OF THE ARCHITECTS

THE ARCHITECTURE

Celebrating Louisiana's history and the influence sports have had on the state, the new Sports Hall of Fame and Regional History Museum will house a collection of sports memorabilia and historic artifacts. The architects' design unites these two seemingly disparate themes in a contemporary venue that recognizes each collection as part of cultural history. The design concept was guided by the fluid shapes of the braided corridors of river channels separated by intermediate bodies of land — this idea becomes the organizing principle for the visitor circulation and gallery arrangement. The focus of the interior is on the atrium, which will serve as a place for community events and general spatial orientation.

THE COLLECTION

The new Louisiana State Sports Hall of Fame and Regional History Museum in Louisiana will bring together two exhibition programs — sports and regional history. The museum will house both a collection of memorabilia, donated by more than 250 outstanding sports figures in Louisiana, and a display of regional historic artifacts. Formerly housed, respectively, in trophy cases lining a university coliseum concourse and on the ground floor of a nineteenth century courthouse these two, apparently unconnected, themes will be displayed together in the new museum. While the museum may appeal to visitors of different interests, the building form allows shared aspects of each topic to be expressed. The site's position, overlooking the historic landscape of the Cane River Lake at the boundary of the Red River valley, makes it possible to unite the apparently disparate themes of sport and historical artifacts by recognizing each as segments of a greater cultural history. The museum offers a view of Louisiana's past, coupled with the experience of a contemporary, state of the art venue. The area will also gain a progressive space for community gatherings and events.

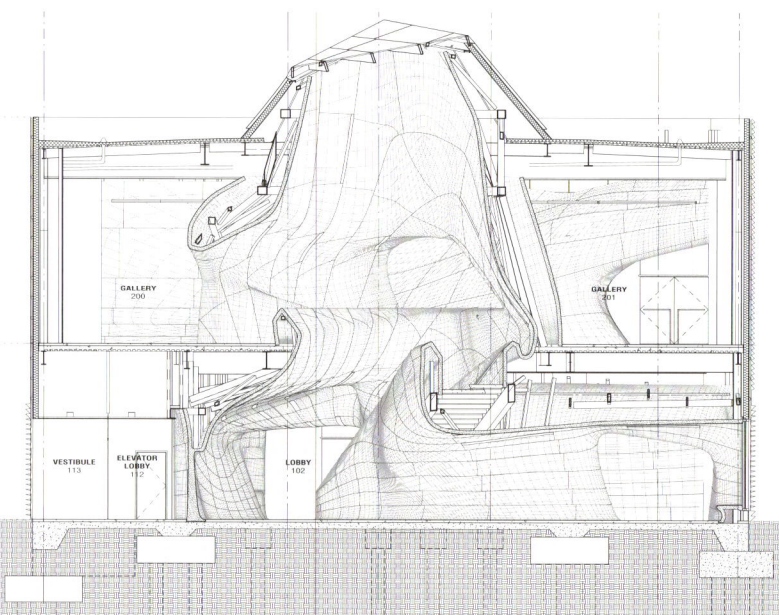

left: Building section_Lobby stairs. right: Atrium_Front entry_Lobby detail.

USA_NEW YORK CITY (NY) **THE BRONX MUSEUM OF THE ARTS**

ARCHITECTS: ARQUITECTONICA_**COMPLETION:** 2006_**TYPE:** ART MUSEUM_**GROSS FLOOR AREA:** 1,551 M² _**PHOTOS:** NORMAN MCGRATH, NEW YORK CITY

THE ARCHITECTURE

The new building is located on Grand Concourse in the Bronx. It emerges from the sidewalk as an irregular folded screen made of fritted glass and metallic panels. The diagonal nature of the panels emphasizes the depth of the crevices. The resulting vertical zones of metal and glass are angled and twisted like architectural origami, making the street wall permeable. One can peek into the ground floor community gallery through the slivers of semitransparent glass that face the approaching pedestrians through their diagonal position. This curtain-like geometry dramatizes the vertical dimension of the otherwise modest structure, turning it into an unexpectedly monumental surface.

THE COLLECTION

The Bronx Museum of the Arts focuses on 20th century and contemporary art, while serving the culturally diverse populations of both the Bronx and the greater New York metropolitan area. Founded in 1971, the Bronx Museum of the Arts was initially housed in the Bronx County Courthouse, located on Grand Concourse and 161st Street. In 1982, the museum was moved five blocks north, to 165th Street. The new location, a former Synagogue, was bought and donated to the Bronx museum by the City of New York. The move to the new location marked the beginning of an ambitious project by the museum to expand its youth and family programs. In February 2004, the museum began construction of the 1,500 square meter extension, to the north of the existing facility. The USD 19 million space was awarded the "Excellence in Design" award, and opened in October 2006. It features a major gallery, flexible events, an outdoor terrace, and an entire floor dedicated to education programs and classrooms. The museum houses a permanent collection of both 20th and 21st century works by artists of African, Asian, Latin and American ancestry, while its permanent collection consists of more than 800 paintings, sculptures, photographs and works on paper.

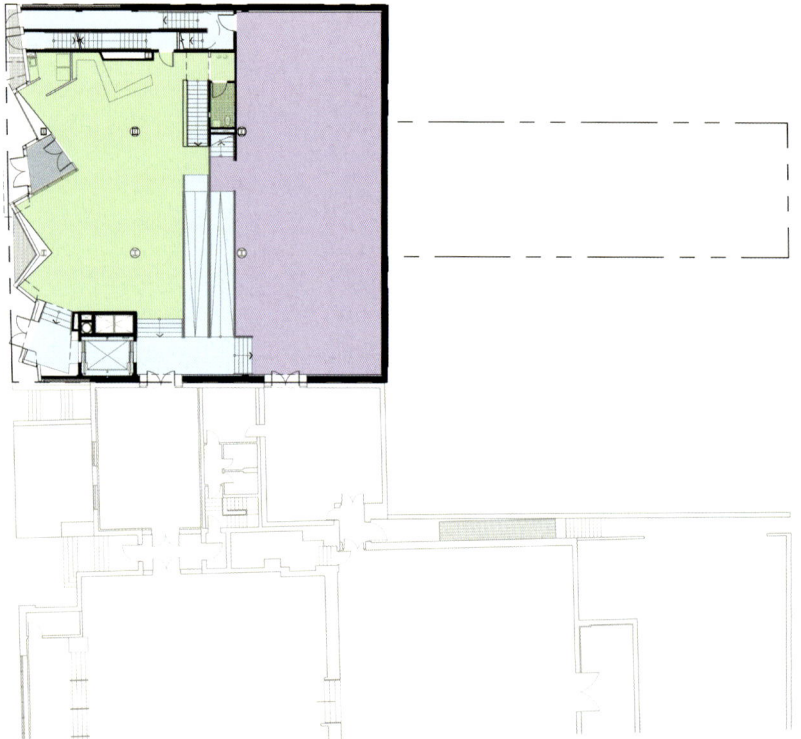

left: Ground floor plan_Façade detail_View looking south-east, night time. right: View looking east Lobby_Stairs.

USA_NEW YORK CITY (NY) **THE SKYSCRAPER MUSEUM**

ARCHITECTS: SKIDMORE, OWINGS & MERRILL LLP
COMPLETION: 2004_**TYPE:** ARCHITECTURE MUSEUM
GROSS FLOOR AREA: 560 M² _**PHOTOS:** ROBERT POLIDORI

THE ARCHITECTURE

The museum conveys the grandeur of a skyscraper, even in its limited space, through the close attention to materials, perspectives, and details. Located on the first floor of the Battery Park Ritz-Carlton, it occupies 560 square meter of donated space. The floors and ceilings are finished with perfectly flat, polished stainless steel panels. Undistorted reflections maximize the apparent volume of the exhibition space, making it seem to extend endlessly in the vertical direction. Together with tall, internally illuminated exhibit showcases, which allow the galleries to be reconfigured for different exhibitions and events, the reflective surfaces create an environment that alludes to a skyscraper.

THE COLLECTION

Founded in 1996, the Skyscraper Museum is a private, non-profit educational corporation, dedicated to the study of the past, present and future of high-rise buildings. Fittingly located in New York City, the world's first vertical metropolis, this museum explores the buildings, trends and historical forces that have shaped the city's own infamous skyline and other influential designs all over the world. Although the museum is now permanently housed in a gallery in the Lower Manhattan area of the city, it previously inhabited four temporary locations. These included 110 Maiden Lane, where the museum was located until September 11, 2001. After the World Trade Center disaster, the museum building was commandeered as an emergency information center to assist downtown businesses. The museum was moved to 55 Broad Street until 2004, when it was given a permanent home in a building at the south end of Battery Park. Amongst the museum's permanent collections are Michael Chesko's Mini-Manhattan models. This exhibition displays detailed hand-carved miniature wooden models of Downtown and Midtown Manhattan. The museum also has a section dedicated to the World Trade Center towers, examining their construction, design and subsequent destruction on the morning of September 11, 2001.

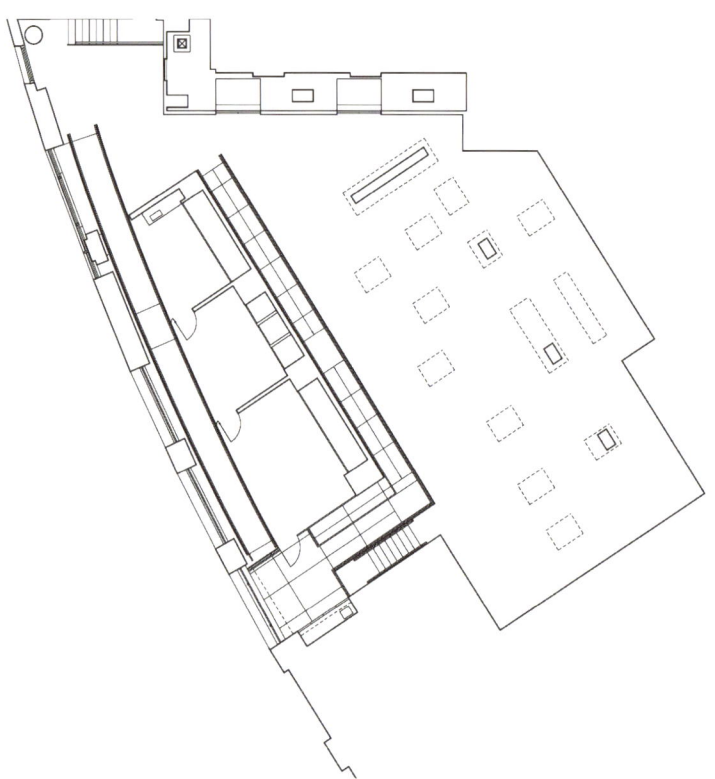

left: Mezzanine floor plan_View of the movable display volumes_View of the entrance ramp. right: View of the gallery_View of the entrance ramp at the ground floor.

USA_OVERLAND PARK (KS) **NERMAN MUSEUM OF CONTEMPORARY ART**

ARCHITECTS: KYU SUNG WOO ARCHITECTS INC. WITH GOULD EVANS ARCHITECTS_**COMPLETION:** 2007
TYPE: ART MUSEUM_**GROSS FLOOR AREA:** 3,865 M²_**PHOTOS:** TIMOTHY HURSLEY, LITTLE ROCK

THE ARCHITECTURE

Located in the suburbs of Kansas City, the museum constitutes an important center for the interchange between art, culture, and education. The design aims to create a space that facilitates the mission of the museum as a home for an outstanding collection of art and that integrates art into the host institution and the daily life of the students, faculty and visitors. The shape of the museum is in contrast with the existing context, marking its presence on campus and the adjoining landscape. The museum space is linked to the outdoors through expansive glazing on the ground floor lobby and strategically placed windows on the upper level, which connect the building to the distant landscape and provide dramatic views.

THE COLLECTION

The Nerman Museum of Contemporary Art is situated on the campus of Johnson County Community College in Overland Park, Kansas. From 1990 to 2007, the museum, formerly called Art Gallery, was housed by the Community College and organized over 80 exhibitions. The Nerman Museum took over this role in 2007, with funding for this USD $15 million project provided by the college and several private investors and foundations. In 2006, the museum was named one of the top ten university campuses for public art in America. Its varied permanent collections and temporary exhibitions include sculpture, ceramics, photography and paper art. The museum presents 16 temporary exhibitions a year, which feature works by international, national and regional artists. The institution's permanent collection consists of works donated to the museum by the Oppenheimer Brothers Foundation and stemming from the college's permanent collection. The museum provides an important space in which culture and education can interact. It strives to be an interdisciplinary academic resource for both students and faculty. Art in different forms is displayed throughout the entire college campus, promoting the idea that art can be integrated into everyday life.

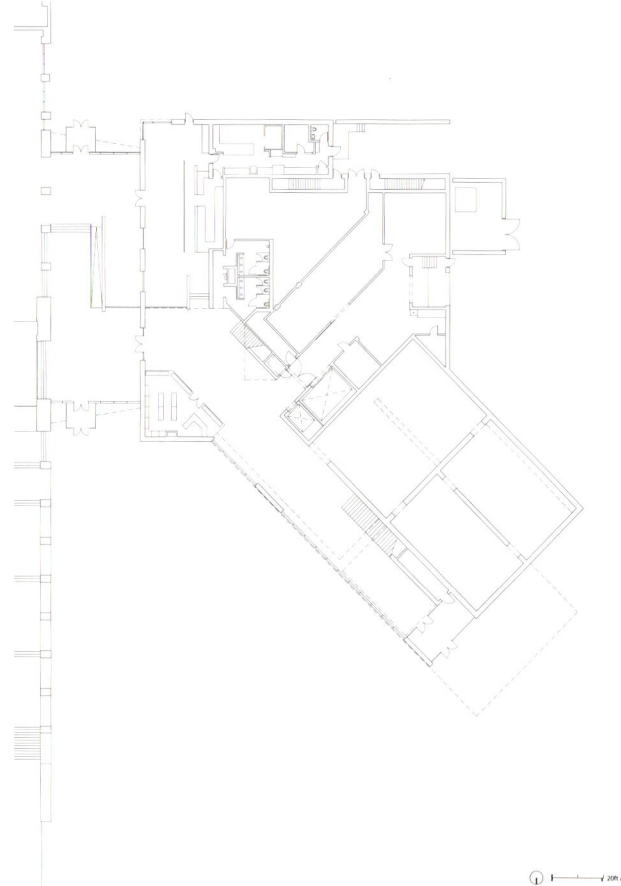

left: Ground floor plan_Exhibition hall_Interior view. right: Exterior_View inside_Glass façade.

USA_ROCHESTER (NY) **STRONG NATIONAL MUSEUM OF PLAY**

ARCHITECTS: CJS ARCHITECTS_**SCENOGRAPHY:** MATT HANDY / STRONG NATIONAL MUSEUM OF PLAY_**COMPLETION:** 2006_**TYPE:** HISTORY MUSEUM_**GROSS FLOOR AREA:** 15,340 M²_**PHOTOS:** COURTESY OF STRONG NATIONAL MUSEUM OF PLAY (112,113 B.), DON COCHRAN PHOTOGRAPHY / ROCHESTER, NEW YORK (113 A., 114, 115)

THE ARCHITECTURE

Whimsical architecture nearly doubled the size of the museum from 15,600 to 26,000 square meter and is a perfect reflection of Strong's playful personality as well as its mission — to explore play. The museum's architectural transformation makes it a striking southeastern gateway to the city. A gigantic, bronze-colored caterpillar atrium organizes and connects galleries and floor levels. An assembly of steel bents covered with colorful resin panels seems like a huge pile of colorful children's blocks and a soaring red tower houses a heating, ventilation, air conditioning system. The butterfly garden is capped with a tensile fabric structure looking like luminous outspread wings.

THE COLLECTION

The Strong National Museum of Play was founded by Margaret Woodbury Strong, a prolific collector of everyday objects, especially dolls and toys. Nearly all the things Mrs. Strong collected were mass-produced, so the museum opened in 1982 with a focus on the ways industrialization changed everyday life. In the mid 1990s, after in-depth market research and strategic analysis, the museum significantly increased its programming for families. In 1997, the museum added a new glass atrium entrance featuring an operating 1918 carousel and 1950s diner. In 2002, the museum, already home to the world's most comprehensive collection of toys, dolls, and play-related objects, acquired the National Toy Hall of Fame. In 2006, Strong changed its mission, becoming the only museum in the world devoted solely to the study of play. The museum also doubled its physical footprint to 26,000 square meter, making it one of the nation's largest family-based history museums. In the late 2000s, the museum began publishing the American Journal of Play, a scholarly quarterly with a global audience; and in 2009, the museum launched the International Center for the History of Electronic Games, home to one of the most comprehensive public collections of electronic games and related materials anywhere.

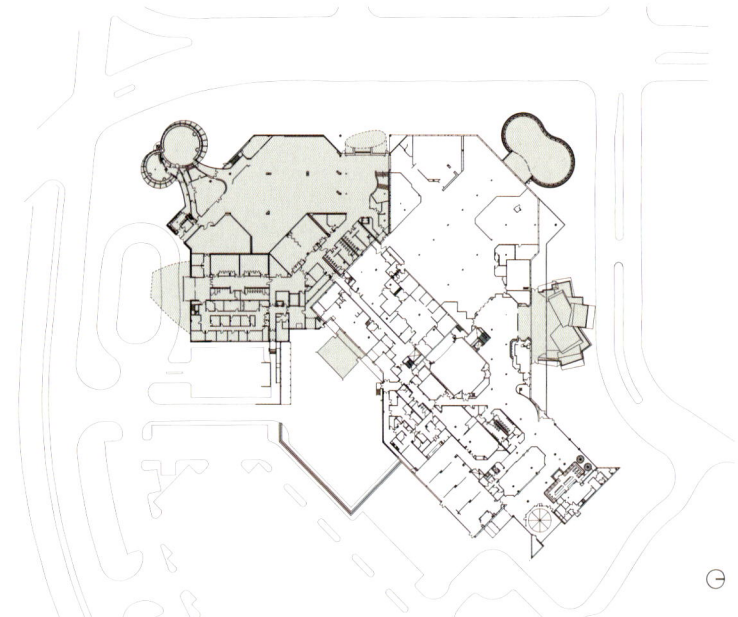

left: Floor plan_Entry to Field of Play exhibition_Overview of exhibition. right: Game Gallery_Toddler "aquarium"_Theater header_Music area.

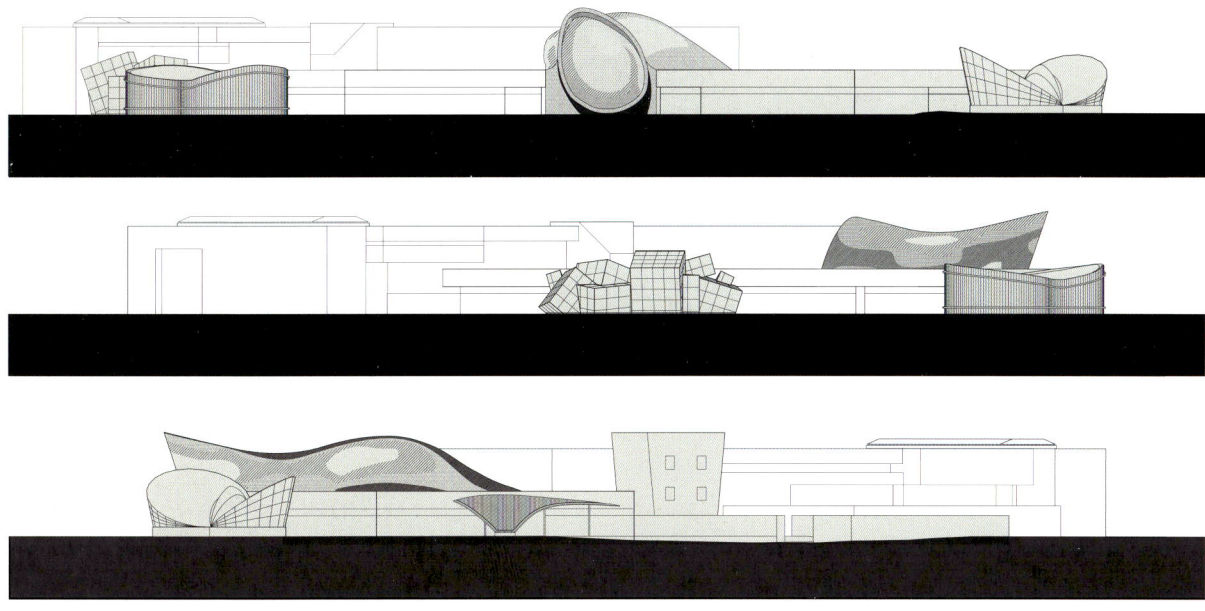

left: Eye Atrium. right: West, north and south elevation_Blue handkerchief canopy_Butterfly Garden pavilion_Exterior view.

ARCHITECTS: STUDIO DANIEL LIBESKIND_**ARCHITECT OF RECORD:** WRNS_**COMPLETION:** 2008_**TYPE:** HISTORY MUSEUM_**GROSS FLOOR AREA:** 5,850 M²_**PHOTOS:** BITTER BREDT FOTOGRAFIE, BERLIN (116, 117 A., 118, 119 A. R., B. R.), MARK DARLEY, MILL VALLEY (117 B., 119 L.)

THE ARCHITECTURE

This museum is a 5,850 square meter facility, located on Mission Street in downtown San Francisco. Since opening in June 2008, the Museum has provided space for temporary exhibitions as well as public and educational programs, and is itself a symbol of dedication to the history and revitalization of Jewish life in San Francisco. Housed in the abandoned, late 19th-century Jessie Street power substation, updated in the first decade of the 20th century by Willis Polk, and landmarked in 1976. The museum literally creates visible relationships between new and old, between tradition and innovation, between the past, present and future, bringing together 19th, 20th and 21st century architecture in one building.

THE COLLECTION

Founded in 1984, the Contemporary Jewish Museum hosts a variety of displays, embracing a range of focused media and artistic disciplines. The museum is a non-collecting institution, collaborating with national and international institutions to keep its exhibitions relevant and current. The displays cover a wide range of topics, from historical objects, to film and music displays. To keep its presentations lively and dynamic, the museum hosts a broad range of programs, including conversations, lectures, live performances and literary readings. Recent exhibitions included a retrospective look at the work of Maurice Sendak, author and illustrator of more than 100 picture books, including the famous children's book, "Where the Wild Things Are". The exhibition aimed to offer an insight into Sendak's life and featured sketches and drawings from more than 40 of his books. Other exhibitions included the first North American showing of "Our Struggle: Responding to Mein Kampf," with a focus on French painter and photographer Linda Ellia's encounter with the book. After personally altering a number of its pages, she invited hundreds of people from all over the world to paint, draw and sculpt directly on the book. These altered pages were then presented in the museum.

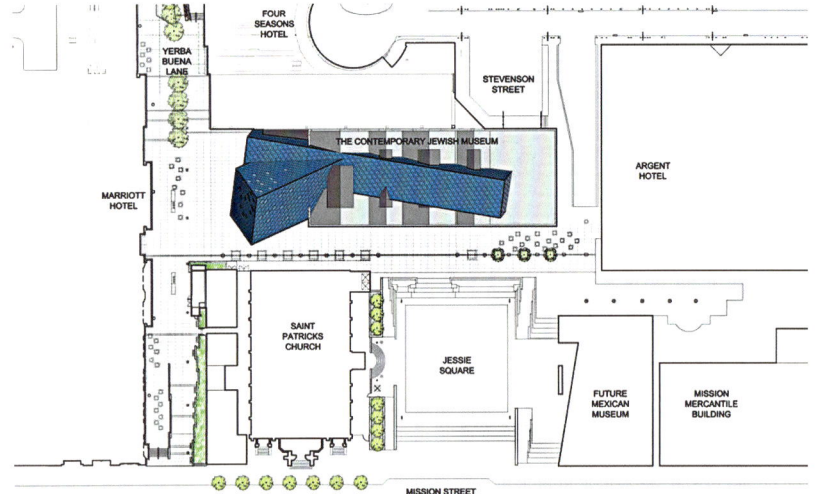

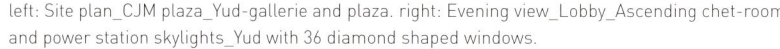
left: Site plan_CJM plaza_Yud-gallerie and plaza. right: Evening view_Lobby_Ascending chet-room and power station skylights_Yud with 36 diamond shaped windows.

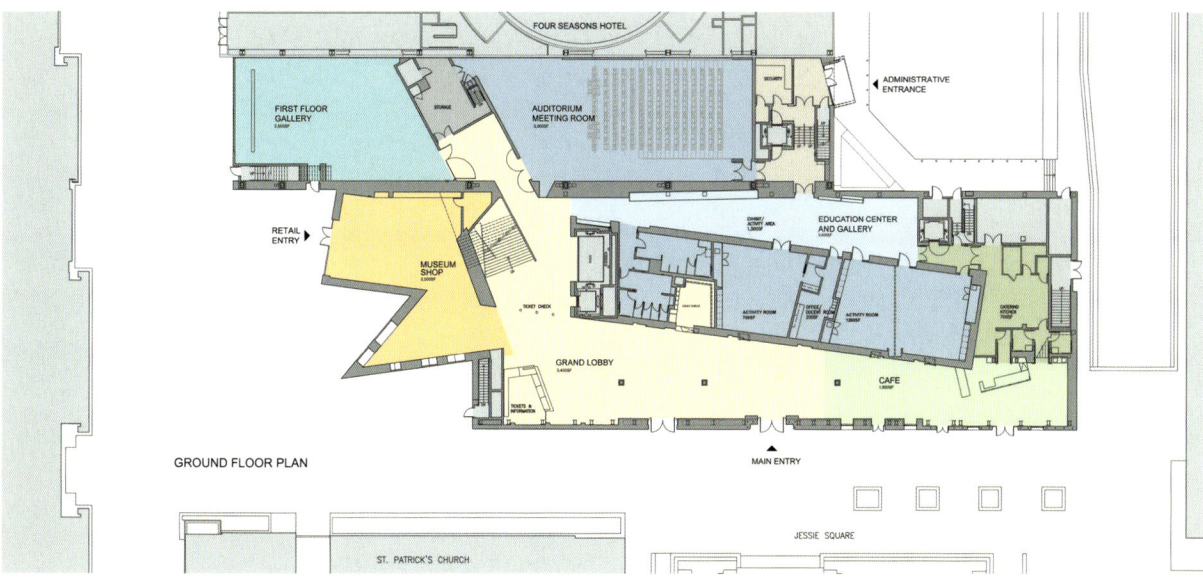

GROUND FLOOR PLAN

FOUR SEASONS HOTEL

ADMINISTRATIVE ENTRANCE

FIRST FLOOR GALLERY

AUDITORIUM MEETING ROOM

SECURITY

RETAIL ENTRY

EDUCATION CENTER AND GALLERY

MUSEUM SHOP

TICKET CHECK

GRAND LOBBY

CAFE

TICKETS & INFORMATION

MAIN ENTRY

ST. PATRICK'S CHURCH

JESSIE SQUARE

left: Staircase. right: Ground floor plan_3,000 steel-blue diamonds emerge into the sky_Detail of blue steel cladding_Gallery.

USA_SAN FRANCISCO (CA) **MH DE YOUNG MUSEUM**

ARCHITECTS: HERZOG & DE MEURON WITH FONG & CHAN
COMPLETION: 2005_**TYPE:** ART MUSEUM
GROSS FLOOR AREA: 27,000 M²
PHOTOS: FINE ARTS MUSEUMS OF SAN FRANCISCO

THE ARCHITECTURE

Constructed in the controversial location of the San Franscisco Bay Area, this new museum serves as a monument, within its surroundings. The flat structure consists of sections, staggered one behind the other in an accordion-like shape. The structure is completed by a tower, whose shape resembles that of a funnel. The individual sections are divided by slits and courtyards, creating a connection between the museum's collection and the surrounding park. The exterior hull consists of 7,200 copper plates, perforated with a pattern of five circles, of various sizes, which are detailed with concave sections and indentations. This design appears uniform from a distance but naturally diverse and changeable when seen from close up.

THE COLLECTION

Founded in 1985, the MH De Young Museum is today an integral part of the city of San Francisco. The building was originally decorated with concrete ornaments, which had to be removed in 1949 as they began to disintegrate, creating a hazard for passers-by. The museum was also severely damaged in 1989 by the Loma Prieta earthquake. The new structure was opened in 2005, providing new facilities and increased exhibition space. One of the museum's largest exhibitions is of American art. Its collection consists of over 1,000 paintings, 800 sculptures and 3,000 objects of decorative art from 1670 to the present day. The museum is among one of ten national collections that encompass the entire history of non-indigenous American art. Although the permanent collection is of national art, works made in California from the Gold Rush era to the present day is also on display in the de MH De Young Museum. The museum exhibits important California collections that also have national significance. Examples include Spanish colonial artwork, Arts and Crafts, and Bay Area Figurative and Assemblage art. The permanent collection galleries integrate decorative art objects with paintings and sculptures, elaborating on the artistic, social, and political context of the works on display.

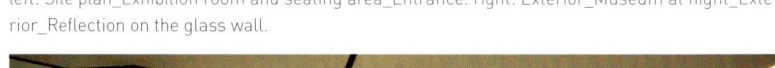

left: Site plan_Exhibition room and seating area_Entrance. right: Exterior_Museum at night_Exterior_Reflection on the glass wall.

USA_SEATTLE (WA) **OLYMPIC SCULPTURE PARK**

ARCHITECTS: WEISS/MANFREDI_**COMPLETION:** 2007
TYPE: ART MUSEUM_**GROSS FLOOR AREA:** 1,116 M²
PHOTOS: BENJAMIN BENSCHNEIDER

THE ARCHITECTURE

This new urban model for a sculpture park connects three separate sites sliced by train tracks and an arterial road with an uninterrupted Z-shaped "green" platform, which descends twelve meter from the city to the water, rising over the existing infrastructure to reconnect the urban core to the revitalized waterfront. The enhanced landform re-establishes the original topography of the site, as it crosses the highway and train tracks and descends to meet the city. At the top of the park, the 1,600 square meter exhibition pavilion, which appears to hover over the parking spaces underneath, accommodates art installations, performances, and educational programming beneath its cantilevered roof.

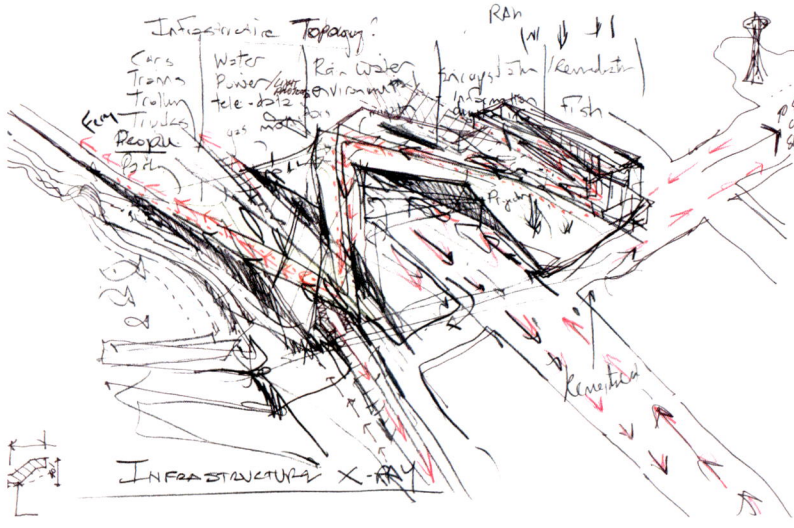

THE COLLECTION

The Olympic Sculpture Park, owned by the Seattle Art Museum, has transformed a 36,000 square meter industrial site into an open and vibrant space for art exhibitions. The former industrial site was occupied by oil and gas corporations and subsequently became a contaminated brownfield, before the museum proposed to transform the area into one of the few green spaces in downtown Seattle. Evolving out of a mutual commitment by both the Seattle Art Museum and the Trust for Public Land, the aim of the park was to preserve downtown Seattle's last remaining undeveloped waterfront property. In 1999 the museum purchased property on the central waterfront from Union Oil of California, and later acquired additional land to ensure that the park was fully accessible to and from the waterfront. From the project's beginnings, the Seattle Art Museum aimed to restore the former industrial site. The "Restorative Engineering" process used on the site introduced a 90 centimeter thick layer of engineered soil that reduces run-off more than ordinary soil. Trees and vegetation were also re-introduced to the area to retain the maximum amount of rainfall. The park offers Seattle residents and visitors the opportunity to experience a wide variety of sculptures in an outdoor setting.

left: Infrastructural X-Ray Sketch_Pavilion interior. right: Pavilion exterior at dusk_Pavilion detail, mirror fritted glass_Elliot Avenue Bridge.

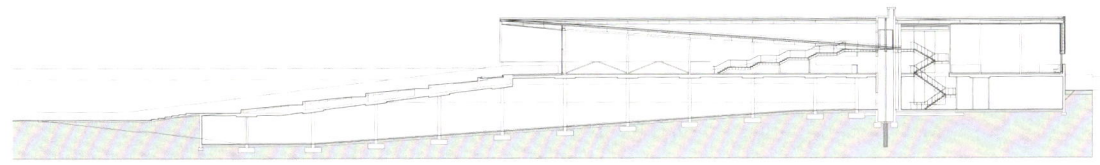

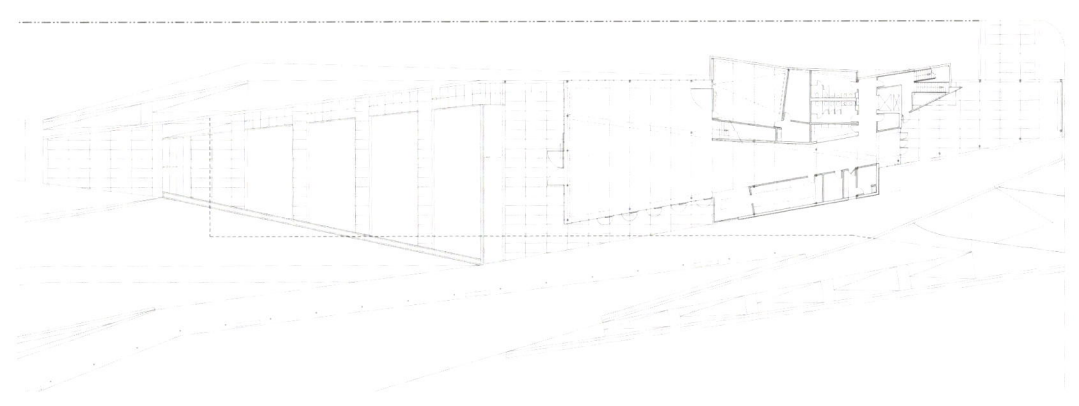

left: Aerial view. right: Pavilion section and plan_Pavilion interior_Urban context_Ascending Route, Park to Pavilion.

europe

ARCHÄOLOGISCHES MUSEUM AGUNTUM_AUSTRIA_DÖLSACH_LAPID...
...UM EGGENBERG_AUSTRIA_GRAZ ARCHÄOLOGISCHES MUSEUM EGGE...
...RG_AUSTRIA_GRAZ_VOLKSKUNDEMUSEUMGRAZ_AUSTRIA_GRAZ_KUNSTHAU...
...AZ_AUSTRIA_GRAZ_AUT – ARCHITEKTURFORUM TIROL ARCHIV FÜR BA...
...UNST_AUSTRIA_INNSBRUCK_ARS ELECTRONICA CENTER_AUSTRIA_LINZ...
...NTOS KUNSTMUSEUM_AUSTRIA_LINZ_BESUCHERZENTRUM MAUTHAUSE...
...EMORIAL_AUSTRIA_MAUTHAUSEN_ML MUSEUM LIAUNIG_AUSTRIA_NEU...
...AUS_MUSEUM DER MODERNE_AUSTRIA_SALZBURG_GIRONCOLI MUSE...
...M_AUSTRIA_ST JOHANN / HERBERSTEIN MUSEUMSQUARTIER_AUSTRIA_VI...
...NA_GROENINGEMUSEUM_BELGIUM_BRUGES_MAC'S – MUSEE DES ART...
...ONTEMPOTAINS_BELGIUM_HORNUMONS_DOX-CENTRUMSOUˇCASNÉHOUMˇEN...
...ECHREPUBLIC_PRAGUE_DANSKJØDISKMUSEUM_DENMARK_COPENHAGEN...
...ANDELS- OG SØFARTSMUSEET_DENMARK_HELSINGØR_RANDERS KUNSTM...
...UM_DENMARK_RANDERS_FUGLSANG KUNSTMUSEUM_DENMARK_TOREB...

AUSTRIA_DÖLSACH **ARCHÄOLOGISCHES MUSEUM AGUNTUM**

ARCHITECTS: MOSER KLEON ARCHITEKTEN_**COMPLETION:** 2005
TYPE: ARCHEOLOGY MUSEUM_**GROSS FLOOR AREA:** 1,200 M²
PHOTOS: NIKOLAUS SCHLETTERER, INNSBRUCK
(128, 129, 130, 131 R.), BARTH, BRIXEN (131 L.)

THE ARCHITECTURE

With its simple geometry, this building still indicates its earlier function, as a protective shell, while its fully glazed southern side provides views of the adjacent forest. The northern side is dominated by a Corten steel façade that shields the site from traffic. The museum's interior features rhythmic skylights that affect the view and the lighting of the room settings. Mastic asphalt and perforated birch plywood slabs are the predominant surfaces. Black and red MDF panels are the main material used for fittings and furnishings. Only the showcases are painted in various colors, which sets them apart.

THE COLLECTION

Aguntum was a Roman settlement that was given autonomous city status under Emperor Claudius. The ruins of the city wall, an atrium house, a thermal bath and the artisan district can be seen today. Due to the danger of flooding by the nearby Debantbach, a protective structure was built right next to the "Atrium house" and converted into a museum. It contains today an exhibition of the culture and civilization of the Roman era in the Alps. The exhibits include life-size dolls wearing the costumes of the local and Roman population, as well as Roman reliefs from Aguntum and other areas of the Noricum province, profane and sacral inscriptions, and a road map from the late Antiquity era. The exhibition furthermore includes ceramics, jewelry, amphorae, tools, coins and a large-scale male bronze statue consisting of complemented fragments. The central point of the museum is the 16 by 14.50 meter marble pool of the atrium house. The two erected statues on the gravel of the island in the pool represent Antonia minor and Octavia Claudia, the mother daughter of Emperor Claudius, respectively.

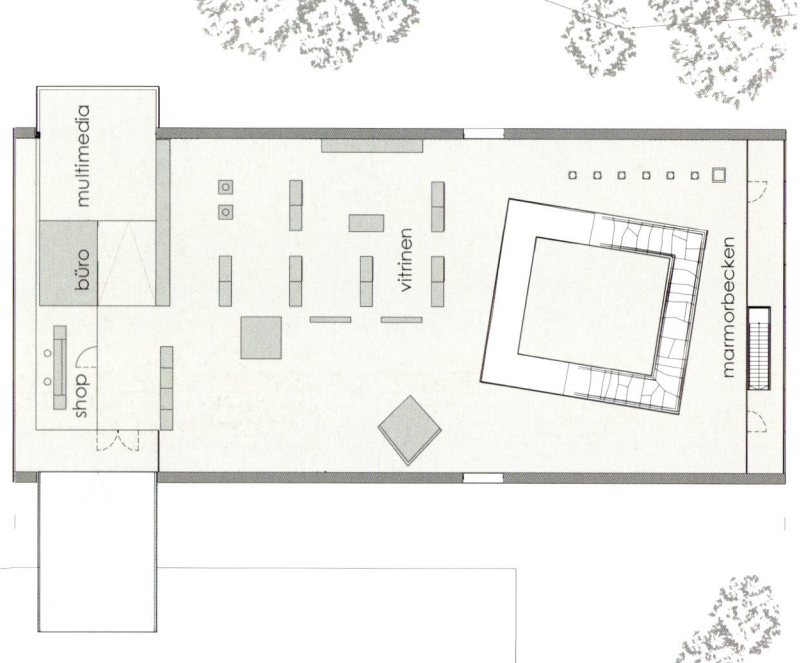

left: Ground floor plan_North façade_Entrance. right: North façade_Entrance area.

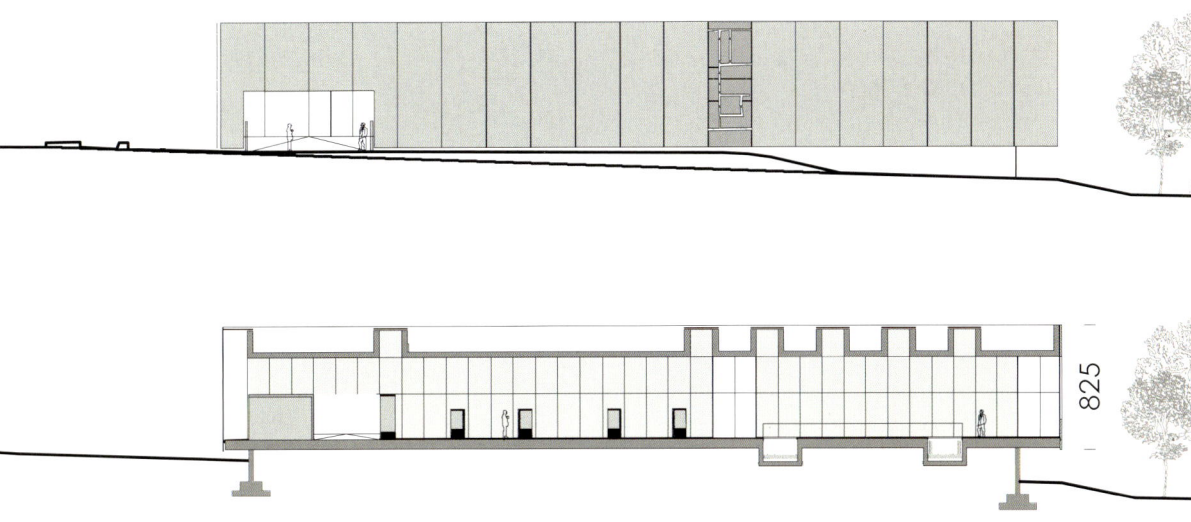

825

left: Exhibition hall. right: Elevations_Museum shop_Exhibition hall, southern part_Exhibition hall, view to north.

AUSTRIA_GRAZ **LAPIDARIUM EGGENBERG**

ARCHITECTS: PURPUR. ARCHITEKTUR ZT GMBH_**COMPLETION:** 2009_**ORIGINAL BUILDING:** PURPUR. ARCHITEKTUR ZT GMBH, 2004_**TYPE:** ARCHEOLOGY MUSEUM_**GROSS FLOOR AREA:** 1,500 M²
PHOTOS: ANGELO KAUNAT, SALZBURG

THE ARCHITECTURE

The new lapidarium is situated at the northern end of the newly constructed Planetary Garden near Eggenberg castle next to the historic 18th century orangery. It was conceived as a "building state" of the present, as a fragment of a continuous process, suspended between the wing walls with the front columns topped by capitals, remnants of the orangery and the northern surrounding wall of the castle. This "in-between" is also reflected in the style and experiences offered by the museum concept — at the core of the exhibition concept is the ambivalence between objective and subjective images and the tension inherent in this duality.

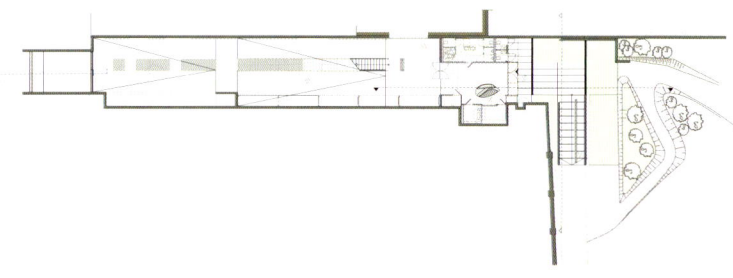

THE COLLECTION

The museum for Roman steles of the Universalmuseum Joanneum contains Austria's and the entire Eastern Alps region's largest and most significant collection, providing an insight into the key aspects of life and cultural development of the region during the Roman era. Located in the park of Schloss Eggenberg, the lapidarium features three floor mosaics among other exhibits. It also contains 96 steles, inscriptions, reliefs, and round sculptures of Styria and the former Lower Styria. Many of the steles are headstones. They feature portraits and provide an insight into the life, work, and wealth of the area's residents through inscriptions, costumes, servants' figures and attributes. Next to the headstones and fragments of grave statues, archeologically significant Roman provincial sculptures are presented, such as a grave stele of L. Cantius of Graz that is almost three meters tall. The museum also contains mythological reliefs that tell of never-ending love and altars that speak of kept vows.

left: Ground floor plan with newly constructed entrance area_Lapidarium in the Planetary Garden Interspace. right: Exhibition space_Exhibition space.

AUSTRIA_GRAZ **ARCHÄOLOGISCHES MUSEUM EGGENBERG**

ARCHITECTS: BWM ARCHITEKTEN UND PARTNER – BERNARD WALTEN MOSER ZIVILTECHNIKER GMBH_**GRAPHICS:** LICHTWITZ
COMPLETION: 2009_**TYPE:** ARCHEOLOGY MUSEUM_**GROSS FLOOR AREA:** 650 M²_**PHOTOS:** RUPERT STEINER, VIENNA (134 B. R., 135, 136, 137 A., B. R.), PAUL OTT, GRAZ (134 B. L., 137 B. L.)

THE ARCHITECTURE

The purpose of the new building for this museum was the underground extension of the existing lapidarium along with the new presentation of the Joanneum's archeological exhibition. The zones of the two-part exhibition hall with a skylight extending through its center are defined by different floor levels. Exposed concrete walls and flooring create an understated background for the small-scale exhibits that seem to float in highly transparent, fully glazed showcases. Architecture and showcases are combined into a contemporary and elegant room structure that is very light and bright.

THE COLLECTION

Established in 1811, the Joanneum established the foundation of the collection as part of its history department, the so-called "Archive", which collected pre- and early history sources on the region. In 1869, an independent department entitled Münz- und Antikenkabinett (Coin and antiquities cabinet) was established, which subsequently gained ground as the department of prehistoric collections, antiquity and coins. The specialization of the individual departments, such as pre-history and early history, Roman provincial archeology, and numismatics, resulted in the establishment of independent sections, which are today once more united in a single department — the archeology and coin cabinet. After initial resentment toward the collection, which caused the transfer of all archeological finds to Vienna and the stop to all excavations, the first systematic excavations took place in the late 19th century under Friedrich Pichler, the museum's director at the time. In 1911, intensive excavations were begun, during which first insights into the time from the Paleolithic era up to the early Middle Ages were gained. Since that time, the museum's contents, ranging from the Stone Age to the Modern Era, were continuously expanded.

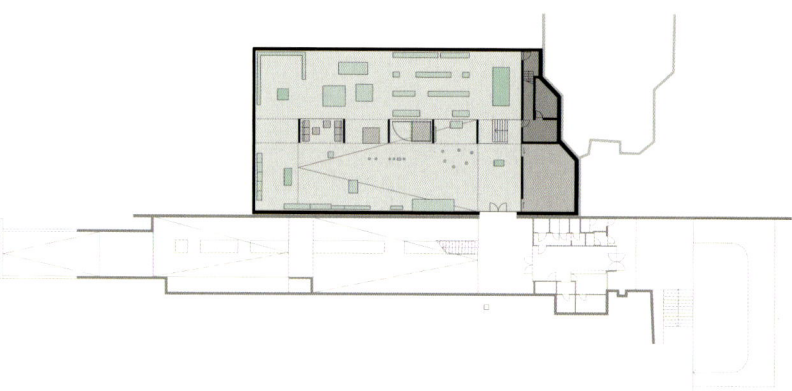

left: Floor plan with furnishing_Exhibition space before furnishing_Excavation container as childrens zone. right: Exhibition space gods_Exhibition space weapons.

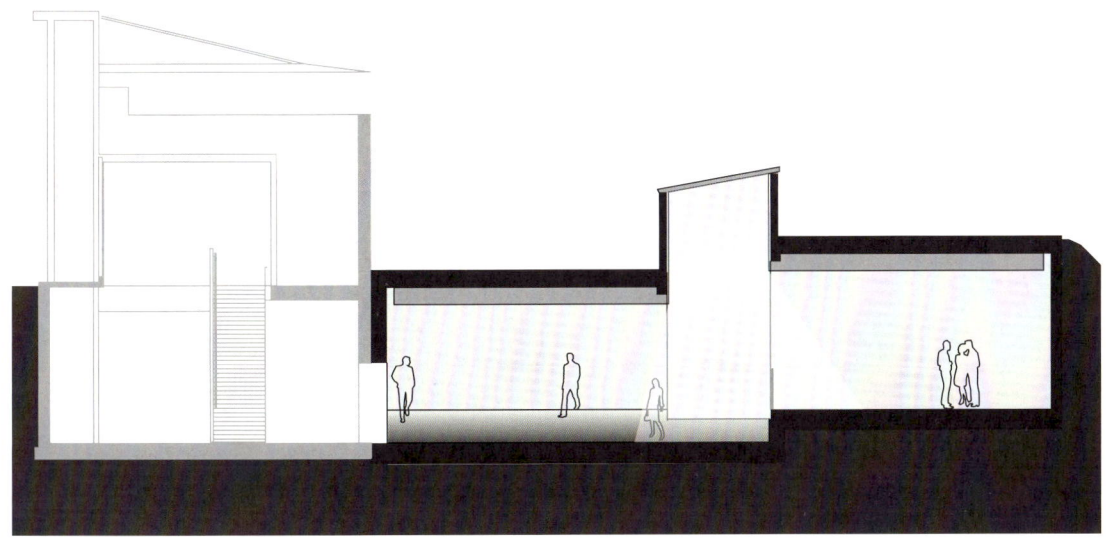

left: Information and recreation area. right: Section with light_Exhibition area vessels_Exhibition area worship_Exhibition area jewelry_Exhibition area vessels.

AUSTRIA_GRAZ **VOLKSKUNDEMUSEUM GRAZ**

ARCHITECTS: BWM ARCHITEKTEN UND PARTNER – BERNARD
WALTEN MOSER ZIVILTECHNIKER GMBH_**COMPLETION:** 2003
ORIGINAL BUILDING: EARLY 17TH CENTURY, 1930_**TYPE:**
CULTURE MUSEUM_**GROSS FLOOR AREA:** 1,500 M²
PHOTOS: ALEXANDER KOLLER, VIENNA

THE ARCHITECTURE
The architects were responsible for the renovation, restructuring and new
adaptation of the existing Volkskundemuseum (ethnology museum) as well as
the rearrangement of the exhibits depicting rural life in the 19th and 20th century. The architectural concept intended to separate the new room structures
from the historic substance. The outer walls of the former monastery premises remained unchanged. The interventions are distinguished by the applied
material: glass, metal, light. The architectural highlight of the redesign is a
glass bridge connection between the main building and the historic costume
hall. Back-lit glass showcases impressively present the ethnological objects
on light tables.

THE COLLECTION
The Volkskundemuseum Graz houses the oldest and most extensive folkloris-
tic collection of the Joanneum universal museum. It was established in 1913
by the folklorist Viktor von Geramb (1884–1958). He designed individual rooms
as overall works of art, for example a "Smoke room" of a farm from the West-
steiermark region and a "Traditional costume hall" with 42 life-size figures
donning traditional costumes of the Styrian region from the Roman era to the
beginning of the 20th century, designed by von Geramb in the 1930s. Both
rooms still exist today. In addition, the museum's permanent collection, which
was opened in fall 2008 entitled "Return with new accents" presents exhibits
related to living, dressing, and believing. A total of more than 40,000 objects
are contained in the museum's collection, documenting the folklore of Styria,
especially during the pre-industrial era. In addition to the exhibits, the museum also contains a specialized folklore library including 14,000 individual
volumes and 80 specialized periodicals, an archive, and an image archive with
around 20,000 color slides and historic photos.

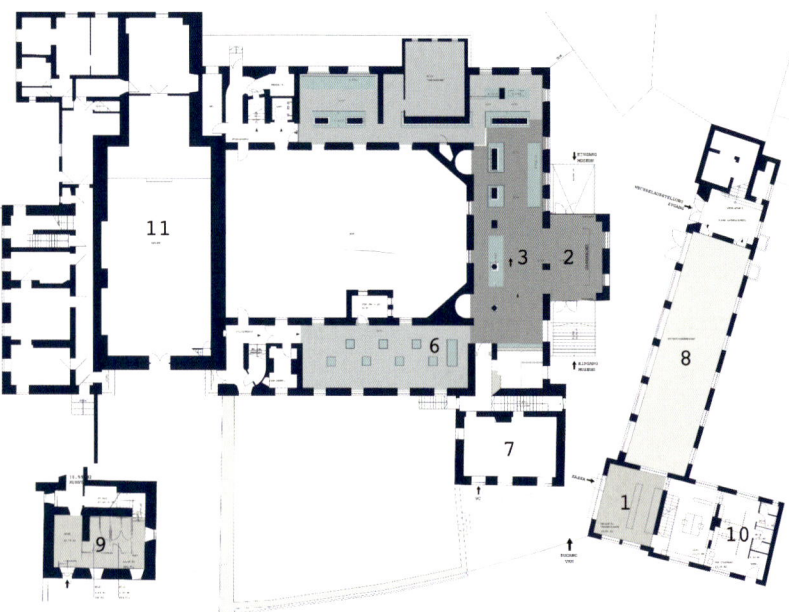

left: Ground floor plan_Entrance at night_Bridge, temporary exhibition space. right: Sleeping room
Exhibition_Smoking room.

AUSTRIA_GRAZ **KUNSTHAUS GRAZ**

ARCHITECTS: SPACELAB COOK / FOURNIER WITH ARCHITEKTUR CONSULT_**COMPLETION:** 2003_**TYPE:** ART MUSEUM_**GROSS FLOOR AREA:** 13,100 M² _**PHOTOS:** NICOLAS LACKNER / UMJ (140, 141 B. R.), PETER GRADISCHNIGG, GRAZ (141 A.), GEORG WALLNER (141 B. L.)

THE ARCHITECTURE

The Kunsthaus Graz, the "Friendly Alien", lovingly dubbed by its architects Peter Cook and Colin Fournier, enriches the historic district of Graz not only with its unusual appearance. Since the year 2003, its exhibition program also enhances the cultural life of the Austrian regional capital with national and international art from the 1960s to this day. A glass gallery — the so-called "Needle"— provides a magnificent view of the city across the river. A smaller, glazed ground floor carries the biomorphic structure, with its acrylic glass skin nestled among the roofs of the ancient city district. Digital art can also be displayed on the building's multimedia façade.

THE COLLECTION

The Kunsthaus Graz was built as part of the European Capital of Culture celebrations in 2003 and has since become an architectural landmark in Graz, Austria. The museum's exhibition program specializes in contemporary art, focusing on works from the last 40 years. The museum also hosts a range of temporary exhibitions, which focus on a variety of different trends, forms and media. The museum aims to embrace different artistic mediums and consider controversial and developing forms of emerging art. A recent exhibition entitled Robot Dreams explores the political, social and artistic implications associated with robots. For this exhibition, eight artists were specifically invited to create a piece of art for the exhibition. The aim was to attempt to explain and investigate the term "robot" and how robotic creations have moved gradually from science-fiction movies to an established place in our society. The display also gave its audience the opportunity to investigate society's association of the word "robot" with the concepts of power, fear and control. Robots in this exhibition act as an artistic medium, a means by which visitors to the museum can explore concepts of ethical considerations and the relationships between man and machine in modern society.

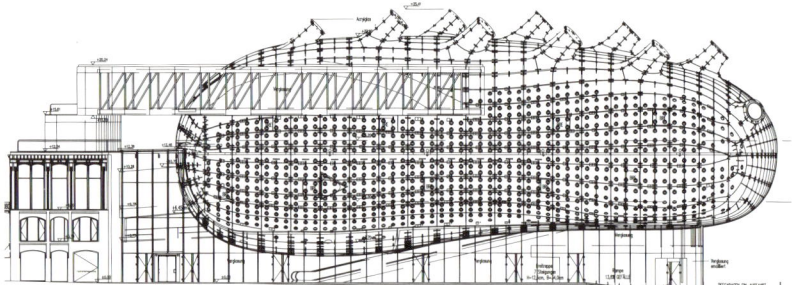

left: Elevation eastside_BIX Media façade and Needle_Space01. right: Exterior_Corridor to Space03 BIX Media façade and Needle.

AUSTRIA_INNSBRUCK

AUT – ARCHITEKTURFORUM TIROL
ARCHIV FÜR BAUKUNST

ARCHITECTS: ARCHITEKTEN ARGE KÖBERL & GINER+WUCHERER, PFEIFER **COMPLETION:** 2004_**ORIGINAL BUILDING:** LOIS WELZENBACHER, 1926/27_**TYPE:** ARCHITECTURE MUSEUM_**GROSS FLOOR AREA:** 1,410 M²_**PHOTOS:** LUKAS SCHALLER

THE ARCHITECTURE

This former brewery was custom-built as a "wrap" around the exceptionally vertical production premises. In the next step, the entire technical plant was removed and the customized building transformed into an architectural forum — "form follows function" became "function follows form." The upper area of the silos was turned into an archive, while the lower boiling and simmering area became the architectural forum, keeping the upstairs/downstairs organization intact. Integration of the silos resulted in a "room layout" on the minimal site plan of 12 x 18 meters — not in the sense of Loos, but rather resembling more complex structures such as Koolhaas' ZKM project for Karlsruhe.

THE COLLECTION

The archive for architecture at the University of Innsbruck is dedicated to the preservation, storage, and research of architecture and constructional engineering in the Alpine region. Established in 1993 upon the initiative of a group of committed architects, the independent association emphasizes the interaction with contemporary design issues. Since its inception, the association organizes numerous events, such as architectural, art and design exhibitions, as well as lectures by national and international architects, discussion rounds, excursions, symposia, tours, thematic movie series, and "on-site" artist talks in new buildings. An online construction data base, which is part of the "nextroom" Internet platform by Juerg Meister, features select Tyrolean buildings that are a representative cross-section of the current architectural scene. Furthermore, an extensive collection of books, newspaper and magazine articles related to architecture and Tyrol are available for research purposes. In addition, a media center containing around 800 examples across all movie genres related to architecture, cities, and design is available, organized by the Viennese architecture and film historian Helmut Weihsmann.

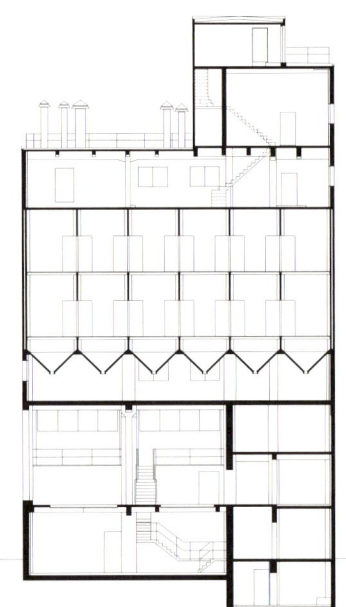

left: Sections_Archives_Exterior_Archives. right: Simmering area_Seminar room_Lower exhibition floor.

AUSTRIA_LINZ **ARS ELECTRONICA CENTER**

ARCHITECTS: TREUSCH ARCHITECTURE ZT GMBH_**COMPLETION:** 2008_**ORIGINAL BUILDING:** KLAUS LEITNER, WALTER MICHL, 1996 **TYPE:** ART AND MEDIA MUSEUM_**GROSS FLOOR AREA:** 4,620 M² **PHOTOS:** RUPERT STEINER (144, 145 B. R.), ANDREA EHRENREICH (145 A., B. L.)

THE ARCHITECTURE

The basic concept of this design is the creation of a sculptural building volume, whose structure is accessible and thus available for visitors to experience. The existing Ars Electronica Center and the expansion are combined into a single unit and perceived as a whole. The shape of a glass cube with a double-glazed façade conveys a homogenous impression. In terms of urban planning, the concept is based on a dialogue with its surroundings, which provide a free view of the Danube River, while maintaining the historic ensemble with a contemporary addition. The exhibition areas can be flexibly subdivided into smaller or larger exhibition spaces.

THE COLLECTION

The Ars Electronica Center (AEC) deals with techno-cultural phenomena and shows how information and communication technologies can change social life today. Human beings are always at the center of all exhibits. Installations allow visitors to fly, while wall and floor projections enable them to delve into virtual worlds or see never observed details of historic works of art. For example, they can look at a reproduction of the Last Supper by Leonardo da Vinci, enter Etruscan underground burial sites, or observe the digital construction of the cathedral of Beauvais. The heart of the center is the so-called "Main Gallery", where visitors can work and experiment together with artists and scientists. In addition to its exhibits, the center also offers a future lab as well as room for seminar and conferences, dining establishments and a forecourt measuring 1,000 square meters for open air events. Once a year, the Prix Ars Electronica for computer art is awarded at the AEC.

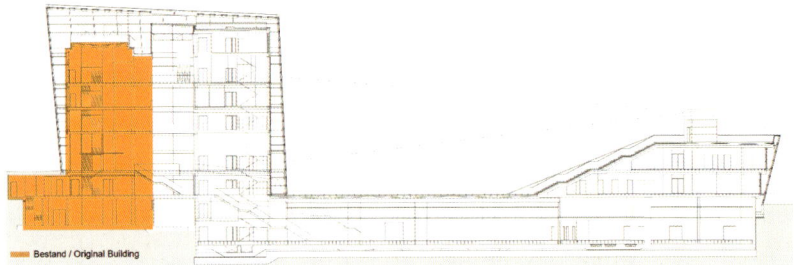

Bestand / Original Building

left: Section_Night view including church_West façade. right: View from Danube river, red_View from Danube river, blue and green_Staircase.

AUSTRIA_LINZ **LENTOS KUNSTMUSEUM**

ARCHITECTS: WEBER HOFER PARTNER AG_**COMPLETION:** 2003_**TYPE:** ART MUSEUM_**GROSS FLOOR AREA:** 7,700 M² **PHOTOS:** DIETMAR TOLLERIAN, LINZ

THE ARCHITECTURE

This museum marks the western edge of the Donaupark and is aligned with the flood levee. Resembling a ship, it lies at the shore of the Danube, surrounded by water on one side and by the park on the other. Spanned by the building structure, the open "sculpture hall" is a room without columns measuring 60 x 24 meters. It is a public square as well as the entrance hall to the museum, and a window to the Danube. The spacious glass façade with its reflective coating reflects the surrounding light. At night, the museum is turned into an illuminated body that is reflected in the Danube.

THE COLLECTION

Based on the collection of 120 works of art of the Berlin art trader Wolfgang Gurlitt (1888-1965), the Neue Galerie of the city of Linz was established after World War II. Subsequently, the city of Linz decided to operate the Neue Galerie from 1953 as a city museum with a constant exhibition program and purchase activities. From 1979, the gallery was housed in the Lentia 2000 until the city decided in 1998 to build the Lentos Kunstmuseum. Today, the collection contains approximately 1,600 paintings, sculptures and pieces of object art. In addition, the museum owns more than 10,000 works on paper, including 1,000 photographs by artists such as Man Ray and Alexander M. Rodtschenko. The museum's earliest works date to the first half of the 19th century and were created by Caspar David Friedrich and Johann Baptist Reiter. The museum's contents are constantly complemented by purchases and donations with a currently discernible focus on contemporary Austrian art. The museum presents works by artists such as Fritz Aigner, Elke Krystufek, as well as Lois and Franziska Weinberger.

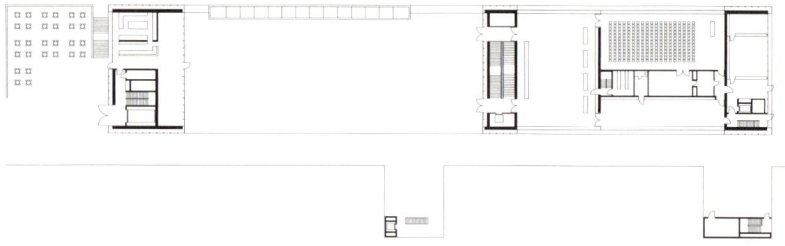

left: Ground floor plan_Townsilhouette_Sculpture hall by night. right: Reflection and view through the building_Large exhibition room.

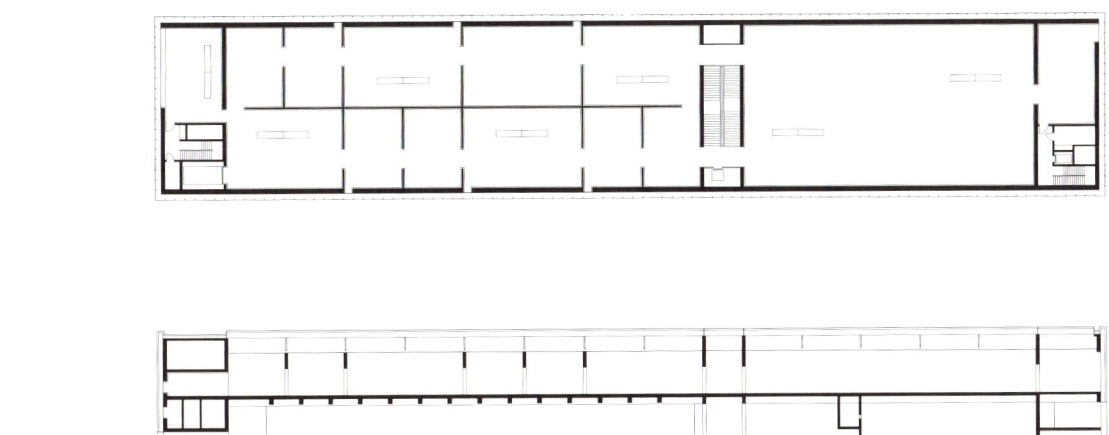

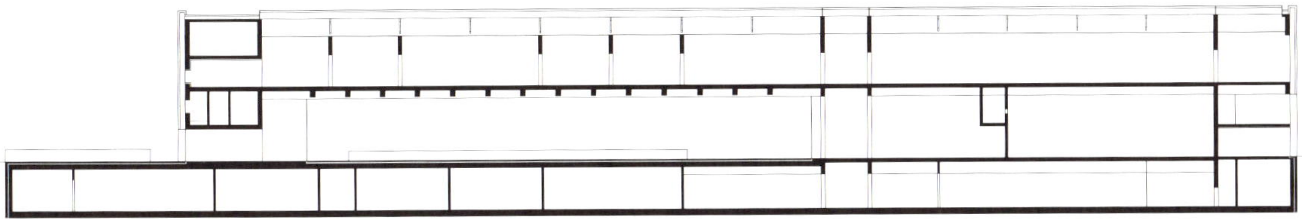

left: Small exhibition room. right: Second floor plan and longitudinal section_Exhibition rooms.

AUSTRIA_MAUTHAUSEN

BESUCHERZENTRUM MAUTHAUSEN MEMORIAL

ARCHITECTS: HERWIG MAYER / CHRISTOPH SCHWARZ / KARL PEYRER-HEIMSTÄTT_**COMPLETION:** 2003_**ORIGINAL BUILDING:** 1938_**TYPE:** HISTORY MUSEUM_**GROSS FLOOR AREA:** 2,845 M²
PHOTOS: JORK WEISSMANN

THE ARCHITECTURE

The aim was to clearly delineate the visitors' center from the actual memorial site. The architectural concept of the visitors' center consists of a compact, interior-oriented venue on two levels. These levels are combined in a prism-shaped building structure almost entirely located underground whose greened flat roof is at ground level. A central inner courtyard and a neighboring two-floor exhibition area with connected raster-shaped access zones constitute the core of the premises. The primary use of exposed concrete, whitewashing and glass defines a minimalist material expression that contrasts with the use of granite during the Nazi regime.

THE COLLECTION

On a round tour of the former prison camp, visitors receive information about the Mauthausen concentration camp. This includes the functions of the individual parts and buildings of the camp, aspects of the inmates' living conditions, and special conditions of individual groups of inmates. At the same time, visitors are told about general structures and mechanisms of the concentration camp system. For example, they can look at files of the SS administration, along with their transport and death lists. Quotes from autobiographical essays as well as statements by former inmates of the concentration camp illustrate the everyday life and the cruelties of the camp. The quotes were chosen from the reports of different types of prisoners from various countries, providing a comprehensive insight into their individual and collective experiences. Approximately 900 audio and around 90 video interviews on the memories of survivors could be collected in an archive. In another area of the memorial, every personal item of survivors tells its own story. The information is complemented by other facilities such as a library and rooms for film screenings and seminars, which provide detailed access to research and knowledge.

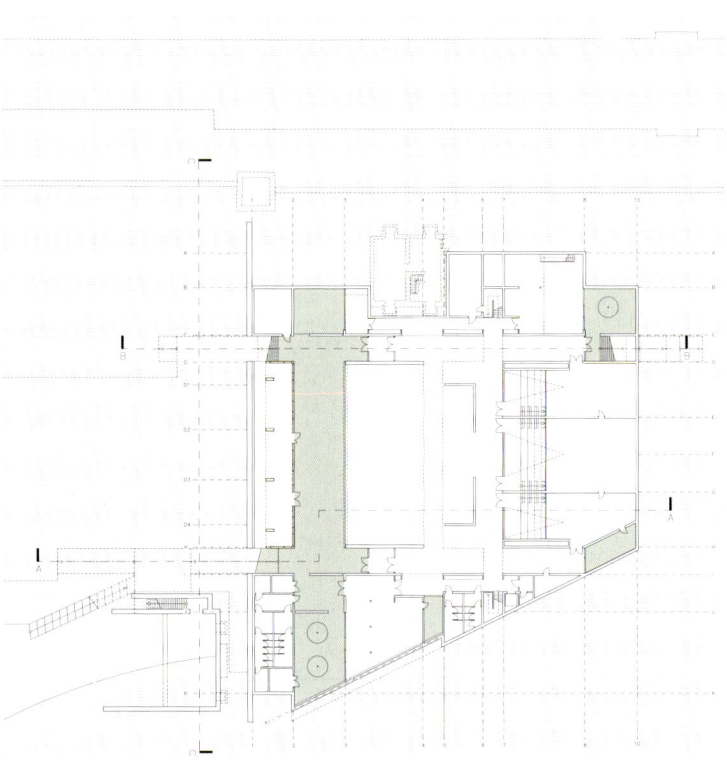

left: Ground floor plan_Entrance_View between cubes. right: Interior_Glass façade_Exhibition_View to the outside.

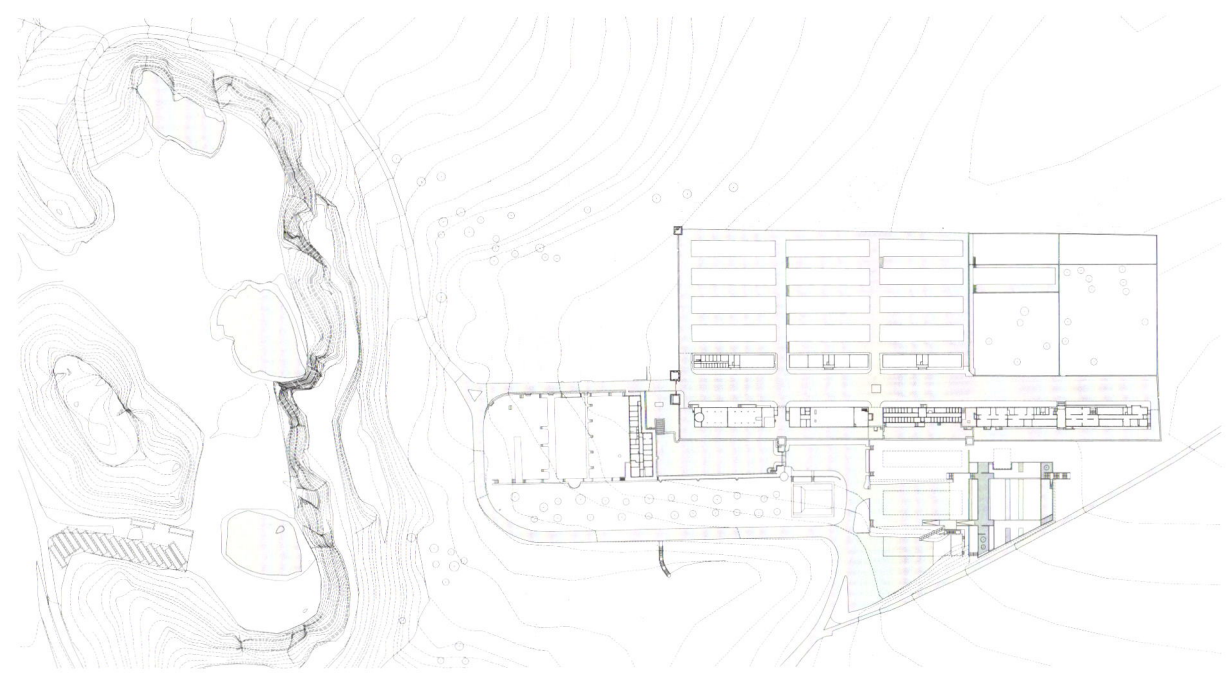

left: View out of the cubes. right: Site plan_Details_Exterior.

AUSTRIA_NEUHAUS **ML MUSEUM LIAUNIG**

ARCHITECTS: QUERKRAFT ARCHITEKTEN ZT GMBH
COMPLETION: 2008_**TYPE:** ART MUSEUM_**GROSS FLOOR AREA:**
4,810 M²_**PHOTOS:** QUERKRAFT / LISA RASTL

THE ARCHITECTURE

This museum, housing the extensive private art collection of Herbert Liaunig, was intended to attract visitors and allow contemplative enjoyment of art far removed from all urban centers with a minimal budget and the lowest possible operational costs. For cost reasons and to optimize the energy concept, 95 percent of the cubature is located underground. Visitors enter the museum via the generously proportioned display repository area, the "Wine cellar of art," and reach the bright, centrally-located main hall. As a counterpoint to the contemplative enjoyment of art, the visitors discover dramatic climaxes by intensely focusing on the landscape, which never gives the impression of being underground.

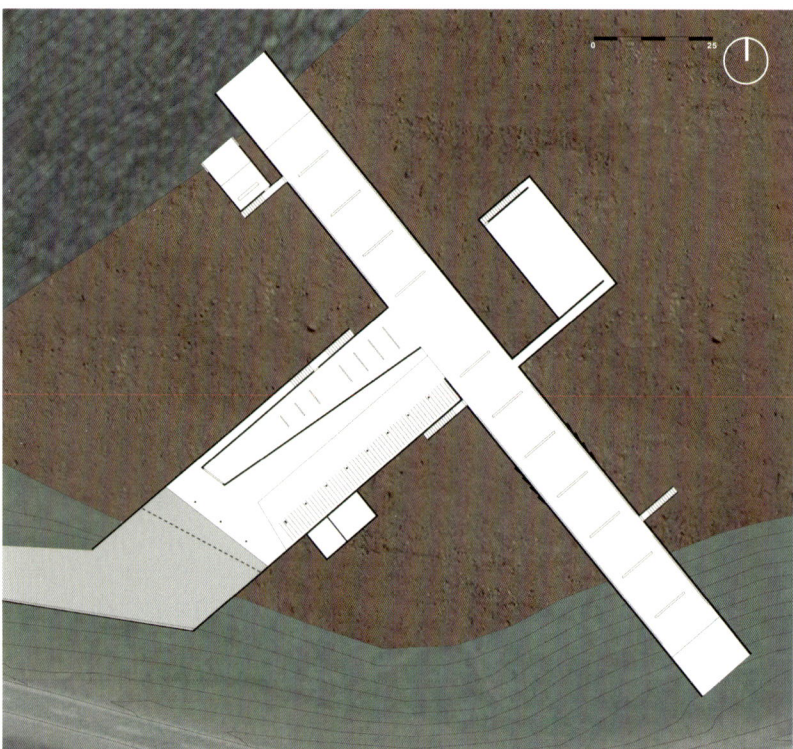

THE COLLECTION

Situated in Neuhaus, Carinthia, the Liaunig Museum was built for art collector Herbert W. Liaunig's project. The museum was opened in late August 2008 and houses Liaunig's collection of contemporary art and, as an interesting counterpoint, a collection of Akan gold objects. Herbert W. Liaunig says of the collection, "The museum represents the fulfillment of a long-term wish of our family to create an adequate home for our collection." The museum also claims to be the only place that exhibits an overview of Austrian Post-war art in a permanent exhibition. One of the highlights of the museum is the permanent exhibition "Akan Gold," which is seen as a counterpoint to the works of contemporary art. A total of 600 pieces of jewelry and cult objects from African tribal kingdoms, including Ashanti, Baule and Fante, are displayed and are directly accessible from the main area of the museum. These valuable exhibits, which mainly date from the 19th and 20th century, form one of the world's largest and most significant collections of this type of art. In view of the geometry of the basic designs and elementary figurative portrayals, the "Akan Gold" exhibition offers a wealth of instructive comparisons with the other art on display.

left: Site plan_Entrance area. right: Terrace_Exhibition space at daylight_Façade.

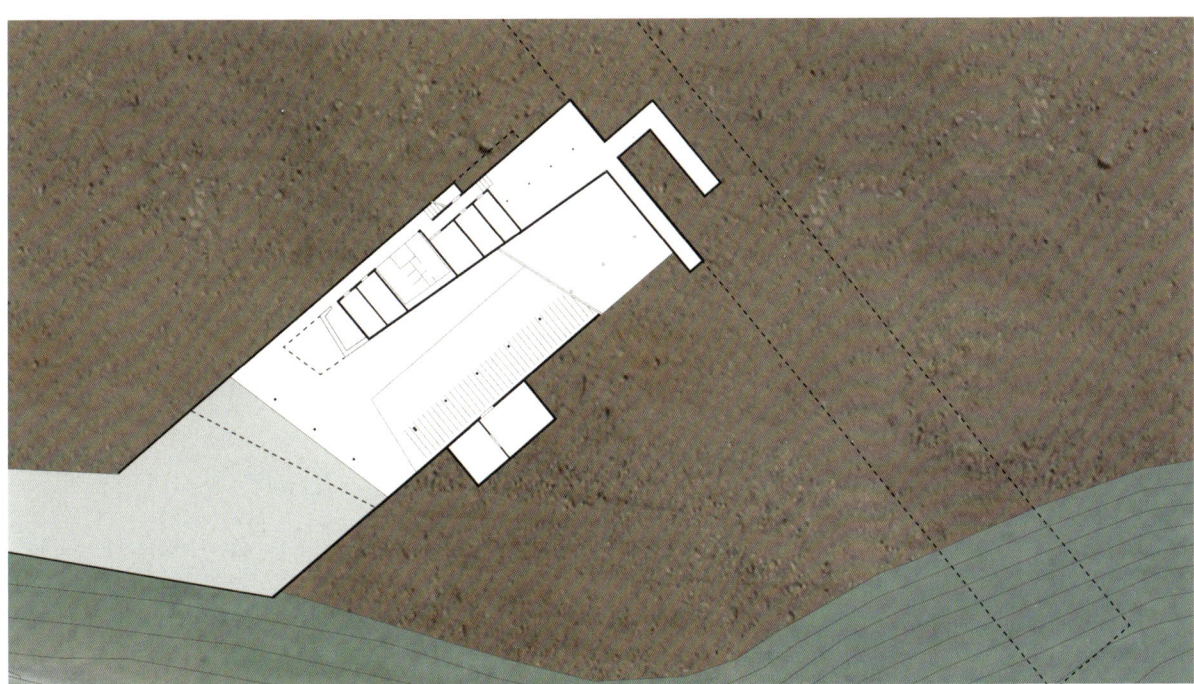

left: Outside view from the street. right: Design sketch_View to the terrace_Connecting hallway to the Gold collection with light art by Brigitte Kowanz.

AUSTRIA_SALZBURG **MUSEUM DER MODERNE**

ARCHITECTS: FRIEDRICH HOFF ZWINK ARCHITEKTEN
COMPLETION: 2004_**TYPE:** ART MUSEUM_**GROSS FLOOR
AREA:** 6,550 M²_**PHOTOS:** SIMONE ROSENBERG

THE ARCHITECTURE

A key purpose of the construction was to anchor and adjust the museum to the peculiarities of the construction site. The Mönchsberg offers a breathtaking view of the old part of Salzburg, which is why the Wasserturm (water tower) was already equipped with an observation platform in 1892. It has now been freed from structures built aorund its base, while the restaurant was kept at its original location. As a monolithic block, the museum reflects the horizontal alignment of the mountain, similarly the vertical incisions into the building structure reflect the vertical fissures in the rock. The path inside the building was conceived as a spiral, resembling the serpentine meandering of the landscape.

THE COLLECTION

The Museum der Moderne consists of two buildings: the Rupertinum in the historic city district and the museum on the Mönchsberg. Both buildings accommodate thematic and monographic exhibitions of 20th and 21st century art as well as the presentation of graphics and photography. The basis of the museum was created by the art dealer Friedrich Welz, who donated large parts of his collection to the state of Salzburg. Due to his friendship with the Austrian artist Oskar Kokoschka, many works of Expressionist artists were added to the Rupertinum collection. In the year 1983, the Rupertinum was handed over to the public as the Salzburger Museum für Moderne Kunst und Graphische Kollektion. In 2004, the museum on the Mönchsberg was opened, thus integrating the former Rupertinum state collection into the new concept of the common Museum der Moderne Salzburg. The thematic focus of the collection is on the image of humans. Featuring works of artists like Arnulf Rainer, Maria Lassnig and Bruno Gironcoli, the museum primarily presents Austrian development as a special form of overall European development.

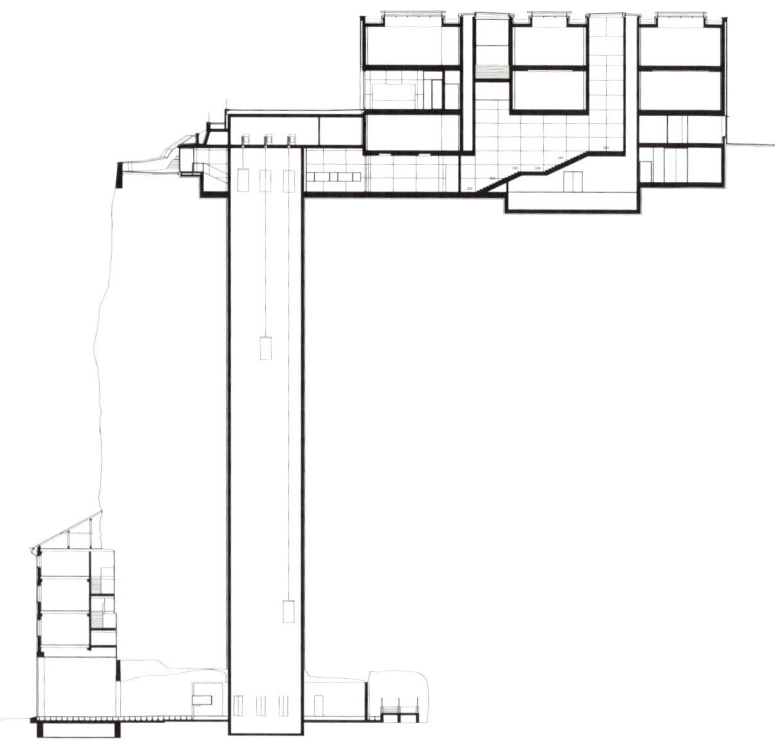

left: Section_South façade_East façade with restaurant terrace. right: Connecting bridge natural light level_View to south_Exhibition space.

AUSTRIA_ST. JOHANN / HERBERSTEIN **GIRONCOLI MUSEUM**

ARCHITECTS: ARCHITEKT DI HERMANN EISENKÖCK
COMPLETION: 2004_**TYPE:** ART MUSEUM_**GROSS FLOOR AREA:** 2,183 M²_**PHOTOS:** PAUL OTT, GRAZ

THE ARCHITECTURE

This project includes a new building and an annex to a historic shed in the Herberstein palace grounds. The museum for the Gironcoli sculptures received great artistic, architectural and touristic acclaim, as it is Austria's first large-scale project interweaving representative contemporary pieces of art with extensive natural and historic building structures in the style of an artistic and landscape entertainment park. Minimalist and lapidary, and subsequently with a special aura, the architectural outer casing creates a suitable artistic frame, with its lucent skin of Rodalux façade elements, on a steel skeleton frame.

THE COLLECTION

Bruno Gironcoli (1936–2010) was professionally trained as a goldsmith and studied painting at the Akademie für angewandte Kunst in Vienna. In 1960/1961, he discovered the work of Alberto Giacometti, which strongly influenced him and his work. In 1977 he became the head of the school of Sculpture at the Akademie der bildenden Künste in Vienna. The professorship provided him for the first time with large studio rooms, allowing him to work independently from the art market. The museum contains the currently largest complete exhibition of works by the Austrian artist Gironcoli. The around 30 exhibited works include torso-like figures, butterfly-like objects, or futuristic tools. Spoons, shovels, and pots, as well as gas hoses and valves, machine and furniture parts are all included in the inventory of the drawings and sculptures by the artist. The theme of change, of constantly alterable shapes, plays a large role in the work of Gironcoli. The materials usually include wood, nylon, iron, aluminum, glass, tar, and wire.

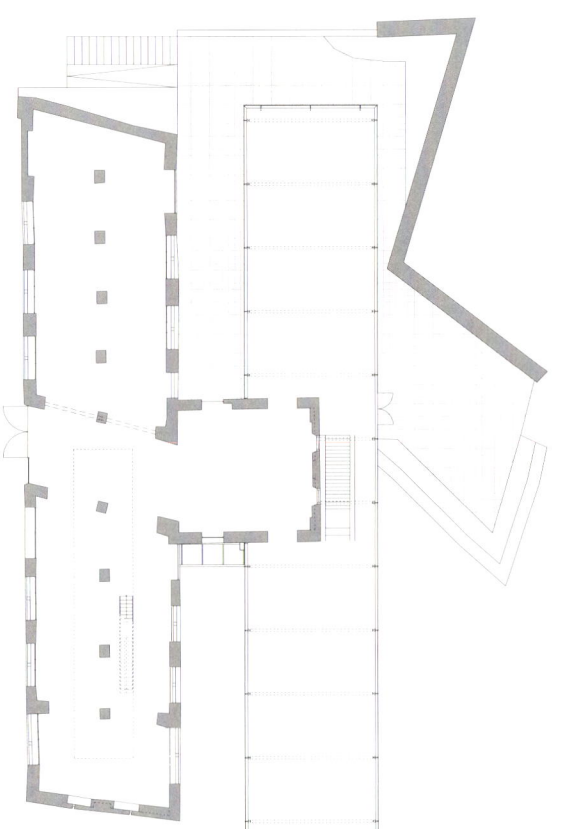

left: First floor plan_South elevation with main entrance_Gallery. right: Stairs and exhibition room View of the museum east.

AUSTRIA_VIENNA **MUSEUMSQUARTIER**

ARCHITECTS: ORTNER&ORTNER BAUKUNST_**COMPLETION:** 2001
TYPE: ART MUSEUM_**GROSS FLOOR AREA:** 53,000 M²_**PHOTOS:**
RUPERT STEINER, VIENNA (162 B. R., 163 B), COURTESY
OF THE ARCHITECTS (162 B. L., 163 A.)

THE ARCHITECTURE

The center of contemporary art, the museum quarter contains various cultural establishments — the Museum für Moderne Kunst (Museum of Modern Art), the Leopold Museum, the Kunsthalle Wien (Art Gallery of Vienna), the E+G event halls, the Architekturzentrum (Architectural center), the Kindermuseum (children's museum) with children's theater, production areas for new media, artists' studios, restaurants, cafés and thematic shops. The location, on the site of the former imperial stables (built in 1723 by J. Fischer von Erlach), and in the immediate vicinity of the Hofburg palace and imperial museums provides the ideal connection between contemporary culture and historical tradition.

THE COLLECTION

The three largest museums of the museum district in Vienna are the Museum der Modernen Kunst, MUMOK, the Leopold Museum, and the Kunsthalle Wien. The MUMOK is also the largest museum for modern and contemporary art in central Europe. It contains an extensive collection of international 20th century and contemporary art. The basic stock of the MUMOK was the Austrian Ludwig foundation of the art collector husband and wife Irene and Peter Ludwig, whose exhibits were previously shown at the 20er Haus and the Palais Liechtenstein. Among other exhibits, the Leopold Museum presents the world's largest collection of paintings by the Austrian painter Egon Schiele. In addition, the Leopold collection contains essential items of turn-of-the-century Austrian arts and crafts, by artists such as Otto Wagner, Josef Hoffmann and Koloman Moser. The collection is complemented by old Japanese and Chinese works of art, as well as objects from Africa and Oceania. The Kunsthalle Wien functions as a workshop, a laboratory, and a place for negotiating contemporary esthetic and social issues. Thematic exhibitions present developments and interrelations from classic modernism to the current art scene. The focus is on photography, video, film, installations, and new media.

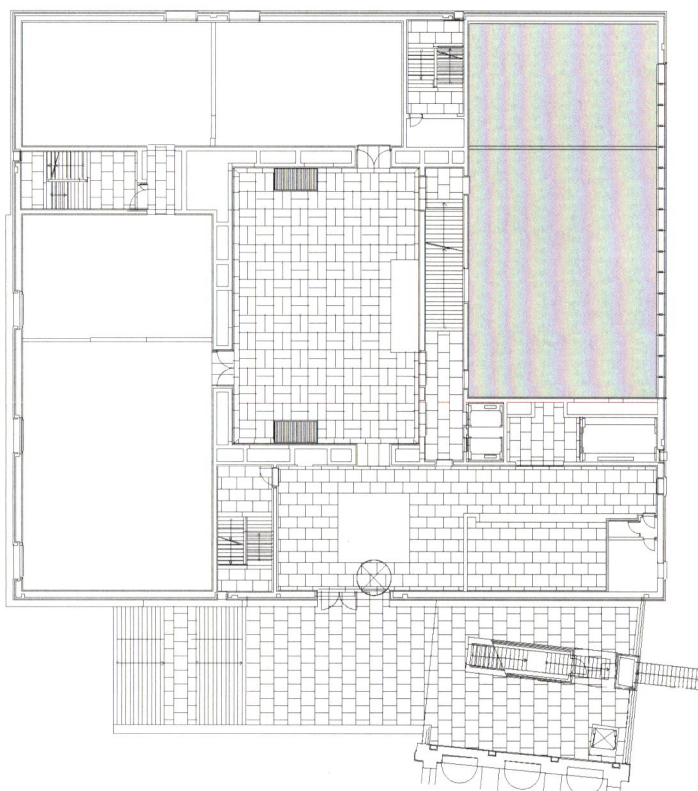

left: Plan of Leopold Museum_Exterior of Museum of Modern Art_Façade of the Art Hall. right: Aerial view_Façade of Leopold Museum_Interior of Leopold Museum.

BELGIUM_BRUGES **GROENINGEMUSEUM**

ARCHITECTS: 51N4E_**COMPLETION:** 2003_**ORIGINAL BUILDING:** 1930s_**TYPE:** ART MUSEUM_**GROSS FLOOR AREA:** 1,170 M² _**PHOTOS:** 51N4E (164 B. R., 165 B. R.), HANS WERLEMANN / 51N4E (164 B. L., 165 A., B. L.)

THE ARCHITECTURE

The Groeningemuseum is not so much a building as it is a collection of linked objects within a garden layout. This garden turns the Groeningemuseum into a potential public domain. Over the years this domain grew organically, leaving a confused impression upon the museum's visitors. The phased refurbishment of the 1930s Groeningemuseum did not merely focus on the creation of a new interior. It is an in-depth inquiry into the museum's capacity as a public interior within the city layout. The new Groeningemuseum layout has two sides — a conventional museum with a "Expo route" and a cocoon-like public domain with a "public route."

THE COLLECTION

The Groeninge Museum is also called "The city museum of Fine Arts". Its large collection was already developed at the beginning of the 18th century, but the building in which it is currently housed is more recent. The name "Groeninge" refers to the nearby "Groeninge straat" but also to the Groeninge fields in the city of Kortrijk, where the army of the Flemish defeated the army of the French king in 1302. The collection in the museum spans art from the 14th to the 20th century and focuses primarily on works by painters who lived and worked in Bruges. A part of the museum's permanent display consists of a very valuable collection of "Flemish masters." This exhibition includes two works by Jan Van Eyck, the first and most important "Flemish Primitive". The museum's centerpiece is "The Madonna with Canon Joris van der Paele", which Van Eyck painted in 1436. The rich details of this painting make it an excellent example of early Flemish medieval painting. Other medieval Flemish masters from the 15th century are also represented here — "Death of the Holy Virgin" by Hugo van der Goes, "The altar of Saint Christopher" by Hans Memling, as well as "The Justice of King Cambyses" and "The baptism of Christ" by Gerard David.

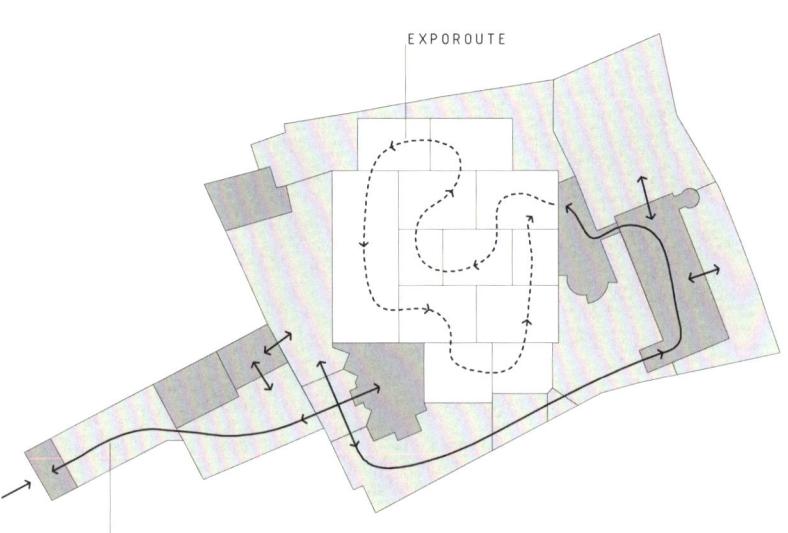

EXPOROUTE

PUBLIEKSROUTE

left: Combination of Expo route and public route_Baroque room_Renaissance room. right: Neoclassicism room_Abstract room_Landscape painting room.

MAC'S – MUSEÉ DES ARTS CONTEMPORAINS

ARCHITECTS: ATELIER D'ARCHITECTURE PIERRE HEBBELINCK & PIERRE DE WIT_**COMPLETION:** 2002_**TYPE:** ART MUSEUM_**GROSS FLOOR AREA:** 7,000 M²_**PHOTOS:** HÉLÈNE BINET, LONDON

THE ARCHITECTURE

For this museum located in a former coal mine, the architect constructed a new building, which both restores the appeal of the older building and disrupts its monumental style. The understated modern and extremely precise architecture undermines the symmetrical monumental-era pathos of the premises, creating new building structures as well as a spatial dialog. However, similarities and differences not only become apparent in the composition of the buildings and the individual structures, but are apparent up to the smallest architectural detail for example the different brick used in both eras.

THE COLLECTION

The former industrial estate settlement Grand Hornu survived as a monument in the vicinity of Mons. The venue was created in 1820-1830 by the mine owner Henri de Georg Legrand based on plans by Bruno Renard. The classicist brick laborer's settlement is a further development and adjustment of Claude-Nicolas Ledoux' royal salt works in Arc-et-Senans (1779). The Belgian mining settlement consists of an oval complex with 425 residential houses, an early version of a garden city, offices, stores, hay barns, stables, workshops, the former sugar factory, warehouses, as well as the family's Château. After coal mining was discontinued in Borinage in the 1950s, the complex deteriorated and was liquidated in 1954. In 1971 it was bought by architect Henry Hornutois Guchez. In 1984 an association was formed to ensure its maintenance and in 1989 the Hainaut province bought the premises including the castle to transform it into a culture and seminar center. Even before the MAC moved to the grounds, the center was able to gain international acclaim with arts and crafts and design exhibitions.

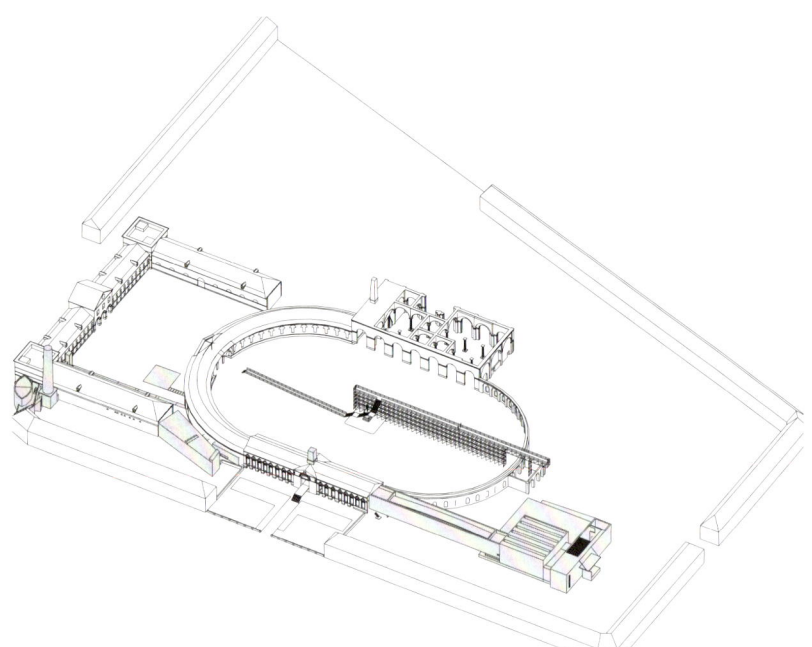

left: Axonometry_Old and new building_Façade details. right: Façade_Exhibition room_Staircase Entrance.

CZECH REPUBLIC_PRAGUE **DOX – CENTRUM SOUČASNÉHO UMĚNÍ**

ARCHITECTS: IVAN KROUPA ARCHITEKTI_**COMPLETION:** 2008
TYPE: ART MUSEUM_**GROSS FLOOR AREA:** 6,250 M²
PHOTOS: COURTESY OF THE ARCHITECTS (168, 171 R.),
JAN KUDEJ, PRAGUE (168 B., 169, 170, 171 L.)

THE ARCHITECTURE

The architecture here is an integral part of this specific quarter, an industrial district from the turn of the 19th to the 20th century, that is currently undergoing intensive development. This project does not exploit the plot with a maximum possible volume, but leaves void space above the original buildings, in which the dense urban structure can rest. The project, which was carried out gradually between 2004 and 2008 as a private initiative, is about taking a sensitive approach to the place and its atmosphere. The process and time span of the construction were strongly controlled by the low budget. Today the complex houses twelve exhibition spaces, a café with a terrace, bookshop and service facilities.

THE COLLECTION

The purpose of the DOX is to present contemporary art within the context of current events by presenting currently debated topics in various art forms, including architecture, design, sculpture, painting, photography, film and new media. In addition, it aims to support the development of local art through cooperation and partnerships with regional and international artists and institutions, creating a productive setting for interaction, development and inspiration of different views and opinions. The DOX Center was established in 2002 by Leoš Válka, along with several partners (Robert Aafjes, Richard Fuxa and Václav Dejŏmar). Válka was active from 1981 to 1995 in the construction and interior design sector in Australia. After his return, he initiated the creation of an international-scale arts exhibition center. When it was found that the state was not capable of creating such a hall, the DOX was created as a private initiative with Válka as the founding director. Only a small part of the budget is covered by subsidies, which is therefore complemented by other means such as renting out space for events. The program of the DOX far exceeds that of a classic art exhibition center, including readings, workshops, symposia, performances and discussions.

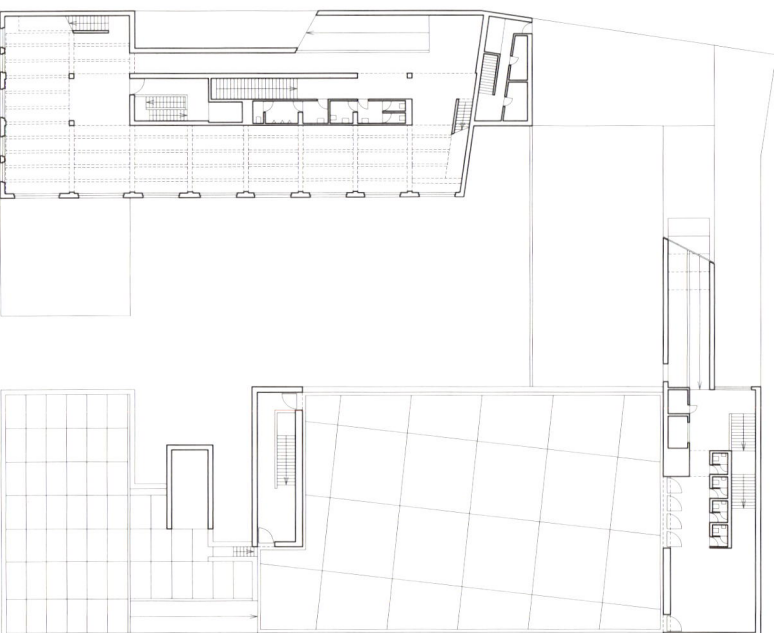

left: Third floor plan_Roof terrace. right: Main entrance ramp.

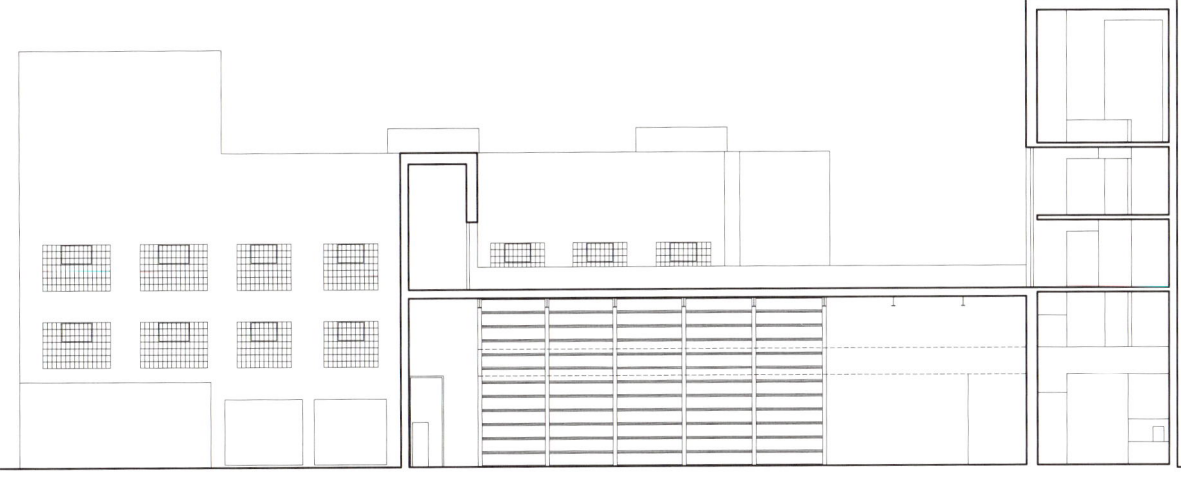

left: Tower building. right: Section_Interior view to tower_Room with skylight_Stairs.

DENMARK_COPENHAGEN **DANSK JØDISK MUSEUM**

ARCHITECTS: STUDIO DANIEL LIBESKIND**_RENOVATION OF GALEJHUSET:** FOGH & FØLNER ARKITEKTFIRMA**_COMPLETION:** 2003**_ORIGINAL BUILDING:** ROYAL BOAT HOUSE, BEGINNING 17TH CENTURY, ROYAL LIBRARY, 1906, BLACK DIAMOND, END 20TH CENTURY**_TYPE:** HISTORY MUSEUM**_GROSS FLOOR AREA:** 450 M² **_PHOTOS:** BITTER BREDT FOTOGRAFIE, BERLIN

THE ARCHITECTURE

This museum is dedicated to the history of Jewish life in Denmark dating back to the 17th century. Located in one of the oldest parts of Copenhagen, the museum is housed inside a 17th century structure built by King Christian IV. The architects designed the museum's interior space while preserving the original building. Visitors enter into an architectural structure in which the artifacts are seamlessly organized. The entire building has been conceived as an adventure, both physical and spiritual, tracing the lineaments that reveal the intersection of different histories and aspects of Jewish Culture.

THE COLLECTION

The Danish-Jewish museum is located in the former royal boathouse built by Joseph Matzen in 1609 for Christian IV. In 1906, the monument of the Nordic late Renaissance was incorporated into the royal library by architect Hans J. Holm, who incorporated early Renaissance and Northern Italian late Gothic elements. The history of Jews in Denmark is also closely associated with Christian IV, who invited in 1622 Sephardic Jews into the newly founded city of Glückstadt/Elbe. The history of Jews in Denmark is much more harmonious than in many other European nations. In 1675, they received residence permits in Fredericia, another newly established city, and in 1684 in Copenhagen. In the early 19th century they were given citizenship. However, the most important episode was the rescue of the Danish Jews from the Nazis. The German diplomat Georg Ferdinand Duckwitz was informed of their imminent deportation into concentration camps in the night of October 1 to 2, 1943. He sent a warning to the head rabbi of Copenhagen, Marcus Melchior and informed neutral Sweden of a mass exodus. Within a very short time, 7,000 of the 8,000 Danish Jews were smuggled into Sweden via the Öresund, the Kattegat, and the Danish Baltic Sea island of Bornholm.

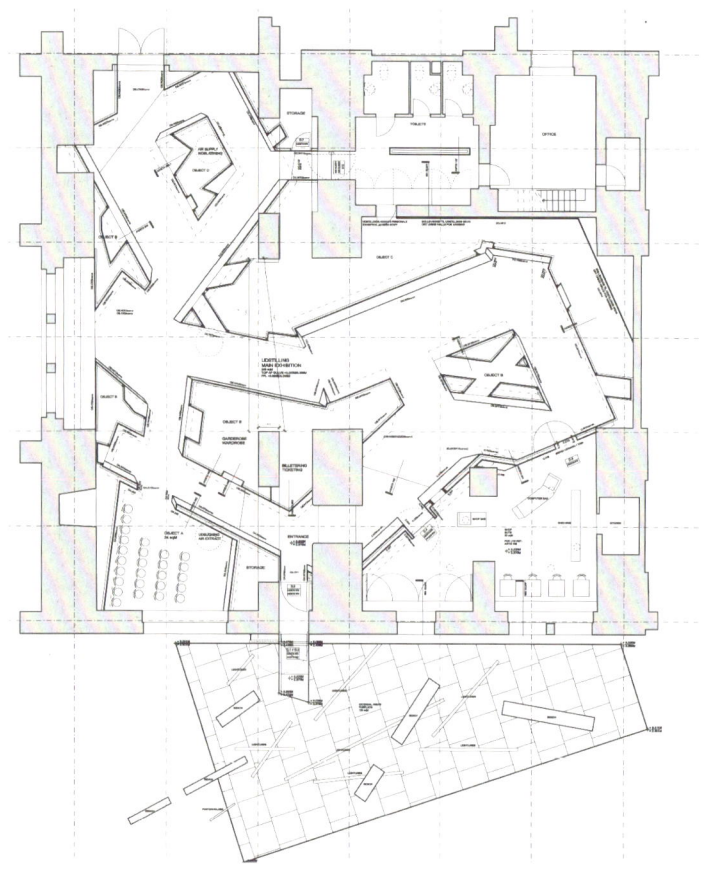

left: Ground floor plan_Museum building_Four intersecting planes structure the interior landscape Exhibition space_Showcases. right: Ancient brick walls, vectors of light, fragments of memory.

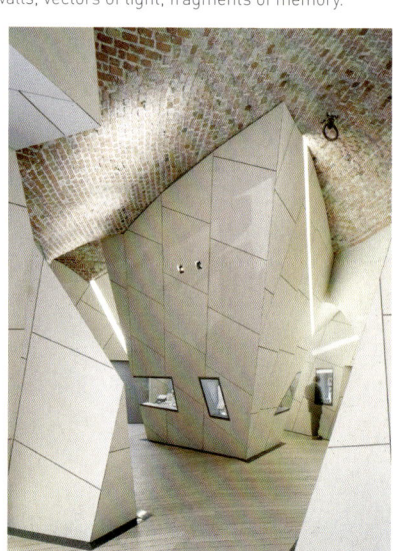

DENMARK_HELSINGØR **HANDELS- OG SØFARTSMUSEET**

ARCHITECTS: BIG_**COMPLETION:** 2013_**TYPE:**
MARITIME MUSEUM_**GROSS FLOOR AREA:** 7,200 M²
PHOTOS: COURTESY OF THE ARCHITECTS

THE ARCHITECTURE

The museum had to find its place in a unique historic and spatial context; between Kronborg Castle and a new, ambitious cultural center, while at the same time manifesting itself as an independent institution. In this context the building will be built as a subterranean museum around a former dry-dock that will be preserved as an open, outdoor display in order to maintain the powerful building structure as the core of the Maritime Museum. This is the basis of the layout of the entire museum. Bridges and ramps structurally and sculpturally dissect the air space, allowing visitors to penetrate the depth of the room.

THE COLLECTION

The Danish Maritime Museum was first opened in 1915 and is housed in the castle of Kronborg in Denmark. The museum's permanent collections and temporary displays cover all aspects of Danish Shipping from 1400 to the present. The museum displays tell the story of the Sound Dues, the Napoleonic Wars, trade with China and trade history between Denmark and the old Danish colonies in India. Featuring several exhibitions on navigation, sea charts, and the history of the lifeboat service, the museum looks at how shipping technologies have progressed throughout history. The permanent collection is strengthened by changing temporary exhibitions based on various maritime and topical subjects. In addition to the museum's vast displays, several thousand paintings are housed in store rooms, along with a photographic display of 150,000 photos. Much of this is being digitalized so that it can one day be available for viewing by the public. A recent display of some of the museum's photographs was entitled "Gale Warning!" and featured photographs of ships enduring stormy conditions at sea. The display includes photographs from Dutch Photographer Herman Ijsseling of ships battling some of the worst storms ever witnessed.

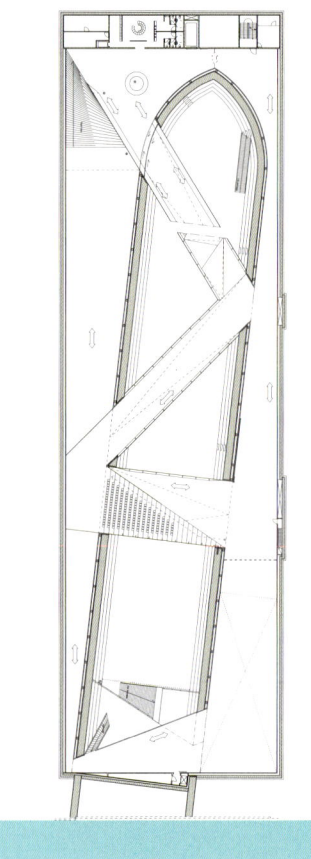

left: Site plan in the dry-dock_Subterranean courtyard_Staircases between levels in courtyard. right: View of courtyard_Exhibition space_View from museum into the courtyard.

DENMARK_RANDERS **RANDERS KUNSTMUSEUM**

ARCHITECTS: 3XN_**COMPLETION:** 2013_**TYPE:** ART MUSEUM
GROSS FLOOR AREA: 7,550 M²
PHOTOS: COURTESY OF THE ARCHITECTS

The Architecture

The new Randers Museum of Art is based on the philosophy that a great museum is extrovert and opens up towards its surroundings, as well as introvert in its concentration on the experience of the works of art within it. The museum consists of a building on one level, rising up towards each end and traversed by a diagonal with a mezzanine deck running full length through the exhibition building. The diagonal creates a bridge between the permanent and the temporary exhibitions. The internal flow is a continuation of the external flow of its surroundings — the city of Randers and the new sculpture park by the river.

THE COLLECTION

The permanent exhibition of the museum contains approximately 2,000 works with a focus on 19th century Danish art, including works of L. A. Ring, Theodor Philipsen and Vilhelm Hammershøj as well as 20th century Danish art. These are especially represented by artists such as Vilhelm Lundstrøm, Wilhelm Freddie and Asger Jorn. Special attention is also given to the work of Sven Dalsgaard of Randers, of whom 1,000 collected works are presented in a separate exhibition. Another main focus of the museum is on international art of the second half of the 20th century. In addition, the graphics collection includes outstanding works of Danish and international artists. The museum was able to procure works by artists such as Paul Cézanne, Paul Gauguin, Georges Rouault and Andy Warhol. It also presents varying temporary exhibitions, some of which are organized in cooperation with other museums. Some exhibitions are organized by the local art association with a main focus on young artists.

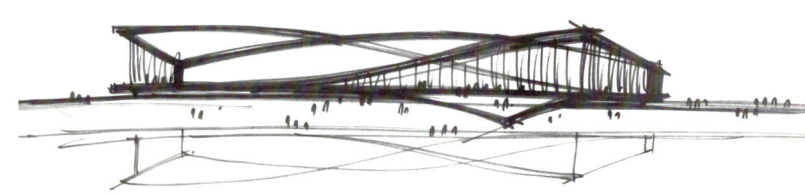

left: Sketch_Side corridor of exhibition_Interior. right: Exterior_Museum in its scenery.

DENMARK_TOREBY L. **FUGLSANG KUNSTMUSEUM**

ARCHITECTS: TONY FRETTON ARCHITECTS_**COMPLETION:** 2008
TYPE: ART MUSEUM_**GROSS FLOOR AREA:** 2,500 M²
PHOTOS: PETER COOK

THE ARCHITECTURE

This new museum is a low-rise building, which sits within a loose assembly of rural buildings. Similar to the red barn and the forge in the surrounding countryside, the museum extends into the fields with an axial but offset relation to the most significant of the buildings, the Manor House and its formal surroundings. Connection between the two buildings is further established by the profile of the museum with its arrangement of three diagonal roof lights. The façades of the museum are constructed from brick. Complementing to the barn on the west side of the court, they are painted white with roof lights of grey brick to match the color of the roofs of the surrounding buildings.

THE COLLECTION

The museum's collection contains samples of Danish art from the 18th century until the present time. The special focus of the paintings and sculptures is on the era of early Danish Modernism (1915-1930). The around 600 paintings include works by prominent Danish artists such as Skagensmalerne, Fynboerne and Th. Philipsen. Furthermore, the museum contains approximately 100 mostly small, original sculptures, such as statues and busts by artists such as Johannes C. Bjerg, Sven Dalsgaard as well as a collection of 16 sculptures by the sculptor Gottfred Eickhoff. Consisting of approximately 2,800 sheets, the collection of drawings, water colors and graphics originates mostly from the 20th century. A special section focuses on artists with biographical connections to or motifs from the region. In addition, the museum features changing temporary exhibitions as well as several special exhibitions every year.

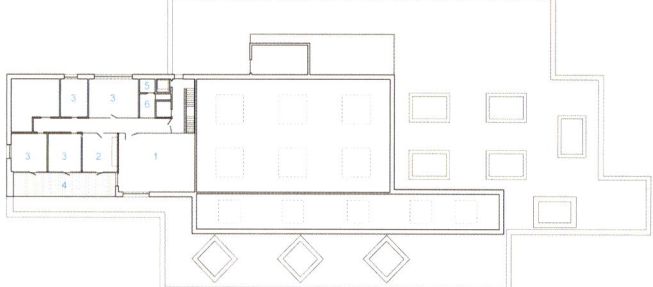

left: Floor plans_South elevation. right: South-west corner with entrance_South-east corner.

left: Sunlight from the roof lights. right: Site plan_Gallery with ornamented ceiling and diagonal roof light_Exhibition room_View of the central gallery.

ESTONIA_TALLINN **KUMU**

ARCHITECTS: VAPAAVUORI ARCHITECTS_**FURNITURE DESIGN:** PILLE LAUSMÄE SAB AND SISUSTUSARKKITEHDIT GULLSTÉN-INKINEN OY_**COMPLETION:** 2006_**TYPE:** ART MUSEUM_**GROSS FLOOR AREA:** 23,900 M²_**PHOTOS:** JUSSI TIAINEN, HELSINKI

THE ARCHITECTURE

The site with a 20 meter high limestone slope is located at the southern end of the Kadriorg Park, three kilometers from Tallinn city center. In order to leave the park as intact as possible and to reduce the impact of this large building, the museum was integrated into the slope, partly underground. A curved wall unifies the plan, externally enclosing a courtyard and internally dividing the functions. The exhibition halls are simple and unassuming, directing the focus on the artwork. The ascetics of the interior continue in the exterior, which relies on the power of plain geometric forms. The main façade materials are limestone, green-aeruginous copper, and glass.

THE COLLECTION

One of northern European largest museums, the KUMU is the largest museum of the Baltic nations. Next to temporary exhibitions, the museum contains a permanent exhibition, including a collection of Estonian art from the 18th century to the end of World War II. The exhibition moves from one topic to another — from a work of an anonymous Baltic-German portrait artist to Johann Köler, Kristjan Raud and Konrad Mägi, and on to the group of Estonian Artists of the Pallas School. The third floor of the building is dedicated to contemporary art starting from the second half of the 20th century, an era dominated by dramatic social changes. This separate section reflects the relationships between the Soviet state and art, which is particularly evident in Socialist Realism. Furthermore, the exhibition presents different artistic phenomena that took place in the 1960s, 1970s and 1980s, such as Modernism, Pop Art and Hyper Realism, along with developments in national landscapists' schools and graphics.

left: Site plan_Main entrance_Entrance from courtyard. right: Main entrance_Courtyard, terraced sculpture garden_Passageway.

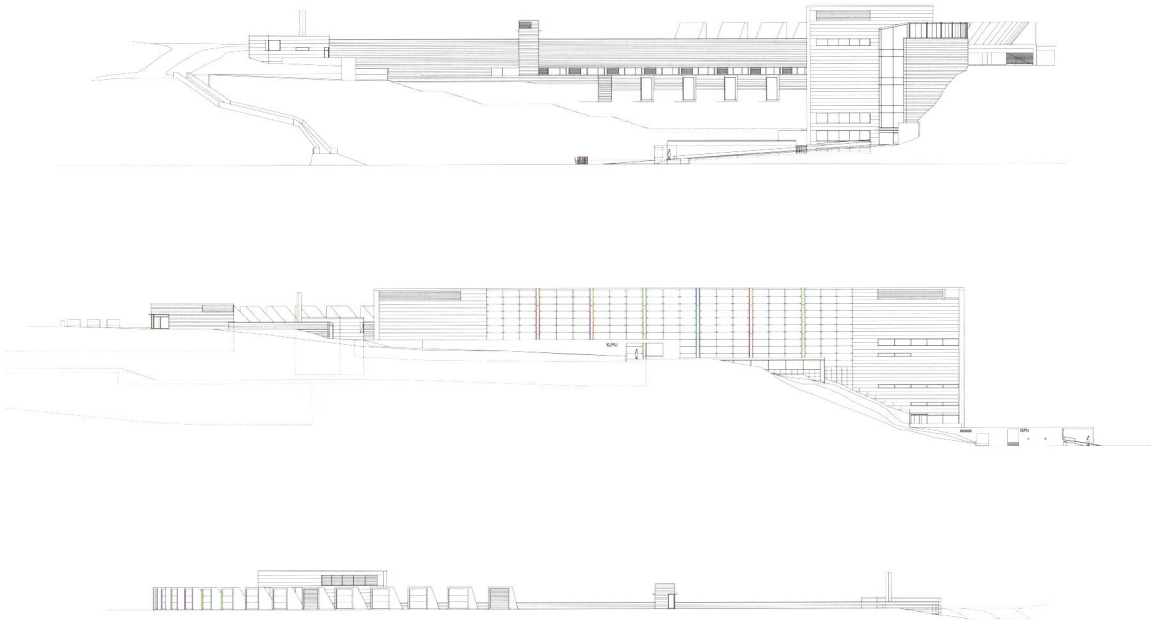

left: Exhibition space. right: Elevations_Lobby_Changing exhibitions hall_Changing exhibitions hall, detail.

FRANCE_CALAIS

CITÉ INTERNATIONALE DE LA DENTELLE ET DE LA MODE DE CALAIS

ARCHITECTS: AGENCE MOATTI ET RIVIÈRE WITH FLINT
SCENOGRAPHY: ATELIER PASCAL PAYEUR_**COMPLETION:**
2009_**ORIGINAL BUILDING:** 19TH CENTURY _**TYPE:** FASHION
MUSEUM_**GROSS FLOOR AREA:** 7,500 M² _**PHOTOS:**
MICHEL DENANCÉ, PARIS (186 B. L., 187 B.), AGENCE MOATTI ET
RIVIÈRE, PARIS (186 B. R., 187 A.)

THE ARCHITECTURE

In this project, technology steps aside in favor of imagination and age-old tradition. The new façade of the "City of Lace and Fashion" arouses curiosity. From the canal, it masks the old mill and fills it out. Like moving images of changing periods, the nearby canal and roads are reflected in anamorphoses on the two façades, one concave, the other convex. Their fine silkscreen patterns, in metallic enamel, reproduce the perforations of the Jacquard weave cards once used on British leaver looms. With the passing of time, these high-tech cards have become artifacts themselves.

THE COLLECTION

The museum houses exhibits dealing with the topic of lace and its production processes. They include images and costumes depicting the chronological development of lace making from the 16th to the 19th century. A special focus of the exhibition is on the lace and tulle industry of Calais. Visitors can witness how a single industry evolved into a city with innovative technologies, new business sectors, and international trade. In addition, a workshop can be visited in which the individual production processes are shown step by step. The museum also features an exhibition of the development of fashion from the early 20th century to the present day. It contains collections of several famous fashion houses such as Poiret, Dior or Chanel. In its final section, the museum contains mini laboratories that present an outlook of lace and the "lace effect" on future fashion. The museum also offers workshops related to the themes of lace, couture and design around the year.

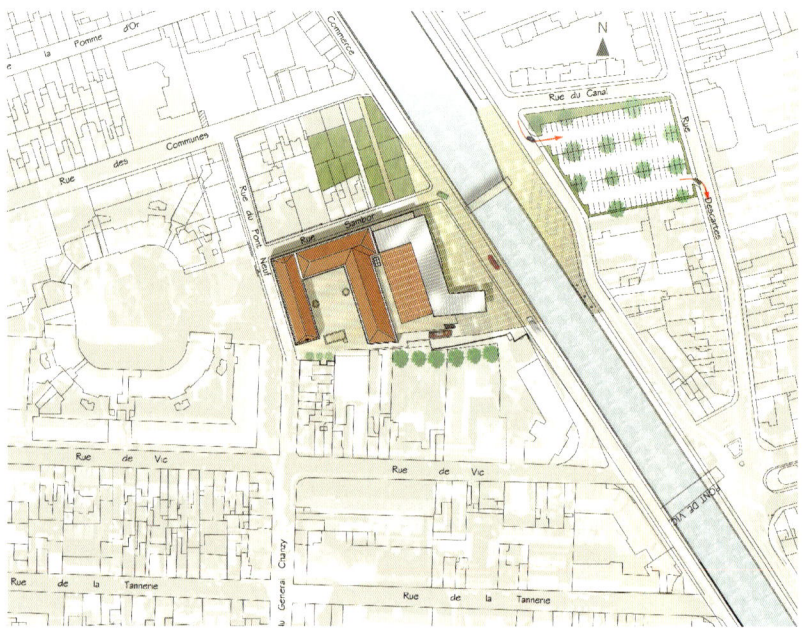

left: Master plan_The interior façade_Construction detail of the glass façade_Interior view. right: Detail façade_New glass façade.

FRANCE_ERSTEIN **MUSEÉ WÜRTH**

ARCHITECTS: JACQUES ET CLÉMENT VERGÉLY_**COMPLETION:** 2008_**TYPE:** ART MUSEUM_**GROSS FLOOR AREA:** 3,416 M²
PHOTOS: COURTESY OF THE ARCHITECTS

THE ARCHITECTURE

The museum is a new two-story rectangular building made of smooth, raw concrete. The entrance to the two 70 meter long rectangular structure is located on the central line of the building. The laterally positioned exhibition halls are illuminated by two rows of sky lights. An auditorium with 224 seats is situated at the "blind" center. The raw concrete and the simple white plastering contrast with the art objects. Two light boxes on the flat roof allow daylight to penetrate the rooms. The amount of this light can be adjusted depending on the weather situation. Shutters and installed artificial lighting can create cold and warm hues.

THE COLLECTION

Starting in the 1960s, the art collection of the Swabian screw manufacturer Reinhold Würth grew to 12,500 objects today. The focus of the collection is on Expressionism, Surrealism, geometric abstraction and neo-figurative painting of the 1980s. In 2003, the 100 most prominent works of old German Masters from the dissolved collection of the Fürsten zu Fürstenberg were added to it. As one of the major private collectors, Würth integrated the works into the "corporate identity" concept of his company — in 1991 the Museum Würth was established as part of the Group headquarters in Künzelsau, and in 2001 the Kunsthalle Würth was opened in Schwäbisch Hall, 20 kilometers away. In the meantime, 13 museums were established in the company locations between Capena near Rome, La Rioja in Spain, Turnhout in Belgium, and Hagan in Norway. This way, the valuable collection – including works by Pablo Picasso, Max Beckmann, Anselm Kiefer, Stephan Balkenhol, Max Ernst, Victor Vasarély, Claude Monet, Gerhard Richter — is presented to the general public and primarily also to the company staff. Consequently, this museum in Erstein is located immediately next to the company constructed by Jacques Vergély in the industrial zone.

left: Ground floor plan_Main entrance_Sculpture courtyard. right: Twilight_Exhibition space_Exhibition space.

FRANCE_FIGEAC **MUSÉE CHAMPOLLION**

ARCHITECTS: AGENCE MOATTI ET RIVIÈRE_**SCENOGRAPHY:** ATELIER PASCAL PAYEUR_**GRAPHIC DESIGN:** PIERRE DI SCIULLO **COMPLETION:** 2007_**ORIGINAL BUILDING:** MEDIEVAL_**TYPE:** ARCHEOLOGY MUSEUM_**GROSS FLOOR AREA:** 1,300 M² _**PHOTOS:** LUC BOEGLY, PARIS (190, 191, 192, 193 L. A., R.), AGENCE MOATTI ET RIVIÈRE, PARIS (193 L. B.)

THE ARCHITECTURE

This museum occupies three buildings in the heritage area of the old town. The screen façade on Place Champollion gives the museum its own identity — it is a metaphor of writing and deciphering of animated alphabets. It represents a "polyglot typographic moucharabieh," expressing poetic modernity inspired by living vibrating light. The old stone façade ensures continuity of the urban fabric. The screen façade is set back from the alignment and designed as a composition of glass and copper. Between these two façades, loggias are open to the public, and higher up there is a soleilo, a feature borrowed from the vernacular architecture of the region. The depth of the façade forms a public space of transition between the square and the museum.

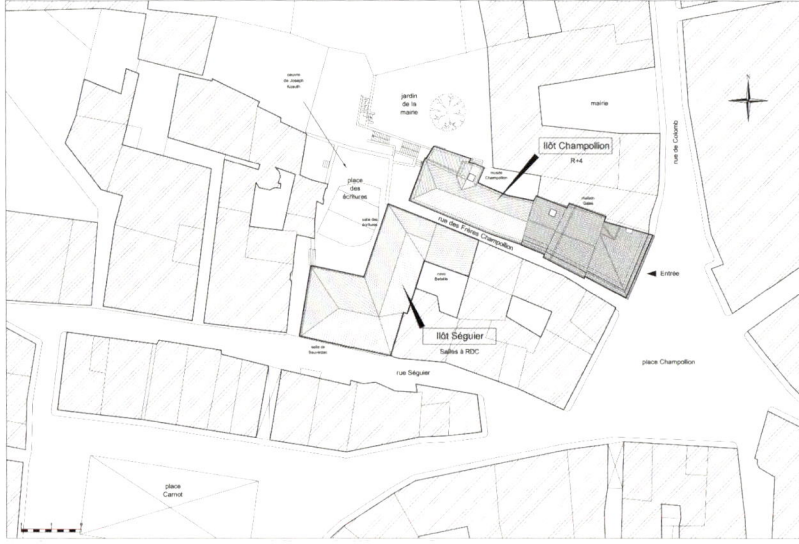

THE COLLECTION

Jean-François Champollion (1790-1832) was a French linguist who succeeded in decoding the Egyptian hieroglyphs with the help of the "Rosetta stone." The Champollion Museum was located from 1986 to 2007 in Figeac in the birthplace of the researcher, presenting exhibitions related to hieroglyphs and ancient Egypt. To this day, the Champollion hall informs visitors about the work of the researcher via objects from ancient Egypt, such as sarcophaguses, mummies, religious statues, and books of the Dead. Jean-François Champollion is even featured himself talking about his Egyptian expedition. Since its renovation and expansion, the museum also presents an exhibition entitled "Les Ecritures du Monde" that focuses on the development of writing around the world. Milestones from the first primitive writing instruments, via the development of the alphabet, pells, and books up to modern word processing, are elaborated. The museum contains exhibition rooms on four floors that currently contain seven thematic areas –"Champollion and Egypt", "Human beings, the world and script", "Development of Scripts", "Invention of the alphabet in the Mediterranean region", "Books, the memories of humanity", "Script, the power of the Bourgeoisie" as well as a "Reading and multimedia room."

left: Master plan_Exhibition, the mediterranean room. right: Façade by night.

left: Detail of the façade. right: Elevations_Detail between the two façades_The museum site, night vision_Façade.

FRANCE_LENS **LOUVRE-LENS**

ARCHITECTS: SANAA_**COMPLETION:** 2012_**TYPE:** ART MUSEUM
GROSS FLOOR AREA: 33,000 M²_**PHOTOS:** FRANCIS BOCQUET
(194 A.), KAZUYO SEJIMA + RYUE NISHIZAWA / SANAA,
TIM CULBERT + CELIA IMREY / IMREY CULBERT,
CATHERINE MOSBACH

THE ARCHITECTURE

To avoid blocking the site, and to reduce the scale of this very large project, this building will be broken up into smaller units, incorporating the dimension and arrangement of the surrounding bastions that are scattered across the calm slope of the site. Housing both the entrance foyer and a large public space, the central glass structure introduces a void between the building volumes, making it possible to pass without visiting the museum. Nature is fused with the building by its highly reflective, polished and anodized aluminum façade that covers the calm curves of the volumes, providing blurred reflections of the surroundings that change according to the scenery, the weather, and the position of the visitor.

THE COLLECTION

As opposed to most other museums, the Louvre-Lens does not own a collection, but will present various temporary exhibitions of items on loan from the Louvre collection. At its opening, more than 300 works will be exhibited at the so-called "Galerie du temps", which will be 120 meters long and cover an area of more than 2,000 square meters. Masterpieces will be presented in chronological order, reflecting the history of the Middle Eastern empires, Egypt, Greece, Rome, Islam and Europe from the 4th century BC to the year 1850. At the adjacent "Pavillon de Verre," annually changing exhibits of individual themes from the "Galerie de temps" will be presented in greater detail. In addition, the museum will feature an annual winter and summer exhibition, which will be coordinated with those of the Louvre in Paris and the museums of the region of the Nord-Pas-de-Calais. The opening exhibition here will focus on the Renaissance era. In addition to the exhibits, the museum also contains storage areas where visitors can observe restoration activities.

left: Bird's eye view_Exterior_Interior. right: Exterior_Panoramic view of the hall.

FRANCE_MOUANS-SARTOUX **ESPACE DE L'ART CONCRET (EAC)**

ARCHITECTS: ANNETTE GIGON / MIKE GUYER, ARCHITEKTEN
COMPLETION: 2003_**TYPE:** ART MUSEUM_**GROSS FLOOR AREA:**
1,829 M² _**PHOTOS:** SERGE DEMAILLY

THE ARCHITECTURE

The new building is located in the immediate vicinity of the small castle of Mouans-Sartoux, in the steeply sloping forest of the surrounding park. Extensions of the tower-like structure with a limited floor area increase the exhibition space while creating various ground floor entrances along the slope. Spiraling stairs connect the split-level, offset exhibition spaces. Light enters the rooms through lateral windows, which illuminate the works, and provide a view of the tree tops and the city. To prevent the moss and algae infection from the nearby trees, the bearing concrete structure was covered with yellow-green mineral paint.

THE COLLECTION

The museum for the collection of concrete art Gottfried Honegger und Sybil Albers was established not far from the Côte d'Azur. The term concrete art was coined by Theo van Doesburg in 1924 to describe art based on mathematic-geometric principles as represented by him and the other De-Stijl members. In 1930 he provided a programmatic manifesto for the style with the establishment of the Art concret group. The core belief of this trend, the Dutch De Stijl, and Russian Suprematism is that the universal language of mathematics is the only concrete art form and even the universe has been created in a mathematical language. Gottfried Honegger, born 1917 in Zurich, was initially a commercial artist before becoming active in this style in 1958. Together with his partner Sybil Albers-Barrier, he established a valuable collection of 500 works by more than 160 exceptional artists. An early 16th century château located ten kilometers north of Cannes served as the museum's venue and in 2000 the collection became state property as an Albers-Honegger donation with which the state financed the new building as the collection did not have enough room anymore in the former premises.

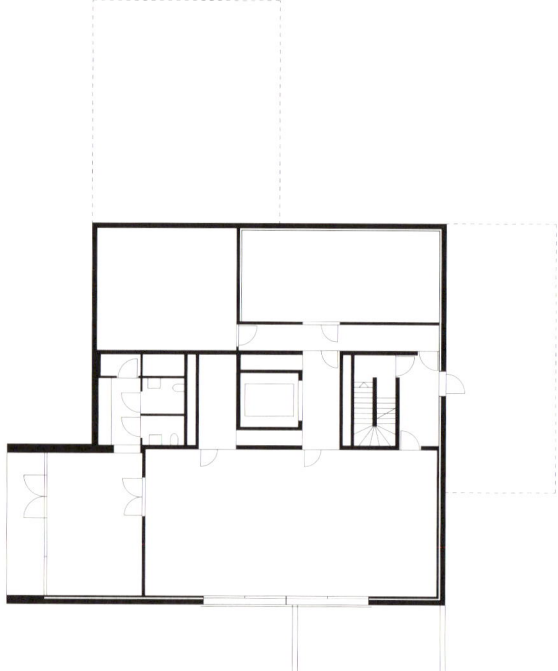

left: First floor plan_Main entrance in twilight_Building on the slope. right: Main entrance_Exhibition room_Visual relation to the exterior.

FRANCE_PARIS **PALAIS DE TOKYO**

ARCHITECTS: LACATON & VASSAL_**COMPLETION:** 2001_**ORIGINAL BUILDING:** ANDRÉ AUBERT, MARCEL HENRI ALBERT DASTUGUE, JEAN-CLAUDE DONDEL, PAUL-JEAN-EMILE VIARD, 1937_**TYPE:** ART MUSEUM_**GROSS FLOOR AREA:** 7,800 M² _**PHOTOS:** CHRIS VAN UFFELEN (198 B. L., 199 B. L., B. R.), PHILIPPE RUAULT (198 B. R., 199 A.)

THE ARCHITECTURE

The aim of this restructuring was not to create an enclosed museum, but an open event venue. A large open space, free of borders or limitations, installations or pressures was created, resembling an urban square. The very elongated concrete building of 1937 was stripped on the inside and now has a raw and industrial look. Construction elements with a light appearance such as stairs and paths were added to the exterior. They reduced the monumental impression of the original building and comply with the temporary nature of the contemporary interior art installation. Behind the monumental façades, the building interior resembles impressive abandoned industrial premises as daylight enters through the large atriums and windows to generously and evenly flood the exhibition rooms.

THE COLLECTION

The original building was constructed in 1934-1937 on the occasion of the World Fair with a design containing the monumental era shapes predominant at the time. The main wing behind the cour d'honneur, which opens up towards the Seine, consists of a portico that connects the lateral wings. Since 1961, the east wing contains the Musée d'art moderne de la Ville de Paris, while the west wing contained the public Musée National d'Art Moderne from 1947 until it moved to the Centre Pompidou in 1977. Plans for its new use began in 1999. After the conversion, the "Palais de Tokyo/Site de création contemporaine" is the city's most prominent exhibition hall of contemporary art. It offers all types of artistic expression — creative art, video films and games, dance, performance, or even fashion. The ground floor offers an almost uninterrupted exhibition space that also accommodates huge installations.

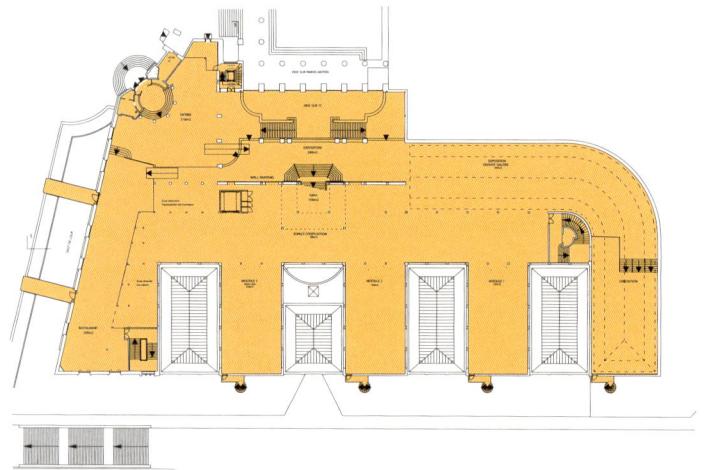

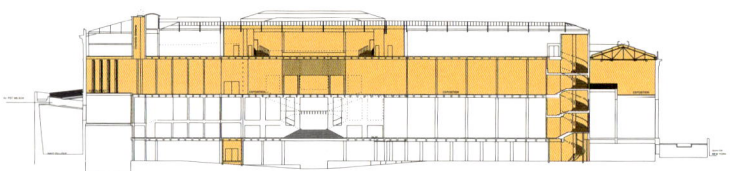

left: Third floor plan and section exhibition level_Exterior_Exhibition hall. right: Exhibition level_Exhibition hall_Book shop.

FRANCE_PARIS **MUSÉE DU QUAI BRANLY**

ARCHITECTS: ATELIERS JEAN NOUVEL_**COMPLETION:** 2006
TYPE: CULTURE MUSEUM_**GROSS FLOOR AREA:** 76,500 M²
PHOTOS: PHILIPPE RUAULT

THE ARCHITECTURE

This building is situated in a park measuring 18,000 sqaure meters. It also extends underneath the ground floor, which remained largely free of construction. A glass wall, 12 meters high and 200 meters long, insulates the premises from the Quai Branly and incorporates the street alignment. A complex path takes visitors to the exhibition halls and cabinets of the main building. These are visible as colored cubes from the outside through the northern glass façade. Horizontal rows of windows dominate the museum's red-brown southern façade. The central element of this façade consists of a rounded building segment with three rows of windows.

THE COLLECTION

The new museum near the Seine combines the exhibits of cultures outside Europe that had previously been divided across several collections. The garden, designed by Gilles Clément, already introduces the various climate zones and the green wall combines the plants of various continents combined on 800 square meters. The collection, which is known as Musée des Arts premiers or Musée des arts et civilisations d'Afrique, d'Asie, d'Océanie et des Amériques, does not categorize the exhibits according to ethnological viewpoints, but emphasizes the artistic and esthetic properties of the items. The creation of a museum for "indigenous arts," was initiated by the art trader Jacques Kerchache, who was specialized on African art and who wanted to introduce these works to the Louvre in the 1990s. When Jacques Chirac was elected president, the section was created in the Louvre, but one year later the politician initiated the construction of the MQB as a new independent museum specialized in these works.

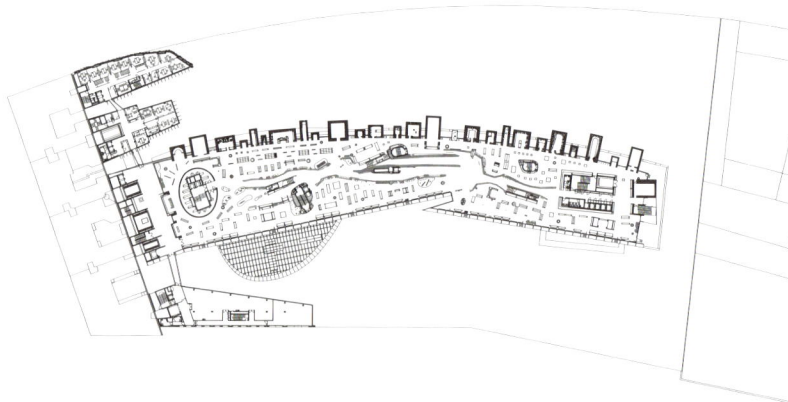

left: First floor plan_Exterior_Façade. right: Main façade and glass screen_Exhibition_Exhibition room.

FRANCE_RENNES **ÉCOMUSÉE DU PAYS DE RENNES**

ARCHITECTS: GUINEE*POTIN ARCHITECTS_**COMPLETION:** 2010
TYPE: NATURE MUSEUM_**GROSS FLOOR AREA:** 990 M²
PHOTOS: S CHALMEAU, NANTES

THE ARCHITECTURE

Within its strong natural context, this project's wooden skin provides a generous scale for a "building-sign", real "eco-museum." The extension of the existing building develops the new entrance hall and the temporary exhibition, built in timber framework and timber cladding. On the southern side, the timber framework extends down an ecological concrete wall base, tinted with natural pigments. Above this, the timber cladding is made of natural wood shingles (chestnut) arranged in graphic patterns. Pillars are made of raw tree trunks, though a maximum number of the site's trees have been conserved.

THE COLLECTION

The agricultural museum of the Rennes region is located in the former farm Ferme de la Bintinais, in whose renovated buildings 500 years of regional history can be experienced. It also showcases the relationship between the capital of the Bretagne and its surrounding areas through numerous exhibits and photographs. Across three floors, replicated scenes, equipment and agricultural machines provide an insight into the everyday working environment of past centuries, while modern audiovisual media, interactive games and films vividly present the working and living conditions of farmers. Rooms authentically decorated with original furniture and household items show how people used to live in earlier days. The open air museum extends across more than 19 hectares and shows how the cultivation of land and animal husbandry were practiced in the Bretagne since the 17th century. Various types of fruits, vegetables and grains are planted here, in addition 19 types of breeding animals, which are threatened by extinction, live on the museum grounds.

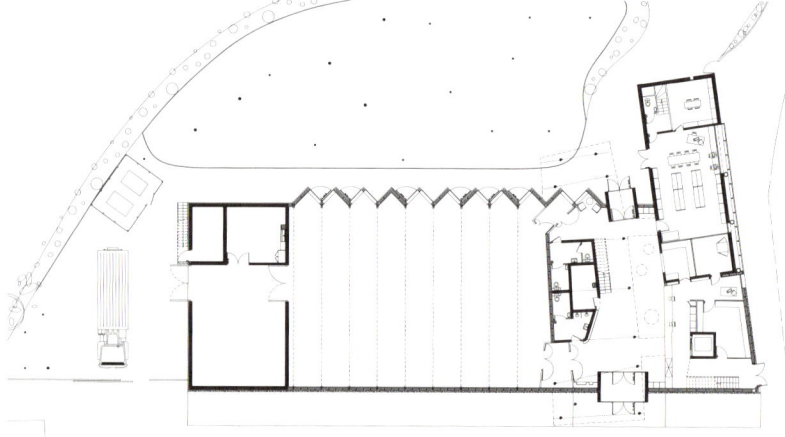

left: Ground floor plan_General view_Context. right: Entrance_Exhibition room_North elevation.

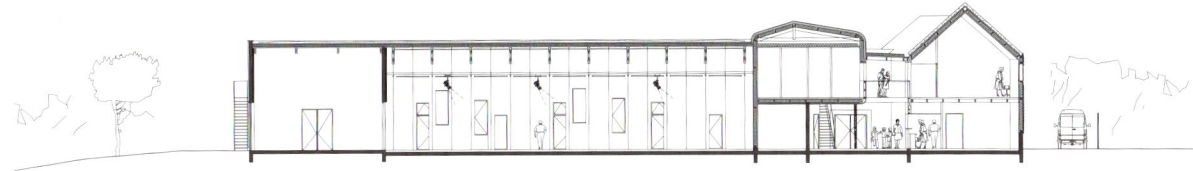

left: Entrance hall with stairs. right: Cross section_Entrance hall.

FRANCE_SABRES **ÉCOMUSÉE DE LA GRANDE LANDE**

ARCHITECTS: BRUNO MADER ARCHITECTE_**COMPLETION:** 2008
TYPE: NATURE MUSEUM_**GROSS FLOOR AREA:** 2,860 M²
PHOTOS: GASTON F. BERGERET, PARIS

THE ARCHITECTURE

The main highlight of the "Pavilion des Landes de Gascogne" building project is the development of a contemporary architecture wihch references the local context. Despite an impressive surface area and an amorphously architectural form, it is integrated without colliding with its environment. It is in sync with the linearity of the tracks, the volume of the neighboring detached houses, and the façades of the traditional sheds. According to the different angles of view, it can be seen as a unique building with supple and broad forms, or as a whole made of several buildings whose masses echo the buildings of the railway station and of the town of Sabres.

THE COLLECTION

The open-air village of Marquèzeone is France's first open-air museum. Located in the back-country of the Aquitan shore of the Atlantic, it can be reached from Sabres via an old steam train. The museum village is located inside the Parc naturel régional (regional natural park) of the Landes de Gascogne, which was established in 1970 and covers an area of 315,000 hectares with 60,500 residents. The park was planned to serve responsible ecologic tourism. The new building next to the railway station provides the functions required for the operation of the museum — exhibition room, depot, lecture room, laboratory, and museum pedagogy. In the old buildings, which replicate life in the first half of the 19th century, the museum conducts traditional types of trades. Planting of grains, beekeeping, poultry and sheep keeping, as well as tapping are carried on and researched. Under Napoleon III., animal husbandry was discontinued in the meager heather landscape and pine trees for tapping planted instead, creating Europe's largest forest. After the middle of the century, the landscape developed in one of France's richest regions due to the resin production for rubber products. However, this was followed by an equally rapid decline after the introduction of synthetics.

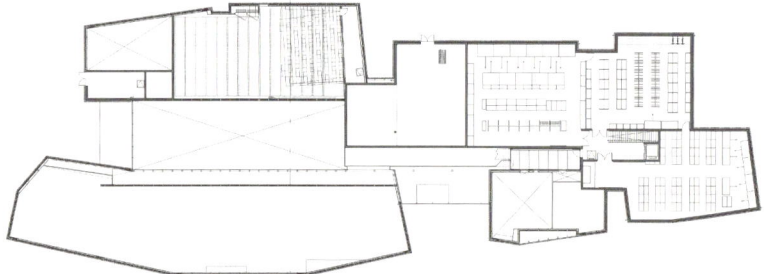

left: First floor plan_General view from west_View of temporary gallery_View from temporary gallery.
right: Exterior view from west_View from south.

FRANCE_SAINT-OURS-LES-ROCHES **VULCANIA**

ARCHITECTS: HANS HOLLEIN_**SCENOGRAPHY:** ATELIER RAINER VERBIZH_**COMPLETION:** 2002_**TYPE:** NATURE MUSEUM_**GROSS FLOOR AREA:** 4,700 M² _**PHOTOS:** ATELIER HOLLEIN / SINA BANIAHMAT (208, 209, 210, 211 A . R., B. R.), VUCANIA / JOEL DAMASE (211 B. L.)

THE ARCHITECTURE

Vulcania is the world's first new volcanology center. Situated within extinct volcanoes at an altitude of 1,000 meters in the Auvergne region, this complex allows visitors to receive information and learn about as well as experience the primeval forces of nature and the creation of our planet. Mostly located underground, it is accessed via a long ramp down towards a metaphorical volcano — a cone clad in dark volcanic stone lined with golden metal animated by light on the inside. The architect creates extreme environments within the scope of this museum. Vulcania is also an educational site dedicated to professional research. The building complex additionally houses research and conference facilities, IMAX theaters, and green houses.

THE COLLECTION

The establishment of the "European Park for Volcanism" was advanced by the former French president Valéry Giscard d'Estaing as regional president of the Auvergne region. It is located in the regional natural park Volcans d'Auvergne, in the Chaîne des Puys volcano chain, also known as Monts Dômes, whose 80 volcano domes from the Quarternary extend in the North-South direction at a length of approximately 30 kilometers. The Puy de Dôme is the highest elevation at 1,464 meters. Its last outbreak took place approximately 7,000 years ago. Vulcania attempts to convey the history of the landscape and volcanism in general in an entertaining and curiosity-evoking way. On the thin line between popularity and science, all contents were confirmed by the international scientific advisory body. Visitors can journey to the center of a lava stream, look at an exterior view of the "machine" of our earth, or witness the eruption of the Great Geyser. On a platform, they can experience a tornado, an earthquake, an avalanche, a meteorite shower or a lava stream up close and personal. At the same time, practical information for emergencies is provided.

left: Sketch_Cone lined inside with golden metal_Exterior view. right: Cone_Exterior view by night Exhibition area.

left: The cone is cladded in dark volcanic stone lined inside with golden metal. right: Section_Aerial view_Interior garden_Exterior view.

FRANCE_VILLENEUVE D'ASCQ

LAM – MUSÉE D'ART MODERNE D'ART CONTEMPORAIN ET D'ART BRUT

ARCHITECTS: MANUELLE GAUTRAND ARCHITECTURE
COMPLETION: 2010_**ORIGINAL BUILDING:** ROLAND SIMOUNET,
1983_**TYPE:** ART MUSEUM_**GROSS FLOOR AREA:** 9,000 M²
PHOTOS: MAX LEROUGE

THE ARCHITECTURE

Rather than install the new section at a distance, the architects chose to wrap the extension around a corner of the "old" building. The project, for the Communauté Urbaine de Lille, aims to reconstitute the museum as a continuous ensemble, by adding new galleries to house a collection of Art Brut works in a travelling movement that extrapolates existing spaces. The architecture of the extension wraps around the northern and eastern ends of the angular brick building in a double splay of long fluid and organic volumes. On one side, the new wing extends in narrow folds to contain a restaurant opening onto a central patio, while on the other it extends in larger folds, each of which houses one of the five Art Brut galleries.

THE COLLECTION

The museum is the only museum in Europe presenting all the main components of 20th and 21st century art side by side. It contains three collections — a collection of modern art, a benchmark anthology of contemporary art, and a collection of outsider art unrivalled in France. Combined, these include 4,500 works of art. The museum was originally constructed to house the donation made by Geneviève and Jean Masurel to the urban community of Lille Métropole in 1979. This collection includes Cubist masterpieces by Georges Braque, Henri Laurens and Pablo Picasso, along with significant series of works by Fernand Léger, Joan Miró and Amedeo Modigliani. It also contains works of Fauvism, Surrealism, the Montparnasse School of Paris, Naïf Art and the artists from northern France. The collection of contemporary art, which can be continuously expanded includes, for example, works by French and foreign artists of the caliber of Lewis Baltz, Christian Boltanski and Dennis Oppenheim. In 1999, the collection was complemented by France's major collection of outsider art, in the form of a donation made by the Aracine Association.

left: Model (1/200)_View of the Patio. right: Exterior night view_Interior of the extension_Exterior.

GERMANY_BERLIN **JÜDISCHES MUSEUM BERLIN**

ARCHITECTS: STUDIO DANIEL LIBESKIND_**LANDSCAPE ARCHITECT:** MÜLLER, KNIPPSCHILD, WEHBERG_**COMPLETION:** 1999, EXTENSION 2007_**TYPE:** HISTORY MUSEUM_**GROSS FLOOR AREA:** 15,500 M²_**PHOTOS:** BITTER BREDT FOTOGRAFIE, BERLIN (214, 215 B. L., B. R., 217 L., A. R.), GUENTER SCHNEIDER, BERLIN (215 A.), MICHELE NASTASI, MILAN (216, 217 B. R.)

THE ARCHITECTURE

This museum, which opened to the public in 2001, exhibits the social, political and cultural history of the Jews in Germany from the 4th century to the present. The museum explicitly presents and integrates, for the first time in postwar Germany, the repercussions of the Holocaust. The new extension is housed on the site of the original Prussian Court of Justice building, which was completed in 1735 and renovated in the 1960s to become a museum for the city of Berlin. The new design, which was created a year before the Berlin Wall came down, started with the identification of a common feature that bound together both East and West Berlin — the relationship between the Germans and the Jews.

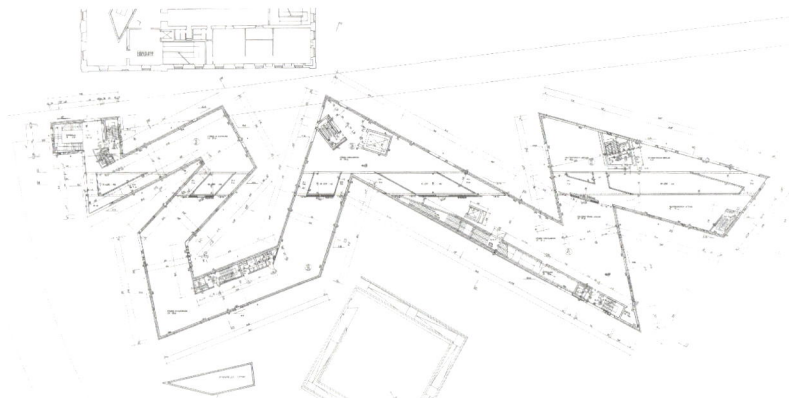

THE COLLECTION

The Jewish museum of Berlin presents 2,000 years of Jewish-German history. The museum contains a permanent and several temporary exhibitions, comprehensive archives, the Rafael Roth Learning Center, as well as research institutions that aim to reflect Jewish history and culture. The museum's collections are based on the Jewish section of the Berlin Museum, the urban history museum of Berlin. In 1981 the Berlin Museum purchased the Judaica collection of the Münster cantor Zvi Sofer, creating a basis for its collection of ceremonial objects. Added to this were important individual pieces such as the Chanukka-candle holder by George Wilhelm Marggraff of 1776 as well as objects of everyday and family use. These objects were presented from 1984 on the ground floor of the Berlin Museum. Two years later, the collection was provided with three additional rooms on the second floor of the Martin-Gropius building. Finally, in 2001 the Jewish museum was established as an independent entity of the federation, incorporating the items of the Berlin Museum. At the same time, the collection's focus was expanded from items related to the Jewish history of Berlin to nation-wide documents.

left: Site plan_JMB next to original baroque building_The void_Holocaust tower. right: Aerial view Main staircase_Overall composition.

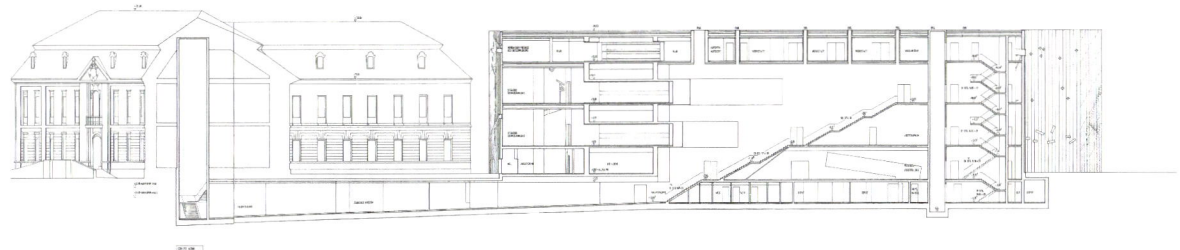

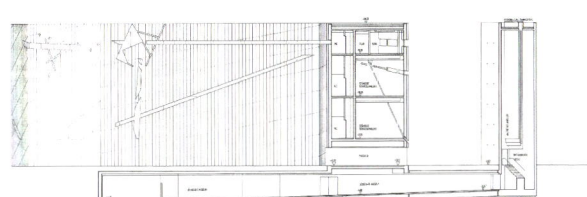

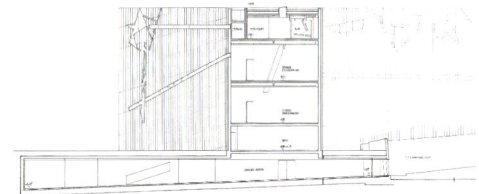

left: Garden of Exile. right: Section with stairs_Paul Celan courtyard_Holocaust Tower and Garden of Exile_Windows as part of Star of David matrix.

ARCHITECTS: DAVID CHIPPERFIELD ARCHITECTS_**COMPLETION:** 2009_**ORIGINAL BUILDING:** FRIEDRICH AUGUST STÜLER, 1855 **TYPE:** ARCHEOLOGY MUSEUM_**GROSS FLOOR AREA:** 20,500 M² **PHOTOS:** SPK / DAVID CHIPPERFIELD ARCHITECTS, PHOTOGRA-PHER: UTE ZSCHARNT (218, 221 L., A. R.), SPK / DAVID CHIPPER-FIELD ARCHITECTS, PHOTOGRAPHER: JÖRG VON BRUCHHAUSEN (219 A., B. M.), SPK / DAVID CHIPPERFIELD ARCHITECTS, PHOTOG-RAPHER: CHRISTIAN RICHTERS (219 B. L., B. R., 220, 221 B. R.)

THE ARCHITECTURE

The reconstruction of this museum, damaged in World War II, features new parts of large-scale pre-fabricated concrete elements consisting of white cement mixed with Saxonian marble chips. Made of the same concrete elements, the new main staircase alludes to the original without replicating it, and sits within a hall that is preserved only as a brick volume, devoid of its original ornamentation. Other new volumes — the northwest wing, with the Egyptian court and the Apollo projection, the apse in the Greek courtyard, and the South Dome — are built of recycled, handmade bricks. The reinstatement and completion of the mostly preserved colonnades on both the eastern and southern sides of the museum re-established a part of the pre-war urban situation.

THE COLLECTION

The Prussian king Friedrich Wilhelm IV decreed on March 8, 1841 the construction of the Neues Museum to provide new space for the growing collections of the Altes Museum. Construction commenced on June 19,1841 under the supervision of chief construction engineer Carl Wilhelm Hoffmann. Two years later the foundation stone was laid. In the year 1850, the Egyptian collection and copper engraving department were opened as the first section in the basement of the Neues Museum. In 1855, the Kunstkammer opened on the third floor. This section contains a collection of architectural models and furniture as well as ceramics and glass vessels. The collection of national antiquities and the plaster cast collection opened on the main floor in 1856. Three years later, the ethnographic collection was the last section to open on the ground floor of the Neues Museum. From 1919 to 1923 the Greek courtyard was turned into the Amarna hall of the Egyptian collection. The building was severely damaged in World War II and parts of the museum had to be demolished as a result. It was not until 1977 that David Chipperfield was commissioned to plan the reconstruction of the Neues Museum, which commenced in 2003. The museum reopened on October 16, 2009.

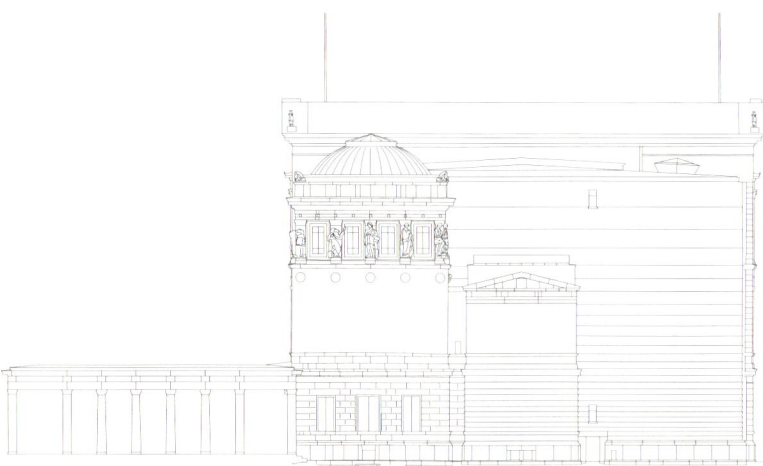

left: North Elevation_West façade. right: Staircase Hall_Staircase Hall, view into the Greek Room Staircase Hall_Room behind the Staircase Hall, view into the Ethnographical Room.

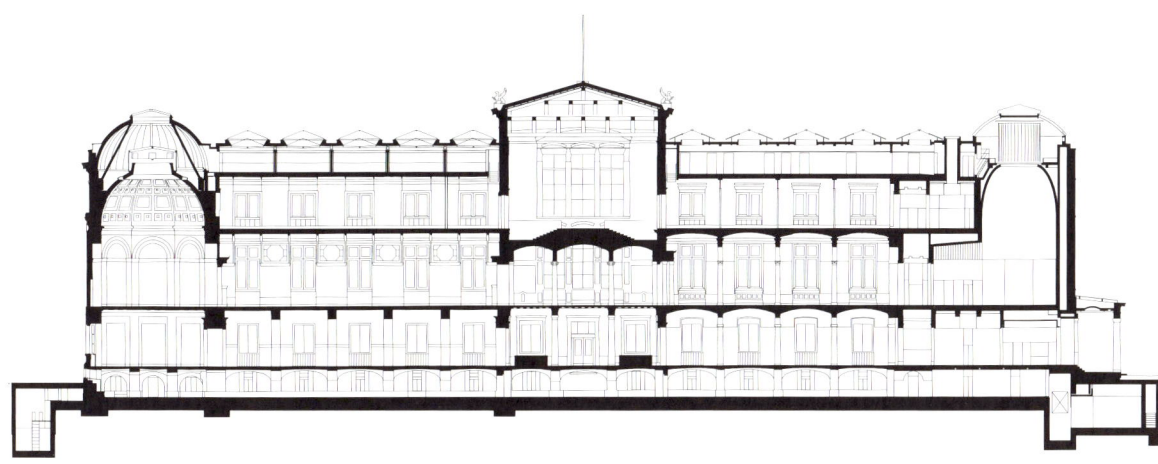

left: Greek courtyard. right: Section through east wing_Enfilade level 2 east wing_Detail Egyptian courtyard_Sternensaal (starroom), view into westerly art collection chamber.

GERMANY_BERLIN **BERLINISCHE GALERIE**

ARCHITECTS: DIPL.-ING. JÖRG FRICKE, ARCHITEKT**_DESIGN STAIRCASE, OFFICE BUILDING, CAFÉTERIA:** ANGELIKA KAMITZEK, BMH A+**_ART, PAVEMENT, STREET FURNITURE:** KÜHN MALVEZZI ARCHITEKTEN, BERLIN**_FAÇADE AND WALL ART:** FRITZ BALTHAUS, BERLIN**_COMPLETION:** 2004**_ORIGINAL BUILDING:** HEINZ GEISTERING, HORST GRÜTZNE, 1965**_TYPE:** ART, PHOTOGRAPHY AND ARCHITECTURE MUSEUM**_GROSS FLOOR AREA:** 14,055 M² **PHOTOS:** HANS PRAEFKE, BERLIN

THE ARCHITECTURE

In the immediate vicinity of the Jewish museum of Daniel Libeskind, a former industrial hall and administration building were converted into a museum, with limited funds, in just under a year. The focus was on optimizing and improving the functionality of the exhibition spaces. Varying room heights, fluid transitions and a multitude of visual connections characterize the building. In addition to the user's requirements, planning criteria included sustainable operations and low operating costs. Sophisticated detail solutions, the use of limited materials and a restrained architectural language create a noble objectivity, which focuses on one thing only — art.

THE COLLECTION

The "Landesmuseum für Moderne Kunst, Fotografie und Architektur" (State museum of modern art, photography and architecture) was founded in 1975 as an association to exhibit art created in Berlin. It was initially based in an office in Charlottenburg. In 1978, the gallery moved to the Landwehr-Kasino, and from 1986 to 1998 it was located in the Martin-Gropius building. In the subsequent years, the gallery did not have a fixed location and was only moved to its current building, a former industrial hall, in 2004. Its creative arts collection contains approximately 5,000 paintings, sculptures, installations and multimedia works of the late 19th century to the present day. A particularly large focus is on entire series of works by individual artists, such as Naum Gabo, Iwan Puni, and Hans Uhlmann. The graphic art section contains around 15,000 works on paper. The Berlinische Galerie also contains a collection of photographs consisting of mostly original photographs as well as authorized new enlarged photos along with a wealth of biographic material about the photographers. The architectural collection occupies a separate section, established in 1987. It includes around 300,000 plans and drawings, as well as around 2,500 architectural models with a focus on documents related to the architectural and urban planning history of the 20th century.

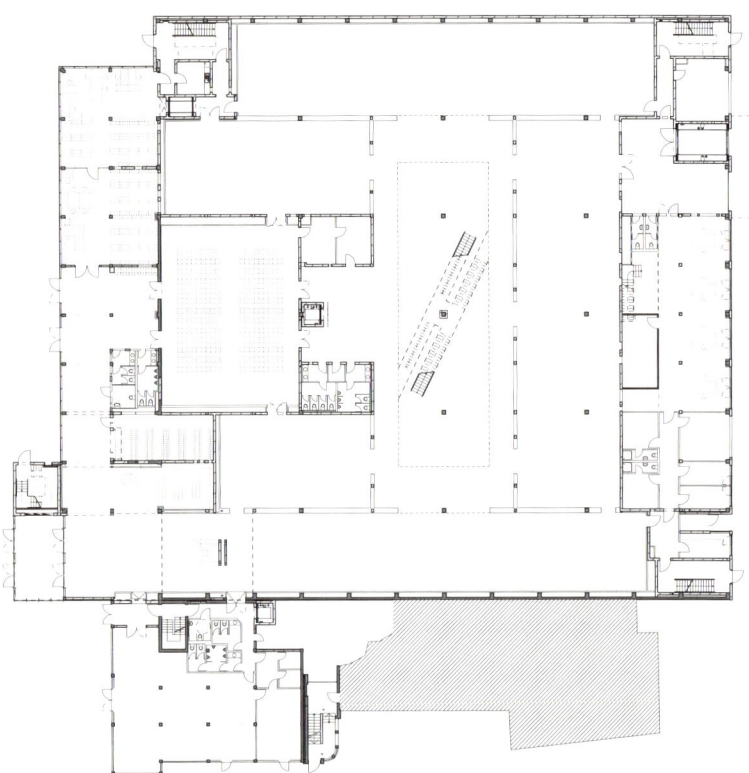

left: Ground floor plan_South elevation with sculpture "Dreiheit (Trinity)" by Brigitte and Martin Matschinsky-Denninghoff_Room in a room. right: Large exhibition room with artwork by Gerold Miller, Stefan Beck, Ronald de Bloeme, Tim Trantenroth and Fritz Balthaus_View from side-room Main staircase.

GERMANY_BRÜHL **MAX ERNST MUSEUM**

ARCHITECTS: ARGE VAN DEN VALENTYN ARCHITEKTUR, SMO ARCHITEKTUR_**COMPLETION:** 2004_**TYPE:** ART MUSEUM **GROSS FLOOR AREA:** 5,400 M² _**PHOTOS:** RAINER MADER

THE ARCHITECTURE

The essence of this classicist three-wing premises, built around the year 1844, was preserved, all annexes removed, and the initial shape with a court-yard opening up towards the park reconstituted. This was complemented by a new building, half of which is located underground and whose roof surface is reflected in the park as a slightly elevated natural stone plateau. Inserted into the inner courtyard, the entrance pavilion constitutes the connecting element between the old and new structures. The area of the temporary exhibitions re-ceives daylight illumination through accessible skylights. An adjacent concert hall is used independently. The work of Max Ernst is primarily situated in the old building, which houses the permanent exhibition in its main section.

THE COLLECTION

The museum is the only museum in the world dedicated to the work of artist Max Ernst. Across approximately 1,100 square meters, the museum presents Dadaist and surreal works from the almost 70 years of the artist's creativity. The exhibition includes the former collection of Dr. Peter Schneppenheim, containing almost the entire graphic works of Max Ernst. In addition, the 36 "D-paintings," birthday and romantic presents by the artist to his wife, are also on show, plus more than 700 photographic documents that reflect the artist's life. In addition to this permanent exhibition, the museum also contains a 500 meter hall for temporary exhibitions. The "rotating exhibition" concept approaches the multifaceted work of Max Ernst in a way that provides continuously fresh insights. For example, in 2009 the museum presented for an entire year the entire "Petals and Garden of Nymph Ancolie" mural, cre-ated by the artist in 1934.

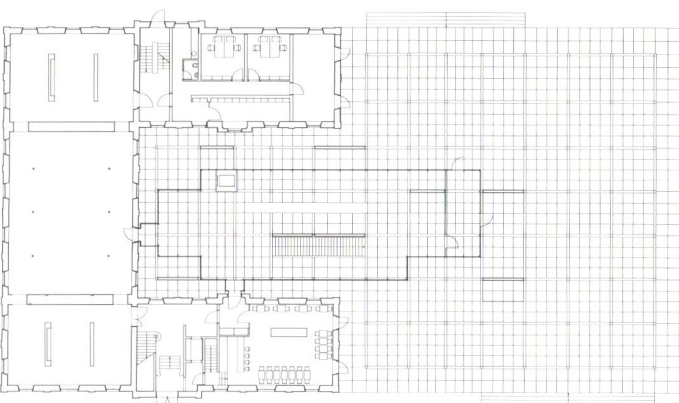

left: Ground floor plan_South elevation. right: Gallery_Elevation from Commesstrasse_Pillared hall.

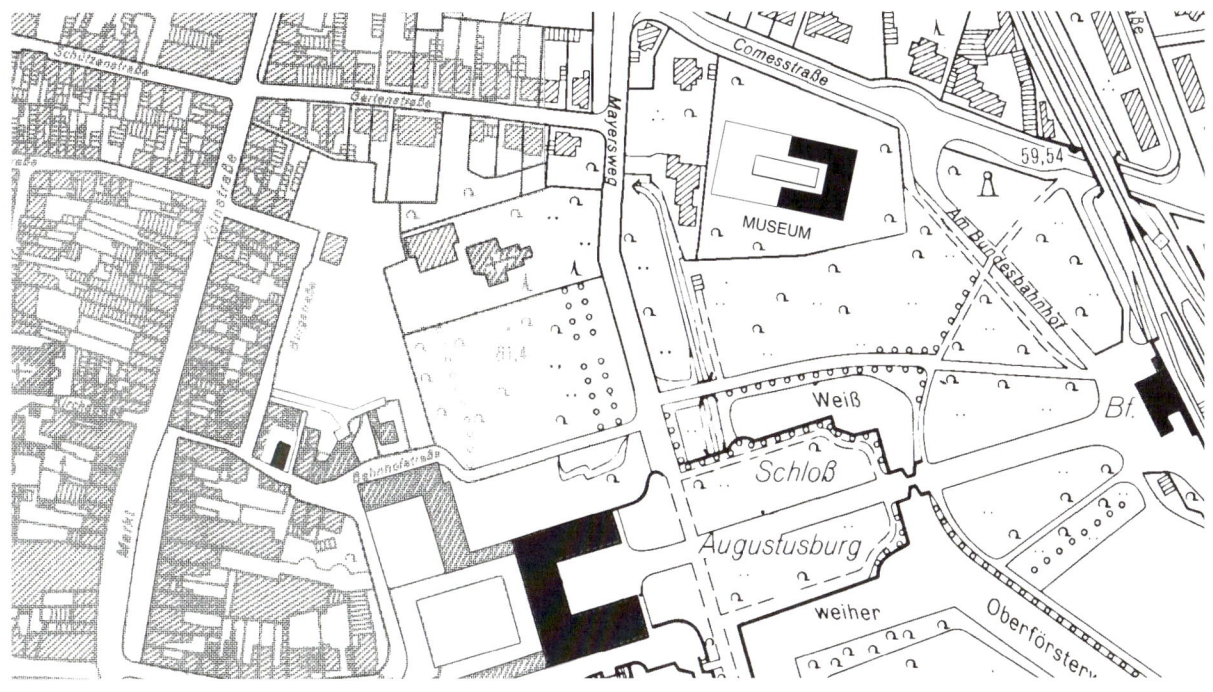

left: Pavilion detail. right: Site plan_Entrance pavilion.

GERMANY_CELLE **KUNSTMUSEUM CELLE**

ARCHITECTS: AHRENS GRABENHORST ARCHITEKTEN BDA
COMPLETION: 2006_**ORIGINAL BUILDING:** WALTER VON LOM, 1992
TYPE: ART MUSEUM_**GROSS FLOOR AREA:** 1,200 M² _**PHOTOS:**
ROLAND HALBE / ARTURIMAGES

THE ARCHITECTURE

Measuring approximately 10 x 10 x 10 meters, the glass cube incorporates the eaves, heights, and building alignments of the Bomann museum and the existing expansion of the year 1992. The two-floor building is colorfully illuminated at night. The roof terrace provides a view of the Residenzschloss palace located opposite. The limited materials employed in the façade design create a dialogue between the old and the new. Evenly reflecting surfaces of clear and white matte glass are fitted onto a level without retaining ledges, visible fixtures or protective steel sheets and reflect the surroundings. The conceptual composition structure consists of surface areas, lines, and volumes.

THE COLLECTION

The museum in Celle is the world's only 24-hour art museum, whose concept was patented by gallery owner and art collector Robert Simon in 1998. Visitors can experience art around the clock. During the day, works ranging from contemporary to the early 20th century are exhibited across an area of 1,000 square meters. One focus of the exhibition is on items from the 1960s. For example, the museum presents a collection of Joseph Beuys work, along with works by Dieter Krieg and Ben Willikens. In addition, visitors can admire Dutch paintings by professors and graduates of the Kunsthochschule Braunschweig and the display cases by Peter Basseler, which present sometimes amusing and sometimes absurd scenes. The collection also presents drawings from the 1920s by New Objectivity artists Grethe Jürgens and Erich Wegner. A highlight of the museum is the "light room" by ZERO artist Otto Piene. When darkness falls, visitors can experience light and sound installations y by artists including Klaus Geldmacher, Francesco Mariotti and Timm Ulrichs from the outside.

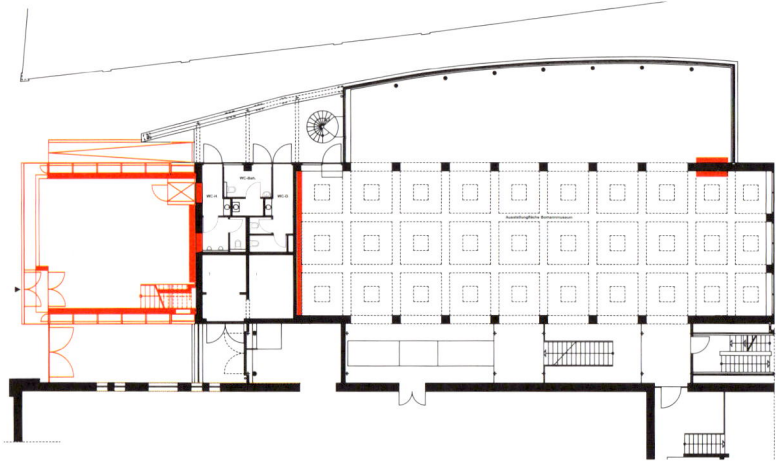

left: Ground floor plan_Ensemble old and new building_In the saddle roof. right: Façade at twilight Different illuminations.

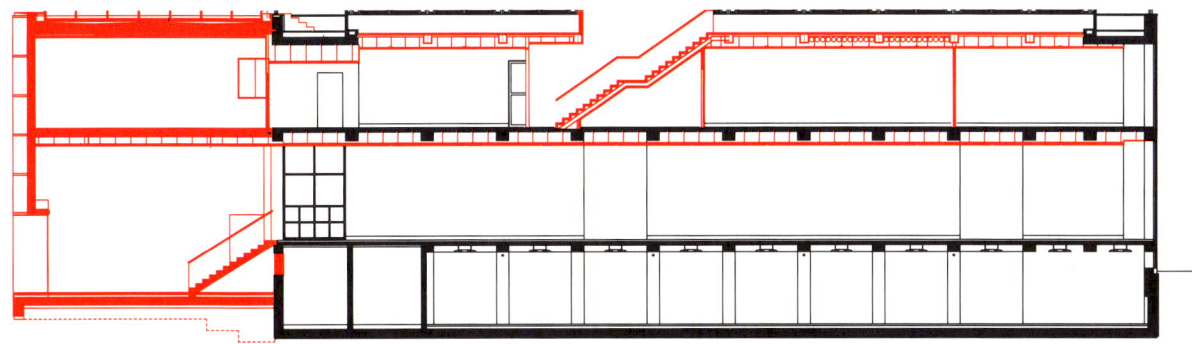

left: Façade. right: Section_View out of the window and window shutter_Roof terrace_Exhibition space.

GERMANY_DRESDEN

MILITÄRHISTORISCHES MUSEUM DER BUNDESWEHR

ARCHITECTS: STUDIO DANIEL LIBESKIND WITH ARCHITEKT DANIEL LIBESKIND AG_**COMPLETION:** 2011_**ORIGINAL BUILDING:** 1877 **TYPE:** HISTORY MUSEUM_**GROSS FLOOR AREA:** 20,000 M²_**PHOTOS:** COURTESY OF THE ARCHITECTS (233), BITTER BREDT FOTOGRAFIE, BERLIN (232 B. L., B. M., B. R.)

THE ARCHITECTURE

This museum will become the official central museum of the German Armed Forces. A new extension was designed by cutting a wedge through the structural order of the arsenal, giving the museum a place for reflection about organized violence. The 140-ton wedge of glass, concrete and steel will intersect the 130-year-old original museum building. A 30-meter viewing platform at the peak provides views of Dresden, while the new extension re-orientates the existing building by opening up the view to the historical center of Dresden. Additionally, its soaring presence above the roof of the original building creates a public symbol of the museum's modernization.

THE COLLECTION

With a collection of more than one million objects, the museum, along with the air force museum, is one of the largest military history museums of the German armed forces. It aims to reflect the German military history within its historical concept from its outset to the present time, including social, technical and cultural aspects. In addition, the history of the building is presented. Constructed between 1873 and 1877, it served as a main arsenal storage building. At the end of World War I it was no longer used as a military depot. The main building continued to serve as a depository for military equipment, and in 1918 housed the Sächsisches Armeemuseum (Saxonian army museum). In 1940 it was renamed Heeresmuseum (Army museum). It was abandoned following world War II after the Red Army had confiscated its contents. Until 1967 the building was managed by the city of Dresden, and known as the "Nordhalle" (north hall) for the presentation of exhibits of the Stadtmuseum (city museum). In the 1972 , the "Armeemuseum der DDR" (Army museum of the German Democratic Republic) moved into the building, focusing mainly on the history of the National People's Army and the Warsaw Pact, which still affects the collection of the museum today. For example, there is ample documentation of the German Peasant's War or the history of the German workers' movement. In 1990 the German federal ministry of defense took over the museum and renamed it "Militärhistorisches Museum" (Military history museum. Since that time, it has focused on the collection of items related to the recent history of the German armed forces.

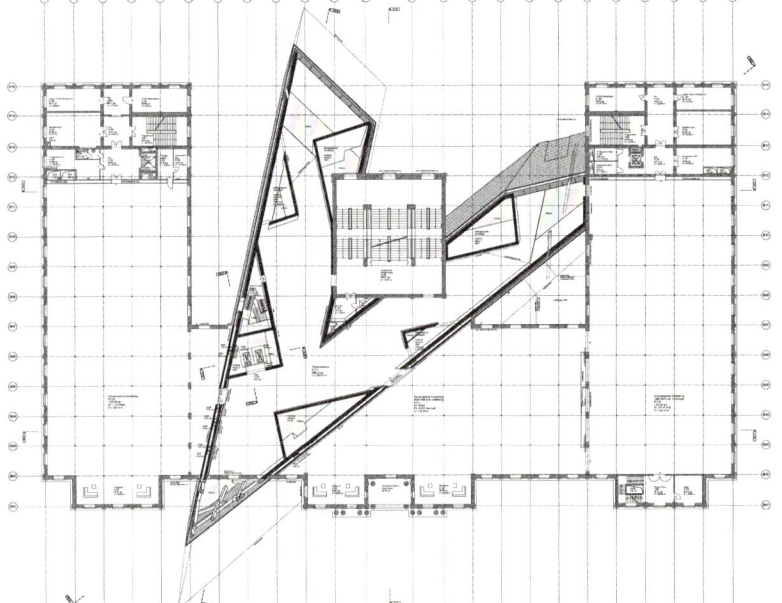

left: Site plan_Old and new construction_Construction photo interior_Construction photo. right: The transparent new façade stands against the opacity of the old façade_View of Café.

GERMANY_DRESDEN **AUSSTELLUNGSGEBÄUDE BRÜHLSCHE TERRASSE**

ARCHITECTS: AUER+WEBER+ASSOZIIERTE_**COMPLETION:** 2005
ORIGINAL BUILDING: CONSTANTIN LIPSIUS, 1894
TYPE: ART MUSEUM_**GROSS FLOOR AREA:** 3,350 M² _**PHOTOS:**
ROLAND HALBE / ARTURIMAGES

THE ARCHITECTURE

This exhibition building is located in the eastern wing of the Dresdener Kunst-akademie, built by Constantin Lipsius in 1894. The "Temple of art near the Brühlsche Terrasse" was severely damaged in World War II and its exterior was not renovated until after 1990. The exhibition areas were renewed based on functional and architectural viewpoints, allowing them to be used once again for temporary fine arts exhibitions and complemented by a new gallery floor, while traces of history were maintained after cleaning and renovation. The new installations respect the quality of the historic rooms, while at the same time their materials and colors contrast with the building substance.

THE COLLECTION

In addition to the art academy, the building also houses the exhibition hall of the Sächsischer Kunstverein. For many decades, it was the venue of highly sensational art exhibitions, for example from 1905 the works of the painters of the at the time newly established "Brücke" artist group. In the year 2005, the exhibition hall reopened with the exhibition "Blick auf Dresden" ("A look at Dresden"). Since that time, the museum has been offering changing tempo-rary exhibitions, with a focus on artists and works of art that have a special relationship to the city of Dresden. Of these, the exhibition hall primarily shows contemporary art, for example "Sigmar Polke. Eine Retrospektive" (Sigmar Polke. A Retrospective"), or "Von Monet bis Mondrian" ("From Monet to Mondrian"). In the year 2010, the museum is presenting a large exhibi-tion of works by the Canadian artist Jeff Wall (*1946). Entitled "Transit," the exhibition features paintings related to transitions and change in the context of historic, sociological, and everyday experiences.

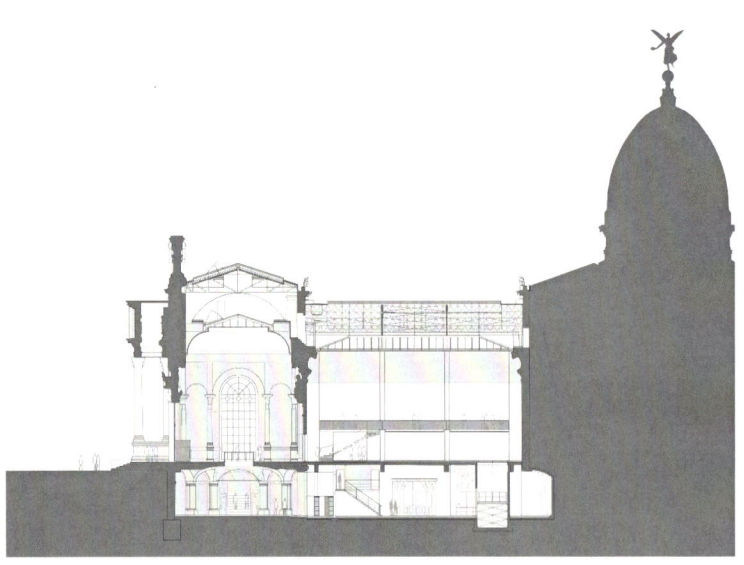

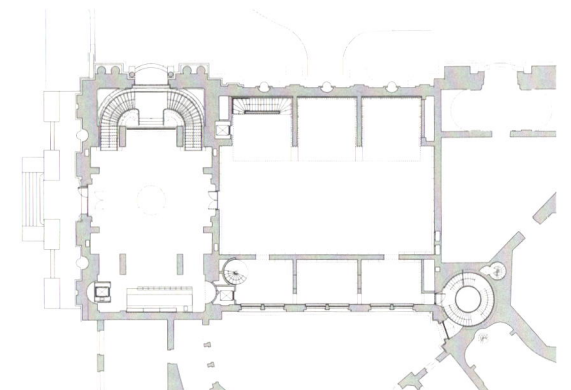

left: Ground floor plan floor_Skylight. right: Supplemented building and vault opening into the base-ment_Adaptation cornice_Exhibition hall_Vault with occulus to the basement.

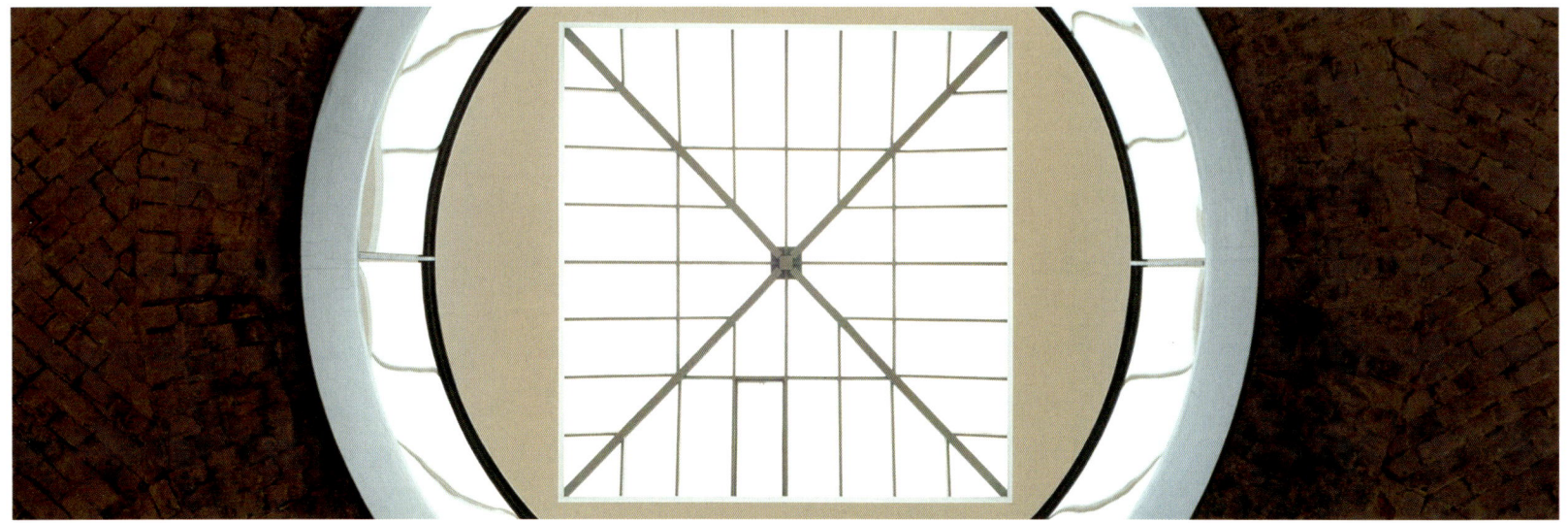

GERMANY_DÜSSELDORF **K21 KUNSTSAMMLUNG STÄNDEHAUS**

ARCHITECTS: KIESSLER + PARTNER ARCHITEKTEN_**COMPLETION:** 2002_**ORIGINAL BUILDING:** JULIUS CARL RASCHDORFF, 1880 **TYPE:** ART MUSEUM_**GROSS FLOOR AREA:** 13,600 M² _**PHOTOS:** RALPH RICHTER, DÜSSELDORF (236 B. L., B. R., 237 B. L., B. R), WOLFGANG SCHWAGER, AACHEN (237 A.)

THE ARCHITECTURE

Within the scope of its restructuring, this building received a new cupola and a large underground exhibition hall. The glass and steel cupola spans the entire building, while the room contained within it provides a panoramic view of the city. The new exhibition hall is used for various temporary exhibitions. Located underneath the post and beam house, it is more than six meters high and reaches to the north all the way to the Kaiserteich. Porthole windows provide views over and under the lake's surface. The historic exterior façade was kept intact. Other historic elements, such as the staircase and the twin column, are emphasized by the white ceilings and walls.

THE COLLECTION

On an exhibition area of more than 5,300 square meters, the museum presents international contemporary art. Initially, the museum was supported considerably by many permanent loans from the three private collections from the Rhine area by Simone and Heinz Ackerman, Dr. Reiner Speck, and Gaby and Wilhelm Schürmann. The museum's varied program of collection and exhibition units currently includes works purchased by the Kunstsammlung Nordrhein-Westfalen itself in recent years. These include, for example, sculptures by Thomas Schütte, photographs by Bernd and Hilla Becher and Andreas Gursky, as well as room installations by Marcel Broodthaers and Nam June Paik. The museum also owns Reinhard Mucha's monumental room installation "Das Deutschlandgerät" of the year 1990, one of the most prominent works of German art of the late 20th century. The museum offers visitors an extraordinary presentation located on the fourth floor immediately underneath the building's glass cupola — since summer 2003 visitors can visit the installation "Bijou Gets Undressed" of the British artist Julian Opie.

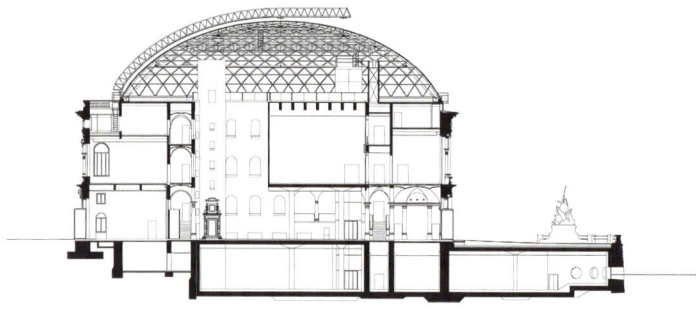

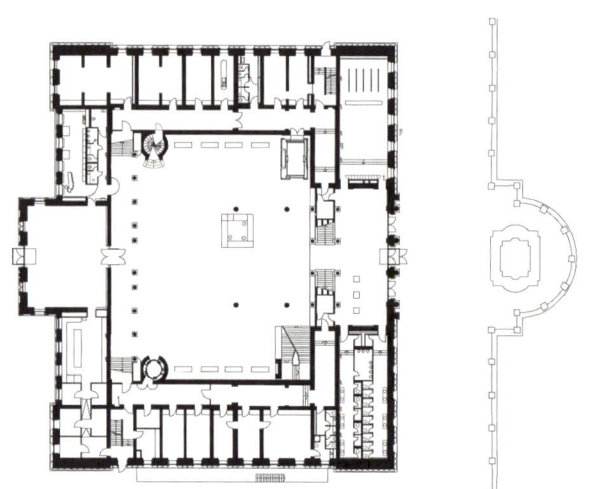

left: Section and ground floor plan_Night version_Café, designed by Jorge Pardo. right: North side with Kaiserteich_Exhibition space under the cupola_Piazza.

GERMANY_DÜSSELDORF **JULIA STOSCHEK COLLECTION**

ARCHITECTS: KUEHN MALVEZZI_**COMPLETION:** 2007
ORIGINAL BUILDING: 1907_**TYPE:** ART MUSEUM **GROSS FLOOR AREA:** 4,350 M² _**PHOTOS:** ULRICH SCHWARZ, BERLIN

THE ARCHITECTURE

The building used to be a factory in the last century. The task was to maintain the exterior of the original layout and to reorganize the interior to suit the new purpose. The interior spaces are stacked up vertically, starting with a cinema space in the basement and culminating in a panoramic terrace at the top of a glass box placed on the factory roof. The collection's focus is on works of video art that are presented to the public with yearly changing themed exhibitions. The exhibition spaces can therefore be changed easily. Areas for watching videos are enclosed by soundproof walls. The spaces dividing each video installation create a break between one piece and another.

THE COLLECTION

Julia Stoschek was born 1975 in Coburg and is a shareholder of Brose Fahrzeugteile GmbH & Co. Since her visit to the private collection of the jurist and entrepreneur Harald Falckenberg in the year 2001, she is also an avid art collector. In 2006 she became a member of the purchasing commission of the "Department of Media and Performance-Art" of the Museum of Modern Art. She increasingly supports young artists by promoting their productions. In the year 2007, the first Julia Stoschek Collection exhibition was held under the title "Distroy, she said." For this exhibition the art collector selected around 40 international artistic positions that deal with the topics of construction and destruction as well as interior and exterior spaces. The Julia Stoschek collection contains approximately 400 works of contemporary art with a focus on time-based media. Video art, photographs, as well as installation are found in the landmarked former production site of the Conzenframe factory. The artists whose works are exhibited across two exhibition floors include Bruce Naumann, Marina Abramovic, Doug Aitken as well as Monica Bonvicini, Isaac Julien and Mika Rottenberg.

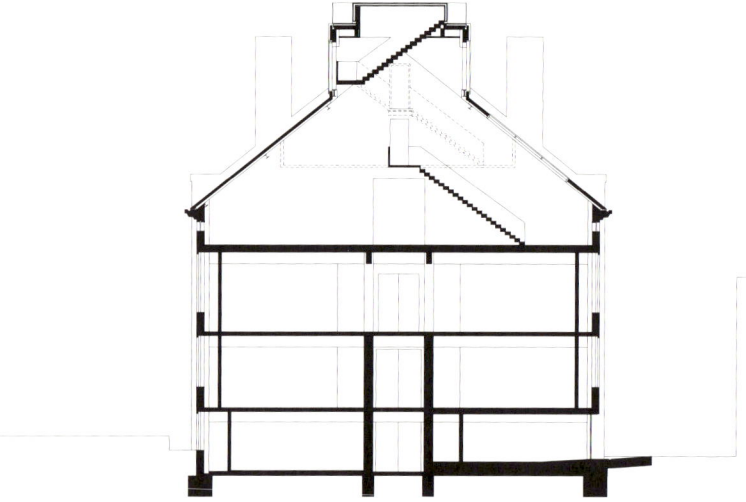

left: Section_Exhibition room, video installation of Doug Aitken_Entrance to the exhibition_Exhibition room with artworks of Tony Oursler and Jeppe Hein. right: Walkway underneath the roof_Roof terrace.

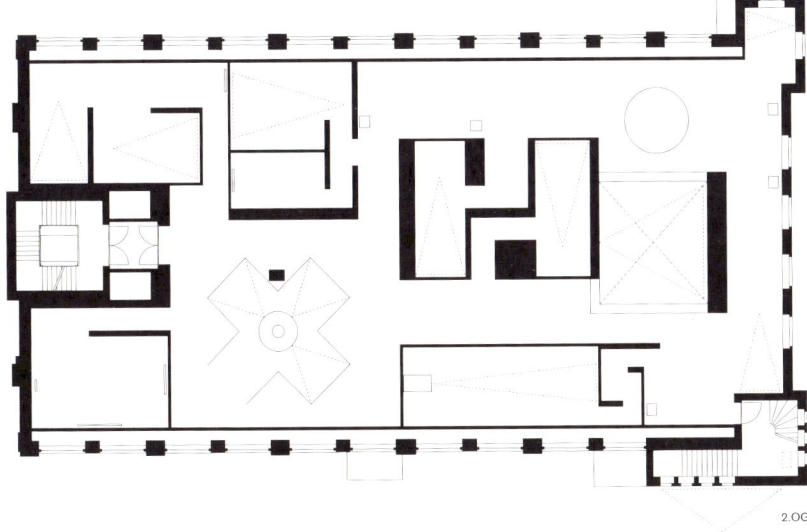

2.OG

left: Exterior and roof terrace. right: Floor plan_Installation of video screens, exhibition: DISTROY, SHE SAID (June 07 - August 08)_Roof terrace with artwork of Dan Graham_Stairs to the roof terrace.

GERMANY_EISLEBEN **MARTIN LUTHER GEBURTSHAUS**

ARCHITECTS: SPRINGER ARCHITEKTEN GESELLSCHAFT VON ARCHITEKTEN MBH_**SCENOGRAPHY:** ILG.FRIEBE.NAUBER ARCHITEKTEN BDA WITH GROUP HOLSTEIN, LEIPZIG_**COMPLE-TION:** 2007_**ORIGINAL BUILDING:** 1693_**TYPE:** HISTORY MUSEUM **GROSS FLOOR AREA:** 1,700 M² _**PHOTOS:** BERND HIEPE, BERLIN

THE ARCHITECTURE

The birthplace of Martin Luther has undergone several changes since its construction in the year 1693. The two most recently constructed new buildings allow its comprehensive use as a museum. The exhibition building provides central access via the courtyard and for the first time enables a round tour of the museum. The visitors' center with peripheral rooms points out the birthplace building which is only marginally visible in the urban space. Despite their independent modern shape, the new buildings feature understated façades of grey-brown exposed concrete. The brick structure continues inside, where new wall spaces are also made of exposed brick and only slightly covered in grey plaster.

THE COLLECTION

The great fire of 1689 severely damaged the upper floor of the house. With the help of donations from across Germany, the city was able to reconstruct the building by the year 1693 and create a memorial and monument for Dr. Martin Luther and the Reformation movement. The building is the only Luther site ever used as a school. As late as 1840, classes were held on the lower floor. In the course of the reconstruction, the "Schöne Saal" was created on the upper floor — one of the oldest historical museums in the German-speaking part of the world solely financed by the population. It features life-size portraits of the two reformers Martin Luther and Philipp Melanchthon and of local rulers of the Electorate of Saxony since the time of the Reformation. The Prussian king Friedrich Wilhelm III in 1817 decreed the preservation of the birthplace with public financing. Subsequently, an extensive Reformation history collection was created. Today, the collection features the life and work of Dr. Martin Luther. In addition to a detailed exhibition of his early years and veneration after his death, the museum also contains a late-Gothic carved altar and a valuable German-language bible of 1483.

left: Ground floor plan_Main stairs exhibition building_Exhibition room_Historic porch, entry to the ensemble. right: Courtyard of the ensemble_Plaster and brick_Timber framework and brick.

GERMANY_FRANKFURT / MAIN **KUNSTHALLE PORTIKUS**

ARCHITECTS: PROF. CHRISTOPH MÄCKLER ARCHITEKTEN
COMPLETION: 2006_**TYPE:** ART MUSEUM_**GROSS FLOOR AREA:**
770 M² _**PHOTOS:** CHRISTOPH LISON (244 B. L., 245),
WOLFGANG GUENZEL (244 B. R., 246, 247)

THE ARCHITECTURE

The exhibition hall for contemporary art is located on Main island near the Alte Brücke. Constructional development of the island was implemented in conjunction with the renovation and expansion of the bridge. The architectural shape of the new building is based on the history of the location, while its typology refers to the medieval houses of Frankfurt. The oxblood-red color of the façades resembles the traditional color of the Frankfurter Römer building. It harmonizes with the red Main sandstone of the Alte Brücke yet is distinguished from it at the same time. The building consists of a clear and well-proportioned exhibition hall, which is structured by a surrounding gallery.

THE COLLECTION

The name of the exhibition hall is derived from the surviving portico of the city library that was destroyed in World War II. The construction was secured in the year 1958 and landmarked as a memorial. Frankfurt architects Marie-Theres Deutsch and Klaus Dreißigacker added a very simply styled exhibition hall to these remnants in the year 1987. The windowless interior space had a floor space of 8 x 16 meters and presented itself as a simple and unadorned cubic structure. The first exhibition of the exhibition hall was dedicated to the artist Diter Rot (1930–1998). After more than 100 exhibitions, due to the reconstruction of the library, the Portikus temporarily moved to the ground floor of the Frankfurt Leinwandhaus. In cooperation with artist Tobias Rehberger a room concept was developed in which the insertion of box and platform elements allowed the integration of the exhibition space, office, bookstore, and storage space jointly in the hall. In 2006, the Kunsthalle im Neuen Portikus moved to the Main island. It is today part of the Hochschule für bildende Künste — Städelschule and is considered to be an important institution in the world of international arts.

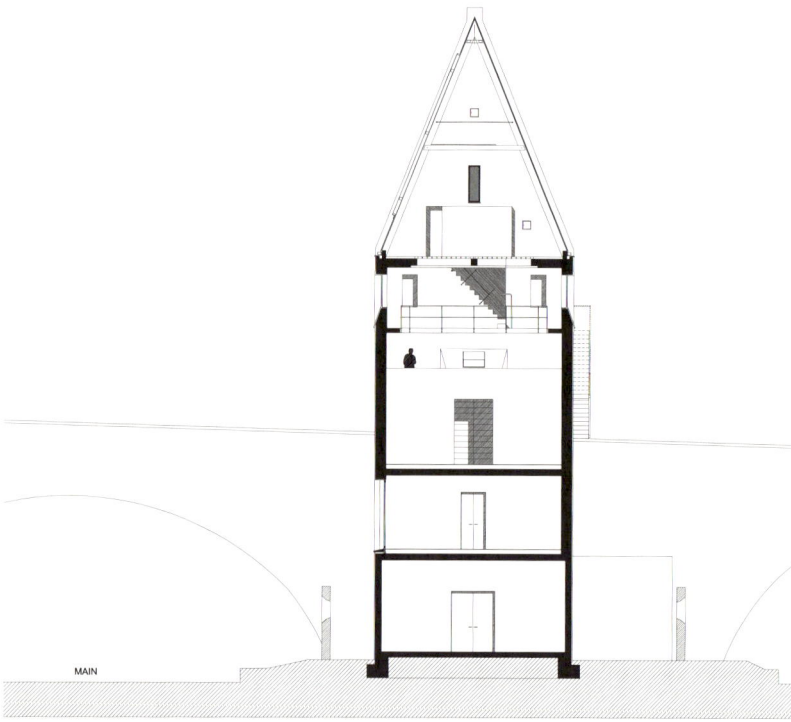

MAIN

left: Section_Façade, detail_Bird's eye view. right: Façade.

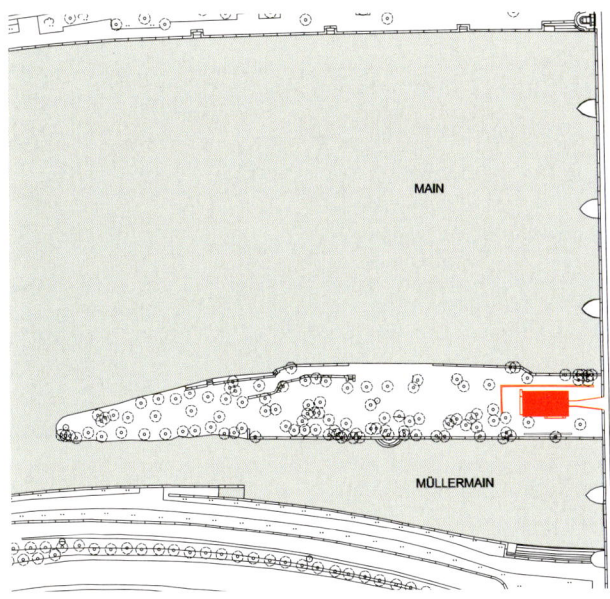

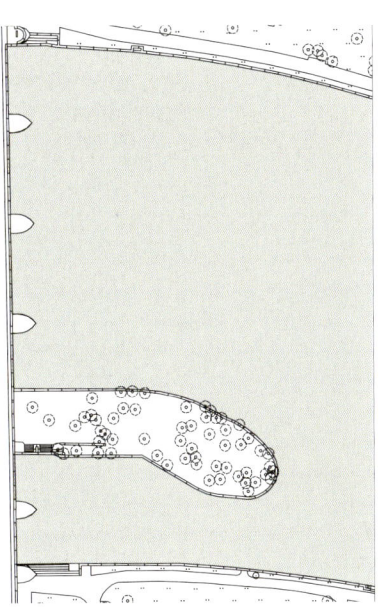

left: Dan Perjovschi, "On the other hand", 2007. right: Site plan_Olafur Eliasson, „Light Lab", 2006/07
Exhibition hall with light installation by Olafur Eliasson_Paola Pivi, „It's a cocktail party", 2008.

GERMANY_FREIBURG **AUGUSTINERMUSEUM**

ARCHITECTS: PROF. CHRISTOPH MÄCKLER ARCHITEKTEN
COMPLETION: 2010_**ORIGINAL BUILDING:** MEDIEVAL
TYPE: ART MUSEUM_**GROSS FLOOR AREA:** 4,095 M²
PHOTOS: CHRISTIAN RICHTERS

THE ARCHITECTURE

The basic premise of the restructuring was to reinstate the former spatial effect by inserting a second interior structure into the nave. In this way adequate rooms were created for the collection of ecclesial art. In particular, the 13th and 14th century cathedral sculptures are prominently displayed at the center of the sculpture hall. A new, generously glazed front building at the western façade provides access for visitors, while the large prestigious portal at the Augustinerplatz invites them into the foyer. As an exterior visible highlight, the original "emperor windows" of the Freiburger Münster were integrated into the front building and fully accentuated once more.

THE COLLECTION

The former Augustinian monastery was first mentioned in the year 1278. Secularized in 1810, it was expanded in the 18th century and given a Baroque style. From 1823, the church served as a theater, while the other buildings were used as barracks. The theater was closed in 1910. Because of World War I, the building could only be converted into a museum in the year 1921. Two years later, the "Städtische Sammlungen im Augustinermuseum" (Urban collections in the Augustinermuseum) were inaugurated. In the post-war era, the city council only had limited financial means at its disposal, therefore the building remained in a state of improvisation that was only resolved in 2004 through extensive renovation measures.

In its central hall and surrounding gallery, the Augustinermuseum contains medieval sculptures and paintings. The attic of the building is dedicated to 19th century paintings by artists stemming from the Upper Rhine or Black Forest regions. These include the paintings "Junge Italienerin am Brunnen" (Young Italian girl by the well) (1834) by Franz Xaver Winterhalter and "Nanna als Bacchantin"(Nanna as bacchante) (1861) by Anselm Feuerbach. Equally impressive are the 70,000 sheets of drawings, graphic prints and photographs. These include prints by Hans Baldung and Albrecht Dürer as well as 19th and early 20th century art of Baden. In addition, there is an exhibition of the daily life and folklore of the people living between the Black Forest and the Rhine region.

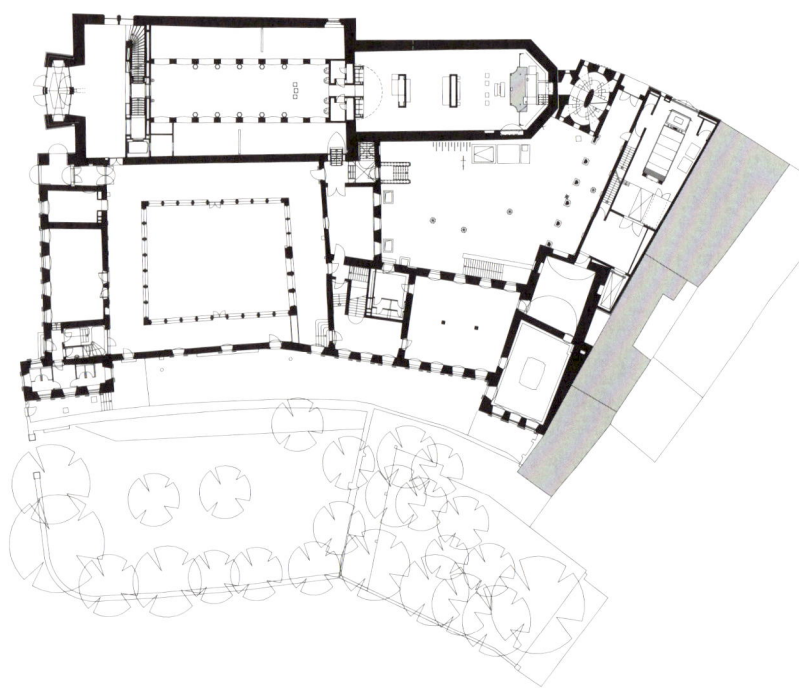

left: Ground floor plan_Staircase. right: View from nave, in direction of Kaiser window in foyer.

Figures of Freiburg Cathedral
...res de la cathédrale de Fribourg

...burger Münsterfiguren
...0–1380

left: Nave. right: Cross section_Gallery_Detail.

GERMANY_GIENGEN **MARGARETE STEIFF MUSEUM**

ARCHITECTS: RAMSEIER & ASSOCIATES LTD._**OTHER CREATIVES:** ERICH MOOSBACHER FRIEDRICHSHAFEN / MILLA & PARTNER / PATZNER ARCHITEKTEN_**COMPLETION:** 2005_**TYPE:** COMPANY MUSEUM_**GROSS FLOOR AREA:** 2,400 M² _**PHOTOS:** COURTESY OF THE ARCHITECTS

THE ARCHITECTURE

This complex consists of two different building structures — the main building and the annex. The museum as such is located in the ellipse-shaped main building. It has a length of 33 meters and was conceived as a column-free steel construction. The exterior of the ellipse is covered in large-scale radial brass panels. With a length of 85 meters, the rectangular extended annex building constitutes the end of the existing factory buildings. Its understated and neutral design of exposed concrete and glass contrasts with the greenish double-glazed windows of the old building. The museum's interior is entirely decorated in white.

THE COLLECTION

The company was established in 1880 as a felt goods retailer. When company founder Margarethe Steiff discovered the sewing pattern for an elephant in a fashion magazine, she created pincushions shaped like an elephant for the Heidenheim market. The so-called "Elefäntle" (little elephant) was a great success that was soon followed by other animals that were featured in 1892 in the first illustrated Steiff catalog. In 1902, Richard Steiff, a nephew of the founder, developed the first teddy bear 55 PB. Following initial great success, Franz Steiff created in 1904 the still protected trademark of the company "Steiff – Knopf im Ohr,", the famed "button in ear," to differentiate their products from those of the competition. The Margarethe Steiff GmbH was established in 1906. The museum with the official name "Die Welt von Steiff" (The world of Steiff) is an interactive museum presenting the production and company history of Margarethe Steiff GmbH as well as the history of teddy bears in particular. Across three levels, more than 2,000 Steiff articles are exhibited on a total area of 2,400 square meters. In addition, the production process of Steiff animals can be observed in a special production display.

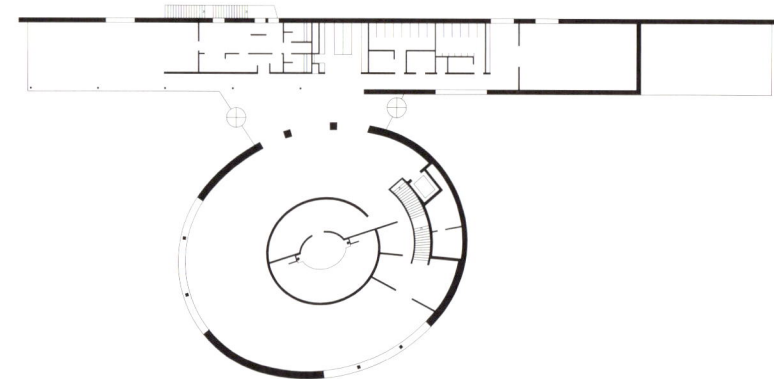

left: Ground floor plan_South façade with main entrance_Façade, detail. right: North façade at night_Entrance parking_View from large window to entrance area.

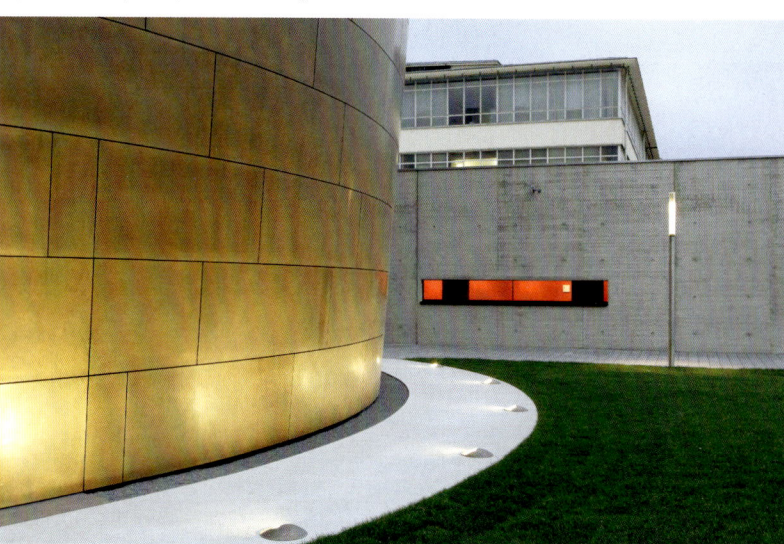

GERMANY_GREVESMÜHLEN **MUSEUM UND VEREINSHAUS**

ARCHITECTS: ARCHITEKT ROLAND SCHULZ_**COMPLETION:** 2005
ORIGINAL BUILDING: 1855_**TYPE:** HISTORY MUSEUM_**GROSS FLOOR**
AREA: 1,378 M²_**PHOTOS:** JÖRN LEHMANN, SCHWERIN

THE ARCHITECTURE

Located on the ground floor of the building, the museum is accessible from the main entrance at the church square. In the course of the renovation, the vertical access was removed from inside the original building and positioned behind it. This resulted in a staircase tower, whose special layout geometry allows it to function as a joint between the old school building and the new event hall. The façades of the old school building made of exposed brickwork were kept intact and contrast with the exposed concrete of the staircase tower.

THE COLLECTION

The building serves several functions. For example, seven clubs with their committee offices moved into it. It also contains a ballroom in which various cultural events and conferences are held. The city museum was established on the ground floor of the former school building. Its permanent exhibition on prehistory and early history presents many archeological findings from the Stone Age to the early German age, providing an insight into the settlement life after the Ice Age in Mecklenburg. The museum's exhibits include a burial model with a large rock grave of the Everstorfer Forst dating back approximately 5,000 years, as well as parts of traditional costumes and jewelry that may provide an insight into burial ceremonies. Other eras, such as the Bronze Age, the Migration period and the Slavic era up to the feudal German east expansion are also represented with various finds. In addition, the museum also features an exhibition of the city's history. Visitors are introduced to the city of Grevesmühlen from its first mention 1230 in the Ratzeburger Zehntregister up to the present day. A further exhibition room of the museum is dedicated to the luxury liner "Cap Arcone." Its exhibits include an original replica of the ship.

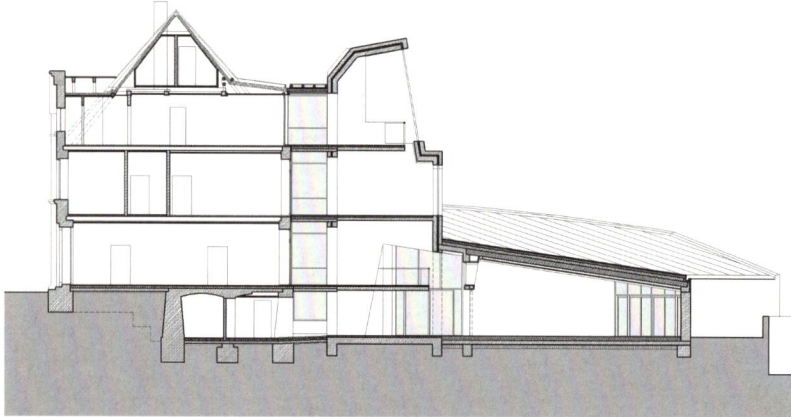

left: Section_Western elevation_Event hall_Collection of buildings on eastern side. right: South-east elevation_Stairway and lift_Event hall_Entrance and stairway.

GERMANY_HALLE **LANDESMUSEUM FÜR VORGESCHICHTE**

ARCHITECTS: DIETZSCH & WEBER ARCHITEKTEN_**RENOVATION:** TOGETHER WITH KOWALSKI & IRMISCH_**COMPLETION:** 2008 **ORIGINAL BUILDING:** WILHELM KREIS, 1918_**TYPE:** ARCHEOLOGY MUSEUM_**GROSS FLOOR AREA:** 7,580 M² _**PHOTOS:** N. BLEUL, A. WEBER / HALLE

THE ARCHITECTURE

This renovation and expansion reconstituted the historic structures and proportions, complementing them with modern elements. A shop, a café, and a lecture hall were newly added in a variable-use room axle on the ground floor. At the same time, a new building for the restoration workshops, which were previously distributed across various locations, was constructed in the vicinity of the museum. Three workshops (stone, metal and wood) with the associated laboratories, offices and storage areas occupy one floor each. The steel concrete building's vertical façade structure and horizontal, cornice-style stratification with a figured glass façade located in front apply industrial construction to express the style of the museum.

THE COLLECTION

The museum was established with the founding of the "Thüringisch-Sächsischer Verein für Erforschung des vaterländischen Alterthums und Erhaltung seiner Denkmale" ("Thuringia-Saxony association for the study of local national history and preservation of local monuments"). In 1825, the collections were set up in the former royal hall of the Neue Residenz. In 1876, the state parliament decided on the establishment of the "Historische Commission der Provinz Sachsen" ("Historic Commission of the Province of Saxony") and approved the creation of a provincial museum in 1882. On April 21, 1886 it was decided to appoint caretakers for the museum. This was the start of the official preservation and care for field monuments in the Saxony province. In 1906 initial plans for the new building of a museum were created, and construction took place from 1911-1913. It was opened in 1918 with a permanent exhibition on prehistory and renamed in 1921 to "Landesanstalt für Vorgeschichte" ("State institution for pre-history"). In 1983, the museum building was designated as a historic monument. Today, the museum is part of the archeological preservation and care of monuments program in the state of Saxony-Anhalt and houses one of Germany's oldest and most extensive archeological collections. The more than 11 million exhibits contain globally unique finds such as the Nebra skydisk and the stone depiction of a horseback rider of Hornhausen. They are exhibited in the correct chronological sequence — from the beginning of the Stone Age up to the early Bronze Age.

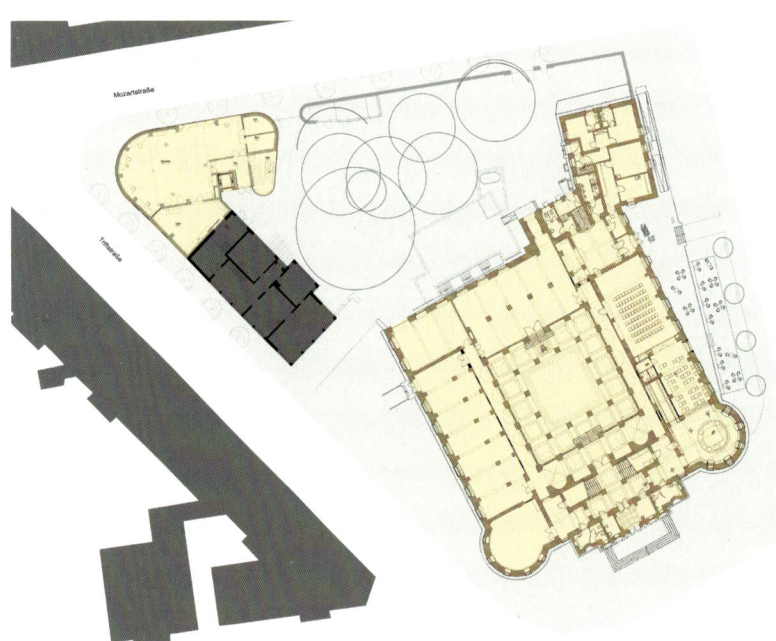

left: Site plan_Main vista_Staircase workshop. right: Courtyard view of the workshop_New building restoration-workshop_Entrance café.

GERMANY_HAMBURG **LOKI SCHMIDT HAUS**

ARCHITECTS: PROF. BERNHARD WINKING ARCHITEKTEN BDA, FRANK WEITENDORF_**SCENOGRAPHY:** ATELIER BRÜCKNER **COMPLETION:** 2006_**TYPE:** NATURE MUSEUM_**GROSS FLOOR AREA:** 460 M² _**PHOTOS:** TOBIAS WILLE (258 B. L., B. M. R., B. R., 259, 260), CHRISTIAN WOLTER (258 B. M. L.,261)

THE ARCHITECTURE

This botanic collection, established in 1870, received its own museum in the botanic garden. The design concept is that of a solitary cube whose outer cover of blue, prismatic broken ceramics represents the blue planet, our earth. It contains the treasures of the earth, its multitude of agricultural crops. The museum features two large display window-style openings as well as a few small windows that present selected views of the garden. The exhibition area extends across three levels. A large eccentric air space connects all levels to each other and highlights what is probably the most spectacular exhibit, a floor-to-ceiling fig tree.

THE COLLECTION

In her lifetime, Loki Schmidt, born 1919 in Hamburg, was dedicated as a German ambassador to the protection of plants and wildlife. Among other activities, she established in 1976 the "Foundation for the protection of endangered plants." In addition, she wrote essential essays in various areas of biology and pedagogy. On her 80th birthday, she was awarded the title of professor and became an honorary doctor of the Russian Academy of Sciences in St. Petersburg and the University of Hamburg. This development history is presented by the museum, which was named after Loki Schmidt. The building also houses a unique botanical collection of plants utilized by humans, their raw products, process stages and varied uses. The basis of today's collection is the donation of the collection of algae of the then mayor of Hamburg Dr. Binder in the year 1870 and the 1879 donation of the "Carpology collection" of the city physician Dr. Bueck. The latter contains fruit and seeds of approximately 10,000 types of plants from all parts of the world as well as 2,700 plant genera. Other donations created a complex and valuable collection of currently almost 50,000 objects. These include collections of medicinal plants, fungi, and types of wood.

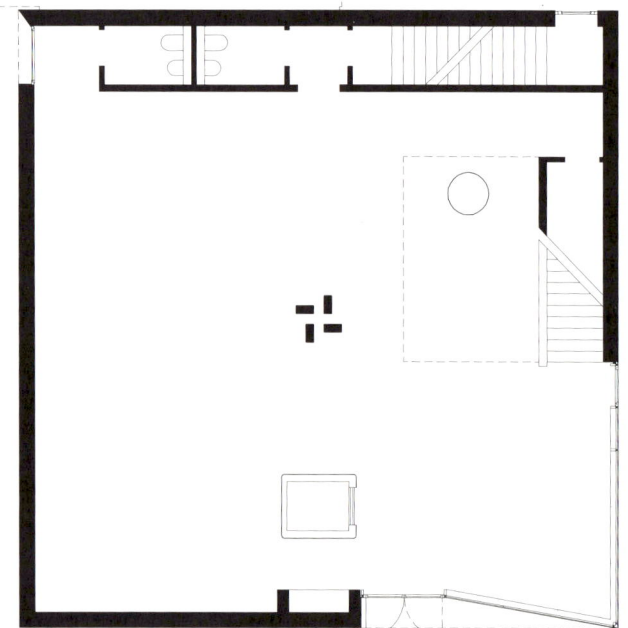

left: Ground floor plan_Entrance_Exhibition second floor_Exterior view from north-east_Staircase. right: View of the entrance.

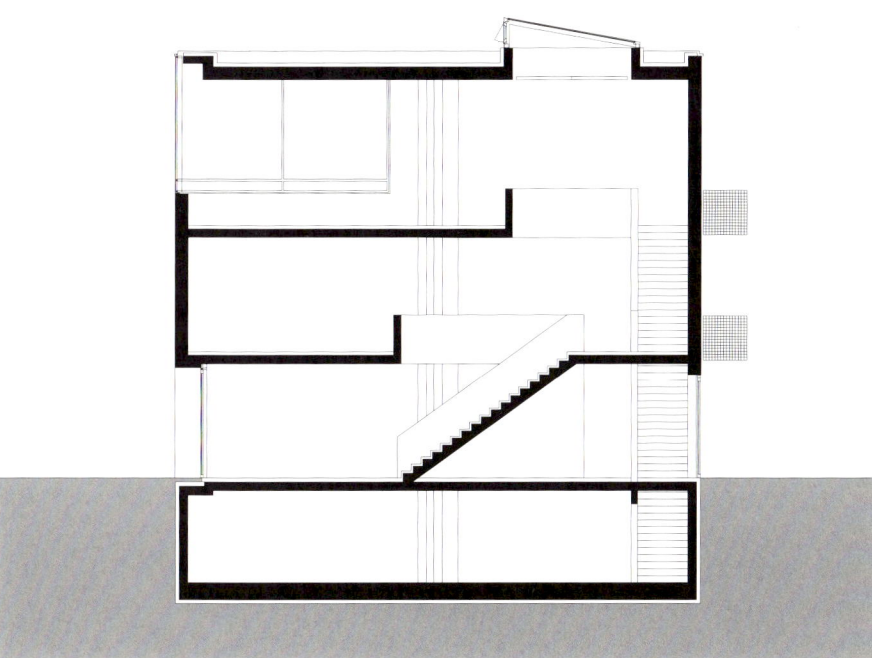

left: View down to entrance area. right: Section_Public archive second floor.

GERMANY_HINZERT **GEDENKSTÄTTE HINZERT**

ARCHITECTS: WANDEL HOEFER LORCH + HIRSCH_**COMPLETION:** 2005_**TYPE:** HISTORY MUSEUM_**GROSS FLOOR AREA:** 471 M²_**PHOTOS:** NORBERT MIGULETZ, FRANKFURT / MAIN

THE ARCHITECTURE

The new memorial and documentation center creates a network of historic sites across the landscape, explaining the system of the former SS concentration camp. The building emerges as a three-dimensional tiled slab structure from the two-dimensional landscape, visualizing borders in a very simple form by interacting with the landscape. The topography resulted in a building that negates the landscape, visualizing the fact that the idyllic appearance of the site is deceptive. The gradual disappearance of the generation of contemporary witnesses makes it increasingly important to inform, learn from and cope with history, which are the basic purposes of this center.

THE COLLECTION

At the graveyard near the memorial site a monument of the former Luxemburg native inmate Lucien Wercollieran was inaugurated in 1986 as a central focal point. On the round granite base the following inscription is found in German and in Latin: "Infused with humanity, peace and justice." In 1989, the "Förderverein Dokumentations- und Begegnungsstätte des ehemaligen KZ Hinzert e. V." (Association to support the documentation and memorial site of the former Hinzert concentration camp) was established by private individuals. In the years 1991 and 1992 the Landeszentrale für politische Bildung Rheinland-Pfalz (Rhineland Palatinate state center for political education) presented a memorial concept, which two years later resulted in the installation of an information system explaining the so-called "sites of inhumanity" in the area surrounding the former camp. The opening of the official documentation and memorial buildings was attended by former inmates from Luxembourg, France and the Netherlands. Since that time, a permanent exhibition provides information about the camp, and its special function in the national socialist concentration camp system, as well as victims and perpetrators.

left: Site plan_Exterior_Tiled outer section. right: Façade_View from exhibition room_Exhibition.

GERMANY_HOMBROICH **LANGEN FOUNDATION**

ARCHITECTS: TADAO ANDO ARCHITECT & ASSOCIATES
COMPLETION: 2004_**TYPE:** ART MUSEUM_**GROSS FLOOR AREA:**
3,050 M² _**PHOTOS:** TOMAS RIEHLE / ARTURIMAGES

THE ARCHITECTURE

The Insel Hombroich museum is located near the river Erft. The entire site consists of an island floating in a vast marshland, a "park" museum. Outdoor sculptures are distributed across 200,000 square meters of forest, together with many handsome "exhibition room" pavilions, that are sculptures themselves. The museum contains a collection of oriental and modern art. Accordingly, its spaces have two different characters. One, for the Oriental art, is a space of "quietude" suffused with soft light. The other, containing modern art, is a space of throbbing "movement" with mixed lighting. The "quiet" space of the permanent exhibition wing is surrounded by a buffer consisting of a nested structure of concrete and glass.

THE COLLECTION

One of the most comprehensive collections belonging to this museum is its collection of Japanese art, developed by Viktor Langen who began developing the comprehensive collection during business trips to Japan in the 1960s. His fascination for Japanese culture led to a love of the country's art. Already an experienced and passionate art collector, Langen enlisted the help of his many and varied contacts, and an interpreter to seek out dealers and gallery owners throughout Japan. From this private interest arose a collection that is unique in Europe both by merit of its size and quality. The collection represents Japanese art from the 12th to the 19th century and includes scrolls, screens and sculptures. The first exhibition of the Japanese collection took place in 1998, under the name "Autumn Wind in the Pines". This exhibition then traveled, visiting various high-profile museums in both Germany and Japan. The museum also houses a collection of 20th century artworks, encompassing almost all of the important and famous artists from the last century. Langen was also responsible for the acquisition of this display. He began by collecting works from expressionists followed by works that simply impressed him.

left: Sketch_Exterior with water basin_Reflection on the water. right: Glass façade_Corridor exhibition building_Exhibition room.

GERMANY_KOCHEL AM SEE **FRANZ MARC MUSEUM**

ARCHITECTS: DIETHELM & SPILLMANN**_COMPLETION:** 2008
ORIGINAL BUILDING: 1893**_TYPE:** ART MUSEUM**_GROSS FLOOR
AREA:** NEW BUILDING: 1,550 M², OLD BUILDING 660 M²
PHOTOS: ROGER FREI, ZURICH

THE ARCHITECTURE

This new three-story building houses the works of Marc as well as exhibits from the Stangl collection, while the old building contains the restaurant, administration and museum pedagogy rooms. Located on a forest clearing, the two buildings and a front courtyard are grouped into a compact ensemble that looks different depending on the viewing angle. With the exception of the foyer, the basic layouts are based on a chamber-like room structure. A concept involving daylight was avoided due to the many light-sensitive works of the collection. Therefore, the main purpose of the few windows is primarily to present a view of the beautiful setting.

THE COLLECTION

Gallery owner Otto Stangl initiated the museum to pay tribute to the life and work of artist Franz Marc (1880–1916). It was established in the year 1986 in Kochel am See, a landscape in which the artist had reportedly stayed repeatedly. The museum presents more than 150 works from the estate of artist Franz Marc along with personal items and written documents. Also exhibited are works by his artist friends including Paul Klee, Wassily Kandinsky and Alexej von Jawlensky, providing an insight into the development and work of the Blauer Reiter (Blue Rider) group of artists. The addition of the collection of the Stiftung Etta und Otto Stangl in the year 2008, including works of contemporaries of Franz Marc, allowed the museum to juxtapose the works with those of the artists of the expressionist "Brücke" (bridge) group. Coupled with key individual works of abstract art from the German post-war era, and representatives of "ZEN 49," the effect and impact of the artist is comprehensibly presented.

left: Site plan_Old and new museum_Façade from Crailsheim shell limestone. right: Exterior new building_View from viewing room_View from lower foyer to staircase.

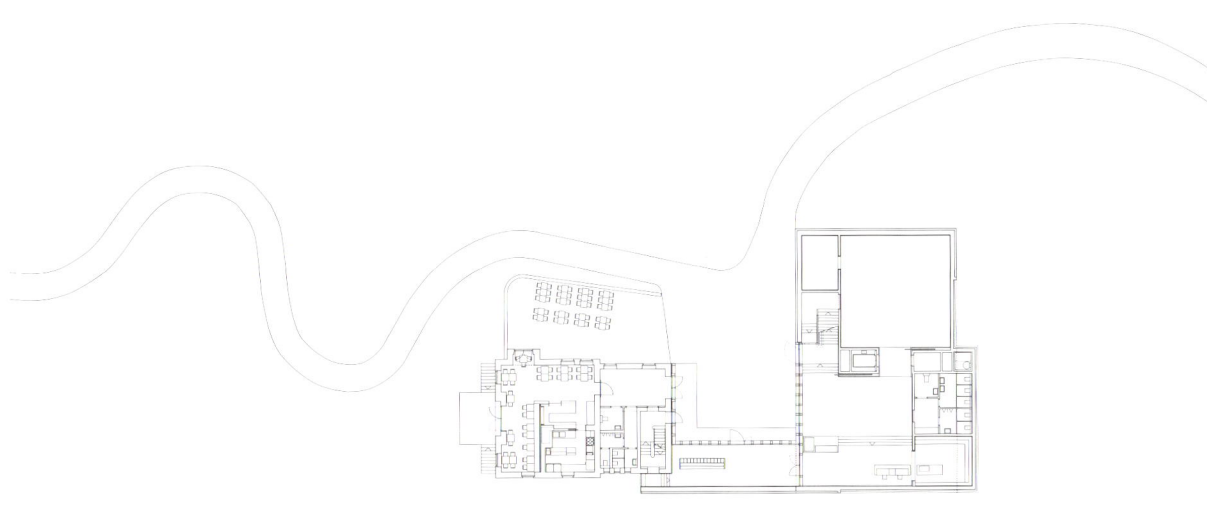

left: Façade detail with casement window. right: Floorplan_Colored walls in the cabinets second floor_Long cabinet third floor_Hallway third floor.

GERMANY_LEIPZIG **MUSEUM DER BILDENDEN KÜNSTE**

ARCHITECTS: HUFNAGEL PÜTZ RAFAELIAN ARCHITEKTEN
COMPLETION: 2004_**TYPE:** ART MUSEUM_**GROSS FLOOR AREA:**
16,732 M² _**PHOTOS:** WERNER HUTHMACHER, BERLIN
(270 B. M., B. R., 271), AZIZI NAMINI (270 B. L.)

THE ARCHITECTURE

This design was based on the premise of replacing an urban setting consisting of small elements with a prestigious large museum building. Rising
high above the surrounding houses, the museum is set back from the street
and surrounded by a ring of small urban structures. The block-shaped new
building seeks to create a balance between an autonomous architecture
and a connection to the site. The autonomy of the glass skin enveloping the
sculptured building contrasts with the stone buildings of the city, while its
large-scale urban interior spaces replicate the glass passages and courtyards
typical of the city of Leipzig.

THE COLLECTION

The art museum was inaugurated in the year 1848 by the "Leipziger Kunstverein" (Leipzig cultural association). In the 19th century, the collection was
financed by public donations. After many works were confiscated by the
national socialist regime and the building destroyed in World War II, many
items were lost from the collection that was repeatedly moved until 1997. It
only received a permanent home in the new museum building at the former
Sachsenplatz in 2004. Currently, the museum's collection contains approximately 3,500 paintings, 1,000 sculptures, and 55,000 drawings and graphic
works from the late Middle Ages until today. These are exhibited in an area of
only 7,000 square meters. Key items include works by the Dutch and German
Old Masters, such as Lucas Cranach the elder and Frans Hals, as well as an
exceptional collection of drawings by Max Beckmann and Max Klinger. With
more than 800 pieces, the museum contains East Germany's third-largest
collection of sculptures.

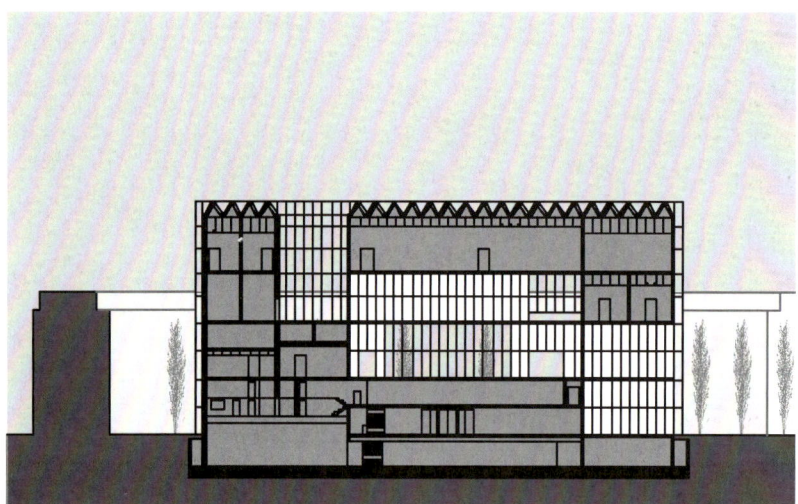

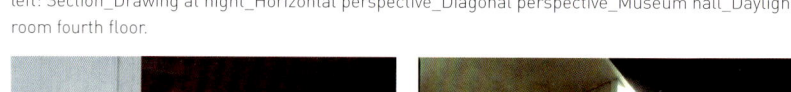

left: Section_Drawing at night_Horizontal perspective_Diagonal perspective_Museum hall_Daylight
room fourth floor.

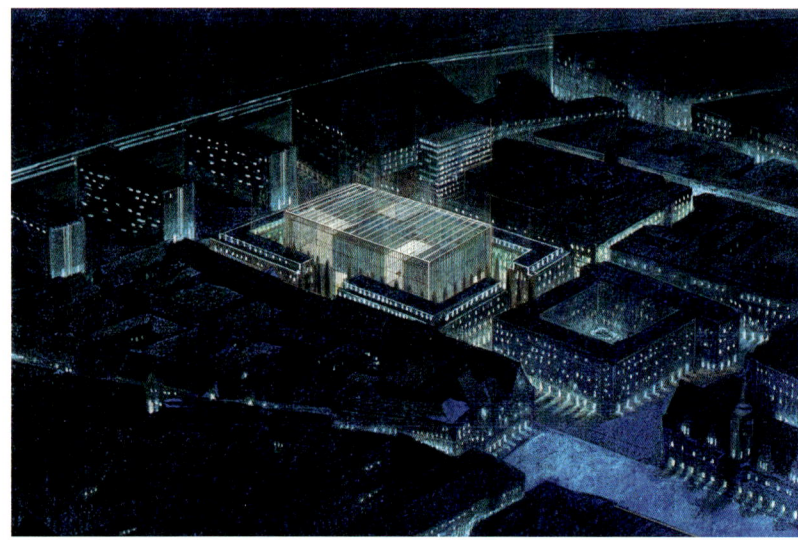

GERMANY_MARBACH / NECKAR **LITERATURMUSEUM DER MODERNE**

ARCHITECTS: DAVID CHIPPERFIELD ARCHITECTS_**COMPLETION:** 2006_**TYPE:** LITERATURE MUSEUM_**GROSS FLOOR AREA:** 3,800 M²
PHOTOS: CHRIS VAN UFFELEN (276 B. L., B. R., 277 B. L.), JÖRG VON BRUCHHAUSEN (277 A.), CHRISTIAN RICHTERS (277 B. R.)

THE ARCHITECTURE

This museum is located in the park of Marbach, on top of a rock plateau. It is made of fair-faced concrete, sandblasted reconstituted stone with limestone aggregate, limestone, wood, felt and glass. The interior spaces of the museum are revealed, as one descends down through the loggia, foyer and staircase spaces, preparing for the dark timber-paneled exhibition galleries, which are illuminated only by artificial light due to the fragility and sensitivity of the works on display. Each of these environmentally controlled spaces borders onto a naturally lit gallery, balancing the interior views of the composed, internalized world of texts and manuscripts with the green valley on the other side of the glass.

THE COLLECTION

The museum is part of the Deutsches Literaturarchiv (Museum of Modern Literature) in Marbach, exhibiting 20th and 21st century items on an area of 1,000 square meters. The permanent exhibition is distributed across three rooms. The room "nexus" presents more than 1,300 exhibits presenting the link between literature and human beings. These include the christening robe of Thomas Mann, manuscripts of Franz Kafka's "Proceß," and Alfred Döblin's "Berlin Alexanderplatz," as well as Hermann Hesse's Nobel Prize document, and Ernst Jünger's diary. These finds are only marked with their respective years and the name of their creator or owner. In the "stilus" room, visitors can practice interacting with literature with the help of a letter catching game with which 56 literary fragments can be decoded. The third room, "fluxus", presents in three-month cycles exhibits from the private collections of curators, such as publisher Klaus Wagenbach, critic Sigrid Löffler, and actor Hanns Zischler. They present their personal views in a video that can be seen in the exhibition area. In addition, the museum presents annually changing exhibits on 400 square meters on specific areas of interest such as "Zeigen" ("Showing") in 2006, "Lassen" ("Letting") in 2008, and "Tauschen" (Swapping) in 2010.

left: Site plan_Lower foyer_Exhibition room. rechts: Exhibition level in the pedestral_Open loggia, Entrance level_West elevation, View towards the main entrance.

GERMANY_MUNICH **BMW MUSEUM**

ARCHITECTS: ATELIER BRÜCKNER_**SCENOGRAPHY:** ATELIER BRÜCKNER_**MEDIA AND INTERACTIVE INSTALLATIONS:** ART+COM **GRAPHIC DESIGN:** INTEGRAL RUEDI BAUR_**COMPLETION:** 2008_**ORIGINAL BUILDING:** KARL SCHWANZER, 1973_**TYPE:** COMPANY MUSEUM_**GROSS FLOOR AREA:** 12,200 M² _**PHOTOS:** MARCUS MEYER, BREMEN

THE ARCHITECTURE

The BMW Museum expresses the contemporary dynamic language of the automotive world. Analogous to the brand, which is synonymous for innovative technology and future-ready design, the museum strikes a new balance in the integrative combination of architecture, exhibition design and communication media. In this historic location, within the landmarked corporate headquarters, visitors are immersed in an urban ambiance. Via paved streets and squares, they reach brightly illuminated exhibition buildings that are each dedicated to a different theme. New media adds to the dynamic nature of the location. All around the central BMW Platz, a symbiosis of media and architecture provides motion to the space and the exhibits, giving an excited and exciting impression.

THE COLLECTION

Architect Karl Schwanzer in 1973 developed the concept of the museum building — visitor's ramps as streets, exhibition areas as public squares. Accordingly, a central visitors ramp in the round building connects a system of apparently floating platforms to take visitors on a spiral-shaped path to the upper floor of the building. Today, this level contains individual exhibition items and a small cinema theater. During renovations in the year 2004, the round building, which is also known as Museumsschüssel (museum bowl) was connected to the neighboring low-rise building via a ramp that connects all 25 exhibition areas. This expanded the exhibition space to 5,000 square meters. Since its reopening in the year 2008, motors and turbines, motorcycles, automotive vehicles and airplanes from the past to the present are shown here along with futuristic studies and forecasts. Visitors can admire approximately 120 original exhibits, such as the Isetta, the BMW 2002, the R32 motorcycle and the BMW 328. While the round building contains temporary exhibitions, the low-rise building , also known as the "four-cylinder", contains a permanent exhibition, reflecting the more than 90 years of history of the BMW brand in seven interrelated thematic blocks.

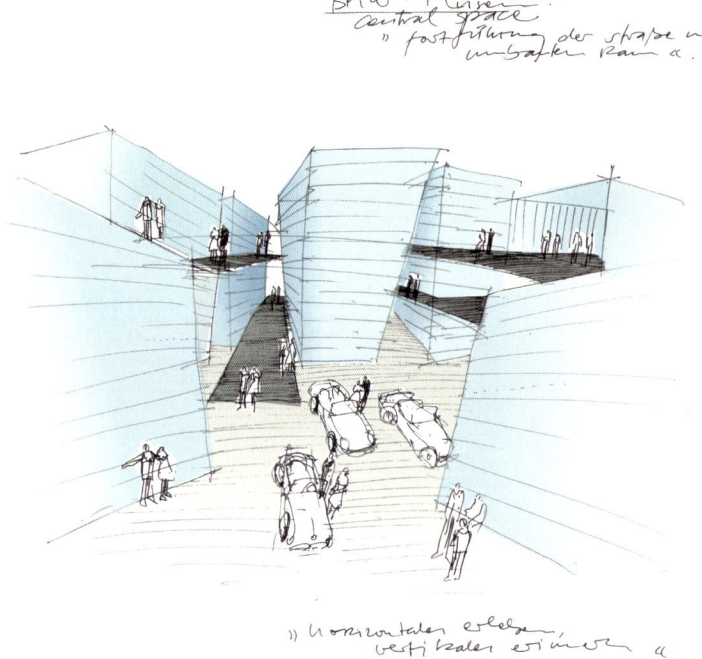

left: Sketch_House of motorsports, touring car_House of the company, meeting room. right: Exhibition room.

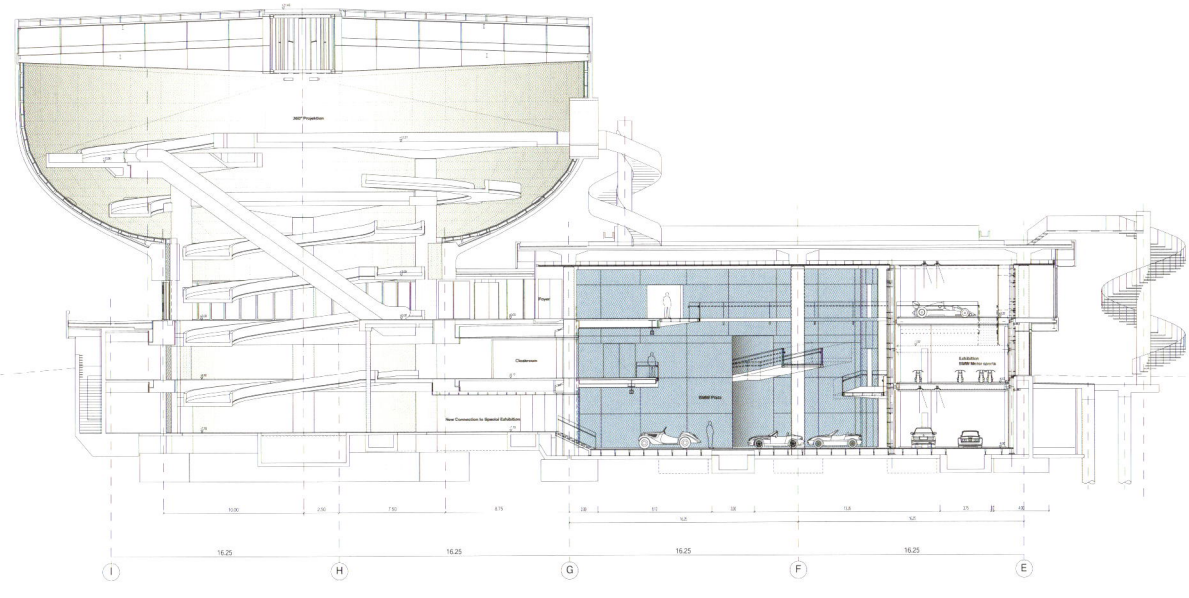

left: BMW Platz. right: Cross section_House of technology, skeletal frame_House of the company, BMW site_BMW Platz.

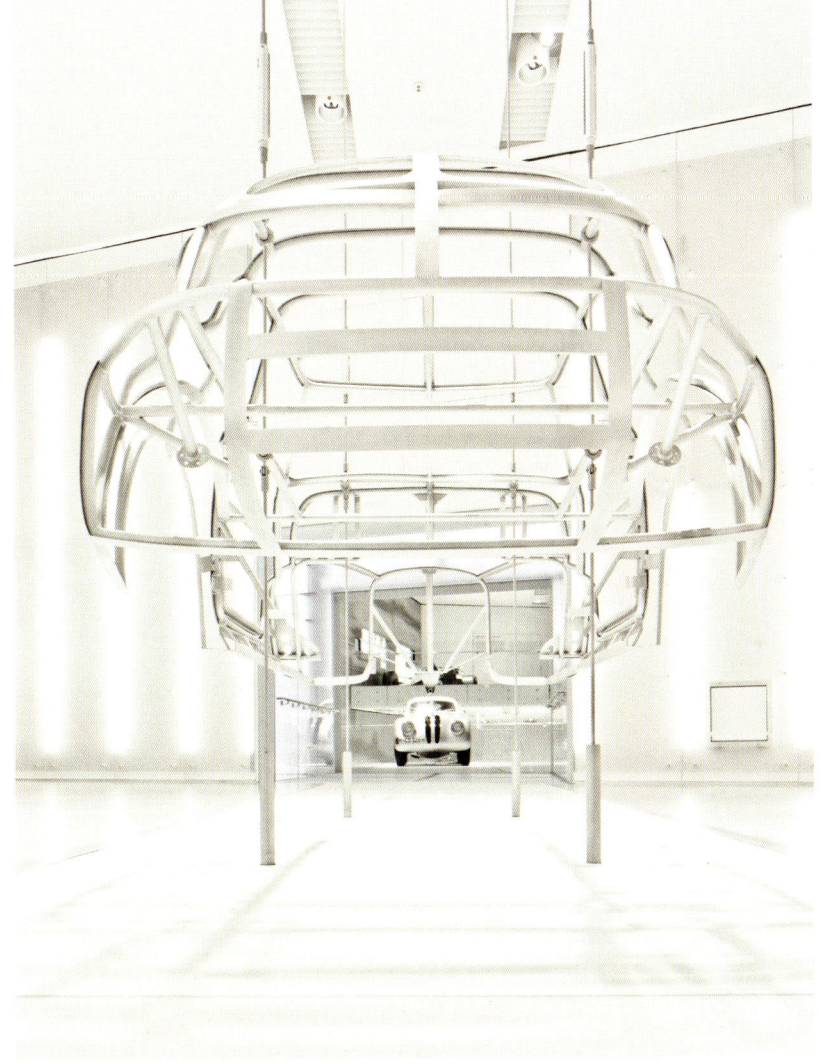

GERMANY_MUNICH **MUSEUM BRANDHORST**

ARCHITECTS: SAUERBRUCH HUTTON_**COMPLETION:** 2008
TYPE: ART MUSEUM_**GROSS FLOOR AREA:** 12,000 M²
PHOTOS: ANNETTE KISLING, BERLIN

THE ARCHITECTURE

Almost all exhibition areas of this three-story building at the north-east corner of Munich's museum district enjoy natural illumination. This is provided by a complex system of reflectors on the ground floor that allow zenith light to evenly enter the galleries. The deliberate variation of lighting, sequencing, size and proportion results in a subtle differentiation of the rooms. The iridescent appearance of the polychrome exterior hull, consisting of ceramic bars glazed in 23 colors as well as a horizontally folded sheet metal façade, changes depending on the location of the observer. The innovative energy concept of the museum saves resources and creates excellent conditions for the exhibited items.

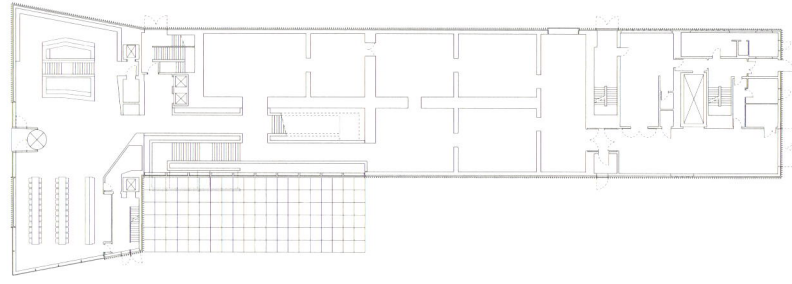

THE COLLECTION

The museum contains the collection of Udo and Anette Brandhorst, who have been collecting modern and contemporary art since the 1970s. In 1993 the collection was transferred to the "Udo und Anette Brandhorst Stiftung." It contains approximately 700 pieces of art. The focus is on paintings, sculptures and installations that have substantially influenced and shaped art since the year 1945. They include works by Andy Warhol, Joseph Beuys and Gerhard Richter. An entire floor of the museum building has been dedicated to the around 60 works of Cy Twombly that offer an incomparable overview of the artist's development. In addition, the interest of Udo and Anette Brandhorst in the cooperation of poets and painters also shapes the collection. For example, the works include 112 original copies of books illustrated by Pablo Picasso, representing almost the entire work of the artist in this area. Other exhibits include drawings and collages by Kasimir Malewitsch, Kurt Schwitters, and Joan Miró.

left: Ground floor plan_Façade to the courtyards_Entrance. right: Façade Türkenstrasse_Exhibition space first floor_Exhibition space ground floor_Café.

GERMANY_MUNICH **PINAKOTHEK DER MODERNE**

ARCHITECT: STEPHAN BRAUNFELS ARCHITEKTEN BDA
COMPLETION: 2002_**TYPE:** ART, ARCHITECTURE AND DESIGN
MUSEUM_**GROSS FLOOR AREA:** 33,500 M² _**PHOTOS:** JENS WEBER

THE ARCHITECTURE

The four museums of the complex — the Staatsgalerie Moderne Kunst (national gallery of modern art), Neue Sammlung (new collection), Architekturmuseum (museum of architecture) and Staatliche Graphische Sammlung (national graphics collection) — are positioned in three exhibition areas that are linked vertically by a large staircase that expands, funnel-like, to the top and the bottom. With a length of 100 meters and an elevation difference of twelve meters, it constitutes an interior sculpture that connects all parts of the building and unites them at its center under a cupola, topped by a sky-light. This results in a variety of room types and perspectives. In the exhibition rooms, the architecture takes a backseat as simple and clearly structured roof-lit halls focus the attention on the exhibits.

THE COLLECTION

A mere six works of art constituted the basis of the collection of modern art of the Pinakothek after 1945. Through collections and private donations, this basis could be turned into an exceptional collection of art. It has been complemented by unique donation series such as the Beckmann collection of Günther Franke and the Brücke artists from the collection of Markus and Martha Kruss. The current focus of the collection is on more recent German painting, including works by Sigmar Polke, Gerhard Richter and Georg Baselitz. The graphic works collection of the Pinakothek contains approximately 400,000 sheets of all eras from the 15th century to today. The origins of this collection date back to the copper engraving and drawing cabinet of the elector Karl Theodor von der Pfalz, which was founded in 1758 and moved to Munich before 1800. The architecture museum of the Pinakothek was established in 1868 as a an educational collection at the time of the foundation of the Technische Hochschule. Continuous new purchases make the architecture collection Germany's largest collection of the kind. It includes approximately 4,500,000 drawings, 100,000 photographs, and 500 models, including works by Theodor Fischer, Le Corbusier and Peter Zumthor. The oldest drawings go back to the 16th century. The Neue Sammlung emerged from the establishment of the Deutscher Werkbund in 1907, and was established as a public museum in 1925. It was the first design museum and contains today approximately 60,000 objects.

left: Ground floor plan_Entrance_Hall in rotunda. right: Entrance and old pinacotheca façade_View from exhibition to rotunda_Exhibition hall_Staircase.

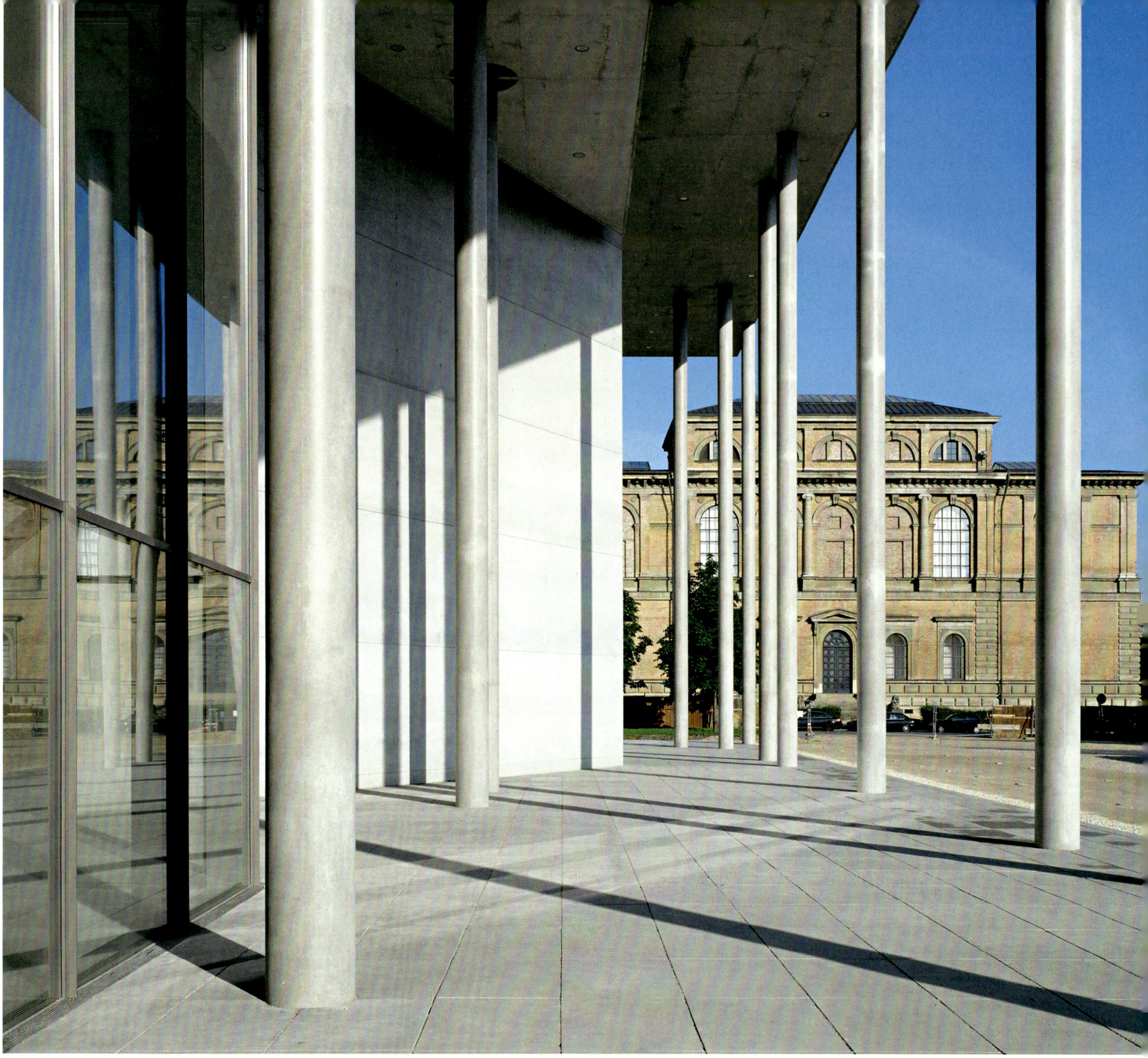

GERMANY_MUNICH **JÜDISCHES MUSEUM MÜNCHEN**

ARCHITECTS: WANDEL HOEFER LORCH_**COMPLETION:** 2007
TYPE: HISTORY MUSEUM_**GROSS FLOOR AREA:** 1,520 M²_**PHOTOS:**
ROLAND HALBE / ARTURIMAGES

THE ARCHITECTURE

This Jewish community center was incorporated into the urban structure of the surroundings at the Jakobsplatz. Its public and open nature can be experienced in public squares, paths and passages in the urban realm. The synagogue, museum and community center constitute a balanced ensemble of independent structures, set in context with each other across the intermediate spaces. As the smallest cubic building on Jakobsplatz, the museum mediates between the synagogue and the community center, offering open and close areas according to the individual needs. Located above an open foyer, blending with the square area into a communication space, lie serveral closed exhibition rooms that offer space for concentration.

THE COLLECTION

There was already interest in and an intention to establish a Jewish museum in 1928. After the Holocaust, the head of the Israelite Community Hans Lamm adopted the endeavor once again, but was unable to implement it. Gallery owner Richard Grimm revived the idea in the 1980s. He opened a small, 28 square meter private Jewish museum. Ten years later, this improvised establishment had to be discontinued for financial reasons. The Israelite Community took over the Richard Grimm collection and provided exhibition space for it in the community center. Until the year 2001, Grimm headed the "interim museum" as a municipal institution. Exhibitions and events were organized in cooperation with the Münchner Stadtmuseum (Munich municipal museum) and the city archive. The Jewish Museum could be constructed in conjunction with the plans of the Israelite community of building its new main synagogue and community center near St.-Jakobs square. The museum's mission is to reflect Jewish culture and history. For example, the permanent exhibition "Stimmen_Orte_Zeiten" ("Voices_Places_Times") includes seven installations with different memorial elements such as the voices of period witnesses, places and images, that present various viewpoints especially regarding the Jewish religion. In addition to various temporary exhibitions, a study library presents information about Jewish life in Munich.

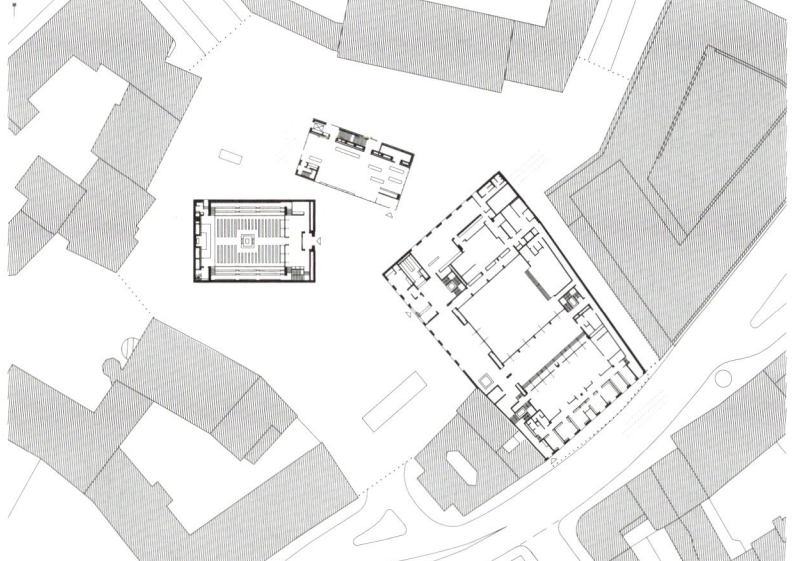

left: Site plan_Exterior_View into synagogue. right: Façade of the museum_Synagogue in the evening_Museum building.

ARCHITECTS: BERSCHNEIDER + BERSCHNEIDER_**COMPLETION:** 2004_**TYPE:** ART MUSEUM_**GROSS FLOOR AREA:** 1,559 M²
PHOTOS: COURTESY OF THE ARCHITECTS

THE ARCHITECTURE

This cubic building, located near the central park of Neumarkt, is a simple, strictly geometrical building. The red square entrance gate and the transparent stairway tower, with a red elevator core, contrast with the otherwise white building. The architects worked in close cooperation with the artist in adjusting the effect of daylight on the various materials of the works of art. Indirect lighting, wall openings and showcases were inserted in the façade. The showcases and glass sections of both floors allow the green of the park to appear as pictures in the wall surfaces. At the same time, they provide insights into the building.

THE COLLECTION

Initiated by the lyricist Margret Hölle, the city of Neumarkt and the artist Lothar Fischer decided in 2002 to erect a museum building about the life and work of the sculptor. Within this scope, the artist donated to the city his entire private collection with over 300 works along with letters and documents. In the same year, the Lothar & Christel Fischer foundation headquartered in Neumarkt was recognized. Today, the museum presents on an exhibition space of 500 square meters about 60 sculptures and around 450 plastic works by Lothar Fischer as well as temporary exhibitions containing information and works related to the artist group "SPUR" (1957–1965), which was co-founded by the artist. The earliest piece of the museum's collection is a "self portrait" from the year 1955, which Fischer created while still completing his education. It was the artist's wish that the works of art were not shown in chronological order at the opening exhibition of the museum in 2004. Instead, select works were arranged according to the type of materials — clay, bronze, iron and gypsum/Styrofoam.

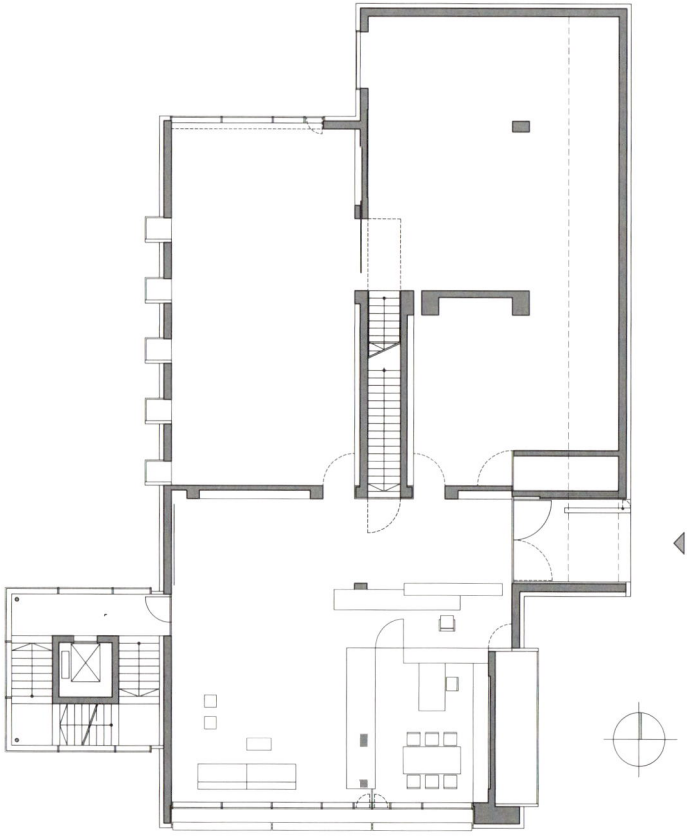

left: Ground floor plan_Showcase_Sculpture gallery. right: Façade_Graduated building structure Stairway in the structure.

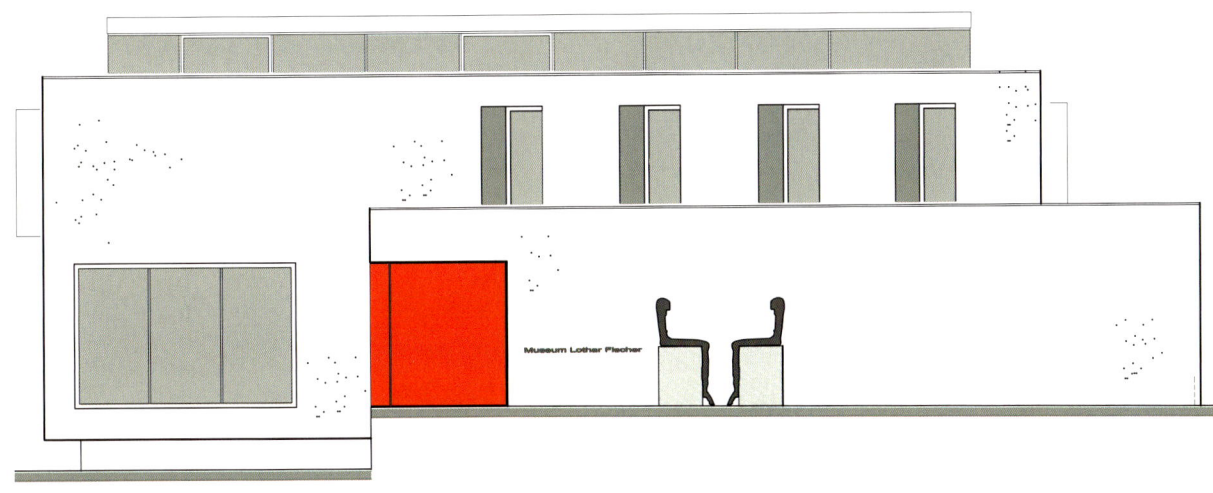

left: Entrance. right: East elevation_Staircase_Exhibition cabinets_Reception.

MUSEUM FÜR HISTORISCHE MAYBACH-FAHRZEUGE

ARCHITECTS: BERSCHNEIDER + BERSCHNEIDER_**COMPLETION:** 2009_**TYPE:** TECHNOLOGY MUSEUM_**GROSS FLOOR AREA:** 6,710 M²_**PHOTOS:** COURTESY OF THE ARCHITECTS

THE ARCHITECTURE

This museum utilizes the historic building structures of the former factory and combines them with modern architecture. Steel sheeting creates angular frames that define new openings and passages within the historic façades and walls. The new foyer building, made of exposed concrete, links the buildings as a central access platform. Showcases and passages appear sharp edged and cut from the concrete surfaces. The halls are illuminated by daylight as well as artificial light, while dark graphite surfaces were deliberately placed behind the exhibits. The floor with the old tarmac tiles, including all the signs of wear and tear from former days, were preserved.

THE COLLECTION

Wilhelm Maybach, together with his son Karl established the later Maybach-Motorenbau GmbH in Dissingen/Enz in 1909. This company produced high performance engines for airships and airplanes. After World War I, Karl Maybach set up the production of luxury automobiles, which continued to be manufactured on order until World War II. Between 1921 and 1941, approximately 1,800 of these cars were built of which around 160 are still in existence today. The Museum für historische Maybach-Fahrzeuge (museum of historic Maybach vehicles) presents a one-of-a-kind exhibition of the history and production of the Maybach brand. The museum was created upon the initiative of Helmut Hofmann, owner of the largest private collection of historic Maybach cars, consisting of 15 vehicles. At the museum, 18 to 20 historic Maybach cars in different conditions are exhibited on an area of approximately 2,500 square meters. The museum also presents historic engines, transmission systems and axles. The exhibited items are accompanied by visual aids, models, and short films.

left: Ground floor plan_Main entrance_Foyer building. right: Courtyard in twilight_Exhibition hall Reconstruction.

1938 Maybach SW 38

GERMANY_LEIPZIG **GFZK-2 – GALERIE FÜR ZEITGENÖSSISCHE KUNST**

ARCHITECTS: AS-IF BERLINWIEN_**COMPLETION:** 2005
TYPE: ART MUSEUM_**GROSS FLOOR AREA:** 1,020 M^2
PHOTOS: WOLFGANG THALER, VIENNA

THE ARCHITECTURE
These new exhibition buildings added approximately 1,000 square meters to the existing ensemble of Museum and peripheral buildings. The building represents a mixture of museum and specialized exhibition architectures. The concept is based on the question of the spatial representation of several work levels, contained in a gallery which has variable links between these levels. The polygonal space structure is an adjustable architectural infrastructure for contemporary exhibitions, with the prerequisites of the institution and the exhibitions as the central theme of the design.

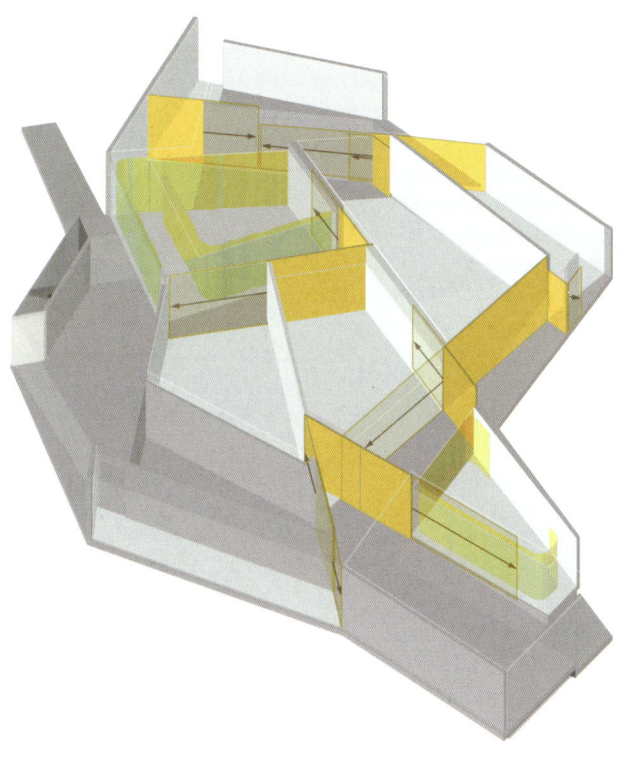

THE COLLECTION
The gallery was established in late 1990 based on an initiative of art historian Klaus Werner with the cooperation of the Kulturkreis der deutschen Wirtschaft im BDI e.V. This association donated works by artists including Marcel Oldenbach and Günther Uecker as the first permanent loans. Following initial exhibitions at various venues, the gallery received its own exhibition space in 1998 in the Herfurth villa of newspaper publisher Paul Herfurth. Items from the "Zentrum für Kunstausstellungen der DDR", which was being dissolved at the time, were added, including works by Hubertus Giebe, Hartwig Ebersbach, and Werner Stötzer. The works were mainly from the years 1979 and the 1980s and did not confirm with the dogma of the German Democratic Republic's cultural policy. In 1992, the Kulturkreis der deutschen Wirtschaft im BDI e.V. already donated "Perlen in Rot und Weiß" (1955) by Ernst Wilhelm Nay, "Große Bewegung vor Braun" (1953) by Fritz Winter and "Monument des Z" (1959) by Emil Schumacher. In 2006, approximately 50 additional works were added, mainly consisting of West German abstract art. These donations substantially determine the nature of the current collection. The gallery presents works that were classified as "degenerate" by the national socialists as well as objects of art reflecting the East and West German politically committed stances of the 1950s and 1960s.

left: Axonometry sliding walls and curtains_Exterior. right: Façade_Internal variability.

GERMANY_MANCHING **KELTEN RÖMER MUSEUM**

ARCHITECTS: FISCHER ARCHITEKTEN, MUNICH – PROF. FLORIAN FISCHER ARCHITEKT BDA DWB, ALEXANDRA ZEILHOFER ARCHITEKTIN_**LANDSCAPE ARCHITECT:** ANNA ZEITZ LANDSCHAFTSARCHITEKTIN_**COMPLETION:** 2006_**TYPE:** ARCHEOLOGY MUSEUM_**GROSS FLOOR AREA:** 1,895 M²
PHOTOS: MICHAEL HEINRICH, MUNICH

THE ARCHITECTURE

Visitors approach this museum in an unconventional way, along a gradually rising pedestrian path of nearly 100 meters which leads to the entrance and foyer. Taking visitors to another time, the museum emphasises the distance between past and present. Like a giant showcase, the exhibition floor is positioned on top of an almost entirely closed monolithic floor with a transparent base. The exhibition rooms increasingly open to the outside in line with the density of the preserved relics. The large northern panorama window in the Celtic exhibition area captures the wild vegetation along the Paar river as a picturesque background, while the two-story hall in which Roman warships are presented opens towards the museum's park.

THE COLLECTION

In the year 1888 the Roman road researcher Hugo Arnold suspected that the eight kilometer long circular fortification near Manching, the so-called "Pfahl", was part of a Celtic Oppidum. Four years later, first archeological excavations were carried out at the site. Today Manching is among the longest continuous excavation sites of the German Archeological Institute inside Germany. The 670 square meter Celtic exhibition of the museum presents findings and exhibits from this Oppidum. The treasure of gold discovered in 1999 is especially noteworthy. It consists of 450 gold coins and is the largest volume of Celtic gold discovered in the 20th century. Another special item is the "Cult tree" discovered in 1984 — a gilded replication of a twig with buds and fruits dating back to the 3rd century BC. After the Celts abandoned their Oppidum, the Romans built a fort in the nearby Oberstimm section of Manching in the first century AD. Across 510 square meters, the Roman exhibition of the museum exhibits findings from the Roman era stemming mainly from the area. A highlight are two well-preserved 15 meter long Roman military ships dating to around 100/110 AD. They were discovered in 1986 in a former side arm of the Danube river.

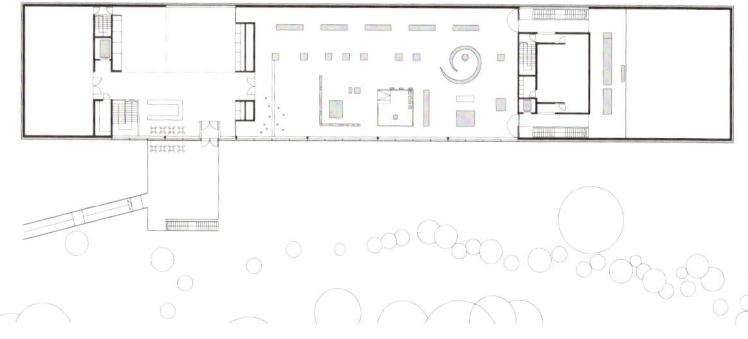

left: Entrance floor plan_Pedestrian path_Celtic exhibition area_North side. right: Roman exhibition area_South-west elevation at day_South-west elevation at night.

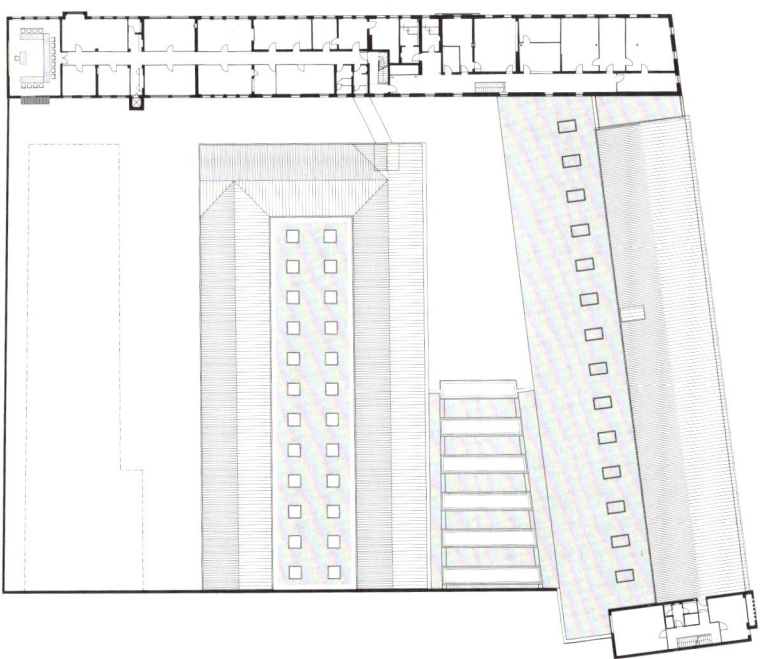

left: View into the exhibition hall. right: First floor plan_Exhibition area_Car exhibition area_Exhibition area with connecting passage way_Staircase.

GERMANY_STRALSUND **OZEANEUM**

ARCHITECTS: BEHNISCH ARCHITEKTEN_**SCENOGRAPHY:** ATELIER LOHRER_**COMPLETION:** 2008_**TYPE:** MARITIME MUSEUM_**GROSS FLOOR AREA:** 17,400 M²_**PHOTOS:** ROLAND HALBE / ARTURIMAGES

THE ARCHITECTURE

The Ozeaneum is an open building which visitors can enter from all sides. The façade is constructed from large-scale pre-curved steel sheets. The surface of the sheets is coated in white and visually links the building to its maritime surroundings. The building is divided into four individual building structures that are assigned to the themes of the exhibition concept. The aquariums are arranged in such a way that they can be viewed in a round tour. The room layouts of the visitor areas and the individual room climate requirements vary largely, reaching from dark exhibition areas to glazed atrium.

THE COLLECTION

May 22, 2010, the Ozeanum was declared the museum of Europe 2010. The exhibitions of the building are reached by a 30 meter escalator, Europe's longest free-standing escalator. On an exhibition area of 8,700 square meters, the museum contains 39 aquariums and an aquarium tunnel, featuring a total volume of approximately six million liters water filled with 7,000 animals and aquatic plants. These reflect the life and environments of the world's oceans. Starting from a frog fish and an animal fossil of ancient times, a round tour takes visitors through the various bodies of water and their biodiversity. From the Stralsund inner harbor and the Baltic Sea, visitors reach the North Sea and North Atlantic exhibition pools. Time-lapsed high and low tide can be observed in a tidal pool. A key attraction is the "Open Atlantic" round pool. measuring 17 meters in diameter and nine meters in depth. On two levels, visitors can observe schools of mackerel, along with various types of rays and breams. At the end of the tour, a hall measuring almost 20 meters in height shows the exhibit "1:1 Giants of the seas," featuring models of various types of whales in their original size.

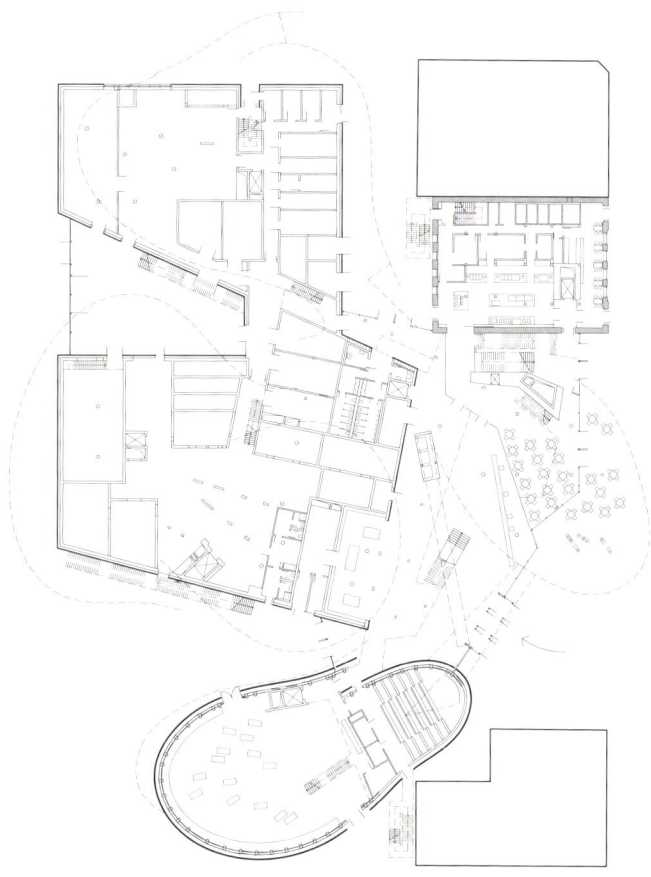

left: Ground floor plan_Whale exhibition_Passage through the aquarium_Foyer with Stairs. right: Exterior_Panorama view.

GERMANY_STUTTGART **KUNSTMUSEUM STUTTGART**

ARCHITECTS: HASCHER JEHLE ARCHITEKTUR_**COMPLETION:** 2004
TYPE: ART MUSEUM_**GROSS FLOOR AREA:** 13,000 M² _**PHOTOS:**
ROLAND HALBE, STUTTGART (298, 299, 300, 301 A. R.),
SVENJA BOCKHOP, BERLIN (301 L., B. R.)

THE ARCHITECTURE

The museum presents itself in the urban setting as a stone cube enclosed in glass. The transparent, permeable entrance level creates a fluid transition from the public space of the adjacent commercial street, to the museum. A generously proportioned staircase leads either into the interior of the multi-story stone core where contemporary exhibitions are located, or into the two-story underground exhibition rooms that contain the permanent exhibition and extend underneath the entire Kleiner Schlossplatz square and a former traffic tunnel. A light strip inserted into the square indicates the art that lies hidden underground.

THE COLLECTION

The museum's collection is based on the donation of the private collection of Swabian Impressionists paintings by Count Silvio della Valle di Casanova in 1924. After World War II, the "Galerie der Stadt Stuttgart" (Stuttgart city gallery) was moved to exhibition rooms in the Kunstgebäude am Schlossplatz in 1961. Eugen Keuerleber, who was in charge of the city art collection since 1945, placed the focus of the collection on Adolf Hölzel and Otto Dix. Starting in 1986, Johann-Karl Schmidt added works by international artists such as Joseph Kosuth, Dieter Roth and Dieter Krieg. In addition, other prominent collections could be added as permanent loans. These include the collection of Rudolf and Bertha Frank and the Konrad Knöpfel-Stiftung of Fritz Winter, which was purchased in 1994. In March 2005, the Stuttgart art collection moved into the central new museum building as the successor of the "Galerie der Stadt Stuttgart." In addition to the prominent permanent exhibition, smaller exhibitions have also been presented in an inoperative tunnel system, such as the "Frischzelle" ("Live cell") series. The same multipurpose room becomes a field of experimentation for young artists three times per year.

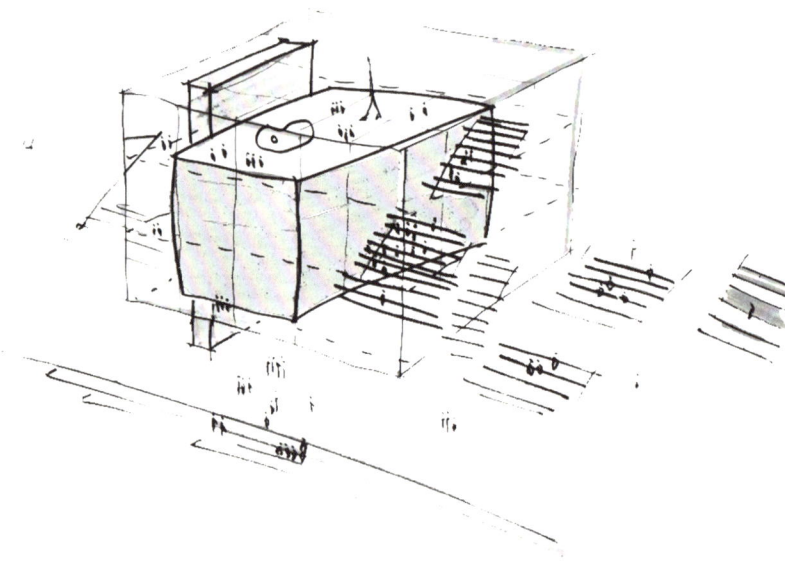

left: Sketch_View from Schlossplatz to the museum. right: Façade_Entrance hall.

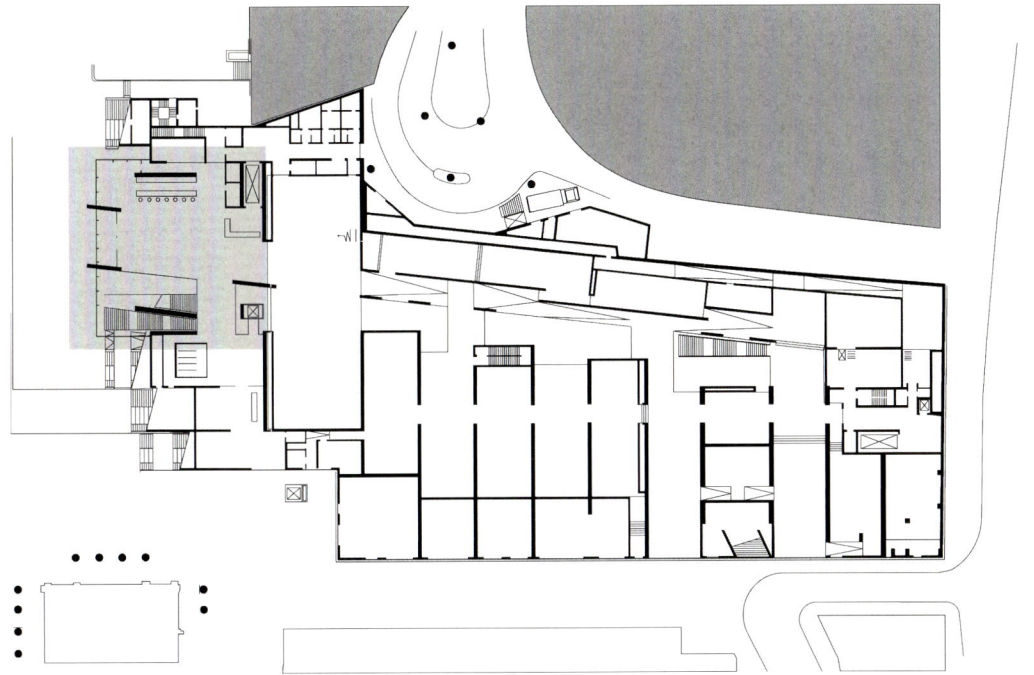

left: Glazed cube with stone core. right: Floor plan entrance area_Skylights of the underground exhibition rooms_Interior_Exhibition space.

MERCEDES-BENZ MUSEUM

ARCHITECTS: UNSTUDIO – BEN VAN BERKEL_**SCENOGRAPHY:** PROF. HG MERZ, STUTTGART_**COMPLETION:** 2006_**TYPE:** COMPANY MUSEUM_**GROSS FLOOR AREA:** 16,500 M²_**PHOTOS:** CHRISTIAN RICHTERS (302, 303 A., 304, 305), CHRIS VAN UFFELEN (303 B.)

THE ARCHITECTURE

In line with its automotive theme, this museum is located next to one of the expressways leading into town. Following a ride in an elevator to the eighth floor, accompanied by multimedia presentations, visitors can embark on one of two round tours that cross each other several times as they wind downwards between the floors as if suspended between the strands of a DNA molecule. A ridge turns into a wall, a ceiling, and finally a room. At the core, the rooms culminate in a building-high atrium open space, which presents constantly new views across the building. The complex geometry was impossible to present in conventional architectural drawings. A digital computer model, which could be altered during the construction process, was used instead.

THE COLLECTION

The basic foundation for the museum was created by Gottlieb Daimler when he exhibited his first experimental engines at the international automotive fair in Berlin in 1899. The first corporate museum was founded in 1923, followed in 1936 by the establishment of the Daimler Benz corporate archives. These currently contain construction sketches and research reports, correspondence documents, protocols, management files, brochures, instruction manuals, photos, films, and rare posters, all of which provide a detailed insight into the company and the history of technology. The museum's collection was constantly expanded, leading to the opening of a new Daimler Benz museum in the 1960s, which was expanded on the 100th anniversary of the automobile. In 2006, the museum moved to its current location in Stuttgart. The museum now contains more than 700 vehicles, including 500 passenger cars, 140 race cars, and 60 commercial vehicles, reflecting the history of the Mercedes-Benz brand. Around 160 exhibits are displayed at the museum; other vehicles are shown at exhibitions and trade fairs or participate in vintage car events and rallies.

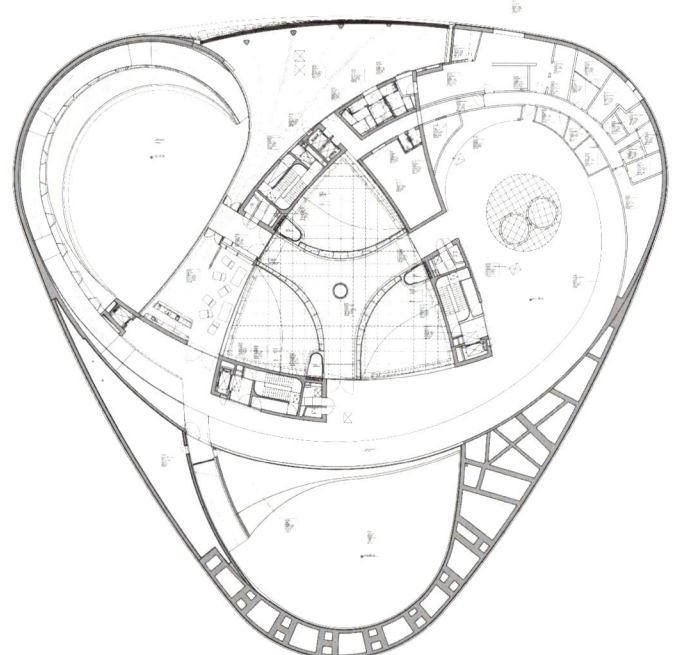

left: Floor plan_Façade_Area view and context. right: Exterior at night_Sports car exhibition_Elevator in the atrium_Atrium skylight.

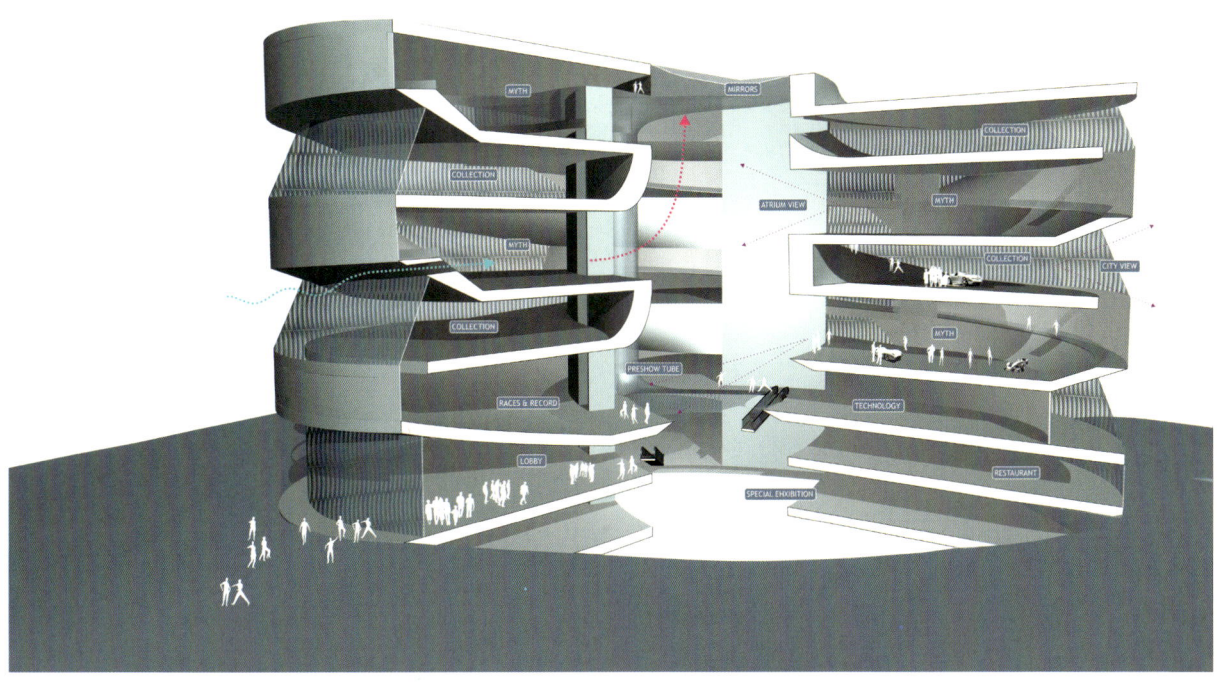

left: Atrium. right: Section_Upper floor_Exhibition space_Cafe.

GERMANY_STUTTGART **MAHLE INSIDE**

ARCHITECTS: HEINISCH.LEMBACH.HUBER ARCHITEKTEN BDA
COMPLETION: 2008_**TYPE:** COMPANY MUSEUM_**GROSS FLOOR**
AREA: 1,970 M² _**PHOTOS:** ZOOEY BRAUN, STUTTGART

THE ARCHITECTURE

The building design is based on a conceptual and spatial exhibition concept, which the architects developed as the groundwork for the development of its shape. The architecture and exhibition thus constitute an inseparable unit. The simple building structure serves as the casing for a complex system of rooms with various proportions and styles that are linked through open spaces and perspectives. The spatial concept of the house represents the various relationships of the exhibition themes with each other. Across four floors, the product lines are presented along with the corporate history, philosophy, methodology and goals.

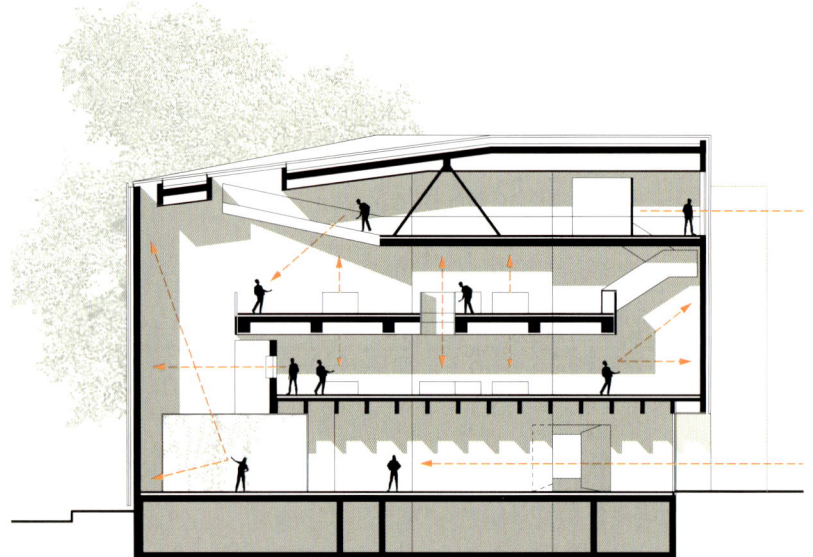

THE COLLECTION

The original plan called for rebuilding and expanding the existing piston museum, but the result was an entirely new museum featuring a corporate exhibition of the automotive supplier MAHLE. On the ground floor of the new MAHLE INSIDE building, visitors are presented with an overview of the company's locations, the MAHLE Foundation, and the ownership structure. A special eye-catcher is a 15 meter high wall, extending from the ground floor to the roof, which is dedicated to the employees. A photo display with about 400 pictures sets an impressive scene of the people of MAHLE. The staircase presents the corporate history, taking visitors through the almost 90 years of company development at every step. The first floor holds functional representations of various engine technologies as well as modules and complete systems from the MAHLE product lines. On the second floor, the individual components of the complete systems and selected historical products are on display. Finally, the top floor is dedicated to motorsports. Visitors can admire exhibits related to the 24-hour race of Le Mans and the Formula 1.

left: Section_South façade at night_West façade at night. right: View Haldenstrasse_Exhibition Basics of motor technology_Exhibition Racing.

GERMANY_WALDENBUCH **MUSEUM RITTER**

ARCHITECTS: MAX DUDLER_**COMPLETION:** 2005
TYPE: ART AND COMPANY MUSEUM_**GROSS FLOOR AREA:** 4,450 M²
PHOTOS: STEFAN MÜLLER, BERLIN

THE ARCHITECTURE

The museum housing the Marli Hoppe-Ritter collection is located at the edge of an extensive meadow in the immediate vicinity of the production premises of chocolate manufacturer Ritter Sport. The impressive limestone building is distinguished by its fascinating interplay of geometric shapes and the discrepancy between open and closed structures. The museum building serves as a prominent border structure between the rural and urban areas, between nature and art. The building consists of two parts and a connecting passage. The technical operational concept with its focus on energy generation from natural resources including solar energy, biomass and geothermal energy, aims to create an environmentally balanced building.

THE COLLECTION

The cubic structure of the museum already introduces the focus of the collection — square shapes. Marli Hoppe-Ritter, granddaughter of chocolate factory founder Alfred Ritter, purchased the first work of the collection in 1993 — the drawing "Square" by Sol LeWitt from 1980. Since that time, she has been collecting objects of art based or focusing on square shapes. The museum's collection contains 20th and 21st century painted and sculptured works, mainly from Europe. It features approximately 700 paintings, objects, sculptures and graphic art works. These objects focus on square shapes in various ways, sometimes mathematical analytical, sometimes playful and witty, and sometimes spiritual. In addition, on the first floor of the smaller wing there is an exhibition on the topic of chocolate in general as well as the corporate history of Ritter Sport in particular. A chocolate workshop is also integrated that shows the production process of the small square pieces of chocolate.

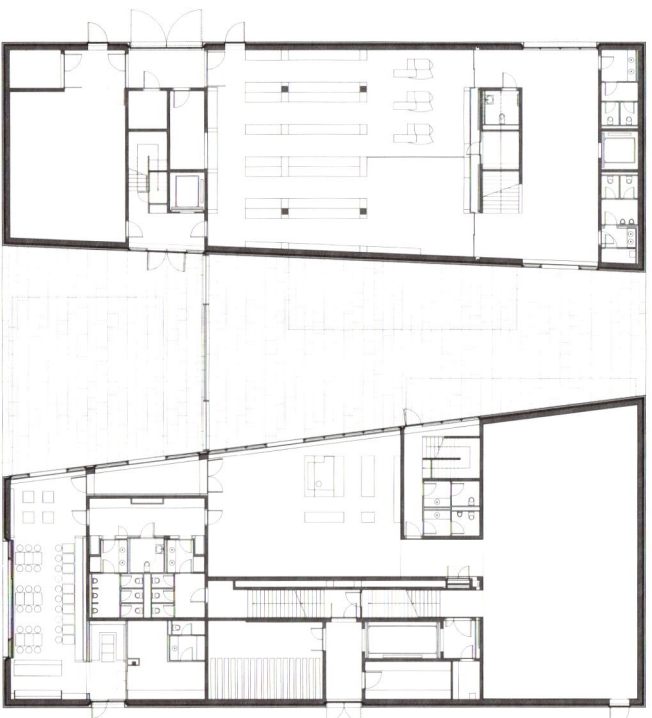

left: Ground floor plan_Passage_Exhibition rooms_Landscape room_Staircase second floor. right: Exterior view from south-east_Exhibition room_Lounge and shop.

GERMANY_WANGEN **BESUCHERZENTRUM ARCHE NEBRA**

ARCHITECTS: HOLZER KOBLER ARCHITEKTUREN / BARBARA HOLZER, TRISTAN KOBLER_**COMPLETION:** 2007_**TYPE:** ARCHEOLOGY MUSEUM_**GROSS FLOOR AREA:** 2,100 M²
PHOTOS: JAN BITTER

THE ARCHITECTURE

The emblematic architecture embeds the history of the Nebra sky disk into the location of its finding with references to archeology and astronomy. A 60 meter long building structure resembles a barque before its launch, containing permanent and temporary exhibitions as well as a planetarium. The transparent entrance floor is located in an opening of the building, with its base extending from the ground underneath. The building is aligned with the 30 meter look-out at the finding site of the sky disk. The leaning tower indicates the prehistoric orientation points of the landscape; it is an architectural interpretation of the sky disk as a measurement instrument.

THE COLLECTION

The skydisk of Nebra is the world's oldest precise depiction of the cosmos. Forged over 3,600 years ago, the bronze disk was found in the year 1999 by tomb raiders in a rock chamber on the Mittelberg mountain. The finding site is marked by the so-called "Himmelsauge" ("Eye to the sky") a slightly arched pane that provides insight into the earth. The visitors' center was erected in its vicinity. It contains scientific information as well as staged events that focus on the sky disk in various ways. These include virtual characters that haunt the showcases of the exhibition halls, as well as a puppet theater that presents a tongue-in-cheek rendition of the search for the sky disk. In addition to this permanent exhibition, temporary exhibitions from the realms of archeology, history, and astronomy are presented. For example, the visitors' center presented in 2010 the exhibition "Von Zeit zu Zeit – Allgegenwärtig und ungreifbar" ("From time to time — omnipresent and ungraspable"), providing information on the topic of time, posing philosophical questions, and presenting various theories. The oldest object of this exhibition is an astrolabe from the 13th/14th century. One of Germany's few digital planetariums is connected to the visitors' center. It presents a staged view of the universe of the Bronze Age.

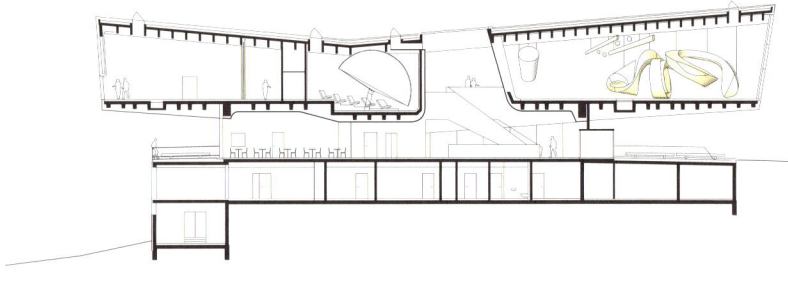

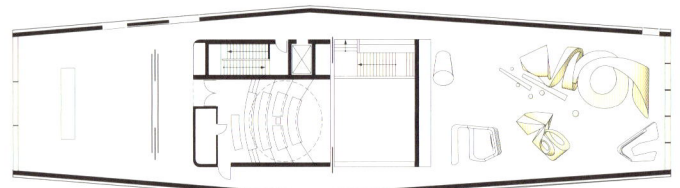

left: Section and second floor plan_Interior. right: Entrance_Exterior.

GERMANY_WAREN **MÜRITZEUM**

ARCHITECTS: WINGÅRDH ARKITEKTKONTOR AB
COMPLETION: 2007_**TYPE:** NATURE MUSEUM_**GROSS FLOOR AREA:**
3,137 M² _**PHOTOS:** ÅKE E:SON LINDMAN, STOCKHOLM

THE ARCHITECTURE

The city of Waren wanted a building that could serve as a center for visitors to the historic town as well as the wildlife of nearby lake Müritz. The project's 2,985 square meters contain areas for temporary exhibitions, an aquarium, a multimedia theater, room for seminars, shops, and animation for children. The circular form is opened up by sharp incisions, of which the entrance is the most prominent. A thin glass shield separates two different kinds of wood panels: a burned, black, panel for the façade, and a light-colored smooth panel for the inside. The "floating" character of the building corresponds to the nearby lake, while the round shape generates special interior spatial qualities.

THE COLLECTION

The Müritzeum is a modern, multimedia-based discovery center featuring exhibits from the Müritz region. The museum intends to offer learning experience to the old and young alike. The center's House of Lakes allows visitors to explore Germany's biggest lakes, located in the region. The exhibition takes a discreet look under the waterline and explores the world of the lake's inhabitants. Other presentations give visitors the chance to discover the local national park and its giant trees, some of which are 1,000 years old. Other themes investigated by the center's many and varied projects, include 24 basin-aquariums, housing 40 local species of fish. The museum's oldest inhabitant is a 27 year old carp that weighs over 20 kilos. The center's largest aquarium has a capacity of over 1,000,000 liters and contains a shoal of 500 white fish. A project investigating the origins of the regions forests presents an in-depth look at the area's history, beginning in the Ice Age before journeying to the Stone Age and then finally to the present day. The museum focuses heavily on hands-on learning for children, and many displays include activities to engage children and begin to teach them about nature and the world in which they live and how best it can be protected in the future.

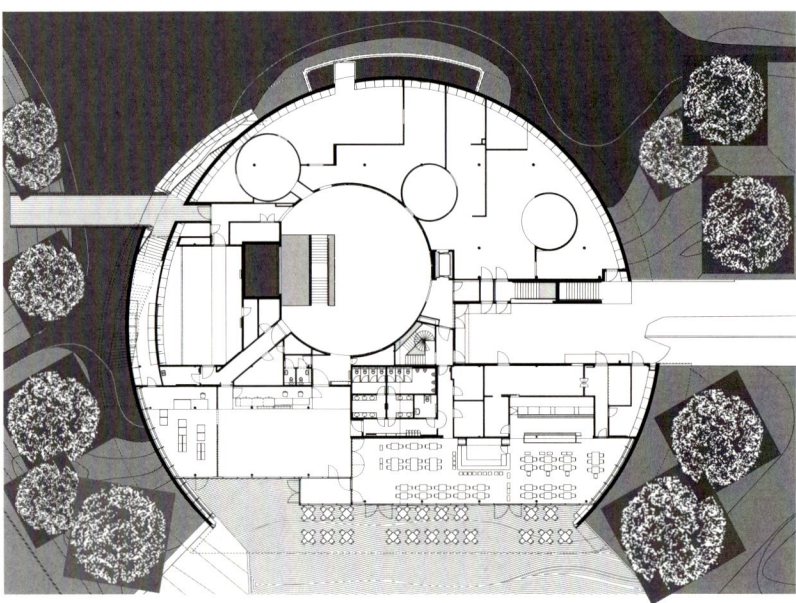

left: Floor plan_Interior detail_View_Exterior staircase_Exterior and bridge. right: Entrance_View of the pond_Water surface.

GREECE_ATHENS **NEW MUSEION AKROPOLIS**

ARCHITECTS: BERNARD TSCHUMI ARCHITECTS WITH MICHAEL PHOTIADIS, ARSY_**COMPLETION:** 2009_**TYPE:** ARCHEOLOGY MUSEUM_**GROSS FLOOR AREA:** 21,000 M² _**PHOTOS:** CHRISTIAN RICHTERS (314, 315, 316), PETER MAUSS / ESTO (317 L., B. R.), NIKOS DANIILIDIS (317 A. R.)

THE ARCHITECTURE

Located at the foot of the Acropolis, this site includes sensitive archeological excavations, the contemporary street grid, and the Parthenon itself. The base of the museum floats on pilotis over the existing archeological excavations, while a network of columns dominates the building. A glass ramp overlooking the archeological excavations leads to the galleries in the middle, in the form of a double-height room. The top, containing of the rectangular Parthenon Gallery, rotates to position the marbles of the Frieze exactly as they were at the Parthenon centuries ago.

THE COLLECTION

The museum presents approximately 300 statues and frieze segments along with around 4,000 other objects from the Archaic Greek, Classic Antiquity and Late Antiquity eras, which were found on the premises of the Acropolis in Athens. The lower part of the museum spans a rich archeological terrain, which was constantly settled from the 5th to the 12th century. The middle floor is dedicated to statues from the Archaic Greek era (the period from the 7th century BC, until 480/479 BC). The top floor presents the marble decorations of the Parthenon temple in a successful combination of originals and copies. Around 40 panels of the 75 meter long Parthenon frieze are located in Athens, while the remaining 56 are at the British Museum in London, to where they were taken around 200 years ago. The new building of the Acropolis museum results in part from the dispute concerning their return — the UK had argued that it could not return the objects as there was no suitable place to exhibit them in Athens.

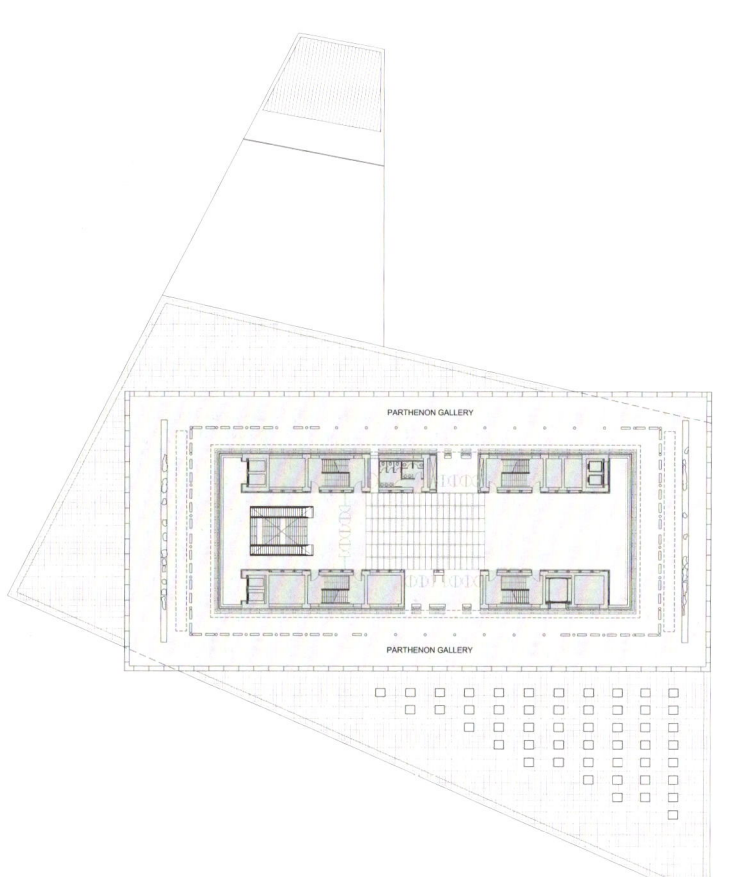

left: Floor plan Parthenon-gallery_Canopy excavations_View from excavations. right: East façade Parthenon-gallery.

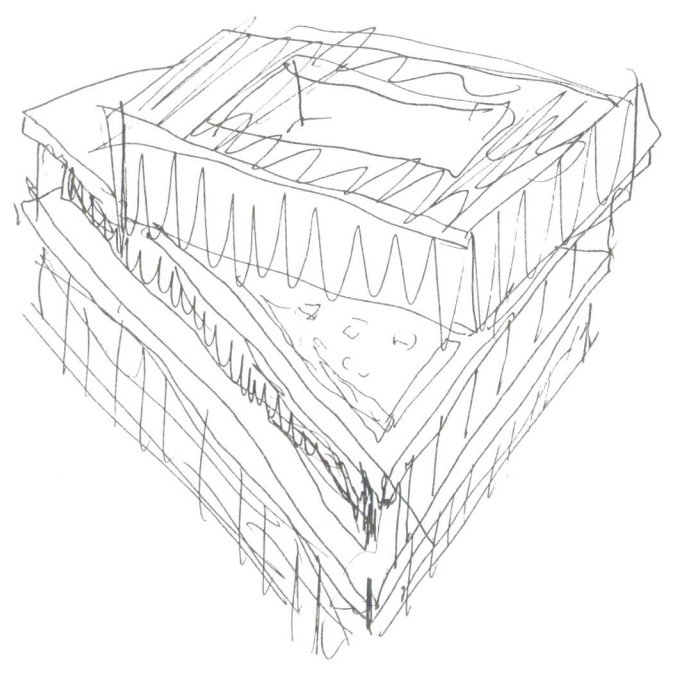

left: North façade. right: Sketch_New building above excavations_Relieffrieze_Sculpture betweeen round pillars.

GREECE_PATRA **MOUSEIO PATRAS**

ARCHITECTS: THEOFANIS BOBOTIS ARCHITECTS
COMPLETION: 2009_**TYPE:** ARCHEOLOGY MUSEUM_**GROSS FLOOR AREA:** 8,000 M² _**PHOTOS:** CHARALAMBOS LOUIZIDIS

THE ARCHITECTURE

A group of asymmetrical prismatic volumes was designed to accommodate the discoveries of a past culture. It is a modern composition which, through its irregular order, attempts to express the harmony of the volumes, the surfaces, the movements and circulation through the spaces where the exhibits are displayed. At the same time, it consists of an organic and functionally structured deconstruction, exempted from a static symmetry that seeks to form a dialogue with the environment, the visitors and the users. The design of the building along the National road of Athens–Patras, an urban central highway, renders the museum a landmark for the area and provides easy and direct access to it.

THE COLLECTION

The Mouseio Patras is one of Greece's largest archeological museums. It contains more than 2,000 valuable archeological finds from the Mycenaean era to the end of the Roman era. These include, for example, mosaics from the Greek and Roman antiquity dating back to the second and third century BC. Some of these are exhibited flat on the floor, while others are standing upright. In addition, the original installation of the floor, along with the stone walls of a Roman "Villa Rustica" provides insights into the working methods of Roman cellar masters. Two foundations of the service building are exhibited here, stemming from an agricultural complex of 14 buildings. They contain various items, such as a winepress, which inform visitors about the production and storage of agricultural products. A further exhibition space is dedicated to local life, language, customs and traditions. The original exhibits include ceramics, jewelry and articles of everyday use.

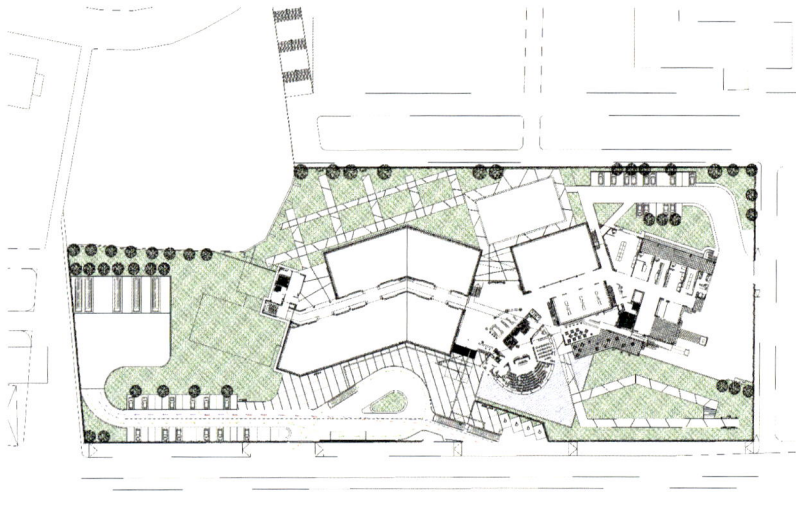

left: Site plan_Exterior view. right: Entrance_Interior_Creased wall.

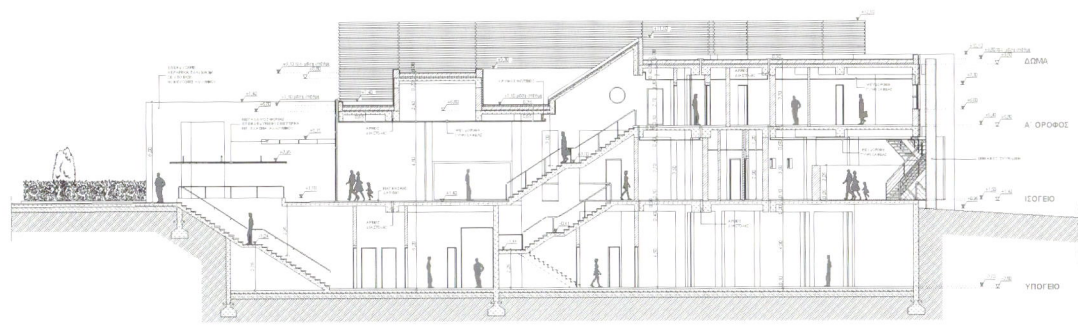

left: Elevated course. right: Section_Elevated museum course_Exterior view_Entrance and traffic distribution area.

ITALY_ROME **ARA PACIS**

ARCHITECTS: RICHARD MEIER & PARTNERS_**COMPLETION:** 2006
TYPE: ARCHEOLOGY MUSEUM_**GROSS FLOOR AREA:** 4,250 M²
PHOTOS: ROLAND HALBE / ARTURIMAGES

THE ARCHITECTURE

This museum, on the bank of the River Tiber has been designed as a new setting for the Ara Pacis, a sacrificial altar dating back to 9 B.C. The structure consists of a long, single-story, glazed loggia. Elevated above a shallow podium, it provides a transparent barrier between the embankment of the Tiber and the existing circular perimeter of the mausoleum of Augustus, built ca. 28 B.C. A predominating feature of the new building is a glass curtain wall that is 45 meter long and 12 meter high. The asymmetrical entry hall, defined by seven slender columns in reinforced concrete finished with white waxed marble plaster, leads to the main hall. The roof over the main hall rests on four columns with skylights to maximize natural lighting.

THE COLLECTION

The Ara Pacis originally stood on the Field of Mars. Today the peace altar has found a new home a hundred meters to the south. First parts of the altar were discovered in 1568. Nine hewn marble blocks were found whose identity was not immediately apparent. Only in the year 1879 were the relief pieces linked to the Ara Pacis. Systematic excavations followed in 1903 and 1937/1938, in which large parts of the altar were found. In addition, around one-third of the relief decorations of the original work was found. These reliefs are found inside and outside the surrounding wall. The reliefs in the southern part are particularly important. They depict the family of Augustus performing the sacrifice. Emperor Augustus is shown at the lead of the depicted succession with a toga pulled over his head. In addition, the consuls of the year 13 BC, four priests, a sacrifice servant shouldering an ax, and members of the imperial family have been identified. At the end of the procession there is an elderly man, who may be Maecenas, a close confidant of the emperor and a patron of the fine arts.

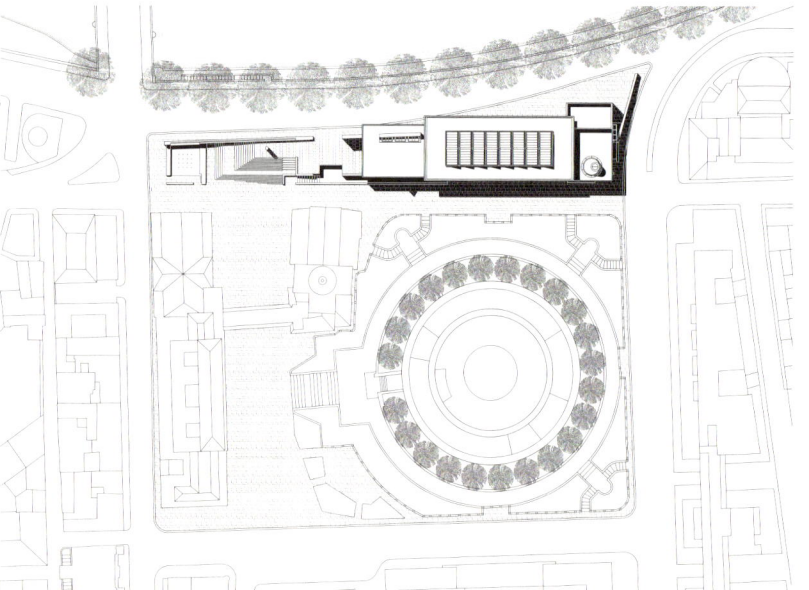

left: Site plan_Exterior_Busts. right: Temples façade_Museum façade_Temple in glass case.

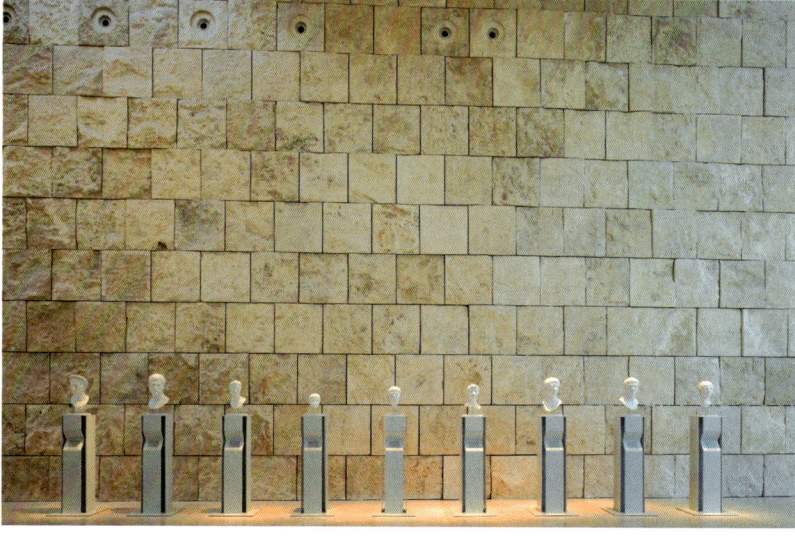

ITALY_ROME **MAXXI – MUSEO NAZIONALE DELLE ARTI DEL XXI SECOLO**

ARCHITECTS: ZAHA HADID ARCHITECTS_**COMPLETION:** 2010
TYPE: ART MUSEUM_**GROSS FLOOR AREA:** 29,000 M²
PHOTOS: ROLAND HALBE / ARTURIMAGES

THE ARCHITECTURE

By intertwining the circulation with the urban context, the center, located in the former army barracks, shares a public dimension with the city. The external as well as internal pathways follow the overall drift of the geometry. Vertical and oblique circulatory elements are located at areas of confluence, interference and turbulence; the notion of a "drift" takes on an embodied form. The drifting emerges, therefore, as both an architectural motif, and as a way to navigate experientially through the museum. The "signature" aspect of an institution of this caliber is sublimated into a more pliable and porous organism that promotes several forms of identification at once.

THE COLLECTION

Even before its opening, the museum presented individual exhibitions and events such as performances of the German choreographer Sasha Waltz. Since that time, the MAXXI has been presenting itself as Rome's first museum for contemporary art, while also housing Italy's first architecture museum. The program of the "MAXXI art" is primarily dedicated to Italian art and its relationship to the international art scene. The collection contains approximately 300 objects, including the work of Anish Kapoor, Mario Merz, and Gerhard Richter. The "MAXXI architecture" presents exhibitions of 20th century works on the ground floor and 21st century architecture on the first floor. The exhibits of the architecture exhibition include the archives of Carlo Scarpa, Aldo Rossi, and Pierluigi Nervi, as well as works of contemporary architects such as Toyo Ito and Giancarlo de Carlo. In addition to the exhibitions, the building offers room for workshops, conferences, shows, projections, educational projects and a laboratory for cultural experimentation and innovation.

left: Study painting_Panoramic view. right: Façade by night_Staircase_Ground floor.

ITALY_ROVERETO

MART – MUSEO DI ARTE MODERNA E CONTEMPORANEA DI TRENTO E ROVERETO

ARCHITECTS: STUDIO ARCHITETTO MARIO BOTTA WITH GIULIO ANDREOLLI_**COMPLETION:** 2002_**TYPE:** ART MUSEUM **GROSS FLOOR AREA:** 29,000 M²_**PHOTOS:** ENRICO CANO, COMO (326, 327, 329 L.), PINO MUSI, MILAN (328, 329 R.)

THE ARCHITECTURE

The museum is set back in relationship to the two historic Palazzos Alberti and Annona on Corso Bettini. The space between them was transformed into an avenue leading to a circular plaza with the different entrances to the museum, library, auditorium and café. The plaza, covered by a glass dome, constitutes the heart of the structure. Starting from here, visitors can access the exhibition spaces on the two upper floors (the last one entirely lit by skylights) or the services area on the ground floor located around the central atrium that proposes different viewpoints and varied uses by alternating mezzanines and large spaces. The basement level houses the library and the 20th century archives.

THE COLLECTION

The collection of the museum was continuously expanded through donations and purchases, as well as bequests of valuable private collections. Today, it includes a total of more than 12,000 paintings, drawings, etchings, and sculptures. These include an extensive collection of Futurist works by artists such as Giacomo Balla, Gino Severini and Tullio Crali, and approximately 3,000 drawings, paintings, sculptures and wall tapestry purchased from the heirs of Fortunato Depero. The MART also contains a valuable collection of 20th century Italian art, including works by Giorgio de Chirico, Massimo Campigli and Giorgio Morandi. It furthermore features the most prominent Italian collection of pop art and minimal art by artists such as Andy Warhol, Robert Rauschenberg and Roy Lichtenstein. The archives of the MART contain an additional historical fund of in excess of 80,000 documents, consisting of letters, manuscripts, drawings, photos and newspaper clippings. The museum's library is stocked with an additional 60,000 works, providing a cross-section of the art and culture of the 20th century.

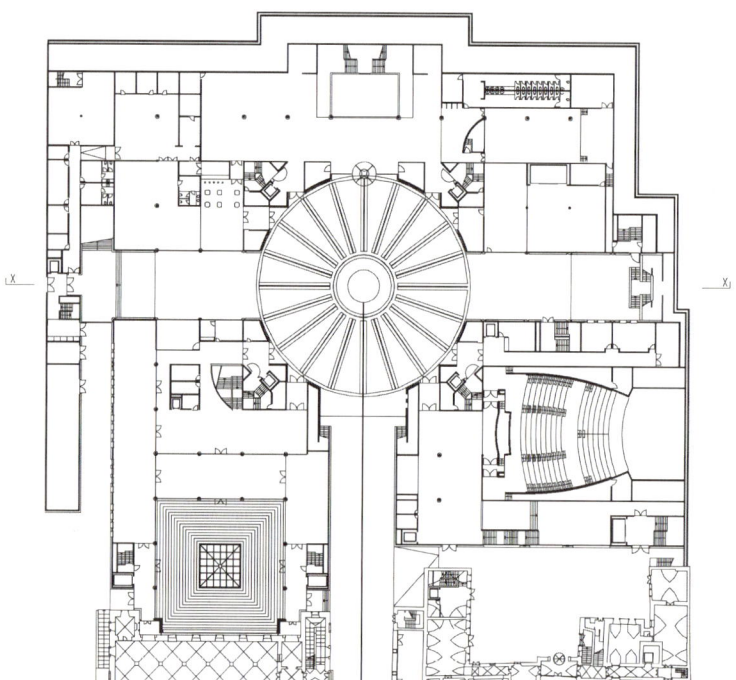

left: Ground floor plan_View from the plaza towards Corso Bettini_Temporary exhibition space. right: The plaza and the glass dome_Exhibition space.

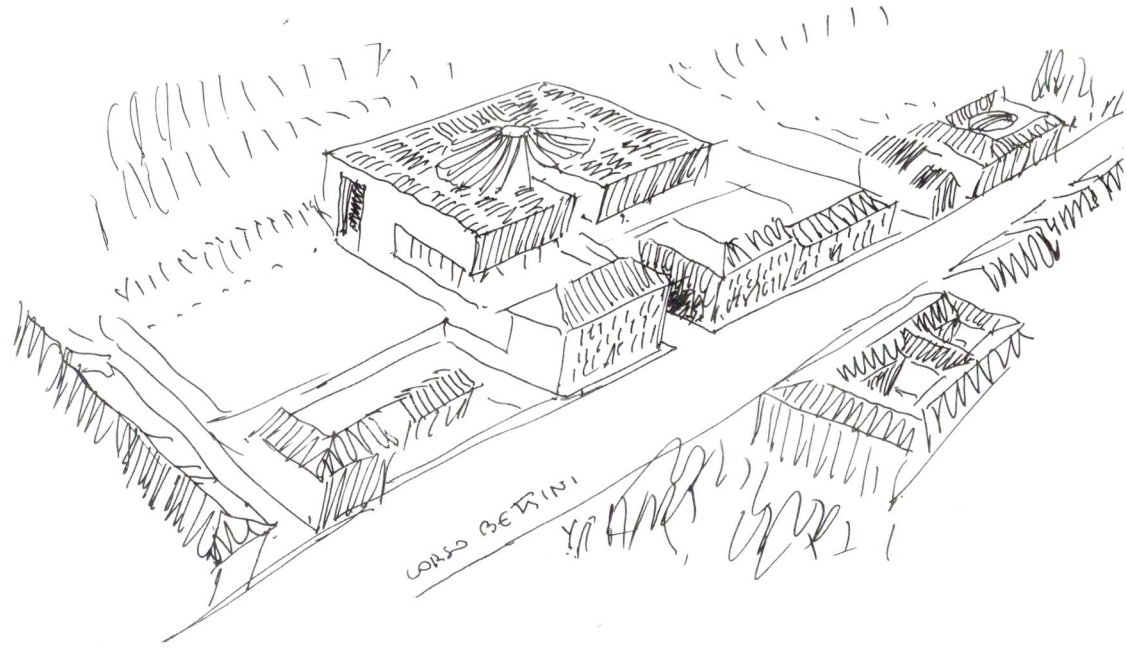

left: Detail of the plaza and the glass dome. right: Overall sketch_Foyer_Skywalk on the second floor_Exhibition space.

NORWAY_HAMARØY **HAMSUNSENTERET**

ARCHITECTS: STEVEN HOLL ARCHITECTS_**COMPLETION:** 2009
TYPE: LITERATURE MUSEUM_**GROSS FLOOR AREA:** 2,508 M²
PHOTOS: STEVEN HOLL ARCHITECTS

THE ARCHITECTURE

This center is dedicated to the writer Knut Hamsun. It is located above the Arctic Circle, near the village of Presteid in Hamarøy and the farm where the writer grew up. The center contains exhibition areas, a library and a reading room, a café and an auditorium equipped with film projection equipment. The concept for the museum is "building as a body," creating a battleground of invisible forces. Many features of the building are inspired by the vernacular style such as the characteristic stained black wood exterior skin of the great wooden stave Norse churches. The long grass on the roof garden is also a modern interpretation of the style of the traditional Norwegian sod roofs.

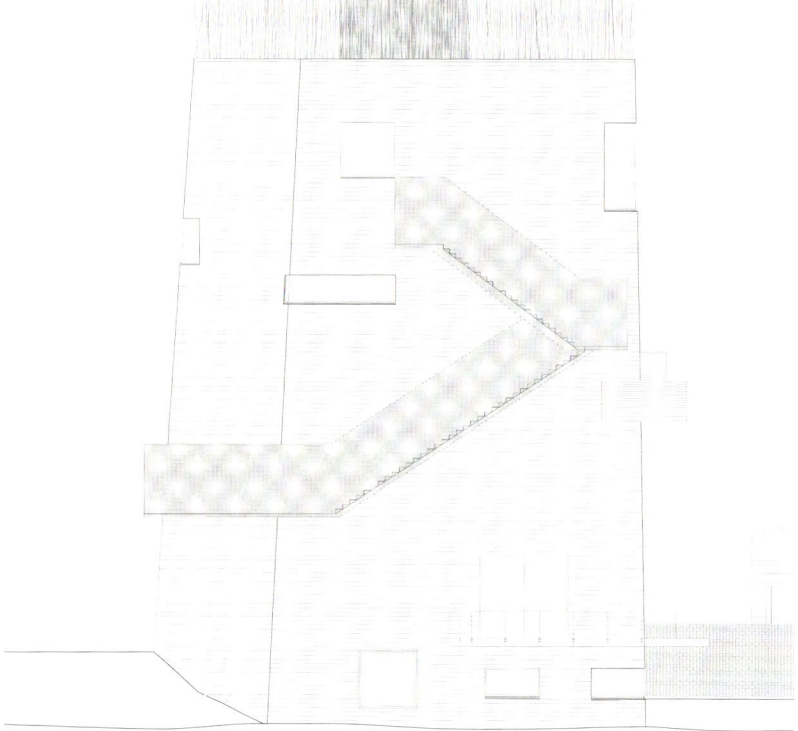

THE COLLECTION

Knut Hamsun (1859-1952) was a prominent Norwegian writer. In 1920, he received the literature Nobel Prize for his epic "Growth of the Soil," which was published in 1917 under the original title "Markens grøde" in Norway. Across four floors, visitors to the center can explore the life and work of the artist. The exhibition rooms provide information about his novels and his criticism of Modernity, as well as his idealization of agricultural life and his love of the Norwegian landscape and nature. In the "Archive" exhibition room, visitors can see objects from some of the author's books, such as Ylajali's veil or Nagel's yellow suit. The walls reflect the author's writing process with handwritten notes, writer's blocks and surges of inspiration. A special focus of the exhibition is on Hamsun's political beliefs, such as his controversial sympathetic stance towards Germany during the two World Wars. The museum presents some of his political essays from 1889 to 1945, while also providing insights into the accusations of treason directed at him after World War II.

left: Façade south_Staircase_Horizontal view_Interior. right: Building in context_Cantilever arm Balcony_View into the landscape_Roof detail with long bamboo.

POLAND_WARSAW **CHOPIN MUZEUM**

ARCHITECTS: MIGLIORE + SERVETTO ARCHITETTI ASSOCIATI
COMPLETION: 2010_**ORIGINAL BUILDING:** OSSOLIŃSKI-PALAIS,
1642_**TYPE:** HISTORY MUSEUM_**GROSS FLOOR AREA:** 1,200 M²
PHOTOS: MARCIN CZECHOWICZ

THE ARCHITECTURE

The permanent exhibition is hosted inside the renewed Ostrogski Palace. In an afford to change the traditional perception of the museum, the architects created a structure able to introduce classical music and the person of Chopin to a wide audience in an entirely individual knowledge experience. Although it shares a dialogue with the architectural and structural elements of the palace, the project goes along with the development of the contents through the definition of eleven different landscapes: emotional landscapes and soundscapes. Each different theme is developed through exhibition structures, designed to integrate music, items of the collection, and interactive systems, by defining a multiplayer and multimodal message.

THE COLLECTION

The palace was originally established in the late 17th century by Duke Janusz Ostrogski. In addition to the museum, the building is also home to the Chopin institute and the headquarters of the internationally active Fryderyk-Chopin-Stiftung. On the occasion of the Chopin anniversary year 2010, the Ostrogski palace was renovated and the previously neglected rooms underneath the terrace turned into a concert hall. The museum contains the world's largest Chopin collection and informs via a multitude of exhibits about the life, work and legacy of the Polish composer Frédéric Chopin (1810–1849). On show are manuscripts of the artist as well as memorabilia, letters, portraits and personal items that were collected from the immediate vicinity of the artist. The exhibition culminates in a room dedicated to the death of Chopin in the year 1849. The sound-proof black cube contains a strand of the pianist's hair as well as a plaster death mask of his face and a book featuring comments from friends and acquaintances at the time, whose pages continually turn.

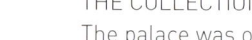

left: Section_Façade_Nohant room. right: Warsaw room_Installation in the Composer room_ Zelazowa Wola room_Travel room.

PORTUGAL_CASCAIS **PAULA RÊGO MUSEUM**

ARCHITECTS: EDUARDO SOUTO DE MOURA_**COMPLETION:** 2008
TYPE: ART MUSEUM_**GROSS FLOOR AREA:** 3,307 M²
PHOTOS: LEONARDO FINOTTI

THE ARCHITECTURE

After surveying the trees, especially the tops, the architects developed a set of buildings with different heights that represent a built "positive" juxtaposed to the "negative" tree top structures. This "Yang" and "Yin" interaction between building and nature was also elemental in deciding the exterior material, a red concrete which is complementary in color to the green wood. In the meantime, the surrounding plant structure was reduced for prophylactic reasons. The architects additionally established a hierarchy by introducing two big pyramids — skylights — in the entrance axis, which house the library and the café. It was considered important that every exhibition room always had an opening to the exterior garden.

THE COLLECTION

The collection of the museum is dedicated to the internationally renowned Portuguese artist Paula Rêgo (born 1935 in Lisbon). The 73 year old artist, who has been residing for several decades in London, donated more than 500 of her works created in the course of 50+ years, to the museum, which presents them at changing temporary exhibitions. The collection contains the entire etchings by the artist, a total of 257, as well as 278 drawings, most of which have never been shown before, and 52 paintings. Most of these works were created in the 1980s, but the collection also includes some of her emblematic pieces from the 1960s (e.g. the "Operas" series or "In and Out of the Sea"), the 1990s (e.g. "Angel", "Love", "The Company of Women"), as well as her later painting "Human Cargo" of 2008. The paintings, drawings, and etchings are produced on a variety of media and using a wide range of techniques. The collection is complemented by 15 oil paintings by her husband, the artist Victor Willing (1928-1988), as well as some of her personal documents.

left: Sketch_General view. right: Courtyard.

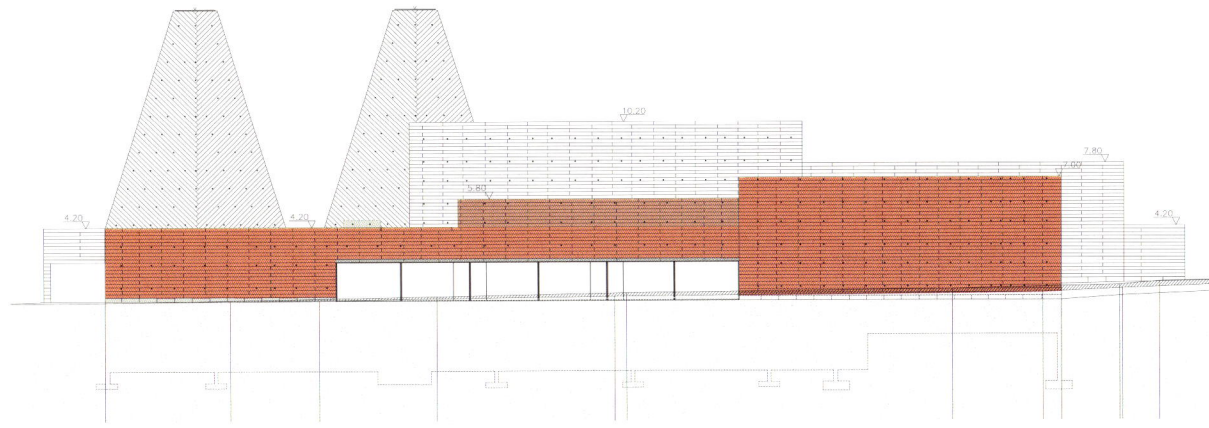

left: Exhibition hall. right: Section_Exhibition hall_Shop.

PORTUGAL_LISBON **MUSEU DO DESIGN E DA MODA**

ARCHITECTS: RICARDO CARVALHO + JOANA VILHENA ARQUITECTOS
COMPLETION: 2009_**ORIGINAL BUILDING:** CRISTINO DA SILVA, 1952
TYPE: DESIGN AND FASHION MUSEUM_**GROSS FLOOR AREA:**
2,634 M² _**PHOTOS:** LEONARDO FINOTTI

THE ARCHITECTURE

This intervention is primarily made with light. The non-material element of light is used to draw attention to the exposed concrete and to the collection, with artificial lighting wrapping around some of the building elements. The project is further characterized by the expressionist, exposed concrete structure and by the scaffolding made of industrial materials. These allude to the street and pallets that function as displays. The floor was partially painted with reflective paint, as the collection occupies the space in an informal way. From the cafeteria, with its single long cork table, one looks through a single glass sheet at the museum, as well as the surrounding streets of Baixa Pombalina.

THE COLLECTION

The Museu do Design e da Moda, also known as MUDE, is one of the world's leading museums of 20th century design. The museum aims to enrich the domestic museum space and exhibits a range of products and designs, forging a strong link between fashion and product design. One of the museum's permanent exhibitions is that of The Francisco Capelo Collection, which started in the 1990s. Showcasing more than 1,000 design and 1,200 fashion pieces, most of it Haute Couture, the Francisco Capelo Collection portrays the history of design and fashion from the 1930s to the present, being an exceptional representation of Portuguese fashion trends and Portugal's relationship to the international scene. The display includes a famous Jean Desses gown that Renée Zellweger wore to the Oscars in 2001. In total, the museum's 1,000 design objects include fashion pieces from famous names like Jean Paul Gaultier and Vivienne Westwood. The museum's design collection consists of works by around 230 designers and represents trends from all over the world, including works by design icons such as Charles Eames, George Nelson, Henning Koppel and Tom Dixon. Trends and designs included in the exhibitions feature innovative furnishings, glass and jewelry dating back to 1937.

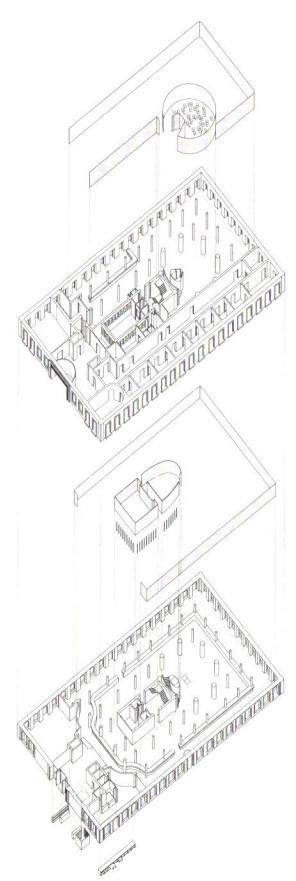

left: Axonometric drawing_Exhibition hall_Façade. right: Exhibition hall_Staircase_Interior.

PORTUGAL_LUZ **MUSEU DA LUZ**

ARCHITECTS: PEDRO PACHECO + MARIE CLÉMENT
COMPLETION: 2003_**TYPE:** CULTURE MUSEUM_**GROSS FLOOR**
AREA: 660 M² _**PHOTOS:** PAULO NUNO SILVA / ÉVORA, PORTUGAL
(340, 343 L., R. B), LEONARDO FINOTTI, SÃO PAULO
(341, 342, 343 R. A.)

THE ARCHITECTURE

The village of Luz was submerged following the construction of the Alqueva Dam. Its inhabitants as well as its culture and origins had to be moved into a new village. This project consists of creating a new place for the church, the cemetery and the museum of Luz as an important memorial landmark between the new and the old village. The museum redesigns the topography of the location as a new foundation, in which paths, walls and light become evident elements of a territory culture. A sequence of interior spaces emphasizes a particular regard for the landscape. Luz room, as the museum's central feature, and the light chimneys, constitute the only visible trace of the building in the landscape.

THE COLLECTION

The Museu da Luz in Portugal was conceived to preserve the memory and identity of the local community. This was necessary as the original village of Luz was destroyed during the Alqueva project, which involved the submersion of the village to make way for the creation of one of Europe's largest reservoirs. The new village retained the functional structure of the old village, both in urban and agrarian terms. It was organized by the rule that village inhabitants received "a house for a house, and a plot of land for a plot of land". The new village was constructed on a site chosen by the community, on two estates: the Herdade dos Pássaros and the Herdade Julioa. The process of the relocation of the village is unique and has been pointed to as an example of how ethical values can be reconciled with the need for the building of a reservoir. The process involved the construction of 212 houses as well as business and community facilities; the village cemetery was also transferred to the new site and a replica of the Church of Our Lady of Light, retaining the architectural features of the original church, was built. Luz Museum was created as a space in the new village for preserving the memory of a community and interpreting the unique process of the relocation of the village, in particular, and the execution of the Alqueva Multipurpose Project in general.

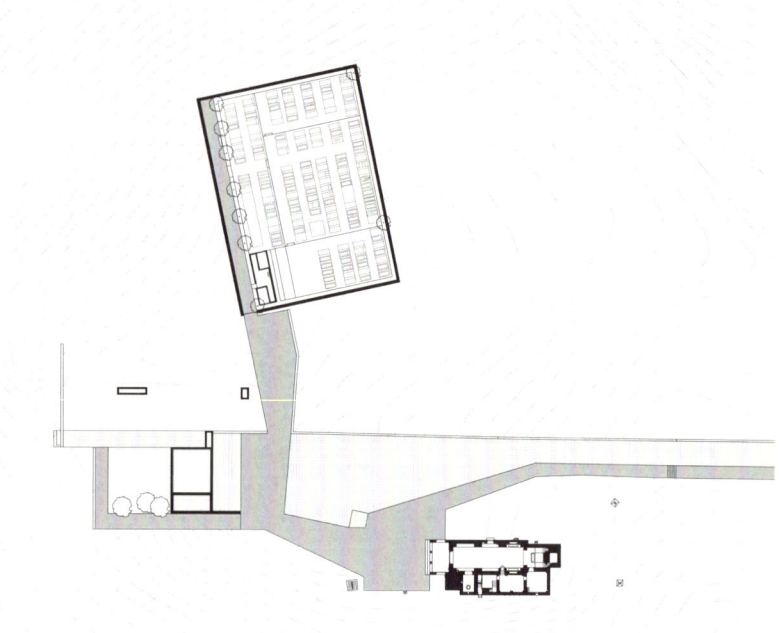

left: Site plan_East view_South view. right: Access ramp and roof platform_Roof landscape and viewpoint over the lake.

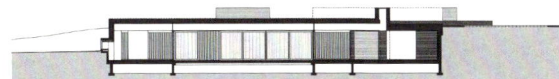

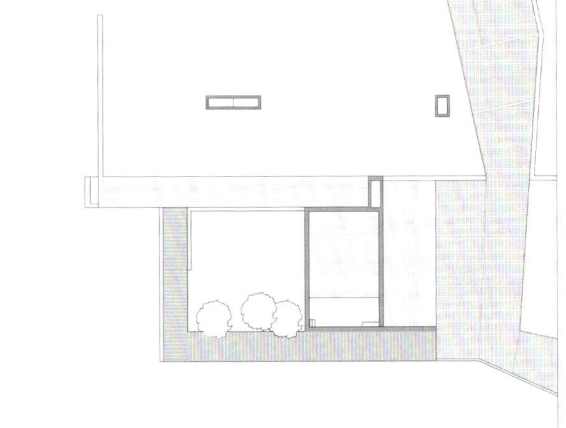

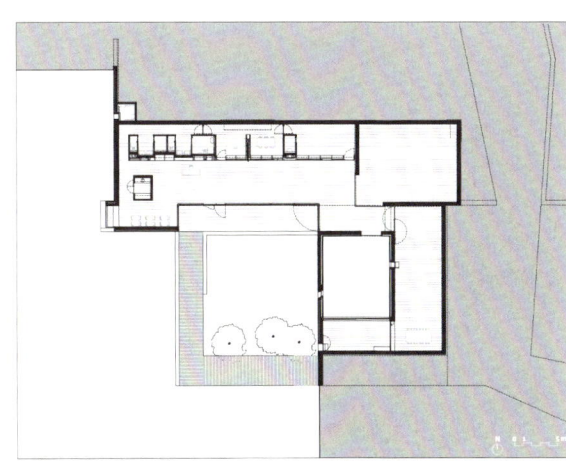

left: Exhibition room. right: Sections and plans_Patio_Room of Luz and patio_Temporary exhibition and memory room.

SLOVENIA_LJUBLJANA **MESTNI MUZEJ LJUBLJANA**

ARCHITECTS: OFIS ARHITEKTI_**OTHER CREATIVES:** ROK OMAN, SPELA VIDECNIK_**COMPLETION:** 2004_**TYPE:** CULTURE MUSEUM **GROSS FLOOR AREA:** 3,250 M²_**PHOTOS:** TOMAZ GREGORIC

THE ARCHITECTURE

The building involves the renovation and extension of the Auersperg Palace, which is located in the heart of the historical city center. The palace and the location have a rich history dating from the prehistoric period to Roman and medieval times. Each era added something to the building. Since the function of the palace changed several times in the course of history, the existing floor plan was not suitable for hosting a museum. The spaces were labyrinthine and disconnected. This successful competition entry suggested a spiral tour for visitors through the exhibition spaces and proposed an added element to connect the wings of the palace.

THE COLLECTION

The Mestni muzej Ljubljana is located in the Slovenian city's Auersperg Palace. A historical building, once owned by the House of Auersperg's, dukes of Carniola. The palace is thought to have been built in 1642, based on several older houses and since that time has undergone several restorations. Its front façade is adorned with a classical entrance portal, which also features an arched courtyard. The museum houses a permanent collection, called "Faces of Ljubljana," dedicated to the city's culture and history. The aim of the museum is to portray the city as both a place for living and as the country's economic, political, administrative and creative hub. Several of the exhibitions feature selected images of Ljubljana and famous people who have lived within the city throughout different historical periods. The museum also contains several themed exhibitions, for example, "Economy", a display focused on the factors that influenced the development of economy in Ljubljana, tracing the history of commerce from prehistory to the era of Internet trade, and the "From State to State" exhibition, showing the transition of the city between different regimes, which were accompanied by varying amounts of violence and conflict.

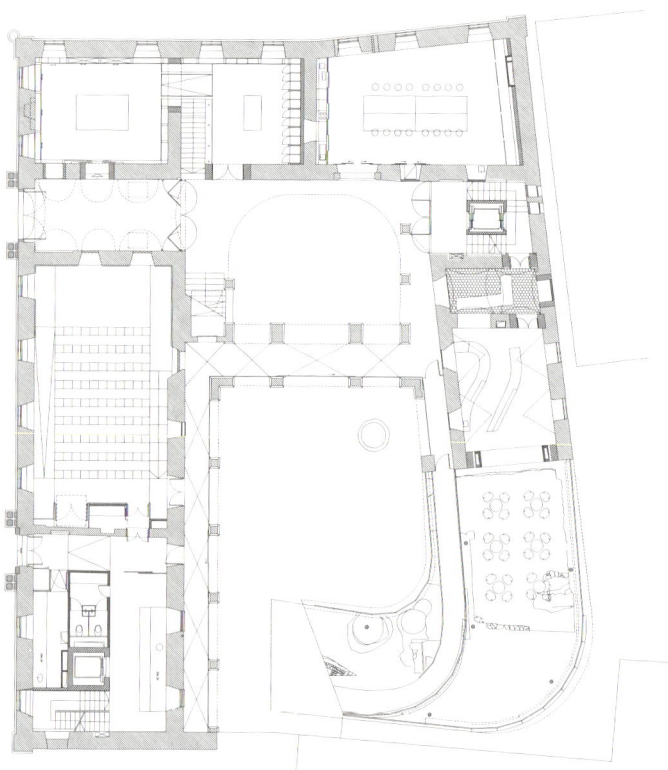

left: Plan_Seating accomodation_Hall. right: View to interior_View restaurant.

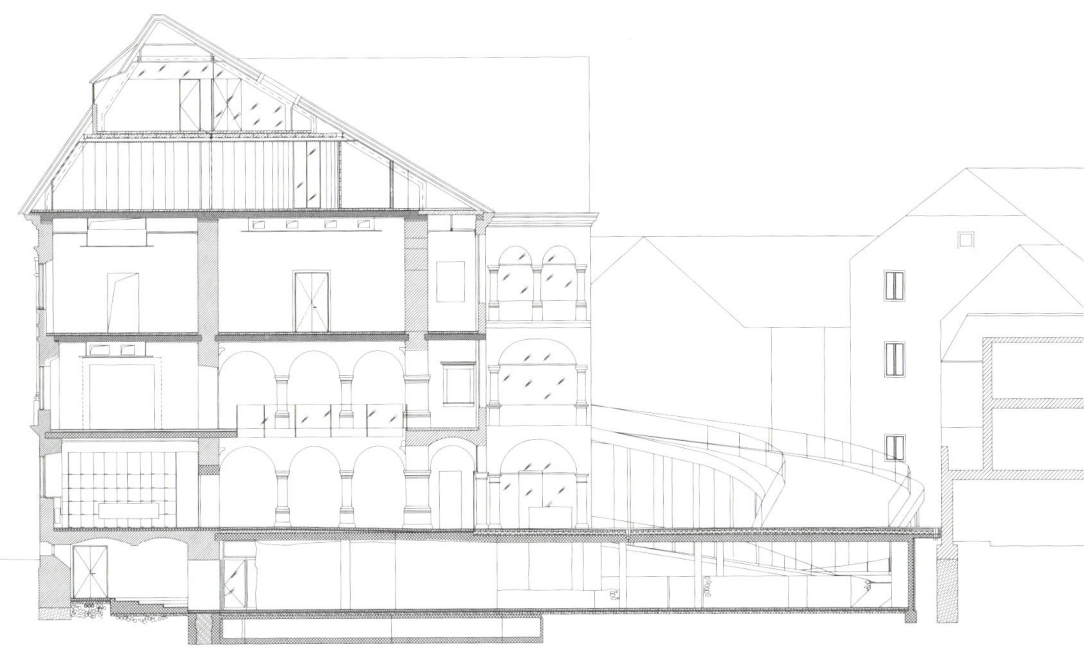

left: Light and reflections. right: Section_Cinema_Model_Exterior.

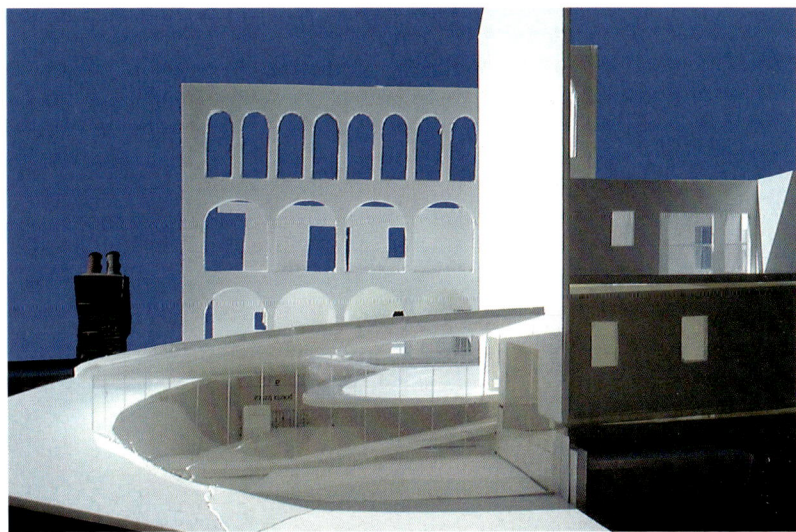

SPAIN_ALMERÍA **MUSEO ARQUEOLÓGICO DE ALMERÍA**

ARCHITECTS: PAREDES PEDROSA ARQUITECTOS_**COMPLETION:** 2003_**TYPE:** ARCHEOLOGY MUSEUM_**GROSS FLOOR AREA:** 6,284 M²_**PHOTOS:** ROLAND HALBE / ARTURIMAGES

THE ARCHITECTURE

The entrance to this building is located at the end of a plaza, which serves as a public space for the city as well as an outdoor lobby for the museum. The existing palm garden situated at the side of the building, was kept and extended to be included within the exhibition space. The museum is intended to host an archeological collection. A number of different spaces are connected by a large void, which orientates the visitor and links the rooms between the permanent collection and the various other activities being held. In some places the exterior walls open up as viewpoints towards the city, while light is provided through skylights in the ceilings. A varnished wooden grid suspended over the exhibition rooms constitutes a filter for direct light.

THE COLLECTION

The Archeological Museum in Almería contains important and varied archeological objects, taken largely from the province of Almería. The core of the collections come from the collection of Juan Cuadrado and was purchased from him by the Provincial Council of Almería. Since this purchase, the museum's collection has grown considerably, due in part to numerous archeological excavations, which have been carried out in the area over the years. The museum also exhibits a wide range of ceramics, regional costumes and weapons, but the main focus of the museum is upon two earlier cultures, which are specific to Almería, those of the Los Millares and El Argar tribes. El Argar is an early Bronze Age culture, which flourished in Almería between 1800 and 1300 BC. This culture was characterized by its early use of bronze, which gave the tribe dominance over other local tribes that continued to use copper. El Argar developed from the earlier civilization of Los Millares. These two cultures shaped Almeria's history and because of their importance to the region, the museum's goal is to become a national center for the study of these ancient societies.

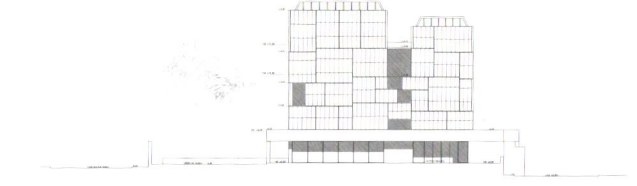

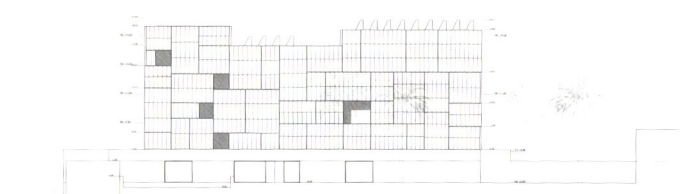

left: Elevations_Interior_Interior with ceiling detail. right: Exterior view_Staircase system_Façade.

SPAIN_BILBAO **GUGGENHEIM BILBAO MUSEOA**

ARCHITECTS: FRANK O. GEHRY – GEHRY PARTNERS
COMPLETION: 1997_**TYPE:** ART MUSEUM_**GROSS FLOOR AREA:**
11,000 M² _**PHOTOS:** JOCHEN HELLE / ARTURIMAGES (350 B. L.),
KARIN HESSMANN / ARTURIMAGES (351 B. L.),
BARBARA STAUBACH / ARTURIMAGES (351 A., B. R.),
PAUL RAFTERY / ARTURIMAGES (350 B. R.)
© FMGB GUGGENHEIM BILBAO MUSEOA,
FRANK O.GEHRY, 1997 (350 A. L.)

THE ARCHITECTURE

Following the rise and fall of the city as an industrial location, the city administration and the competition organizers wanted the museum to act as a symbol of reorientation. Staggered in its height and depth, the building's many curved sections evolve asymmetrically around its center. One wing is crossed by an urban highway, while the entrance side is reflected in the Nervíon river. The complex geometry of undulating and broken façades made of titan sheets was calculated with the computer program CATIA, which was originally developed for the aircraft industry. The extensive press coverage, the tourist appeal and symbolism of the building — the "Bilbao effect," rang in a new era for museum construction.

THE COLLECTION

Solomon Robert Guggenheim (1861–1949) dedicated his whole life to art patronage. From 1927 he collected modern and contemporary art exclusively. In the year 1937 he established the Solomon R. Guggenheim Foundation with the aim of enhancing the public appreciation of modern art. Two years later, the US-based foundation established the Museum of Non-Objective Painting in New York, which was renamed in 1952 into the Solomon R. Guggenheim Museum in honor of the art collector. His niece, Peggy Guggenheim (1898–1979), also began collecting modern art in the 1930s, complementing the collection of her uncle with works of the artist Jackson Pollock. The contents of these two collections are exhibited at the seven currently existing Guggenheim museums, providing a comprehensive overview of 20th century art. For example, the Bilbao museum shows the works of some of the most influential artists of the second half of the 20th century. These include Eduardo Chillida, Yves Klein, Robert Rauschenberg and Andy Warhol. The museum focuses primarily on installations and video art.

left: Sketch Frank O. Gehry_Panorama view_Foyer. right: Main entrance_Titan cladding_Exterior.

SPAIN_CARTAGENA **MUSEO DEL TEATRO ROMANO**

ARCHITECTS: RAFAEL MONEO_**COMPLETION:** 2008_**TYPE:**
ARCHEOLOGY MUSEUM_**GROSS FLOOR AREA:** 17,000 M²
PHOTOS: ROLAND HALBE / ARTURIMAGES

THE ARCHITECTURE

The aim of this project was to incorporate the Roman Theater into the city by connecting pre-existing buildings and voids with the urban framework, thereby creating a museum-like route that leads from the lower levels of the port up to the Cerro de la Concepción. The Center for Roman Studies and the museum are located along this itinerary, culminating in the space of the Roman Theater. The "promenade" flows through exhibition spaces lit by a system of skylights. The construction encompasses two buildings, connected by a corridor, surrounding a yard. The first one contains service rooms and provides access from the Riquelme Palace. The second building is located in General Ordoñez, connected by a terrace to the Old Cathedral.

THE COLLECTION

This ancient site is focused around the Teatro Romano, a large open-air amphitheater, which had previously been hidden for centuries. The site was abandoned, after suffering both flood and earthquake damage, so that by the Renaissance it has already been reduced to ruins and a church and convent were actually built on the site. Restoration began in 1988, as an archeological project but the complete restoration of the ruin has since become the driving force behind the regeneration of one of the city's most underprivileged areas. The project included the restoration of the theater, some parts of the "Old Town" and the construction of the museum and a research center dedicated to the excavation of the site. The museum was one of the central elements of the huge project as it was created to exhibit artifacts uncovered during the excavation process. The museum joins the Riquelme Palace and the Church of Santa Maria La Vieja to the theater complex: with the theater being the final and most important component in the ensemble. The construction consists of two buildings joined by a corridor. One of them provides access from the Riquelme Palace and surrounds a courtyard. It offers service rooms on its various floors, such as the lobby, cafeteria, temporary show room, library, record and study room, and meeting rooms.

left: Section and elevation_Old and new in harmony_Bird's eye view_Entrance. right: Façade.

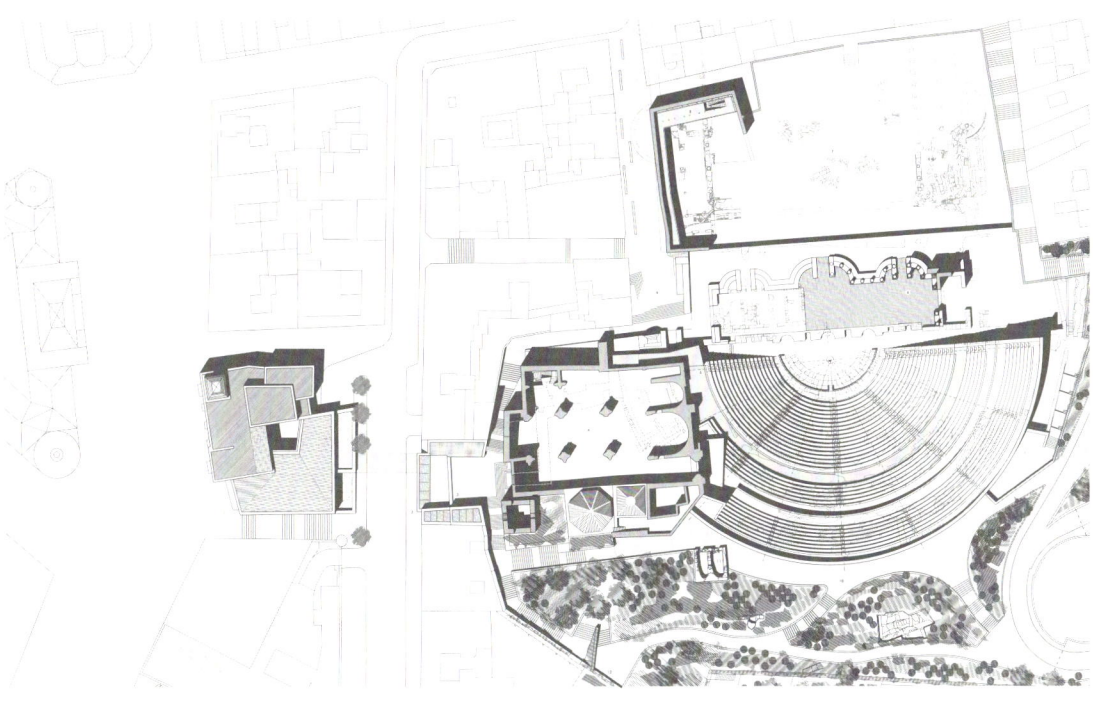

left: Museum next to the roman theater. right: Site plan_Corridor_Foyer_Exhibition room.

SPAIN_CORDOBA **MADINAT AL ZAHRA**

ARCHITECTS: NIETO SOBEJANO ARQUITECTOS, S.L.P.
COMPLETION: 2008_**TYPE:** ARCHEOLOGY MUSEUM_**GROSS FLOOR AREA:** 9,125 M² _**PHOTOS:** ROLAND HALBE / ARTURIMAGES

THE ARCHITECTURE

This building will structure its new uses around a sequence of full and empty spaces, covered rooms and open patios. From the main vestibule, a blue broad patio spreads out on a square plan. The main public spaces will be organized around it like a cloister. Another long, deep patio, green from the surrounding vegetation, will structure the private areas. The walls unearthed during excavations, will consist of white-face concrete with wooden frames; the roofs resting on them will be made of thin slabs; while the patio will be paved in limestone. The concept of this project is implicitly prepared for future growth, especially in the museum and workshop areas where new pavilions can be added.

THE COLLECTION

Madinat al Zahra is an Islamic palace town, founded in the year 936 AD by the Caliph Abd al-Rahman III to serve as his residence. The palace grounds were set up on three graded terraces separated by walls. The lowest terrace was inhibited by common people and contained stables, workshops, a market and homes. The next terrace was reserved for administrators and government officials. Serving as the reception and administration level, it contained many parks and gardens. The top level was the seat of the power and the palace of the Caliph. Ruins of the palace premises can still be seen at the site today. However, as yet only ten percent of the overall 112 hectares could be excavated. The museum contains workshops for the conservation and research of the archeological finds. In addition, the building contains several exhibition rooms such as the "Caliphate city 936-1013" presenting information about the history of the palace city through 162 exhibits. The exhibition also presents the architecture, type and origins of building materials, as well as the palace town in correlation with its surroundings and the orient. Visitors can also received detailed information related to topics such as "The Mosque", "The Caliph and the Crown Prince" or "The barber and the Hammams."

left: Situation_General view. right: Patio_Entrance_The "sunken" museum.

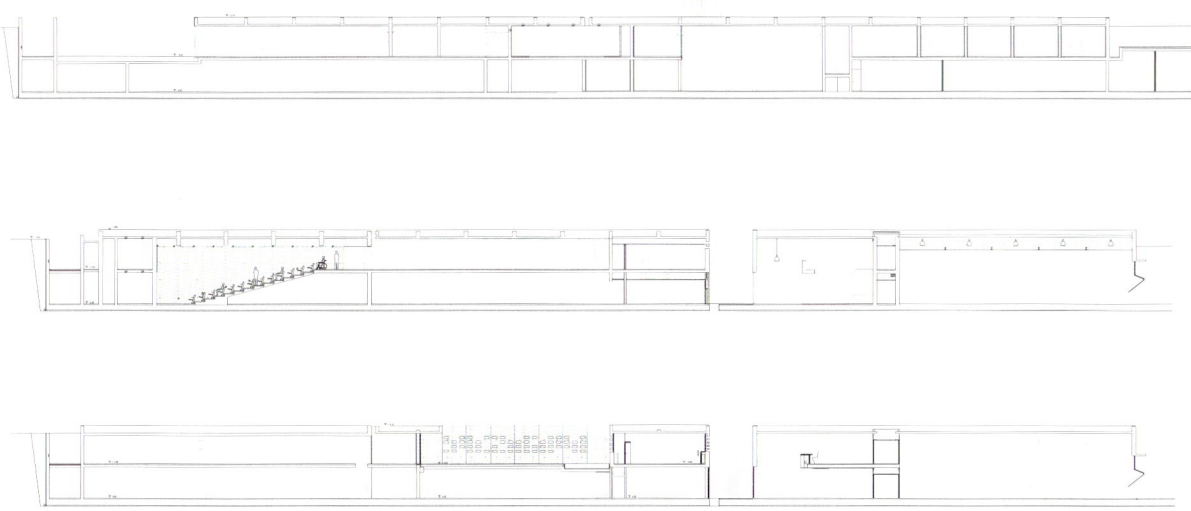

left: View over roofs. right: Sections_View from foyer to patio_Pool in patio.

SPAIN_CORUÑA **MUSEO NACIONAL DE CIENCIA Y TECNOLOGÍA**

ARCHITECTS: ACEBOXALONSO. ARCHITECTS_**COMPLETION:** 2010
TYPE: SCIENCE MUSEUM_**GROSS FLOOR AREA:** 6,000 M²
PHOTOS: HECTOR SANTOS, CORUÑA (360 B. L., 361),
ANGEL ALONSO + VICTORIA ACEBO, MADRID (360 B. R.)

THE ARCHITECTURE

This project combines two different functions — a dance school and a museum for which the architects designed a single volume. The basic shape contains the school while the outer section, in the space between the form and the limit, contains the museum. The architects changed the function of the dance school, turning it into the service area of the museum. The entire exhibition area space is structured in six different heights that can be perceived simultaneously. This space will operate as a versatile environment for many different activities. The roof is turned into a technical floor from which the space for each exhibition is adapted.

THE COLLECTION

The national museum for science and technology presents exhibits from the 16th century to the present time, representing the scientific and technological development starting with the Renaissance. The oldest collections are related to the development in Astronomy, Mathematics, Physics, and Geophysics. They include the cross-staff of Walterius Arsenius from 1563, the Astrolabe of Gemma Cornelli from the 17th century, and a telescope from Ramsden of the 18th century. In addition, a large number of surgery materials, a great selection of sun dials and a 19th century laboratory collection are shown. Another highlight is the industrial exhibition section, where all types of machinery, from a newspaper rotary printing press of the year 1916, to a large number of gramophones, telephones, typewriters, up to radio and television sets are presented.

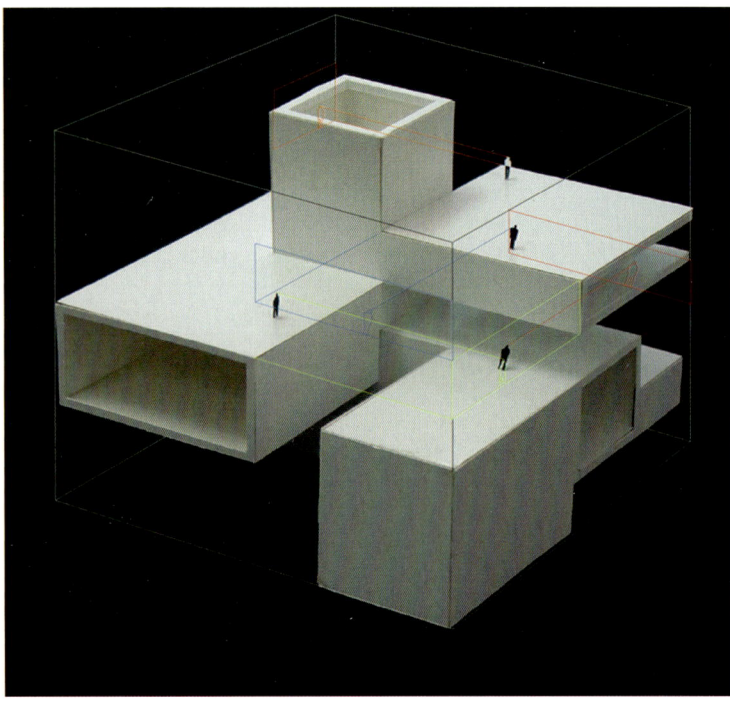

left: Concept model_Interior façade_Exterior. right: Exhibition space_Technical floor_Roof detail.

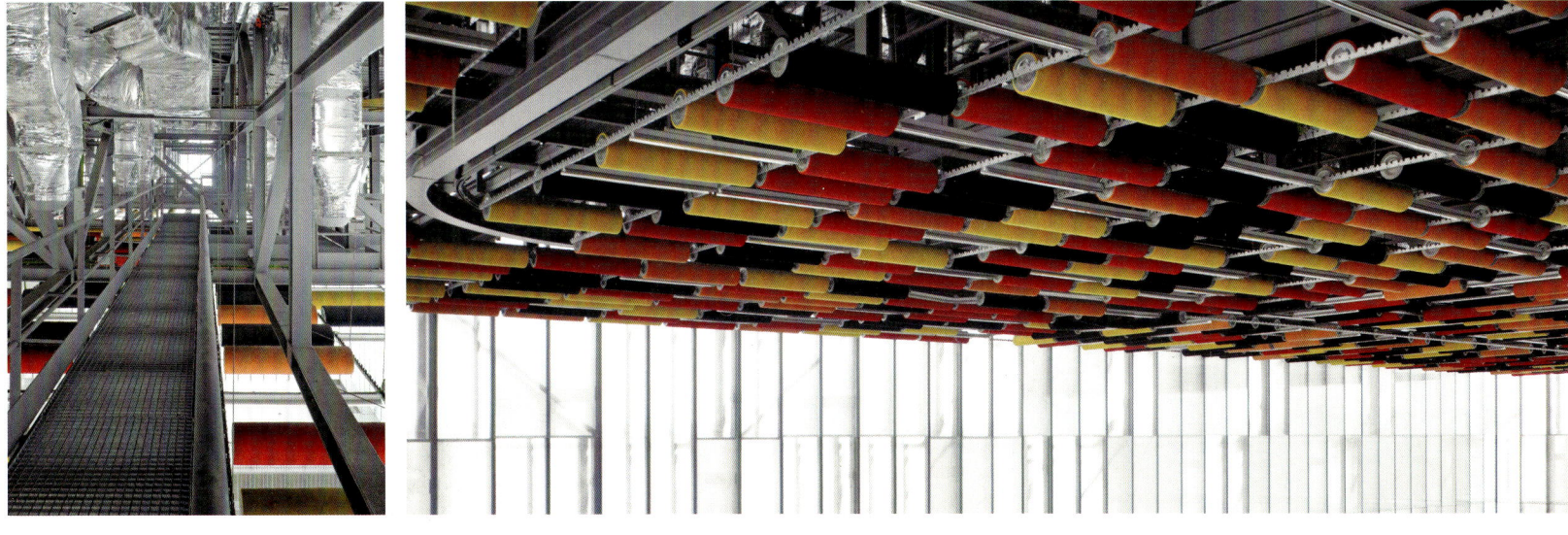

SPAIN_GRANADA **MUSEO MEMORIA DE ANDALUCÍA**

ARCHITECTS: ALBERTO CAMPO BAEZA_**COMPLETION:** 2009
TYPE: HISTORY MUSEUM_**GROSS FLOOR AREA:** 15,000 M²
PHOTOS: JAVIER CALLEJAS

THE ARCHITECTURE

This project compliments the central headquarters of the Caja Granada Savings Bank of 2001, by the same architects. A podium building, measuring 60 x 120 meters, is three stories high, so that its upper floor coincides with the podium of the main Caja Granada building. Everything is arranged around a central courtyard, in elliptical form in which circular ramps rise, connecting the three levels and creating a spatial tension. Like a gate to the city, a strong vertical piece emerges, the same height and width as the main building of the Caja Granada. To finish the entire operation, a large horizontal platform serves as a public space running all the way to the river.

THE COLLECTION

The Museo Memoria De Andalucía was opened in May 2009, and is the first museum dedicated to investigating the territory, history and culture of the area of Andalusia. The museum's exhibitions include interactive and audio-visual displays, which allow visitors to experience a glimpse of Andalusia's colorful past. Visitors to the museum are invited to choose their own route through the exhibitions, and are not guided by signs or plans. This open design was conceived to allow the visitors to select a route through the displays by viewing the exhibits or aspects of past history that interests them most. The museum's primary goal is to create a place where the Andalusian people can get to know their own history and identity as a group of people, exploring the natural diversity, as well as social and cultural development. The interactive nature of the museum's displays promote participation and exploration, rather than focusing solely on contemplative displays and presentations. The museum is divided into four separate rooms, which allow different paths depending on individual preferences and needs. Curators challenge visitor to "get to know Andalusia."

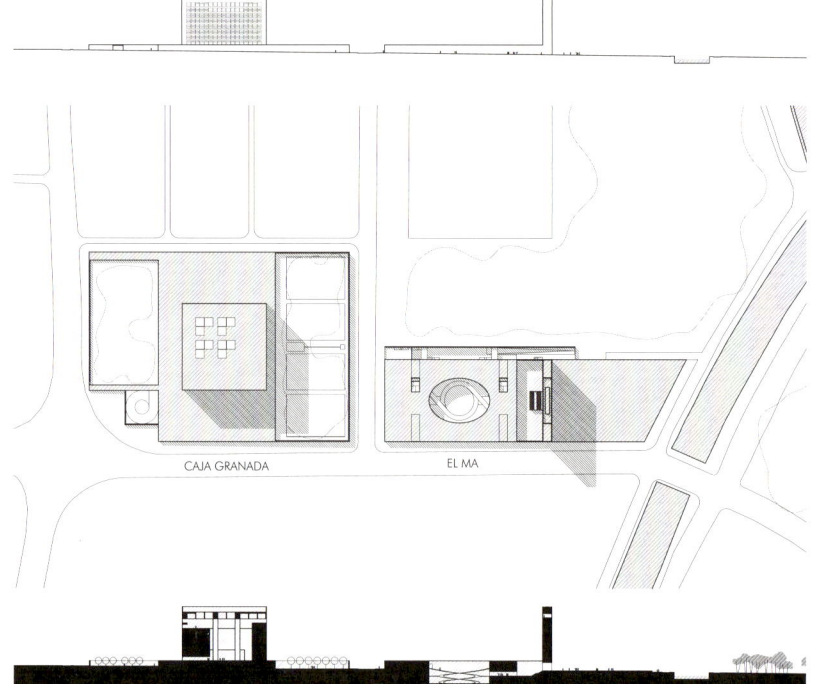

CAJA GRANADA   EL MA

left: Site plan_Bird's eye view_Frontal view. right: Elliptical courtyard.

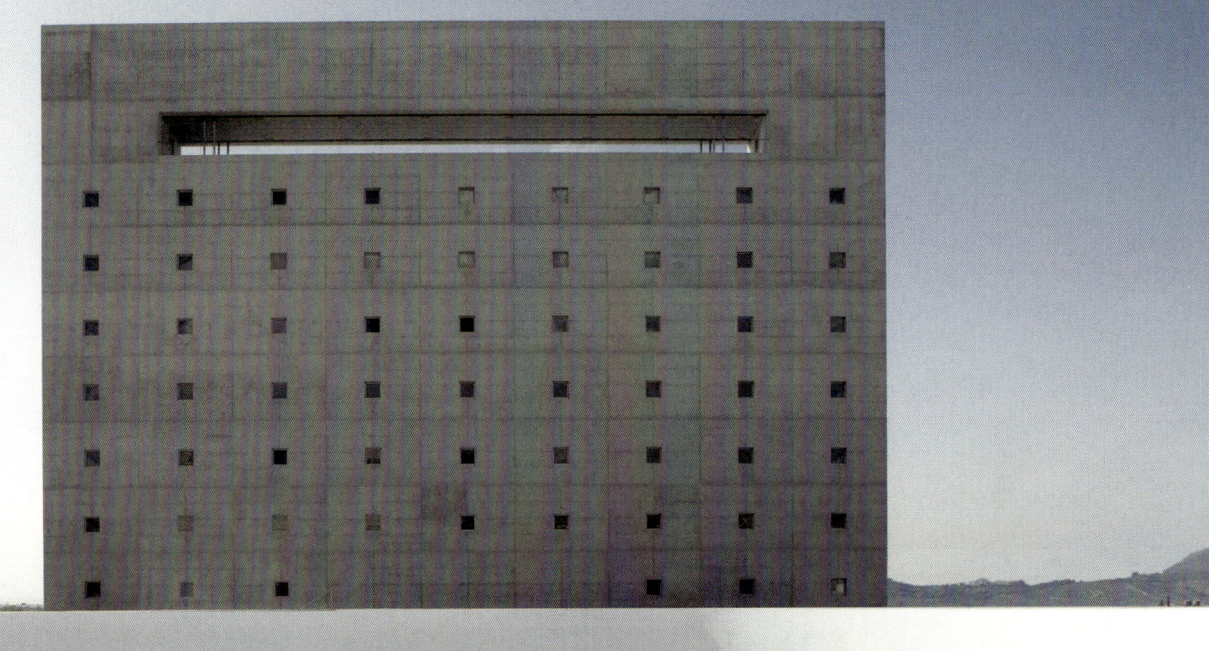

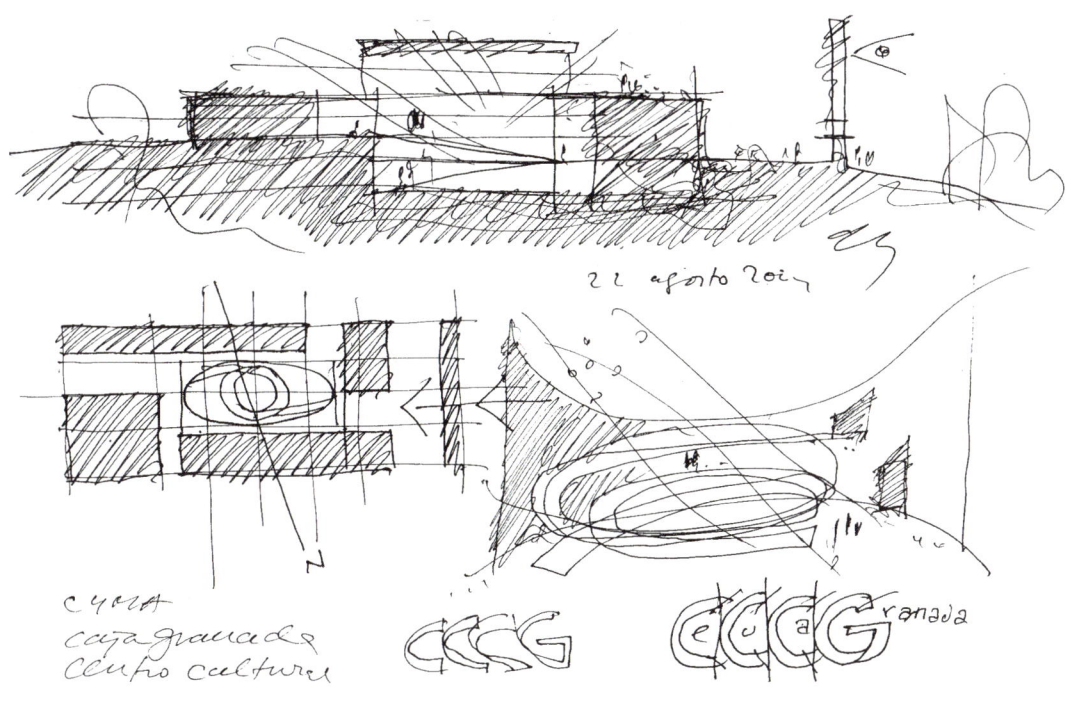

CYMA
caja granada
Centro cultural

left: Screen building. right: Sketch_Elliptical courtyard_Swinging ramps_Crossing of the ramps.

SPAIN_MADRID **MUSEO DEL PRADO**

ARCHITECTS: RAFAEL MONEO_**COMPLETION:** 2007_**ORIGINAL BUILDING:** JUAN DE VILLANUEVA, 1785_**TYPE:** ART MUSEUM_**GROSS FLOOR AREA:** 22,040 M² _**PHOTOS:** ROLAND HALBE / ARTURIMAGES

THE ARCHITECTURE

This property, containing the Jerónimos Cloister is used as a venue for temporary exhibitions, restoration workshops and technical offices, contained in a new building connected at its lower levels with the Villanueva building. This connection presumes the maximum occupation of the available lot on two levels. The restored cloister maintains its original position both in plan and section. Its ashlar masonry is protected by a concrete wall and crowned by a glass roof that will let natural light into all the spaces surrounding it. A large lantern in the center introduces light into the temporary exhibition rooms on the two floors immediately below the cloister.

THE COLLECTION

The building that now houses the Museo del Prado was designed based on the orders of Charles III in 1785 to house the National History Cabinet. Despite this, it was eventually decided that the building would instead house the Royal Museum, which later became known as the Museum del Prado. The museum was created with the purpose of demonstrating to the rest of Europe that Spain had artwork equal in quality of that of any other country. The first museum catalog was published in 1819 and was solely devoted to Spanish paintings. The royal collection forms the heart of the current collection of the museum but other works have also been added, increasing the museum's collection; for example, masterpieces like the two Majas by Goya. The royal collection started to increase in size in the 16th century, during the time of Charles V, and continued under the succeeding Habsburg and Bourbon monarchs. Since the beginning of the Museo del Prado, more than 2,300 paintings have been incorporated into its collection, along with a large number of sculptures, prints and drawings. The best known work on display at the museum is "Las Meninas" by Velázquez. Velázquez not only provided the Prado with his own works, but was also responsible for bringing much of the museum's fine collection of Italian masters to Spain.

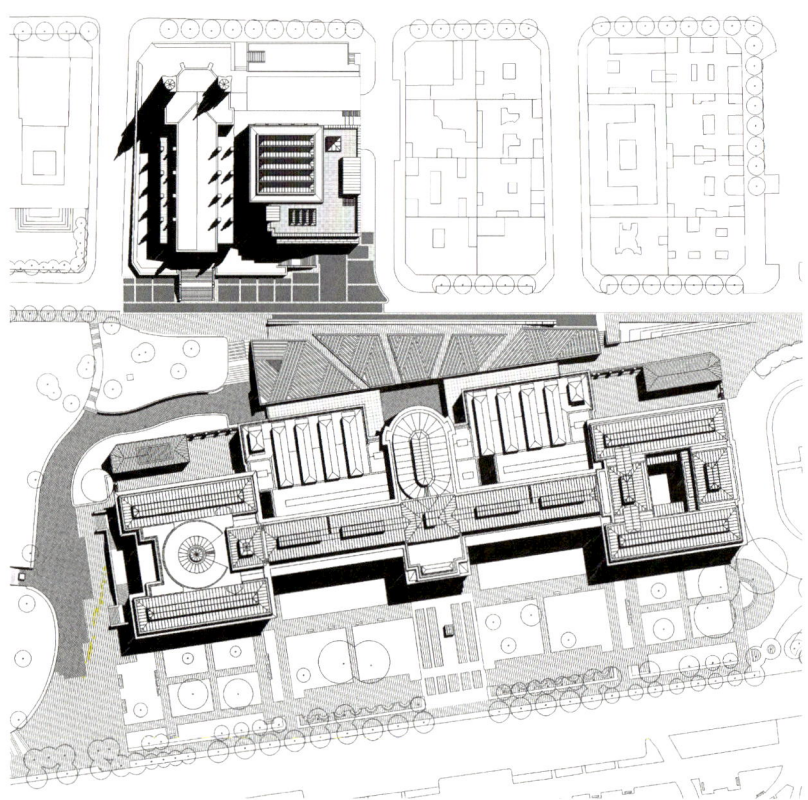

left: Situation_Entrance_Façade. right: Patio and view into the foyer.

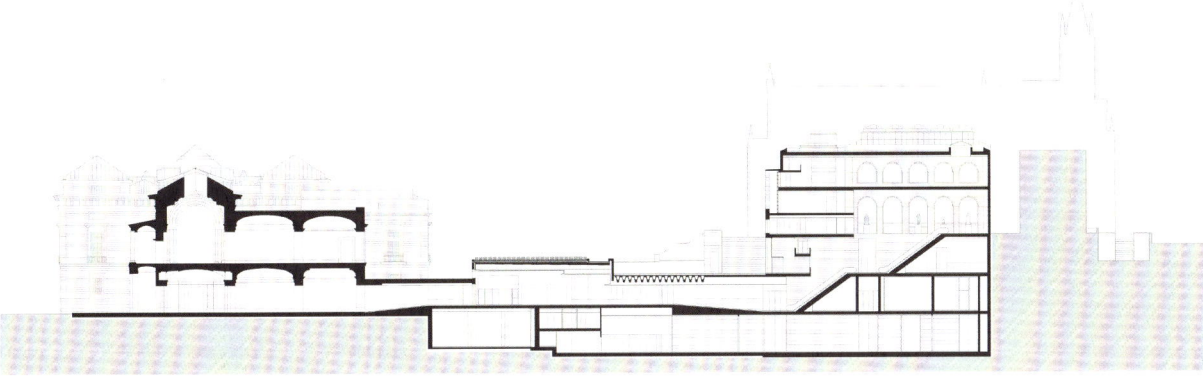

left: View into the cloisters with its lantern. right: Longitudinal section_In the cloisters_Hall of muses_Lantern into the exhibition.

SPAIN_MONTENMEDIO **NMAC – MUSEO MONTENMEDIO**

ARCHITECTS: ALBERTO CAMPO BAEZA_**COMPLETION:** ONGOING
TYPE: ART MUSEUM_**GROSS FLOOR AREA:** 2,000 M²
PHOTOS: COURTESY OF THE ARCHITECTS

THE ARCHITECTURE

The architects proposed an architectural concept of white walls that accentuate the design's horizontality. These walls follow a north-south axis that will serve as the recognizable basis of the building. The walls will be roofed to form spaces that accommodate cultural uses, such as exhibition galleries, a library, lecture hall and cafeteria. Some of these structures are single-story low buildings, while some are two-story, adapted to the slope of the terrain. At different points the earth will be excavated to provide greater vertical space where needed. The different areas include large courtyards with water and flowering vines.

THE COLLECTION

A contemporary art center that specializes in the relationship between art and nature, the Museo Montenmedio is run by the NMAC Foundation. The NMAC was conceived as an institution that would offer support to contemporary artists who are capable of creating specific projects to support and promote social dialogue and understanding, through art. The foundation invites artists from all over the world to undertake projects that can take the form of installations, sculptures, photography and architectural projects within nature. Each of the works produced maintains a close relationship with the surroundings. To date, more than 40 artists have taken part in NMAC projects. 20 of these projects are included in the museum's permanent collection, which is open to the general public. The foundation strives to offer visitors and artists a vision of contemporary art in which the natural landscape and social environment are strongly present. The entire creative process is implemented by local companies and technicians, who are personally directed through the construction stages by the artist. The foundation also puts a strong emphasis on education and teaching techniques. It hosts various activities, downloadable booklets, games and forums to encourage visitors to learn about everything related to contemporary art and the environment.

left: Site plan and section_Exhibition room_Library. right: Patio_Exterior_Café.

SPAIN_PEDROSA DE LA VEGA **VILLA ROMANA LA OLMEDA**

ARCHITECTS: PAREDES PEDROSA ARQUITECTOS_**COMPLETION:** 2009_**TYPE:** ARCHEOLOGY MUSEUM_**GROSS FLOOR AREA:** 7,130 M² _**PHOTOS:** ROLAND HALBE / ARTURIMAGES

THE ARCHITECTURE

The protection of an archeological find included a number of measures in which antiquities are confronted with modernity, and the finding site is confronted with the landscape. The project includes the construction of a roof for the excavations, the protection of the mosaics, and an exhibition and study center for tourists and archeologists. These built spaces are placed inside the archeological settlement as pavilions that do not interfere with the wide metallic roof covering the area. The mosaics are framed by a translucent perimeter of metal mesh that delineates the original layout of the rooms. A wooden raised floor runs through the area connecting the spaces and the display of the mosaics.

THE COLLECTION

The Roman Villa La Olmeda is located in the municipality of Pedrosa de la Vega, Spain. While the existence of this site was already known, it was not until the summer of 1968 that the importance of the remains was realized. The site was built in the 4th century and consists of 3,000 square meters, organized around a patio with four galleries, each decorated with mosaics. Two of these galleries access the villa through doors flanked by white marble columns and out of the 27 rooms, 12 have an underground heating system, demonstrating the former grandeur of this site. One of the most important rooms that has been excavated is the "Del Oecus", which is decorated with mosaics that depict the legend of Ulysses and Achilles. Since excavations on the area began, three cemeteries have been discovered on the outskirts of the village. The one situated to the northwest of the town is the oldest. Some of the remains are believed to date back to the 1st century AD and the cemetery was believed to have been in use until the 4th century. A second cemetery to the south has been the site of over 500 exhumations and finds have included items of clothing, knives, belts, necklaces and other items of jewelry.

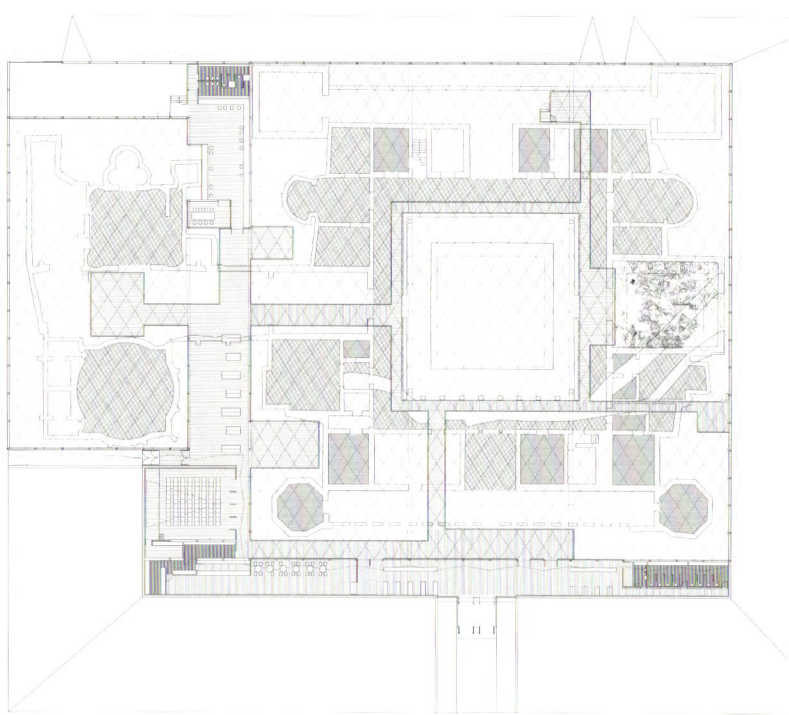

left: Floor plan_Entrance_Corner. right: Façade detail_Exterior.

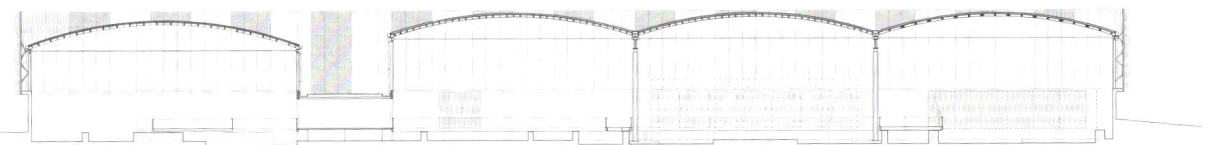

left: Metal curtains as room dividers. right: Section_View of the excavations_Long-span roof structure_Visitors walkways.

SPAIN_VALENCIA **CIUDAD DE LAS ARTES Y DE LAS CIENCIAS**

ARCHITECTS: SANTIAGO CALATRAVA ARCHITECT & ENGINEER
COMPLETION: 2004_**TYPE:** ART AND SCIENCE MUSEUM
GROSS FLOOR AREA: 42,000 M² _**PHOTOS:** © OLIVER SCHUH /
BARBARA BURG / WWW.PALLADIUM.DE

THE ARCHITECTURE

This site is located in the dry bed of the Turia River. The Opera House, Planetarium/IMAX Theater (Hemispheric Theater) and Príncipe Felipe Science Museum constitute a linear sequence from west to east. A fifth structure, "L'Umbracle," functions as both a promenade and parking garage, built within an open arcade. The Science Museum is 104 meters wide and 241 meters long. Five concrete "trees," organized in a row, branch out to support the connection between roof and façade, on a scale that permits the integration of service facilities and elevators. The white concrete, supporting framework of the southern façade is filled with glass, while the northern façade is a continuous glass-and-steel curtain along the building's full length.

THE COLLECTION

The Ciudad de las Artes y de la s Ciencias is an institution dedicated to scientific and cultural investigation. The complex is made up of five separate parts – the Hemisfèric, which contains an IMAX cinema and digital projections, the Umbracle, the Príncipe Felipe Science Museum, which is the heart of the museum's exhibition space, the Oceanográfico, which is the biggest aquarium in Europe and houses over 5,000 marine species, and the Palau de les Arts Reina Sofía. These five parts all serve different functions and work together to provide an ever-changing and enlightening experience. The Principe Felípe Science Museum has become a world renowned institution for interactive science and is one of the most visited museums in Spain, with over 23 million visitors since 2000. The main goal of the museum is to promote discovery and encourage curiosity through interactive learning and experimentation. The aquatic section of the museum houses species of marine life from all over the world. A main feature of this area of the museum is the dolphinarium, which contains 24 million liters of water and has a depth of over ten meters. The five separate exhibition spaces of the Oceanográfic feature exhibits from different aquatic environments, including the Mediterranean, the Arctic Ocean, the Red Sea and more.

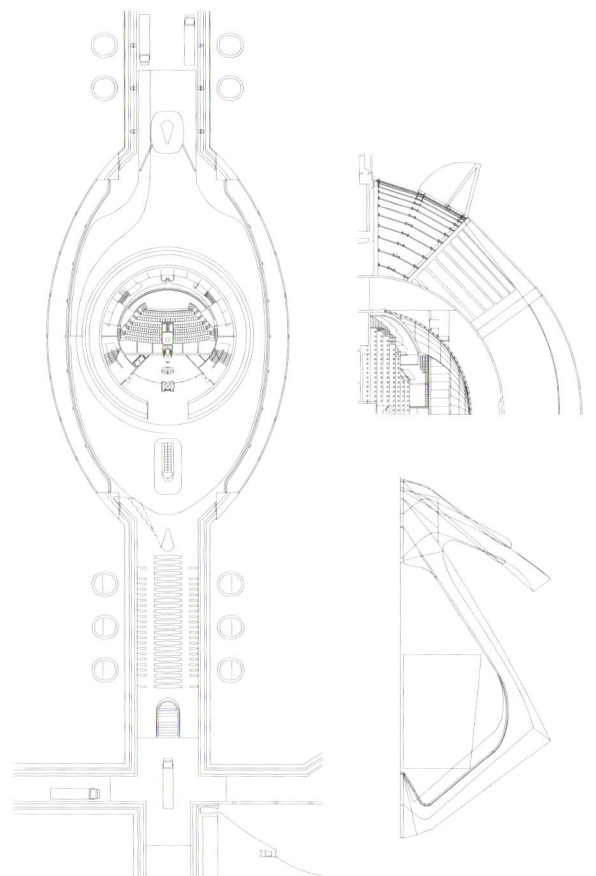

left: Floor plan Hemispheric Theater_Hemispheric Theater_Entrance Science Museum. right: Science Museum_Exhibition space_Treelike pillars.

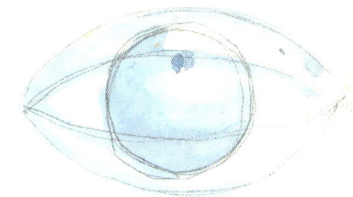

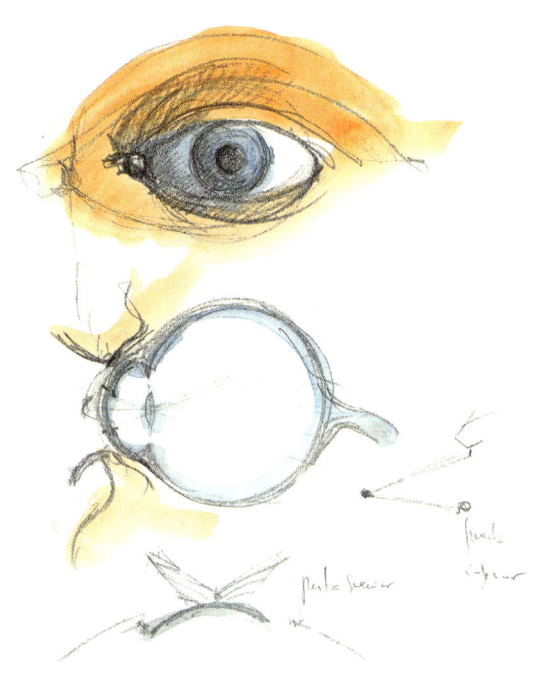

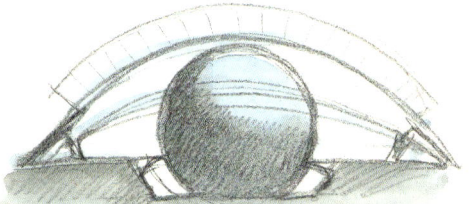

left: Façade. right: Sketch_Hemispheric Theater_Bird's eye view.

SPAIN_VIGO **MUSEO DO MAR DE GALICIA**

ARCHITECTS: CESAR PORTELA_**BASIC PROJECT:** ALDO ROSSI AND CESAR PORTELA_**COMPLETION:** 2002_**TYPE:** MARITIME MUSEUM **GROSS FLOOR AREA:** 10,463 M²_**PHOTOS:** EDUARDO MARTÍNEZ (380 B.), HISAO SUZUKI (381)

THE ARCHITECTURE

The Galicia Sea Museum consists of a peninsula or cape that is half natural and half man-made. It lies along the shoreline and incorporates the estuary into its design. It is defined, in part, by a perimeter wall and at times by the sea itself. A walk through the museum reveals gardens, buildings, patios, courtyards, passageways and piers, from terra firma to the water's edge. It is a movement from land to water without any sense of interruption. The entire project, consisting of two groups of vaulted galleries, connected by an elevated walkway, can function as an observation platform. Reflected by the granite, stucco and tile, the light creates ever-changing, geometric patterns on the polished wood floors.

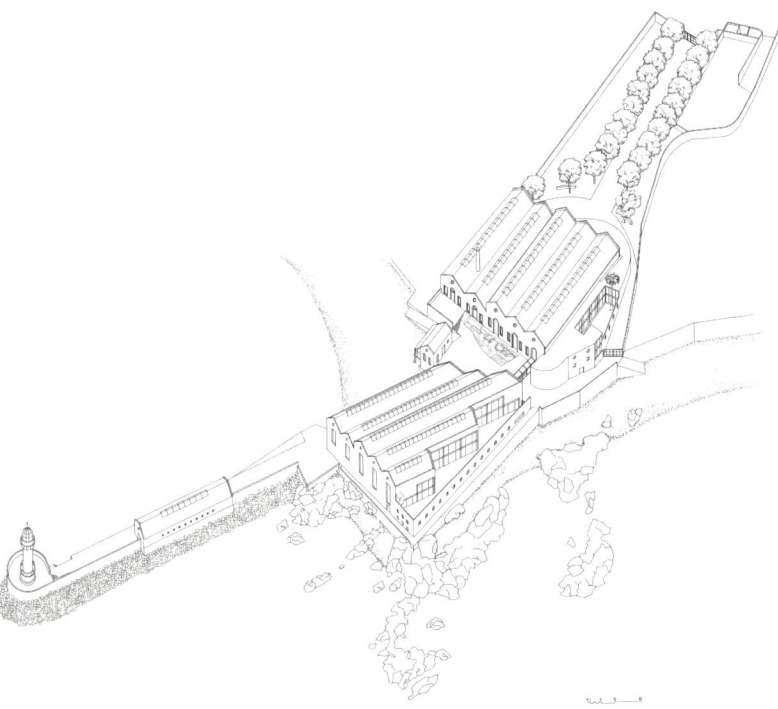

THE COLLECTION

The Museo do Mar de Galicia, (Museum of the Sea), houses a permanent exhibition, which is displayed by large illuminated cubes. Video and audio documents, as well as interactive screens and original objects related to the history of fisheries are on display. In addition to its permanent collection, the museum also hosts a range of temporary exhibitions and displays. Access to the museum's permanent collection is via a footbridge, the elevated position of which presents a good view of the general layout of the exhibition. The large illuminated cubes, set out like harbor containers, display objects relating to the relationship between the people of Galicia and the sea, while the displays include objects and information pertaining to the exploitation, preservation and marketing of natural marine resources. The exhibition is organized into a number of thematic areas, each area is linked to one of the essential pillars of the fisheries industry and is accompanied by a scientific section. The museum uses explanatory panels, video and audio documentaries, interactive screens and recorded documents to provide a wealth of information to accompany the exhibitions. There are also displays relating to the descriptions of both shellfish and octopus-related capture activities, which inform visitors about the harvesting processes of these creatures.

left: Axonometry_General view. right: Courtyard_Exhibition space_Aquarium.

SPAIN_VITORIA-GASTEIZ **MUSEO DE ARQUEOLOGÍA DE ÁLAVA**

ARCHITECTS: FRANCISCO MANGADO_**COMPLETION:** 2009
TYPE: ARCHEOLOGY MUSEUM_**GROSS FLOOR AREA:** 6,000 M²
PHOTOS: ROLAND HALBE / ARTURIMAGES

THE ARCHITECTURE
This building adjoins the Palace of Bendaña, currently the museum of Naipes Fournier. Access to the building is through the same courtyard that leads to the palace. Because of the slope of the terrain, the courtyard is accessed via a bridge over a garden that lets light into the lower areas, which would otherwise have no natural illumination on this side. In the permanent exhibition halls, all horizontal surfaces are dark, the wooden floors are almost black, and the continuous ceilings are black. However, the exhibition pieces are organized around white glazed prisms which draw light in from the roof during daytime.

THE COLLECTION
The Museo de Arqueología de Álava is one part of a new cultural facility, which houses Álava's Fournier Museum of Playing Cards and Álava's Archeological Museum. The two museums are situated in close proximity to each other, in the very heart of Victoria-Gasteiz's historic town. The building that houses the archeological display has 4,200 square meters of floor space, spread across four floors and two basements. The permanent exhibition of Álava's Archeology Museum displays around 1,500 items, covering the period from Álava's prehistoric origins to the Middle Ages. The museum houses the oldest existing evidence of Álava's history. The first floor is devoted to exploring the archeological methods and different historic periods, dating from the Palaeolithic to the Bronze Age, allowing visitors to explore the area's history throughout the ages. The second floor presents the developments in the region during the Iron Age and showcases objects and tools from different villages, telling the story of domestic life and the culture of that time, as well as documenting changes in trend and culture as the years progressed towards the present day. In the third hall, objects from Roman times and the middle ages occupy the displays.

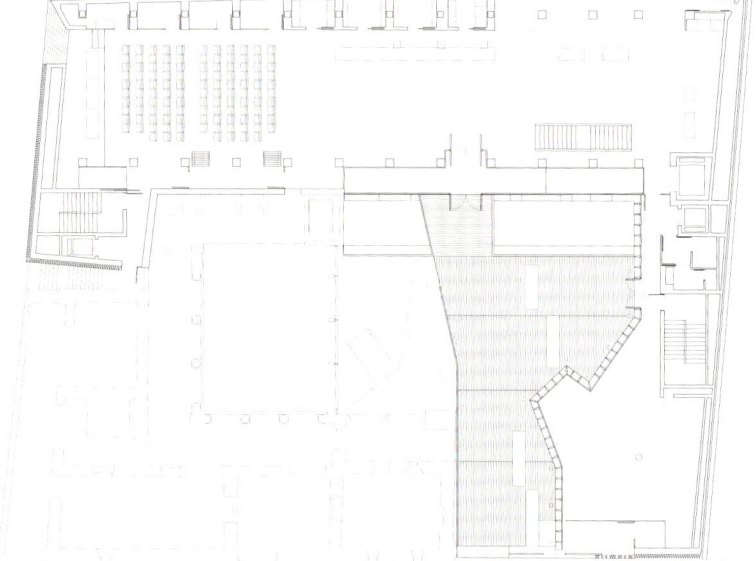

left: Ground floor plan_Façades defining the courtyard_Night view. right: Exterior.

left: Staircase next to the courtyard façade. right: Sketch_Brazen façade_Glazed prisms in the exhibition_General view.

SWEDEN_GOTHENBURG **VÄRLDSKULTURMUSEET**

ARCHITECTS: BRISAC GONZALEZ_**COMPLETION:** 2004
TYPE: CULTURE MUSEUM_**GROSS FLOOR AREA:**
10,950 M² **PHOTOS:** HÉLÈNE BINET

THE ARCHITECTURE

This museum provides a new public platform for the ethnographic collections of Sweden. It also serves as a new forum for international and local events. Situated at the foot of a hill in the city center, the museum incorporates an auditorium, research center, library, seminar rooms, restaurant and administrative offices. The design strategy revolved around creating a clearly marked difference between a solid west wing, containing the gallery spaces and offices along the street, and an open east wing, facing towards the hill, where public activities take place. Between the solid west and the open east is a canyon-like zone containing the building services, with public circulation weaving its way through all three areas.

THE COLLECTION

The documents and collections of many researchers and travelers laid the foundation for today's collection of the museum. Initially, the collection consisted of unrelated objects, photos and archives, which had been given to the museum by sailors, officers, and other travelers. It was not until 1913 that the then director Erland Nordenskiöld introduced a system and order. After he assumed his post, he embarked on an extensive journey to Bolivia, Peru and Ecuador, returning with more than 4,000 objects that established the museum's focus on Latin American culture. In addition, the museum today also contains valuable collections from Africa and Asia that present information about the various cultures and religions, pointing out cultural history and ethnographic problems. At the same time, the exhibition always maintains a link to the present. The building thus functions as a meeting place of individuals from various backgrounds that raises controversial issues and gives new food for thought. The objects on display are not only exhibited in the museum, but are also available for scientific research.

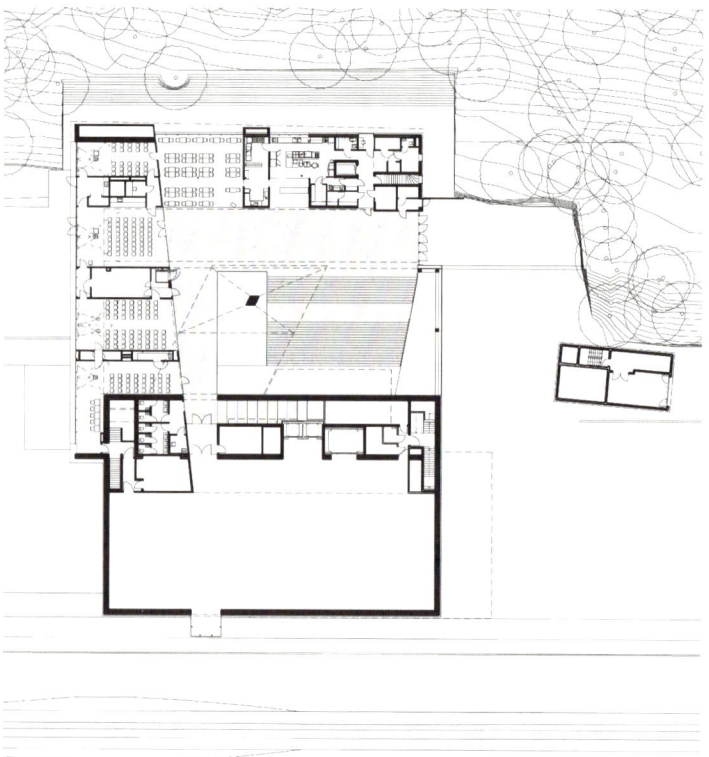

left: Second floor plan_Main hall_Atrium wall. right: Entrance_Exterior_East elevation.

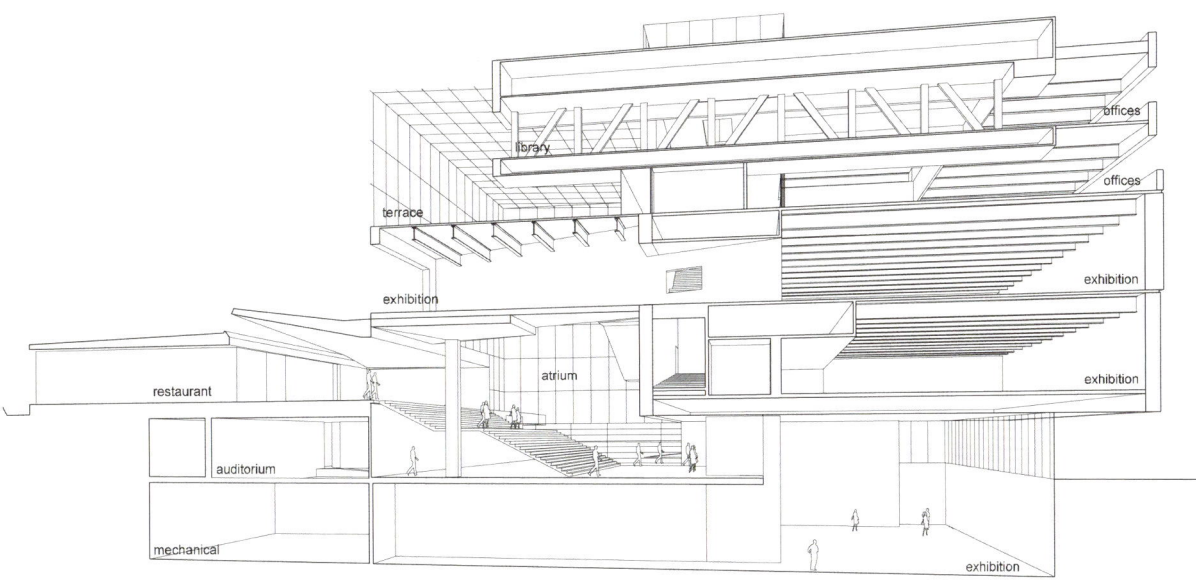

offices
offices
library
terrace
exhibition
exhibition
exhibition
restaurant
atrium
auditorium
mechanical
exhibition

left: Sunken exhibition space. right: Section_Terrace_Gallery_Restaurant.

SWEDEN_KALMAR **KALMAR KONSTMUSEUM**

ARCHITECTS: THAM & VIDEGÅRD ARKITEKTER
COMPLETION: 2008_**TYPE:** ART MUSEUM_**GROSS FLOOR**
AREA: 1,600 M² _**PHOTOS:** ÅKE E:SON LINDMAN

THE ARCHITECTURE
Situated in the city park of the renaissance town of Kalmar, the art museum is located next to a restaurant dating from the 1930s. The brief called for a platform and the plan includes a series of open platforms for art-related activities. The museum is constructed with large spans for maximum flexibility on each level, allowing light and space to be transformed and adjusted to meet the specific needs of each exhibit. The four floors, each with a different style, are stacked on top of each other and create a vertical walk up into the greenery of the trees offering different experiences and views of the surroundings — Kalmar castle, the lake and the city center.

THE COLLECTION
The Kalmar Art Association was established in 1917 and created the basis of its collection from purchases and donations. In the year 1942 the museum moved to the former hospital building in Slottsvägen. Subsequently, plans were made for another move as well as the renovation and extension of the exhibition spaces, but it was not until the year 2004 that it was decided to build a new museum building in the central park. In 1978, the "Arkiv för Svensk Formgivning" was established, which purchased the design sketches of artist Arthur Percy – the first of today's more than 100,000 works contained in the design sketches collection. The museum today presents a collection of more than 3,250 works in three major categories — Swedish Romanticism and Modernism, Kalmar regional art, and contemporary art. Works of artists like Anders Zorn and Carl Larssonder reflect the artistic evolution of Swedish Romanticism and Modernism in the 19th and 20th century. Also noteworthy in this respect is the collection of drawings and sketches of the Swedish artist Carl Wahlbom. Other currently active Swedish artists like Stig Sjölund, Alba Stefan Engström, Magnus Persson, and Hans Jörgen Johansen are represented in the contemporary Swedish collection.

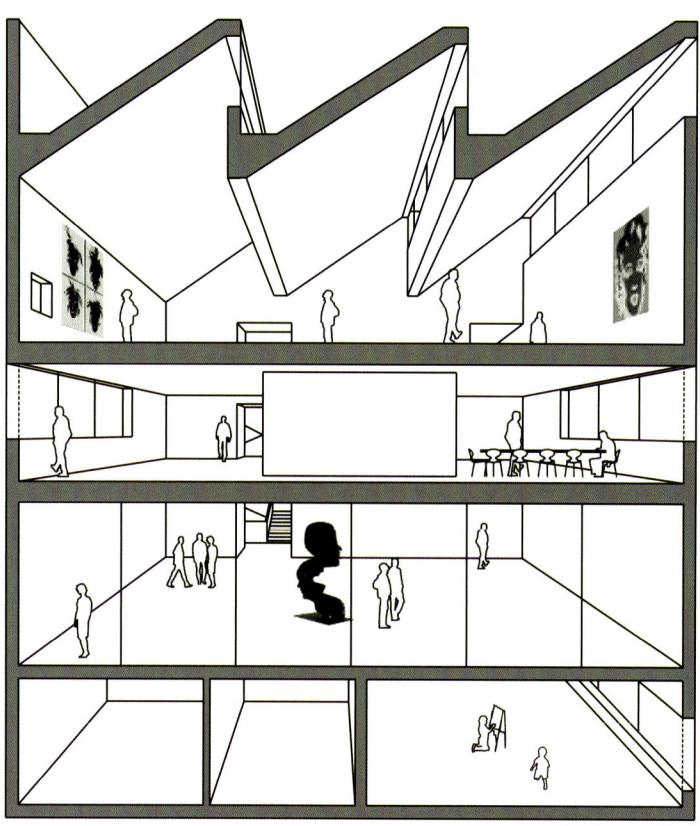

left: Section_Main façade_Stairs_Museum in its enviroment. right: Frontal view_View outside.

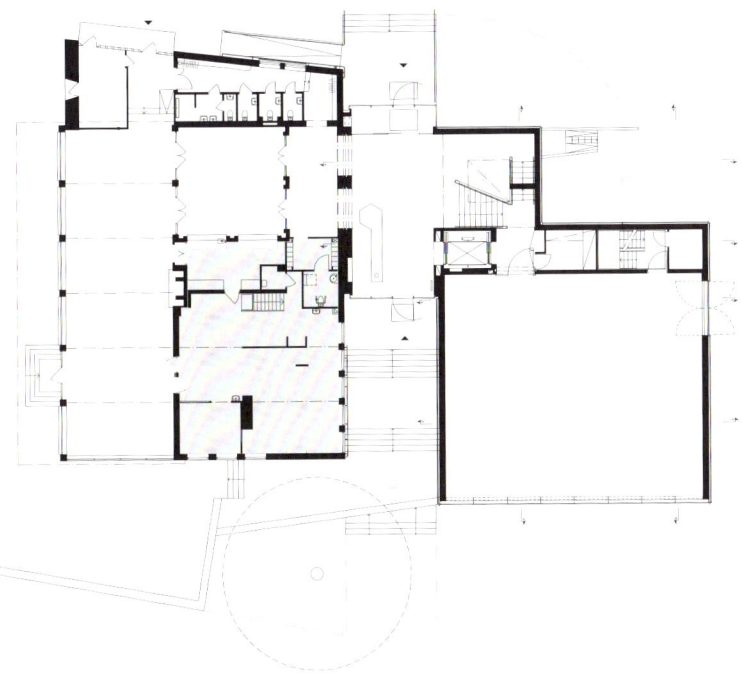

left: Edgewise view of exterior. right: Plan_Stairway_Shed-roof_View outside from stairs.

ARCHITECTS: THAM & VIDEGÅRD ARKITEKTER_**COMPLETION:** 2009
ORIGINAL BUILDING: 1900_**TYPE:** ART MUSEUM_**GROSS FLOOR
AREA:** 2,650 M²_**PHOTOS:** ÅKE E:SON LINDMAN, STOCKHOLM

THE ARCHITECTURE

A new art museum, a public and cultural building, was considered to represent a rare opportunity to create a new node within the city. The museum is located in a former electricity plant with a newly added extension. The new volume marks the arrival of the new museum in the city and houses the main entrance and reception space, as well as a cafeteria and a new upper gallery. Inside, the building was spatially reconstructed. Two new staircases allow the visitor to move in a loop between the grand turbine hall and the upper exhibition rooms.

THE COLLECTION

The museum contains one of the most valuable collections of art from 1900 to this day. It includes, for example, the main works of artists such as Marcel Duchamp, Louise Bourgeois, Pablo Picasso, Salvador Dalí and Henri Matisse, shown in the exhibition space. Immediately upon entering the museum, visitors are faced with the installation "Monogram" of the US artist Robert Rauschenberg. The collection also contains works of contemporary artists, such as contemporary films and videos that are shown in the new video aisle. The photographic collection contains works starting from the 1840s. Another focus of the museum is on Swedish artists, such as Vera Nilsson and Siri Derkert. In addition to the exhibited works of art, the museum also regularly organizes projects and events. One example is the project entitled "Zon Moderna", a cooperative effort to increase art appreciation among upper secondary school students. The "Malmö Gallery Night" is another event at which artist Mattias Kristersson carries out a performance for six hours in an empty turbine hall while visitors can simultaneously visit the permanent exhibition at night.

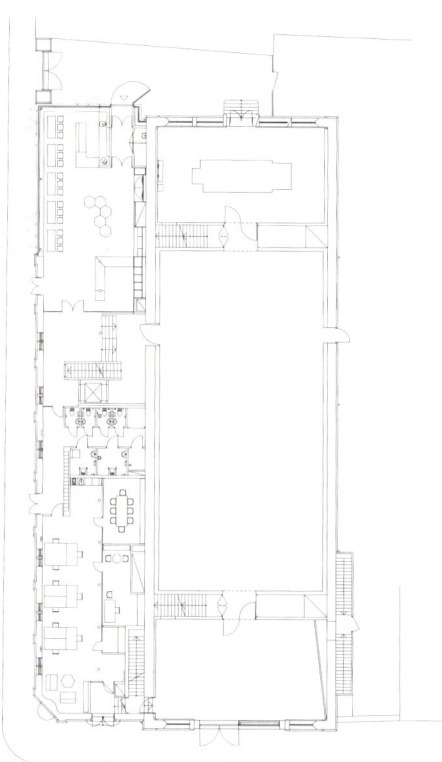

left: Ground floor plan_Exhibition room_Exhibition room, detail ceiling. right: Façade_Lettering name of museum.

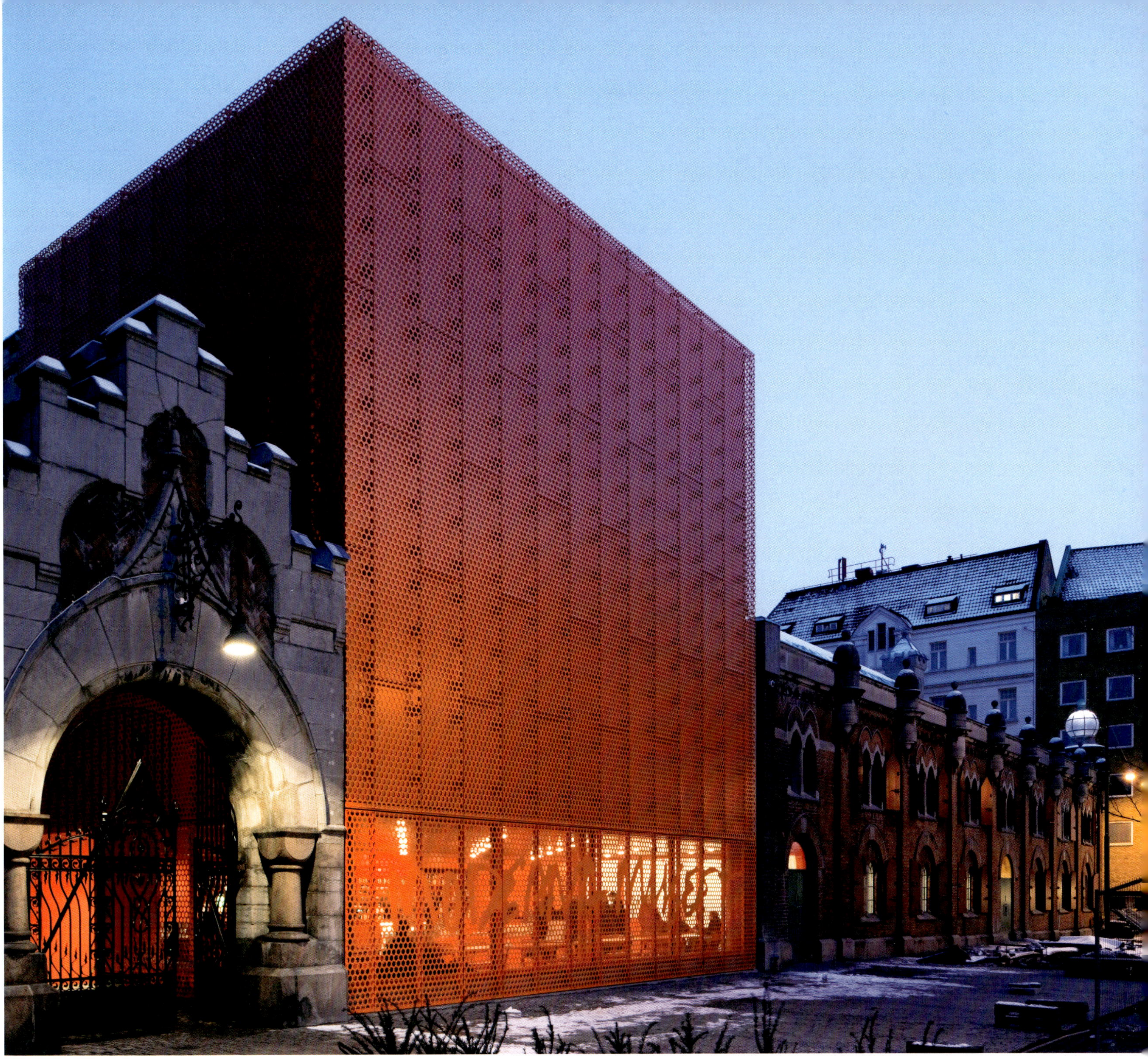

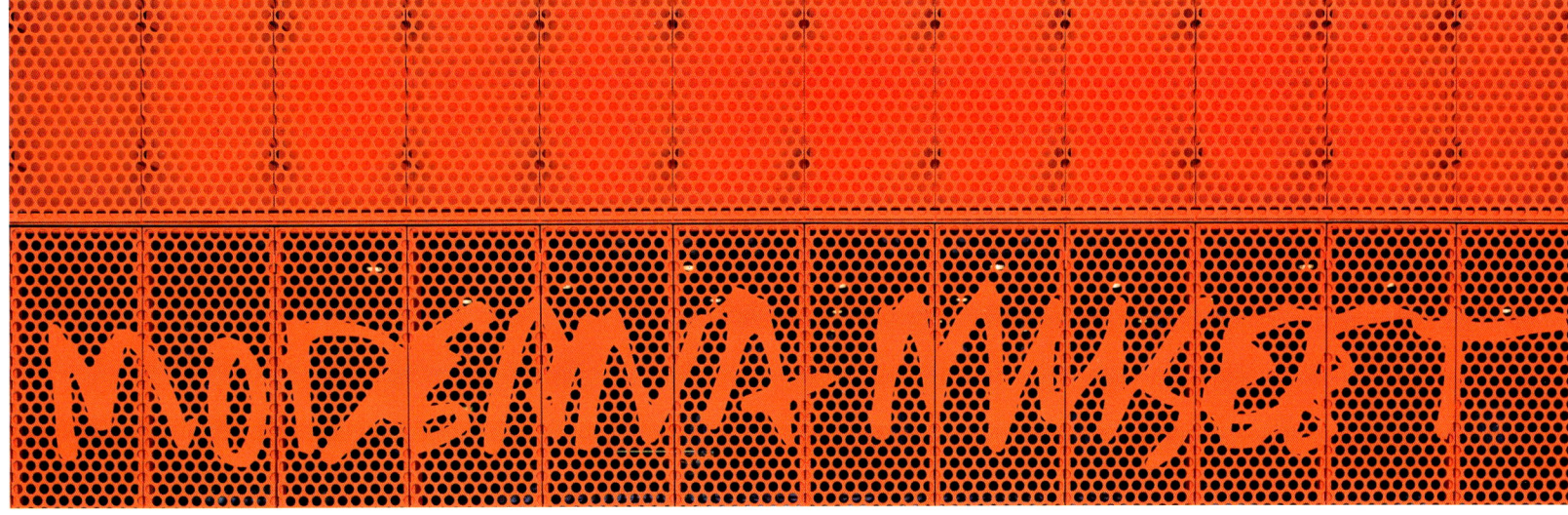

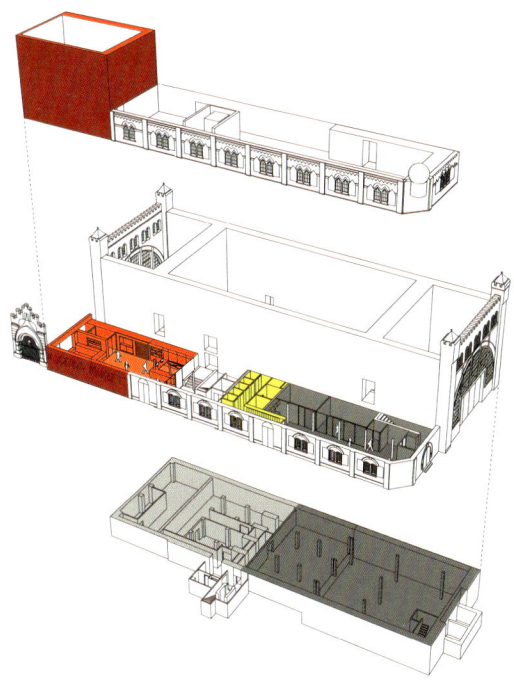

left: Machine hall. right: Exploded view drawing_Café_Entrance Café_Lettering name of museum from café.

ARCHITECTS: MILLER & MARANTA**_COMPLETION:** 2004
ORIGINAL BUILDING: JOHANN JACOB STEHLIN, 1872
TYPE: ART MUSEUM**_GROSS FLOOR AREA:** 1,680 M²
PHOTOS: COURTESY OF THE ARCHITECTS (399 B.),
KUNSTHALLE BASEL (398, 399 A.)

THE ARCHITECTURE

Commissioned by the Basler Kunstverein (Artist Association of Basel), the building complex, dating back to 1872, was renovated and matched to the requirements of contemporary art operations. The renovation incorporated the exhibition rooms, the restoration department, and the garden at the heart of the premises. The room climate and technical security of the exhibition areas were improved. At the same time, the wooden floors and the illumination were replaced. The first floor of the restoration section was refurbished. The Union Hall and bar constitute a unit once again. In the garden, the link between the back wing and the city cinema was improved and the open-air bar replaced.

THE COLLECTION

The Kunsthalle Basel offers temporary exhibitions, which are frequently updated. Current art is reflected upon by means of lectures, performance, and film screenings related to discussions of different viewpoints of contemporary art trends and practices. It was as early as 1840 that the idea of constructing an "Artists' House" was first considered by the city's Art Association. The museum was first opened in 1872, on behalf of the Basel Art Association, and was funded, in part, by a ferry service operated to transport passengers across the Rhine. Since this time the museum has become world renowned for exploring themes of contemporary art and aiming to expand the accepted boundaries of modern art. The institution was the first in Europe to introduce the "New American Painting" to its visitors, organizing a comprehensive presentation of such works in 1958. This open-minded approach to embracing new artistic trends led to its broadened perspective on art soon being embraced by other public art collections. The ground floor of the building offers exhibition halls for the museum's permanent collection and space for the library and conference rooms. The first floor is reserved for displaying temporary exhibitions, which have featured artwork by Van Gogh, Ernst Ludwig, Emil Nolde, and Edvard Munch.

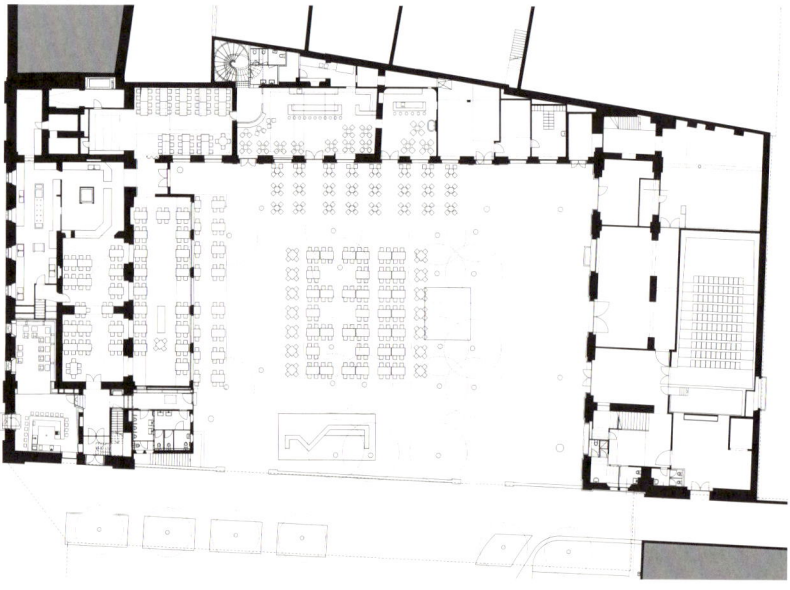

left: Ground floor plan_Exterior_Exhibition hall. right: Exhibition hall_Bar_Seating in the bar.

SWITZERLAND_BERNE **ZENTRUM PAUL KLEE**

ARCHITECTS: RENZO PIANO BUILDING WORKSHOP, ARCHITECTS WITH ARB, ARCHITECTS_**COMPLETION:** 2005_**TYPE:** ART MUSEUM_**GROSS FLOOR AREA:** 16,000 M²_**PHOTOS:** ENRICO CANO (400 B. R.), MICHEL DENANCÉ (400 B. L., 401)

THE ARCHITECTURE

At the heart of this new cultural institution is the artist Paul Klee (1879–1940), his life and his work. Featuring around 4,000 pieces of art, the center's collection is considered to be the largest collection of a single, world-famous artist. The architects devised the concept of creating a spacious island of green from which the architecture would emerge, in the form of three undulating waves. The three hills of steel and glass are divided into a programmatic structure, characterized by an interdisciplinary approach. In addition to generous exhibition space, the premises also include a state-of-the-art music and performance venue, a children's museum, a multifunctional promenade, and seminar rooms.

THE COLLECTION

The Zentrum Paul Klee opened in 2005 and is dedicated to collecting the works of artist Paul Klee. The museum is evolving into a world renowned center of excellence for the research and presentation of artist Paul Klee. Around 40 percent of the artists life's work is housed in the museum and the 4,000 exhibits comprise what is widely considered to be the largest collection of a single artist in the world. The museum presents many varied exhibitions relating to Paul Klee, including the "Rare Fruits" display. This exhibition is arranged in chronological order, with the first part focusing on Klee's landscape painting and then moving on to cover urban-centered works of art. "Klee Meets Picasso" is a representation of work by the two artists who are regarded as modern art's exact opposites. Picasso is said to have made an impression on Klee's work, as both artists worked in the same historical era. The museum also features both Klee's abstract work, and the artistic approach that characterized the Bauhaus era. Other notable features of the museum include an interactive children's museum, Creaviva, where children are engaged in activities that allow them to learn about art and its connection to the world.

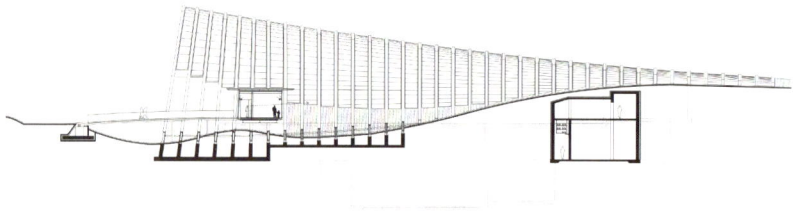

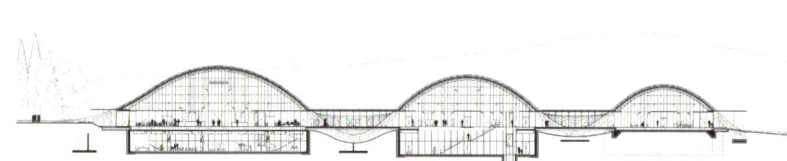

left: Sections_"Creativa" children's workshop_Exhibition room. right: Rollercoaster profiles of the archedsteel members_View from east.

SWITZERLAND_COLOGNY-GENÈVE **FONDATION MARTIN BODMER**

ARCHITECTS: STUDIO ARCHITETTO MARIO BOTTA WITH ARCHILAB_**COMPLETION:** 2003_**TYPE:** ART MUSEUM
GROSS FLOOR AREA: NET 1,280 M²; EXHIBITION AREA: 750 M²
PHOTOS: PINO MUSI, MILAN

THE ARCHITECTURE

The extension consists of a two-story underground construction between two classical-looking villas. The exceptional nature of the preserved documents suggested the idea of a buried presentation case with nothing emerging from the ground except five parallelepiped volumes made of glass, on a square base. They rise to about three-and-a-half meters and are aligned with the entrance like a set of perspective screens. These glassed in shapes rising from the ground act as skylights, letting natural light into the underground exhibition area. Their transparency and geometrical shape combine to change the perception of the space.

THE COLLECTION

Martin Bodmer (1899–1971) was a Swiss collector and patron of the arts. In 1921 he established the Gottfried Keller award. All through his life, Bodmer collected books and manuscripts. In the year 1928 he already purchased a former school building to contain his collection, which had become too large for Villa Freudenberg. In 1951, he moved together with his collection to Cologny near Geneva. He described his collection as a "library of global literature," with which he wanted to encompass "comprehensive humanity." The collection, containing 150,000 items, has been exhibited at the museum in Cologny since 2003. The collection contains manuscripts in 80 languages and from three millennia. They include rarities such as the oldest, almost completely preserved script of the Gospel according to John, the original version of the Grimm fairy tales, and Switzerland's only Gutenberg Bible. Other unique items include the only almost entirely preserved copy of a comedy of the Athenian writer Menandros, the autographs of a string quintet by Wolfgang Amadeus Mozart, as well as many first editions of valuable books.

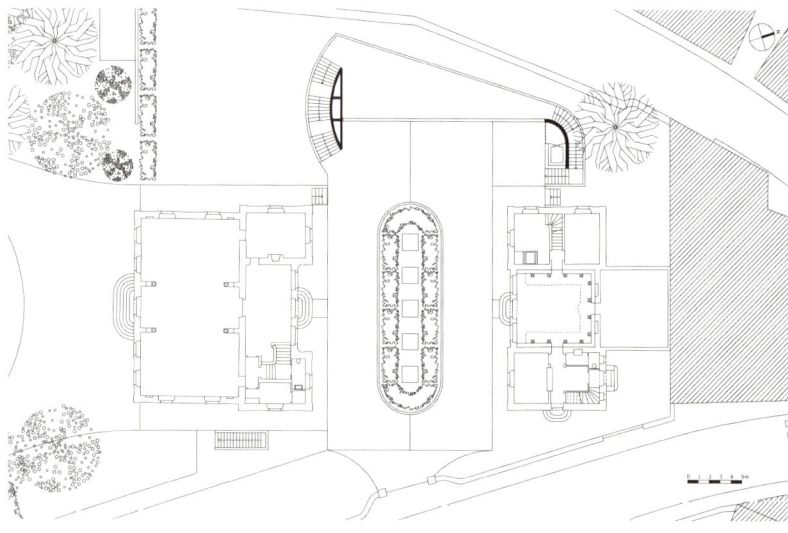

left: Site plan_Exterior view of the five parallelepiped volumes made of glass_Foyer. right: First floor underground, permanent exhibition_Second floor underground, permanent exhibition.

SWITZERLAND_LUCERNE **VERKEHRSHAUS DER SCHWEIZ**

ARCHITECTS: ANNETTE GIGON / MIKE GUYER, ARCHITEKTEN_**COMPLETION:** 2009_**TYPE:** CULTURE MUSEUM_**GROSS FLOOR AREA:** 10,553 M² _**PHOTOS:** LEONARDO FINOTTI (404 B. L., 406), HEINRICH HELFENSTEIN, ZURICH (405 A., B. L., 407), GIGON / GUYER (404 B. R., 405 B. R.)

THE ARCHITECTURE

The 1999 competition requirements included the gradual renewal of the Verkehrshaus premises with its various buildings for the different modes of transport and a new building for road traffic. In the first building phase, the road traffic hall and a new entrance building were constructed. The entrance building constitutes a bridge-like connection to the existing buildings, while the façades were designed as showcases for tires, propellers, wheel rims, etc. The new hall for road traffic is a two-floor, inexpensive multi-purpose black box with an automated parking system and recycled traffic signs as façade covers.

THE COLLECTION

The history of the Verkehrshaus goes back to the year 1897 and the expressed wish to establish a railroad museum in Switzerland. Initial attempts were implemented within the scope of the national exhibition of 1914, where various original objects related to railroad history were exhibited. Based on this collection, the Schweizerische Bundesbahnen (SBB – Swiss national railroads) opened the Schweizerische Eisenbahnmuseum in Zurich in 1918. In the ensuing period, the idea of a museum for transportation in general evolved and consequently, in 1942 the "Verein Verkehrshaus der Schweiz," with headquarters in Zurich, was established. As the city of Zurich was not able to provide suitable premises for the planned museum, the founders accepted the offer of the city of Lucerne of a site measuring 40,000 square meters as well as financial support for the construction that commenced in 1957. Two years later, the Verkehrshaus could be inaugurated. The range of exhibits related to the development of transportation has constantly expanded since that time. More than 3,000 exhibits inform about the history of individual means of transportation and their social ramifications. They include rarities such as Switzerland's first railway train (Spanisch-Brötli-Bahn), the first successful Swiss airplane (Dufaux biplane) or the oldest steam ship still in existence, the "Rigi" of 1848. In addition, the archives and warehouse of the museum contain more than 150,000 documents related to the history of transportation.

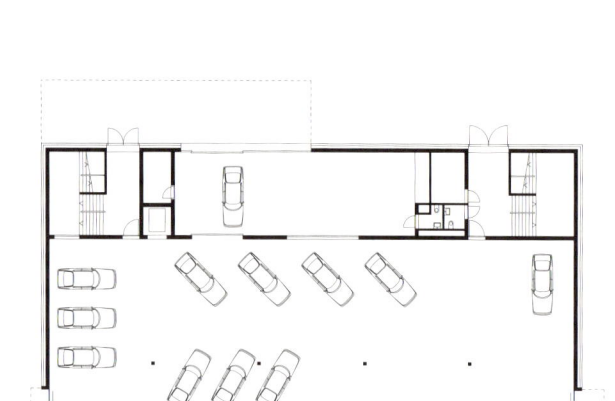

left: Ground floor of individual and street traffic hall_Blue façade, west_Green façade and rear of building, south-east. right: Hall, north-east_Space between buildings_Exhibition rack.

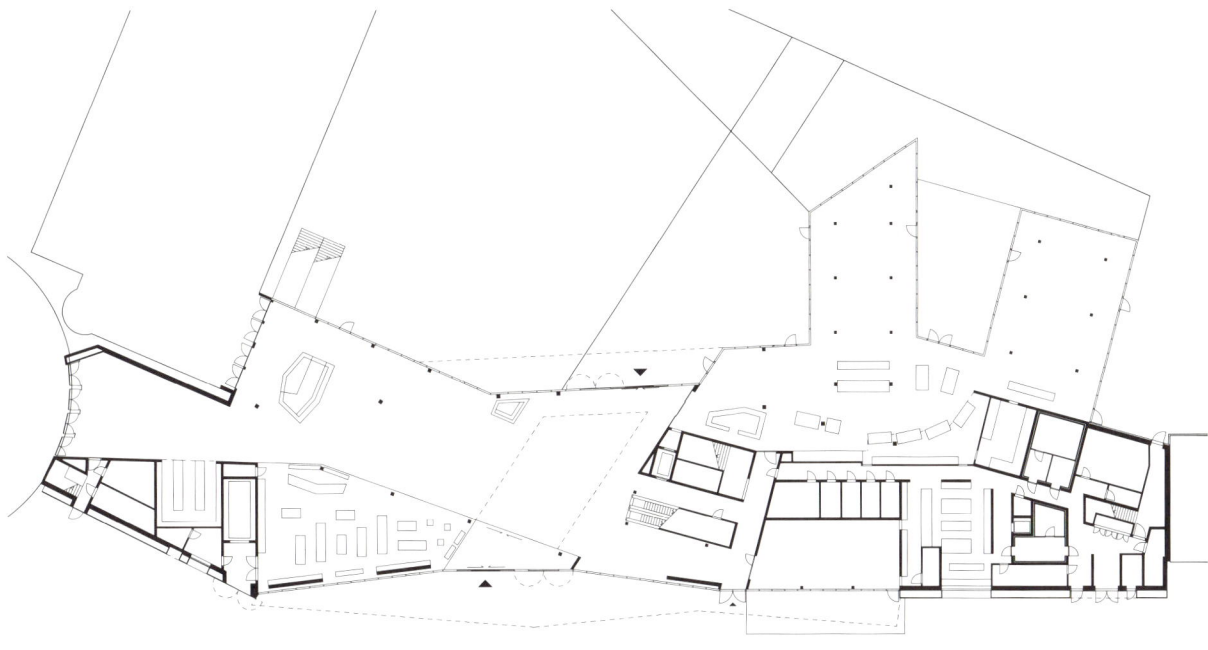

left: Detail showing the transparent façade of the building's entrance. right: Entrance on ground floor_View of outside_Façade.

SWITZERLAND_ZERNEZ **SCHWEIZERISCHES NATIONALPARK-ZENTRUM**

ARCHITECTS: VALERIO OLGIATI_**COMPLETION:** 2008_**TYPE:** NATURE MUSEUM_**GROSS FLOOR AREA:** 1,780 M²
PHOTOS: MIGUEL VERME, CHUR

THE ARCHITECTURE

From outside, the new Visitor's Center seems extremely unexceptional with its two cubes shuffled into each other. The bright in-situ concrete, the only material used for the building, contrasts with the natural surroundings. The inner spatial development of the three floors is the product of various antitheses — concealing and revealing, heaviness and lightness, regularity and irregularity. The exhibition rooms are all alike, connected by a hidden corridor and staircase systems. The broad windows are slightly more horizontal in format, creating an "observing" view of all directions from each room. The exhibition spaces, one room on each floor, can be completely blacked out.

THE COLLECTION

In a permanent exhibition extending across four rooms, visitors can discover the secrets of nature and receive information about ecological interactions. Natural processes, along with human influence and reliability on the landscape of the national park have left traces that can be discovered at the museum. In addition, visitors can watch video clips or the flight of the bearded vulture to gain extraordinary insights into the national park. In another part of the exhibition, impressive survival strategies of animals and plants are shown along with an overview of the founding fathers of the Swiss national park. Interesting questions, for example about the signet bird or why red deer first vanished from the region and returned to it subsequently are found throughout the exhibition rooms. In addition, the visitors' center contains another room that is used for changing special exhibitions. For example, from June 2010 to April 2011 it focused on the ibex —"ein wunderlich verwegenes Thier" ("a wonderfully daring animal").

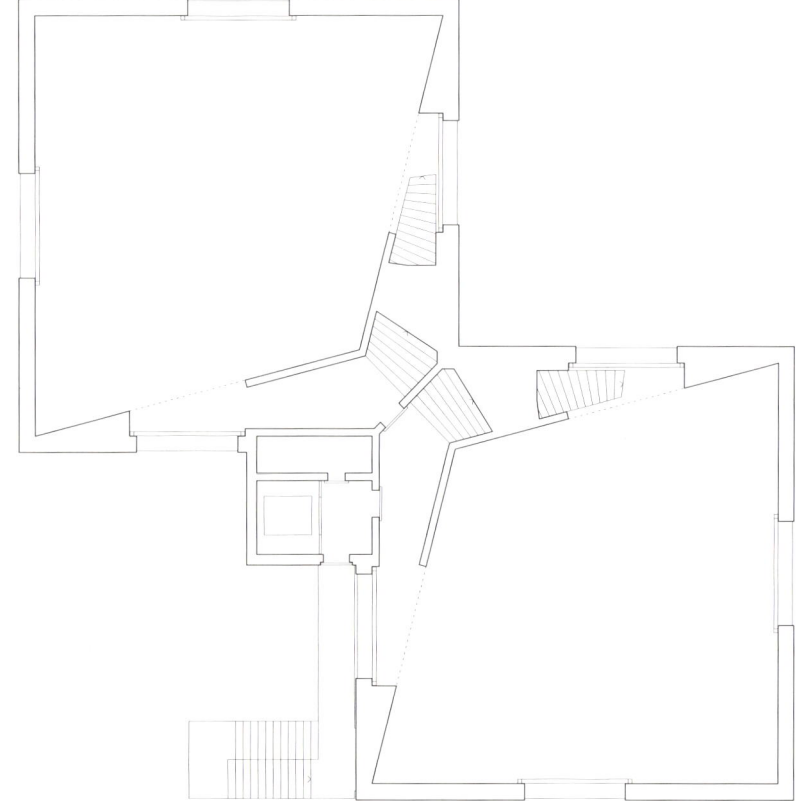

left: First floor plan_Split staircase_Entrance. right: Exterior view_Window bay_Exhibition room.

SWITZERLAND_ZURICH **MUSEUM RIETBERG**

ARCHITECTS: GRAZIOLI UND KRISCHANITZ ARCHITEKTEN
ARTIST: GILBERT BRETTERBAUER, HELMUT FEDERLE
COMPLETION: 2008_**ORIGINAL BUILDING:** VILLA WESENDONCK
BY LEONHARD ZEUGHEER, 1857_**TYPE:** CULTURE MUSEUM
GROSS FLOOR AREA: 5,350 M²_**PHOTOS:**
HEINRICH HELFENSTEIN, ZURICH (410 B. L., 411),
MARGHERITA SPILUTTINI, VIENNA (410 B. R.)

THE ARCHITECTURE

The glass building — in itself a symbol of visibility — provides a view inside the world of the museum. The entrance building of the underground expansion, which nearly doubles the ground floor area of the museum, provides a view of the old building of Villa Wesendonck. As a preliminary building for the actual exhibition area, and connecting to the neighboring event hall, it is a stylish and functional venue for a variety of uses. Its name, "Baldachine von Smaragd" ("canopies of emerald") alludes to a poem by Mathilde Wesendonck, which Richard Wagner set to music. Immediately connected to the glass house is a room level with descending stairs, elevator and mobile functional elements, such as pay decks, showcases and cloak rooms.

THE COLLECTION

In 1945, the city of Zurich purchased the Rieterpark and the Villa Wesendonck. Four years later, a popular vote decided the conversion of the villa into a museum for the collection of Baron Eduard von der Heydt (1882 – 1964), which was implemented in the years 1951 and 1952 by the architect Alfred Gradmann. In 1976, the city bought the Villa Schönberg, which was opened two years later as an annex to the museum. Today the museum is Switzerland's only museum exclusively dedicated to non-European cultures. It contains an international renowned collection of works from Asia, Africa, America, and Oceania. The museum collection was based on donations by Eduard von der Heydt and expanded over the years through the support of other collectors and patrons. For example, the African art collection features prominent work groups such as masks and figurines of the Ivory Coast, sculptures of Gabon's Fang region, and masks from the grasslands of Cameroon. The small collection of indigenous American art includes an in-depth look at Mexican art. For example, it includes a sculpture of a rattle snake from the Aztec era, which Alexander von Humboldt brought to Europe. In addition, the museum contains one of the world's most outstanding collections of Chinese arts, including a world-famous group of Buddhist stone sculptures of the 6th to the 9th century.

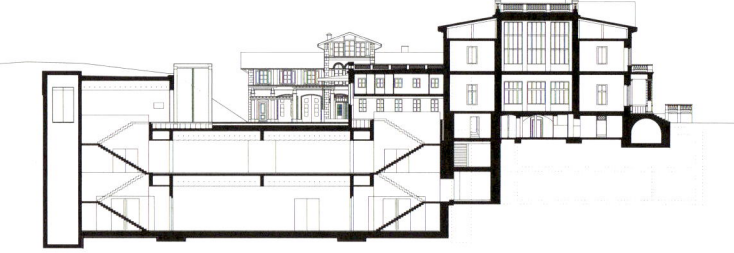

left: Section_Entrance to the new underground construction_Entrance area to the new building.
right: Exhibition room in new building_Museum shop.

THE NETHERLANDS_AMSTERDAM **STEDELIJK MUSEUM AMSTERDAM**

ARCHITECTS: BENTHEM CROUWEL ARCHITECTS_**COMPLETION:** 2011_**ORIGINAL BUILDING:** ADRIAAN W. WEISSMAN, 1895
TYPE: ART MUSEUM_**GROSS FLOOR AREA:** 26,484 M²
PHOTOS: COURTESY OF THE ARCHITECTS

THE ARCHITECTURE

The characteristic qualities of this building — its symmetrical layout with the central staircase and the monumental galleries — were preserved, as was the skylight, so typical of this museum. Moving the main entrance towards the Museumplein was the biggest change. Besides the entrance itself, the new addition will house the information center, library, museum shop, and restaurant. A large number of the new rooms, including Amsterdam's largest museum space (1,100 square meters) are underground. By adding both raised and underground spaces, the original building remains practically untouched and completely visible. A huge white cantilevering roof marks the spacious transparent entrance.

THE COLLECTION

Established in 1874, the urban museum moved in 1895 to the new brick building with the neo-Renaissance style behind the Rijksmuseum. Initially, it contained a very heterogeneous collection including, for example, also military items of the former militia groups, as well as medical and natural history objects. The regular exhibits of the "Association for the creation of a public collection of contemporary art," soon created the basis for the creation of an art museum. In the early 20th century, the museum also started to collect items itself and in 1934 the museum for applied contemporary art also moved into the building, establishing the second collection focusing on modern design. In the late 1950s it was the first Western European museum to set up an extensive collection of photographs. Focal areas within the collection of creative art are the De Stijl artist group and Russian constructivism, CoBrA, Pop art, and video art. The collection consists of approximately 90,000 items, with highlights such as The Beanery by Edward Kienholz (1965), Gerrit Rietveld's Red-blue Chair (1918), numerous works by Kazimir Malevitsch, and Barnett Newman's Who's Afraid of Red, Yellow and Blue III (1968). With its choice of new collections and the presentation of temporary exhibitions, the museum is one of the world's pioneering institutions in the area of modern and contemporary art.

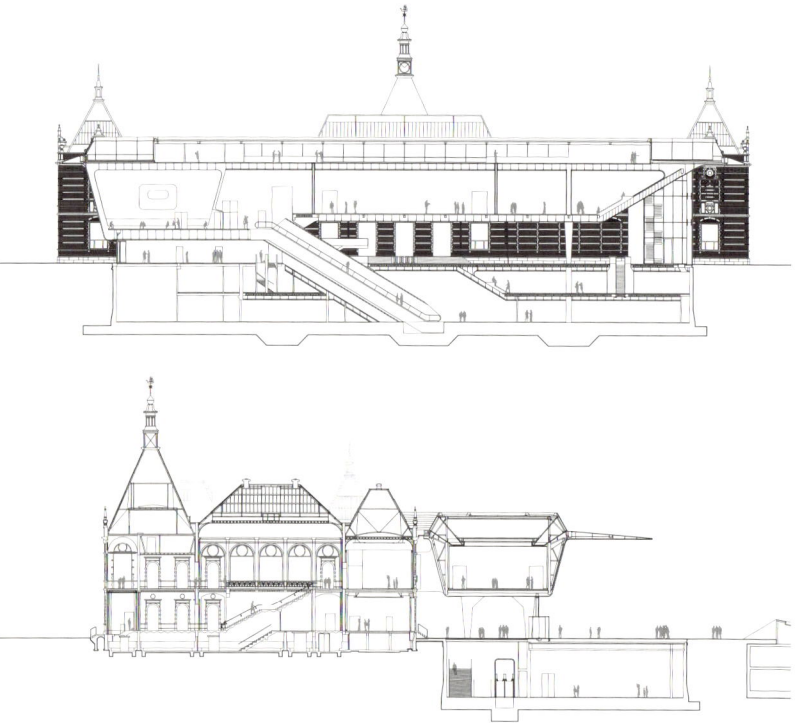

left: Sections_Entrance area. right: Exterior_Interior_Situation.

THE NETHERLANDS_AMSTERDAM

NIEUW RIJKSMUSEUM AMSTERDAM

ARCHITECTS: CRUZ Y ORTIZ ARQUITECTOS_**COMPLETION:** 2013
ORIGINAL BUILDING: PIERRE CUYPERS, 1885_**TYPE:** ART MUSEUM
GROSS FLOOR AREA: 39,000 M²_**PHOTOS:** CRUZ Y ORTIZ
ARQUITECTOS / SEVILLA (414 B. L., 415 A.), DUCCIO MALAGAMBA,
BARCELONA (414 B. R., 415 B.)

THE ARCHITECTURE

This museum building was designed in the 19th century as a connecting element between the existing city and the newer southern developments. A walkway runs through the building, splitting it into two parts. The New Rijksmuseum interventions use this central axis as a natural point of access by clearing the ancient courtyards. Additional space is located in various external pavilions. The new atelier building of the Rijksmuseum in its immediate vicinity has been elaborated with a similar functional effectiveness and style. With its unique façade, it presents itself as a mark between, and in connection with, original villas and urban structures.

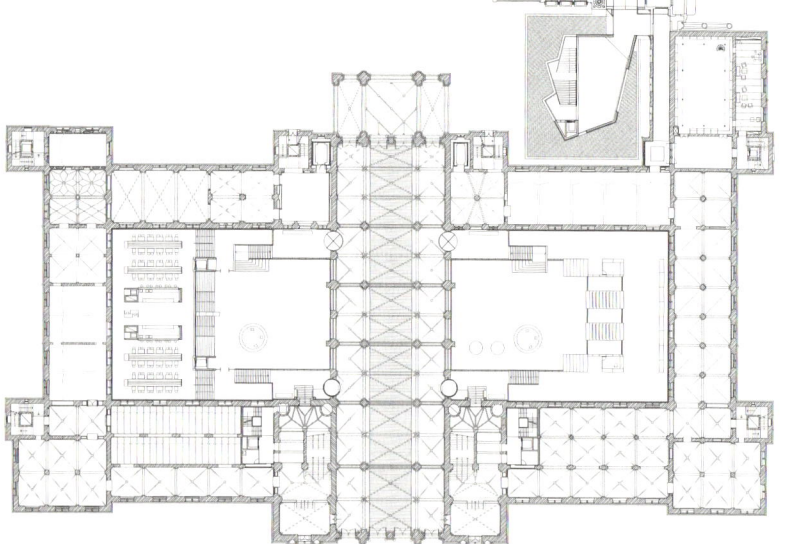

THE COLLECTION

The Netherland's largest and most prominent museum provides an overview of the art and history of the country in more than 200 exhibition halls. The building also houses the national museum for graphic arts and prints. Its more than one million collection items include many masterpieces, especially from the 17th century, the Netherland's "golden century." The many precious pieces of this era include Rembrandt's famous painting "Night Watch" (1642), which is presented in its own hall in conjunction with other group depictions of Amsterdam militiamen of the same era, allowing visitors to conduct their own stylistic comparisons with other painters. The current collection of the museum emerged from the art collection of the city administrators that were confiscated by the Batavian Republic and the bigger part moved to Paris. In 1798 it was decided to erect a national museum for the remaining pieces in Den Haag resembling the style of the Louvre. In 1808, under Ludwig Napoleon, the museum moved to the former city hall, today's palace, in Amsterdam where it was combined with the city collection, including the Night Watch painting. The current museum building was constructed in 1885.

left: Ground floor plan_Central axis_Atelier junction with Villa, façade west. right: Cleared eastern courtyard_Inner view of ateliers_View from atelier building to the old building.

THE NETHERLANDS_APELDOORN **CODA MUSEUM**

ARCHITECTS: ARCHITECTUURSTUDIO HH_**COMPLETION:** 2004
TYPE: ART MUSEUM_**GROSS FLOOR AREA:** 9,000 M² _**PHOTOS:**
HERMAN HERTZBERGER (416 B. L., 417 B.),
HERMAN VAN DOORN (416 B. R., 417 A.)

THE ARCHITECTURE

The existing "House for Fine Arts" is enclosed in an area resembling a court-yard. The front stairs of this fine-arts house were drawn into an undulating indoor landscape covering the museum space below. Entirely without fixed walls, the large museum space is for the most part sunk beneath the court-yard where its curved roof creates a rippling street surface. CODA — "Culture under roof" — features, besides the museum, a public library-extension plus the municipal archives, with a reading room, offices, study spaces and a restaurant. All these components are visible from the outside through fully-glazed skin, which stresses their accessibility and provides a view of them from the courtyard.

THE COLLECTION

The Collection of Contemporary and Modern Art Museum specializes in jewelry and paper art. The foundation of the museum's collection was first de-veloped by the former Van Reekum Museum and encompasses several fields of interest, including paintings, sculptures, graphic art from both Dutch and international artists, and a large jewelry collection. The CODA museum has since added various items to the initial collection, but focuses on two major areas, namely works of art in which paper plays a major role and contem-porary jewelry design. The jewelry collection has been expanded and linked with the paper art displays, by the installment of a paper-jewelry section. The range has also been broadened by the "jewelry with a story" exhibition that aims to breathe new life into old and forgotten traditions. The jewelry collec-tion spans from approximately 1960 until present. Along with Dutch jewelry, the collection documents experimental movements from abroad. Young designers are also supported by the museum. The CODA museum collects, edits, and explores archives of jewelry designers in order to build up a knowl-edge center on jewelry.

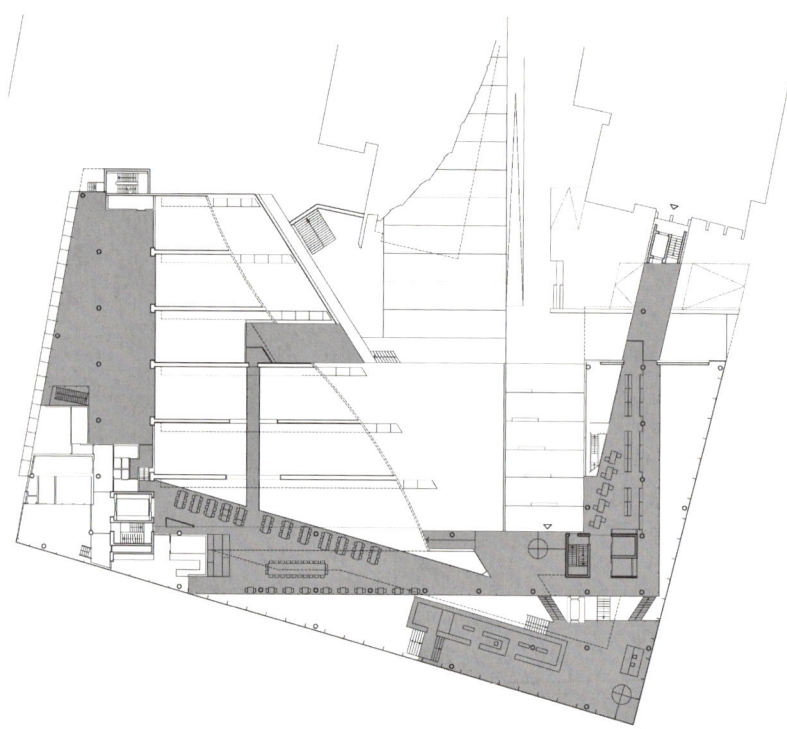

left: Floor plan_Gallery_Courtyard. right: Exterior_Exhibition space_Gangway.

THE NETHERLANDS_ASSEN **DRENTS MUSEUM**

ARCHITECTS: ERICK VAN EGERAAT, FRANK HUIBERS
COMPLETION: 2011_**ORIGINAL BUILDING:** COACH HOUSE,
17TH CENTURY _**TYPE:** HISTORY MUSEUM_**GROSS
FLOOR AREA:** 2,000 M² _**PHOTOS:** VIKTOR FRETYÁN,
PETER HEAVENS, JORNE JONGSMA

THE ARCHITECTURE

The new entrance and extension consistently integrate the museum into the fabric of the city, while a balanced play between building, landscape and water creates a new identity, emphasizing both the scenic character and the cultural-historic face of the city center. The new exhibition wing covers 2,000 square meters, all underground. Its staggered, organic roof consists of a public garden that connects to the existing city parks. The existing coach-house will serve as the new main entrance. Its historic façade will be left untouched, but the entire building will be lifted onto a spectacular glass plinth — allowing light to enter the building at daytime, and highlighting the building by interior lighting at night.

THE COLLECTION

The Drents Museum began developing its collection in 1854 and has slowly accumulated an extensive range of exhibits relating to the cultural history of the area. The collection encompasses a wide range of objects, including jewelry, ornaments, crafts and agricultural tools. A recent temporary exhibition hosted by the museum came from the creators of the famous exhibition "the Terracotta Army of Xi'an". This temporary display featured treasures from ancient Georgia and included around 150 gold, silver and bronze objects, which show that ancient Georgia possessed a high standard of metal-work techniques. One of the central themes of the exhibition was the Greek myth of Jason searching for the Golden Fleece in ancient Georgia. The exhibition displayed highlights from the Bronze Age, the Iron Age and the Roman Era from various places in Georgia, as well as valuable objects from the grave excavations at the famous temple city of Vani. The exhibition objects, all from the National Museum in Tbilisi, have been on show in various different settings around the world, including Berlin, Washington, New York, Athens, Los Angeles, and Stockholm.

left: Sections_Underground exhibition hall_Staircase. right: Exterior_New entrance at Jacob Cramerplein_Landscape design on the roofs.

THE NETHERLANDS_HEERENVEEN **MUSEUM BELVÉDÈRE**

ARCHITECTS: INBO ARCHITECTEN DRACHTEN_**LANDSCAPE ARCHITECT:** MICHEAL VAN GESSEL_**COMPLETION:** 2005 **TYPE:** ART MUSEUM_**GROSS FLOOR AREA:** 1,310 M²
PHOTOS: GER VAN DER VLUGHT, AMSTERDAM

THE ARCHITECTURE

The museum of modern Frisian art extends across the large canal of the restored classic landscape garden of the Villa Oranjewoud. The rectangular main shape of the building fits into the rational landscape, while the façades with mostly closed surfaces made of basalt stones prescind the landscape. Despite the closed volumes, there is a connection between the museum and its surroundings — implicitly in the shape of a glass plinth in the exhibition areas, which also functions as a showroom for paintings; and explicitly in the museum café where the façade at the junction of museum and canal can be pulled up like a curtain.

THE COLLECTION

The museum of modern and contemporary art with a focus on Frisian artists was established in part due to the particular dedication of Thom Mercuur (born 1940). As early as the 1950s, he dreamed of such a museum together with the future artists Boele Bregman and Sjoerd de Vries. Roughly half a century later, he became the founding director of the museum that contained, in addition to the above-mentioned artists, works of Jan Mankes, Thijs Rinsema, Tames Oud, Gerrit Benner and Willem van Althuis. The building showcases the development of styles from Realism via Impressionism and Expressionism and Constructivism up to the new configuration with a focus on artists from the surrounding artistic environment. The name of the museum is derived from the Belvédère in the Oranjewoud park, the Landgoed Oranjewoud museum park contains, in addition to the museum and the modern surrounding landscape (Michael R. van Gessel), also the old Oranjewoud manor.

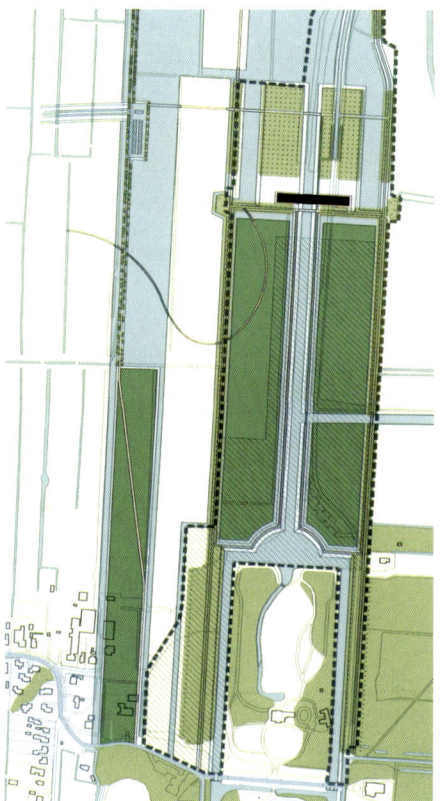

left: Situation plan_Restaurant seen from outside_The façade out of basalt stone. right: Exhibition room_Museum crossing the "Grand Canal"_Approach to the museum.

THE NETHERLANDS_NIJMEGEN **MUSEUM HET VALKHOF**

ARCHITECTS: UNSTUDIO_**COMPLETION:** 1999_**TYPE:** ART MUSEUM
GROSS FLOOR AREA: 39,400 M² _**PHOTOS:** CHRISTIAN RICHTERS

THE ARCHITECTURE

Two main structures organize this museum — the staircase and the ceiling. The staircase forms the structural core of the building and is also a distributor in that its branches shoot off to the various program parts, such as the café, library and museum. The ceiling incorporates all installations and lends coherence to the museum. Divided lengthways into parallel streets with multiple lateral openings, the structure of the museum floor hybridizes the strictly structured with the informal. The ceiling covers, without disguising or concealing, the many installations for lighting and climate control, as well as the multitude of wires. The undulating ceiling has a wave-like structure, which varies according to the expected movement of visitors.

THE COLLECTION

The Het Valkhof museum was established in 1999 from the merger of the archeological museum G.M. Kam and the Commanderie van St. Jan. A main part of the collection is an exhibition of items related to Roman Antiquity in the southern region of the Netherlands along with modern art. Nijmegen was known as Novomagus, and served for four centuries as the most important Roman city of today's Netherlands, while the Valkhof, which lends the museum its name, is a chapel built in the central construction style in 1030 and the country's oldest intact building. It was established as a palace chapel under Emperor Konrad II as a successor of the Aachen palace chapel. The Commanderie, one of its two predecessor institutions, is the city's second-oldest building. It was created in 1196 and became a community museum after a very diverse history. The collection of modern art focuses on the time since Pop Art, with a focus on Dutch artists, as well as some international artists.

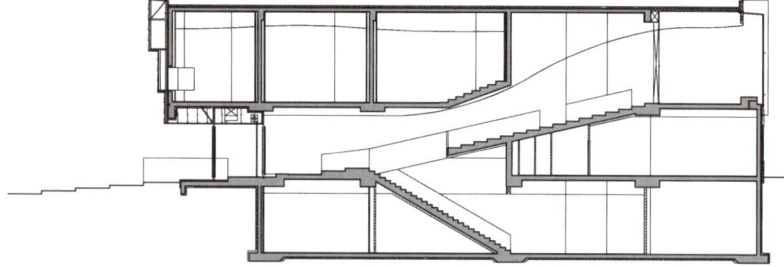

left: Section_Staircase_Steps. right: Gallery_Front façade.

MUSEUM BOIJMANS-VAN BEUNINGEN

ARCHITECTS: ROBBRECHT EN DAEM ARCHITECTEN**_COMPLETION:** 2003**_ORIGINAL BUILDING:** ADRIANUS J. VAN DER STEUR, 1935, EXTENSION: ALEXANDER BODON, 1971 / 1990**_TYPE:** ART MUSEUM **GROSS FLOOR AREA:** 4,000 M²**_PHOTOS:** KRISTIEN DAEM

THE ARCHITECTURE

The Museum Boijmans-Van Beuningen in Rotterdam is a complex amalgam of sections all built at different times. The new building transforms the museum into a single entity again. Green-tinted glass sheets introduce a rhythm into the façade that looks austere and elegant, while its layering also gives a hint of the complexity of the building. Inside, there is a striking link between Adrianus Van der Steur's 1935 brick building and the new one: old and new interlock without any brusque movements and turn the museum into a building that is both coherent and flexible. A feature of the museum is the range of small exhibition rooms around the Bodon wing, similar to the apsidal chapels in a cathedral.

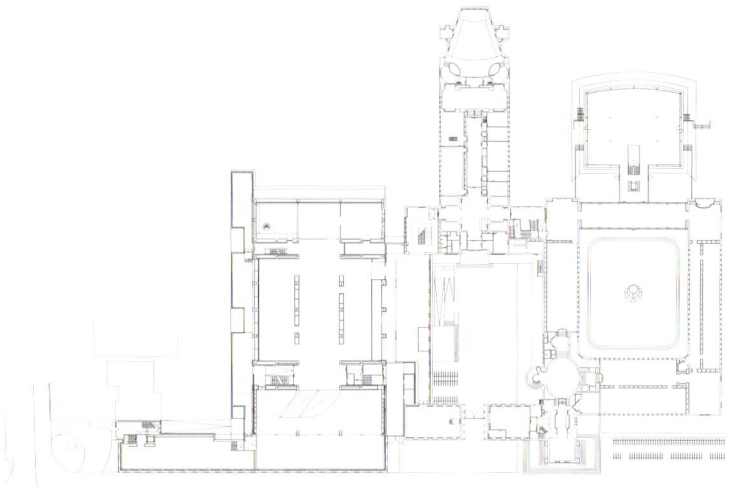

THE COLLECTION

The collection of the museum is based on a donation by the collector Frans Jacob Otto Boijmans in 1841. In 1849, the Museum Boijmans was opened at the Schielandshuis, the only 17th century house (by Pieter Post, 1665), which was preserved at the center of Rotterdam. Part of the collection burned in 1864. In 1935 the core section of today's museum was occupied by Ad van der Steur. After the extensive collection of Daniël George van Beuningen was received by the museum in 1958, it was given today's name. In 1971, the building was expanded by a large exhibition building designed by Alexander Bodon, who expanded the complex again in 1990. Architect Hubert-Jan Henket added the pavilion located in the back. The museum's collection of works by many prominent artists extends from the Middle Ages to modernity, with a focus on Dutch art. The museum contains famous works by artists ranging from Hieronymus Bosch and Pieter Bruegel the Elder, via Rembrandt, up to René Magritte and Salvador Dalí.

left: Ground floor plan_Glass façade_Main façade. right: Exhibiton hall_Bird's eye view_Exhibition.

THE NETHERLANDS_VUGHT **NATIONAL MONUMENT KAMP VUGHT**

ARCHITECTS: CLAUS EN KAAN ARCHITECTEN_**COMPLETION:** 2002
TYPE: HISTORY MUSEUM_**GROSS FLOOR AREA:** 1,830 M²
PHOTOS: CHRISTIAN RICHTERS

THE ARCHITECTURE

Little remains of the Vught concentration camp but a small area with what is left of the crematorium. The façade is composed of a long Roman tile structure. Bonds of this thin terracotta are alternated with thick bricks, which are recessed so that the space between the terracotta tiles can be filled with a thick layer of grout. There are two routes through the building that the visitors follow when they enter and when they leave the site. The exhibition rooms have a pre-modern arrangement, consisting of a sequence of rooms without any connecting corridors. Each of these spaces has its own unique length, width and height. This again illustrates the difference between the indoor and the outdoor world.

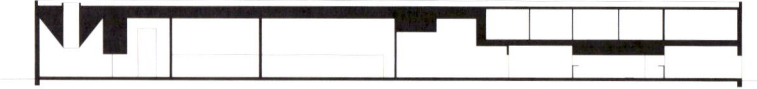

THE COLLECTION

Kamp Vught, officially the concentration camp Herzogenbusch, was one of the five concentration camps in the part of the Netherlands occupied by the German national socialist regime. It was the only Western European concentration camp outside of Germany which was subject to the SS, and served as a "model camp." The one kilometer long and 350 meter wide camp was erected by the prisoners themselves. In the following years, 31,000 people were imprisoned here, including 12,0000 Jews. Also included were 1,666 children who were moved from there to concentration camps in Poland, where they perished. The guards were Dutch members of the SS who also carried out the executions. After World War II, the camp was used as a prison for collaborators and later as emergency accommodation for native Indonesian soldiers of the Dutch army. One part of the camp was turned into a prison and another into a residential area. The original construction was mostly demolished by 1992 but some parts, such as the camp prison, were kept intact. The national memorial contains an original crematorium, along with reconstructed watchtowers and barracks.

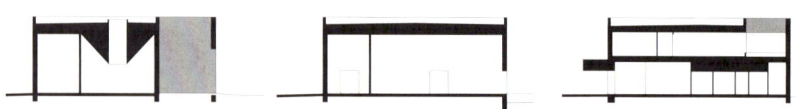

left: Sections_Entrance_Skylight. right: Exterior_Piece of original fence and a model of the camp in front of the museum.

UNITED KINGDOM_CHICHESTER **WEALD AND DOWNLAND OPEN AIR MUSEUM**

ARCHITECTS: EDWARD CULLINAN ARCHITECTS_**STRUCTURAL ENGINEERS:** BURO HAPPOLD_**COMPLETION:** 2002_**TYPE:** CULTURE MUSEUM_**GROSS FLOOR AREA:**1,200 M²_**PHOTOS:** SIMON FENELEY, LONDON (428 B.), EDWARD CULLINAN ARCHITECTS, LONDON (429 A.), KEEGAN DUIGENAN, LONDON

THE ARCHITECTURE

This building provided the museum with a more valuable building than the originally planned workshop and artifacts store. The double-curved form of the building was achieved by laying out flat a grid shell lattice made from four layers of green oak laths on scaffolding seven meters above the ground. The support was then taken away around the edges of the grid, allowing the shape to drop towards an arched cross section. With the ridge pushed up by the central scaffold, the sides were then pulled down and bolted into place. The resulting eco-rating of the Downland grid shell has an impact of about 47 percent of the alternative solution, while the rating of the green oak upper story structural elements is only about three percent of that of steel or concrete.

THE COLLECTION

The Weald and Downland Open Air Museum is the leading museum of historic buildings in England. The museum occupies a 202,000 square meter site in Sussex. It consists of a collection of nearly 50 historic buildings, which date from the 13th up to the 19th century. Narrowly escaping destruction, the buildings in the museum's collection were dismantled and removed from their actual sites, before being reconstructed and restored to their original form. Many of the structures feature period gardens, and the site also includes farm animals, woodland walks and a lake. The buildings renovated by the museum include a timber-framed farmhouse from Kent, a market hall from Hampshire, a granary from the South Downs and a Victorian school. The interiors of many of the buildings have been re-furnished, to recreate the designs and trends of the time when the buildings were in use. The gardens are planted with herbs, vegetables and flowers from the correct time periods to match the buildings. The museum also includes demonstrations and workshops from carpentry to bread making, with a functional Tudor kitchen where experts demonstrate Tudor techniques of cookery and food preparation.

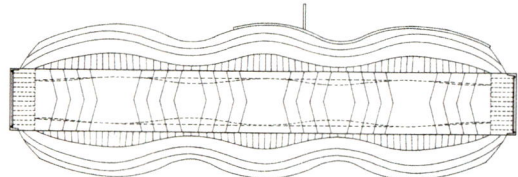

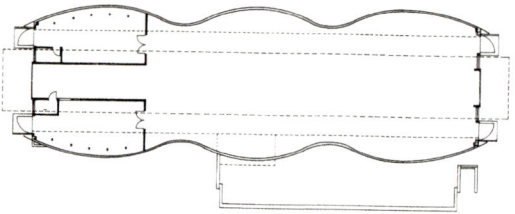

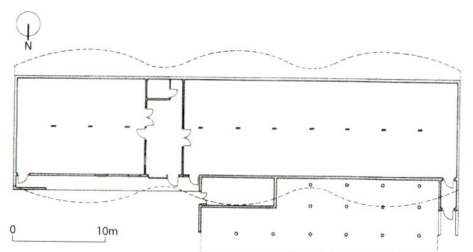

left: Roof, upper and lower floor plans_Entrance_Workshop interior. right: Cladding_Interior_Detail.

UNITED KINGDOM_LONDON **DARWIN CENTRE**

ARCHITECTS: C. F. MØLLER ARCHITECTS_**SCENOGRAPHY:** AT LARGE_**LANDSCAPE ARCHITECTURE:** C.F. MØLLER LANDSCAPE **COMPLETION:** 2009_**ORIGINAL BUILDING:** ALFRED WATERHOUSE, 1881_**TYPE:** NATURE MUSEUM_**GROSS FLOOR AREA:** 16,000 M² **PHOTOS:** TORBEN ESKEROD

THE ARCHITECTURE

The extension of the Natural History Museum takes the form of a huge concrete cocoon, surrounded by a glass atrium. The architecture reflects the museum's dual role as a visitors' attraction and a scientific research center. The cocoon forms the inner protective element, while its shape and size give an understanding of the collections' volume. The exposed thermal mass of the continuous sprayed and reinforced concrete shell provides a stable internal environment and minimizes energy loading. Public access to the scientific core of the center takes the form of a visitor route up and through the cocoon, overlooking the science and collection areas.

THE COLLECTION

The Darwin Center is a state-of-the-art science and collections facility that is part of London's Natural History Museum. The Natural History Museum houses life and earth science specimens, comprising some 70 million items within five main categories: Botany, Entomology, Mineralogy, Paleontology and Zoology. The home for the museum's vast collection of preserved species, the newly developed Darwin Center also provides new work spaces for the museum's scientific staff. One section of the Darwin Center houses the Zoological department's "Spirit Collections" — organisms preserved in alcohol. Another section, opened in 2009, is designed in the shape of a cocoon and houses entomology and botanical collections. The cocoon exhibition features vital plant and insect collections that go back 400 years to the museum's origins. Visitors can learn about the great collectors and naturalists of the past and view detailed 17th century illustrations. The exhibition also includes many interactive activities and real specimens, from huge tarantulas to meter-high plants. Arguably, the museum's most renowned creature is the 8.62 meter long giant squid, affectionately named Archie.

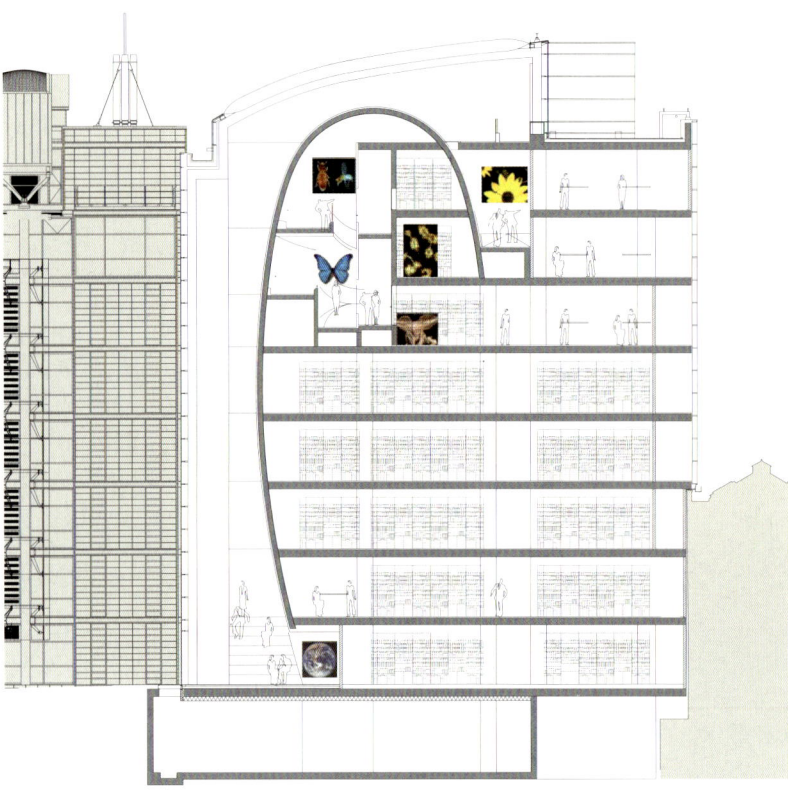

left: Section_New and old together_Cocoon in its glass atrium. right: Façade.

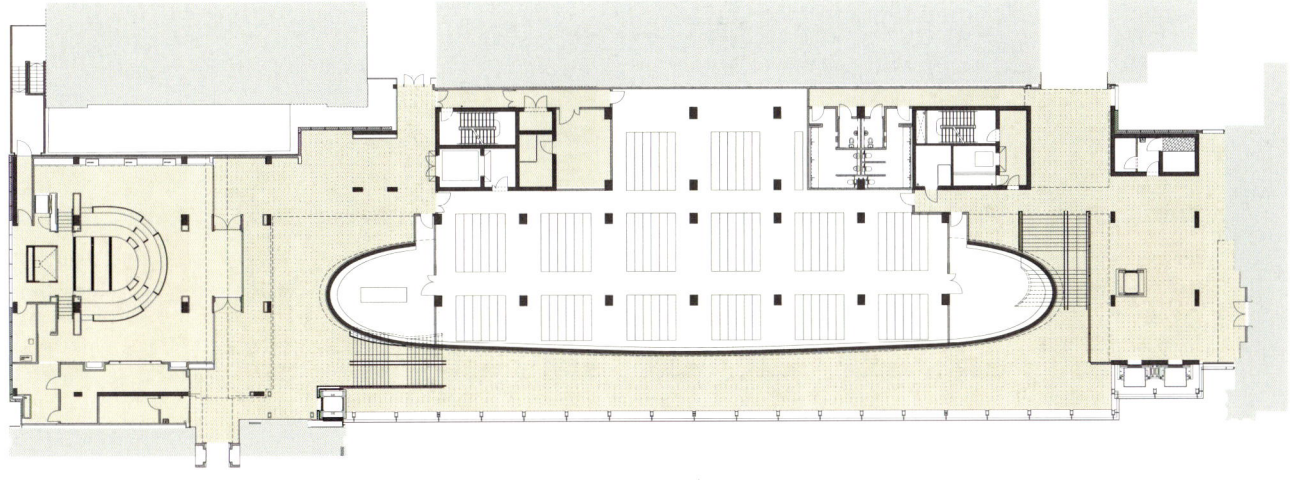

left: Atrium with cocoon. right: Ground floor plan_In the cocoon_Exhibition space_View into the laboratories.

UNITED KINGDOM_LONDON **GARDEN MUSEUM**

ARCHITECTS: DOW JONES ARCHITECTS**_LIGHTING DESIGN:** MINDS EYE**_COMPLETION:** 2008**_ORIGINAL BUILDING:** 17TH CENTURY**_TYPE:** NATURE MUSEUM**_GROSS FLOOR AREA:** 700 M²**_PHOTOS:** DAVID GRANDORGE, LONDON

THE ARCHITECTURE

In October 2000, the architects won an architectural competition to redesign the Garden Museum. The competition brief asked for a new gallery space where temporary exhibitions could be housed in secure and environmentally-controlled conditions. Creation of a dedicated place for the museum's permanent collection was equally important, as the exhibits were frequently moved to make space for events. The architects developed a strategy that addressed both issues. The idea was to create a belvedere within the existing building. This houses the new galleries and provides a raised ground from which a new perspective of the existing building is attained.

THE COLLECTION

The museum was founded in 1977, following the rediscovery of the tombs of two 17th century botanists, a father and son both called John Tradescant, in the churchyard of St Mary-at-Lambeth. The discovery led John and Rosemary Nicholson to found what was then called the Museum of Garden History, in the same church. As the 20th century progressed, the venue struggled to operate as a modern museum and it was decided to re-design the interior. The Garden Museum re-opened its doors in 2008, after undergoing significant interior renovations. The building's historic structure was left intact, but the interior was redesigned, providing new space for exhibitions. Remodeling has allowed the display of light-sensitive items for the first time, including books and photographs. The permanent collection holds more than 9,000 objects and covers the topic of gardening in the broadest possible sense. Objects range from specialist equipment to improvised tools and include ceramic exhibits made several hundred years ago. The museum's goal is to explore British gardens and gardening, through both its permanent collection and temporary exhibitions. The curators also organize a program of events, talks and activities for children, which run throughout the year.

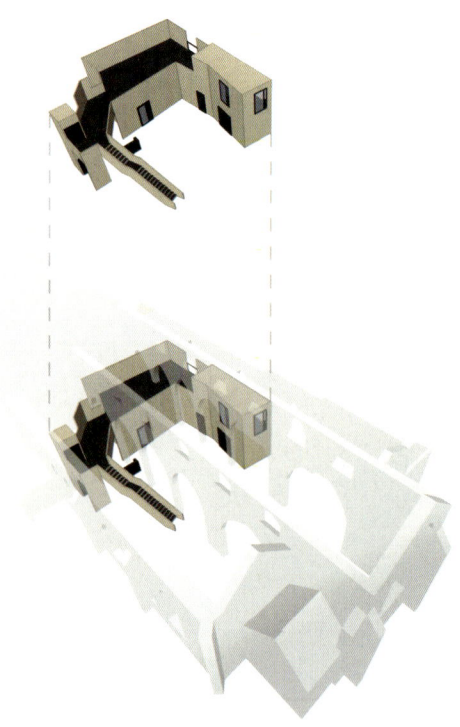

left: Belvedere in 3D_Reception_Education room. right: Event space_Stairs_Permanent exhibition space.

UNITED KINGDOM_LONDON **BRITISH MUSEUM**

ARCHITECTS: FOSTER + PARTNERS_**COMPLETION:** 2000
ORIGINAL BUILDING: ROBERT SMIRKE, 1831_**TYPE:** ART AND
CULTURE MUSEUM_**GROSS FLOOR AREA:** 15,335 M²
PHOTOS: NIGEL YOUNG / FOSTER + PARTNERS

THE ARCHITECTURE

The courtyard at the center of the British Museum was originally an open garden, which after its completion was occupied by the round Reading Room. The move of the British Library to St. Pancras provided the opportunity to recapture the courtyard and to give the building a new public focus. The Great Court connects all surrounding galleries. Within the space – the largest enclosed public space in Europe – there are information points, a bookshop and a cafe. The glazed canopy is a fusion of state-of-the-art engineering and economy of form. Its unique geometry is designed to span the irregular gap between the drum of the Reading Room and the courtyard façades, creating a square footprint.

THE COLLECTION

The British Museum is the national museum of the UK that was founded upon an initiative of naturalist and collector, Sir Hans Sloane. In the course of his life, Sloane collected more than 71,000 objects, which he wished to be preserved after his death. To achieve this goal, he bequeathed the entire collection to King George II for the nation, in return for a payment of 20,000 pounds to his heirs. The king accepted the offer and on June 7, 1753 the British Museum was established. Two other collections were also purchased during the museum's first years. These were the Cottonian Library of books and manuscripts and the Harleian collection of manuscripts. Other important acquisitions included the first ancient Egyptian mummy, bequeathed in 1756. In 1772 the museum acquired its first major collection of classical antiques. George VI donated the Kings Library in 1853, prompting the construction of today's quadrangular building, which houses the vast collection. The 20th century saw an increase in public services and by the 1970s the publishing house had been established. The museum also increased its educational programs, while public facilities were added by a series of newly constructed buildings.

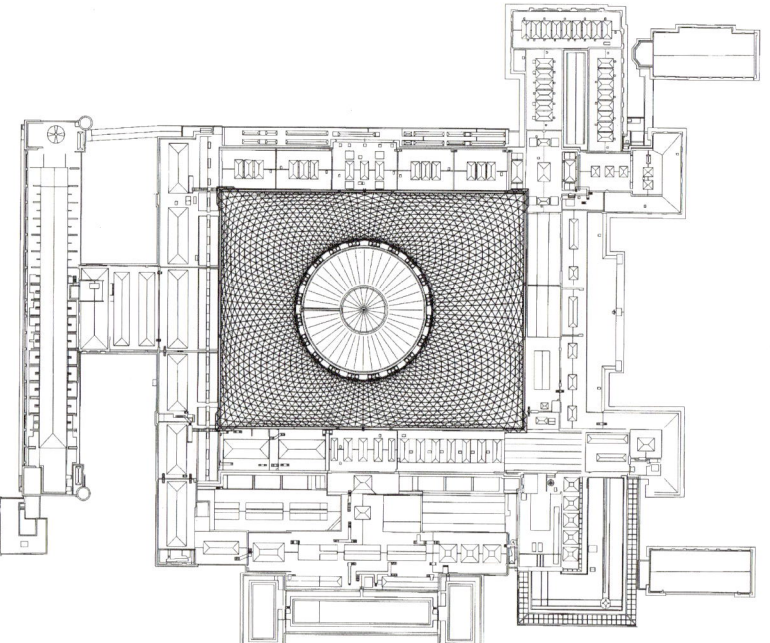

left: Roof plan_Glazed canopy next to the rotunda. right: Glazed canopy in the quadratic court.

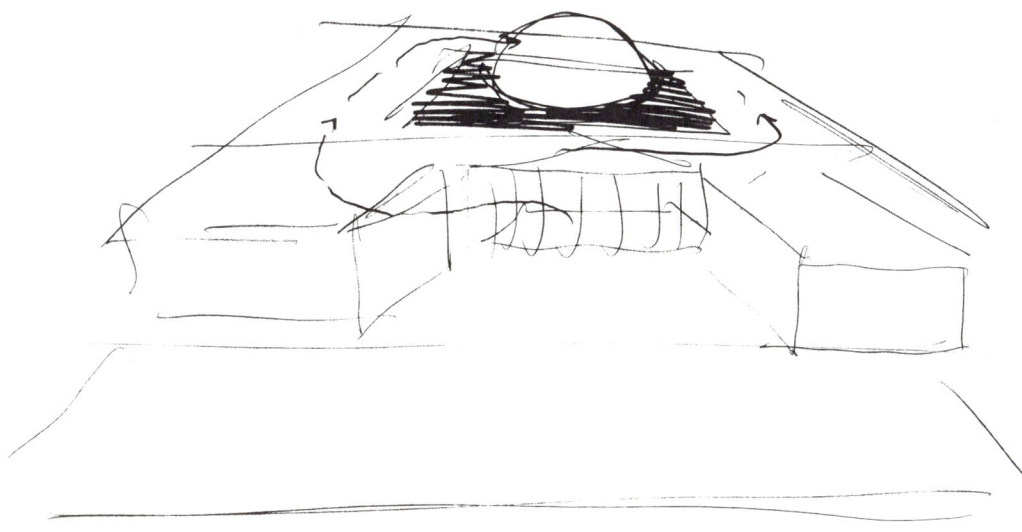

left: Glazed canopy and façade of the court. right: Sketch_New room_Exhibition room_Exhibition.

ARCHITECTS: STUDIO DANIEL LIBESKIND WITH LEACH RHODES WALKER_**COMPLETION:** 2001_**TYPE:** HISTORY MUSEUM_**GROSS FLOOR AREA:** 6,500 M²_**PHOTOS:** BITTER BREDT FOTOGRAFIE, BERLIN (440, 441 B., 442, 443 L.), WEBB AVIATION, GEVELSBERG (441 A.), LEN GRANT, MANCHESTER (443 A. R.), IWMN, MANCHESTER (443 B. R.)

THE ARCHITECTURE

This museum tells the story of how war has affected the lives of British and Commonwealth citizens since 1914. The design concept is that of a shattered and then reassembled globe. The building represents the interlocking of the elements earth, air, and water, substantiating the 20th century conflicts, which took place not on an abstract piece of paper, but were fought by men and women, by land, sky, and sea. The earth shard forms the generous and flexible museum space, signifying the open, earthly realm of conflict and war. The air shard serves as a dramatic entry into the museum, with its projected images, observatories and education spaces. The water shard forms the platform for viewing the canal.

THE COLLECTION

Situated in Manchester, the Imperial War Museum North is one of five branches of the Imperial War Museum, located in different locations throughout the UK. Founded in 1917, the museum's original aim was to serve as a memorial to those who died or suffered in World War I. Since these beginnings, the museum has expanded its remit to include all armed conflicts, focusing on British and Commonwealth involvement. The museum's exhibits explore the impact of armed conflict on both individuals and society. The museum occupies a site overlooking the Manchester Ship Canal, a key industrial area during World War II, which was heavily bombed during the war due to its importance. Alongside its permanent collection, the museum hosts a program of temporary exhibitions. Permanent collections include the Woman's Work display, which is categorized into the various forms of employment undertaken by women. The museum has also operated a successful volunteer program since opening in 2002. The program promotes the museum's aims of seeking to engage local residents who are at risk of social exclusion and to support individuals seeking to return to employment.

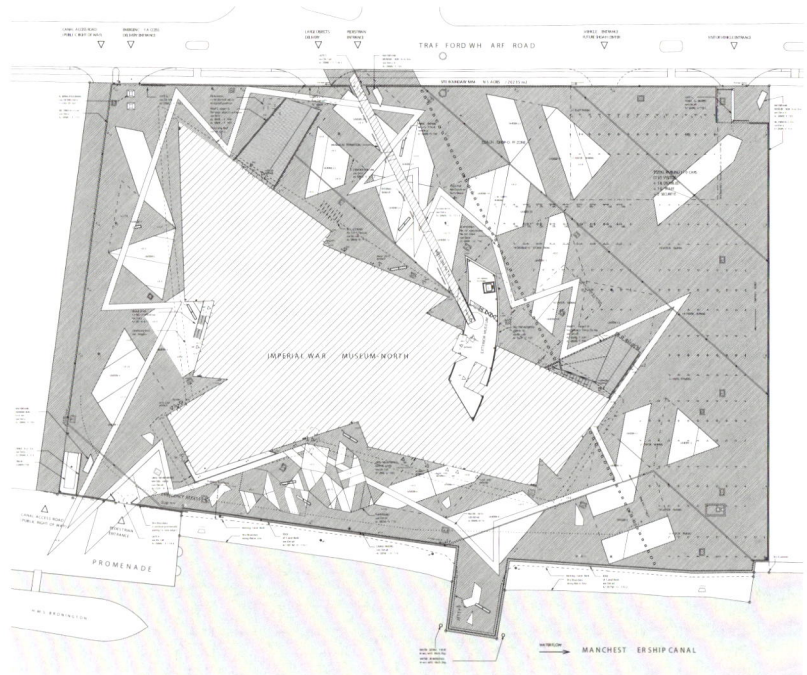

left: Site plan_View from Trafford Wharf Road_View from across the ship canal. right: Aerial view Exhibition space with projections_Exhibition silo.

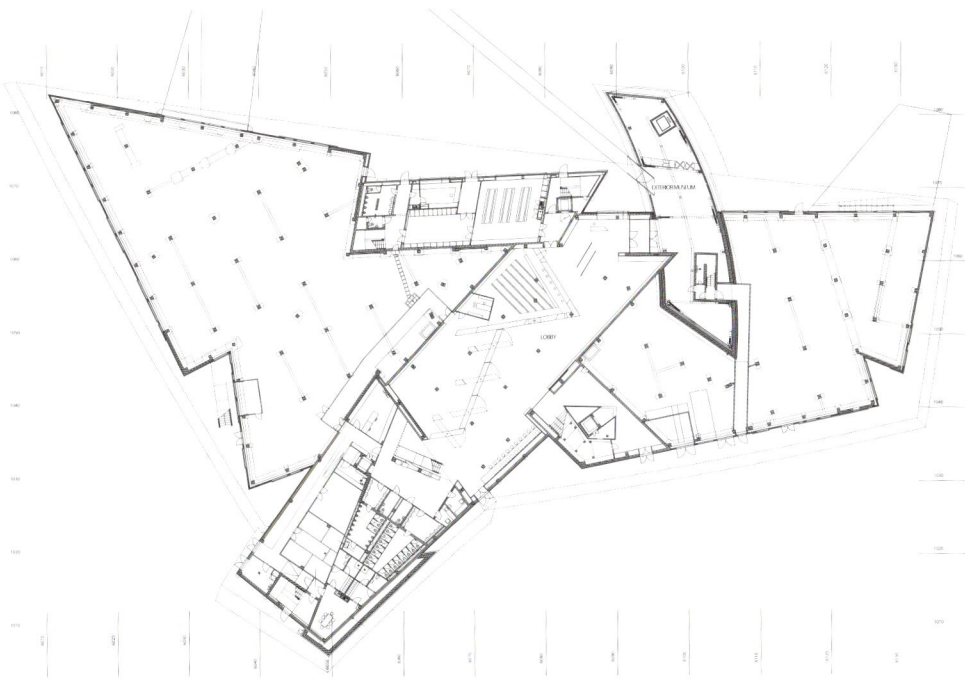

left: View over the canal right: Ground floor plan_Entrance_Water, earth and air shards_Inside the air shard.

UNITED KINGDOM_MIDDLESBROUGH **MIMA – INSTITUTE OF MODERN ART**

ARCHITECTS: ERICK VAN EGERAAT, ROD ALLAN, ANTONIA INFANGER_**LANDSCAPE ARCHITECTURE:** WEST 8
COMPLETION: 2007_**TYPE:** ART MUSEUM_**GROSS FLOOR AREA:** 4,000 M² _**PHOTOS:** CHRISTIAN RICHTERS

THE ARCHITECTURE

The MIMA is part of an urban regeneration scheme, intended to revitalize the heart of the city. The applied materials and scales respect and relate to the existing surroundings. The new public square, an integral part of the project, was designed in co-operation with West 8. The foyer, the defining space within the gallery, forms a transition between gallery and public square. Its height, of more than 16 meters, reveals a central staircase, which is framed by a suspended stone curtain. Interaction between the two is stimulated by the enormous transparent façade, inviting visitors and inhabitants to embrace the gallery as the heart of the new cultural quarter of Middlesbrough.

THE COLLECTION

The Middlesbrough Institute of Modern Art is one of the leading galleries of modern and contemporary art and crafts in the UK. MIMA hosts temporary exhibitions of fine art dating from the 1900s to the present and features work by internationally renowned artists. Exhibitions change on a quarterly basis and include the annual collection show, which brings together the best of the town's art collections, exhibiting art from both the Middlesbrough Art Gallery and the Cleveland Craft Center. The museum boasts five exhibition galleries, a conservation studio and an education suite. The entire collection is comprised of over 1,000 paintings, drawings, prints and photographs and includes the UK's second largest collection of Picassos and works by Andy Warhol, Henry Matisse and Damien Hirst. The contemporary jewelry collection contains both precious and non-precious jewelry, examples have been loaned to other museums and toured widely around the country. The ceramics collection is also one of the most important in the country, as it charts trends and movements of ceramics design since the 1920s. Surrounding the museum building is the town's overhauled Victoria Square and Central Gardens, which together constitute the largest civic space in Europe.

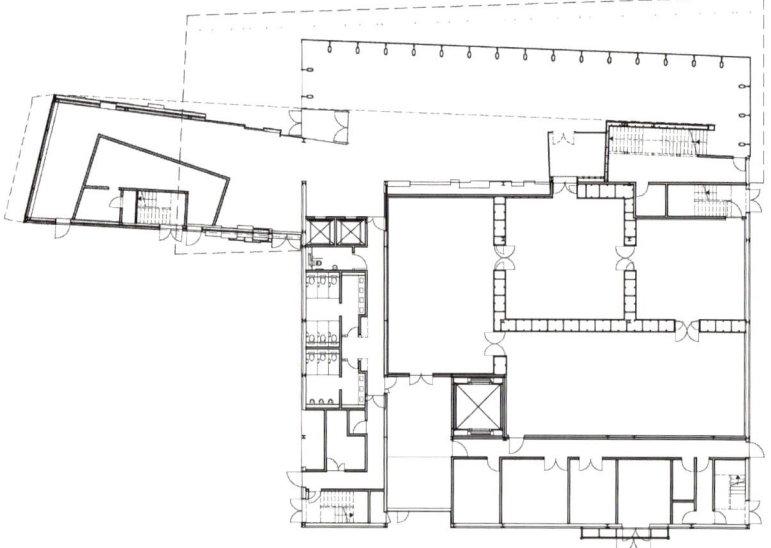

left: Ground floor plan_Café_Exhibition room. right: Foyer at night.

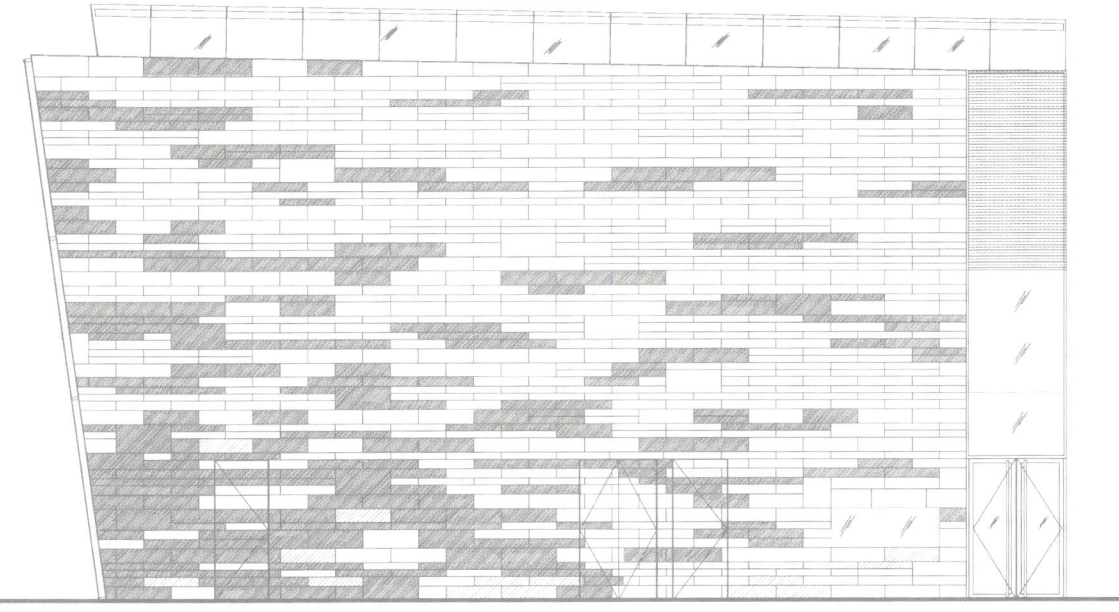

left: Structure façade. right: Elevation_Staircase_Suspended stone curtain.

africa &
australia

EGYPT_GIZA **GRAND EGYPTIAN MUSEUM (GEM)**

ARCHITECTS: HENEGHAN.PENG.ARCHITECTS_**SERVICES:** BURO HAPPOLD_**STRUCTURE / FAÇADE:** ARUP_**COMPLETION:** 2014_**TYPE:** ARCHEOLOGY MUSEUM_**GROSS FLOOR AREA:** 100,000 M²
PHOTOS: COURTESY OF THE ARCHITECTS

THE ARCHITECTURE

The Grand Egyptian Museum is to be located on a 50 hectare site in the desert plateau between the Pyramids of Giza and Cairo. It is envisaged as a cultural complex of activities devoted to Egyptology and will include conference, library and multimedia facilities. The concept was developed around the premise that the key artifacts, the pyramids, are located beyond the building and connected to it visually. A translucent stone wall constitutes the main façade of the Grand Egyptian Museum. By day, the façade forms the plateau edge, its surface delicately fractured and structured by geometry. At night it echoes the precision and glow of the glass-like polished surface of stone veneer which once covered the pyramids.

THE COLLECTION

The Grand Egyptian Museum is due to be completed in 2013, with a total estimated cost of USD $ 550 million. The building will be located just two kilometers away from some of Egypt's most important pyramids and the designers were chosen through a competition. The organizers received 1,557 entries from 82 different countries, making it the largest architectural competition in history. The new museum boasts the largest conservation labs anywhere in the world. These labs contain state of the art equipment for the preservation and restoration of artifacts on site. To improve security and help minimize the impact of the museum labs are located underground. The museum has been designed to allow use of the latest technology, including virtual reality. The museum is also intended to be the international center of museum communication, with direct contact to other local and international museums. Other measures taken to protect this important site include a new road for electric cars. Visitors will park outside the site and use the electric cars provided to reach the pyramids, thus helping to protect the pyramids from the harmful effects of traffic emissions.

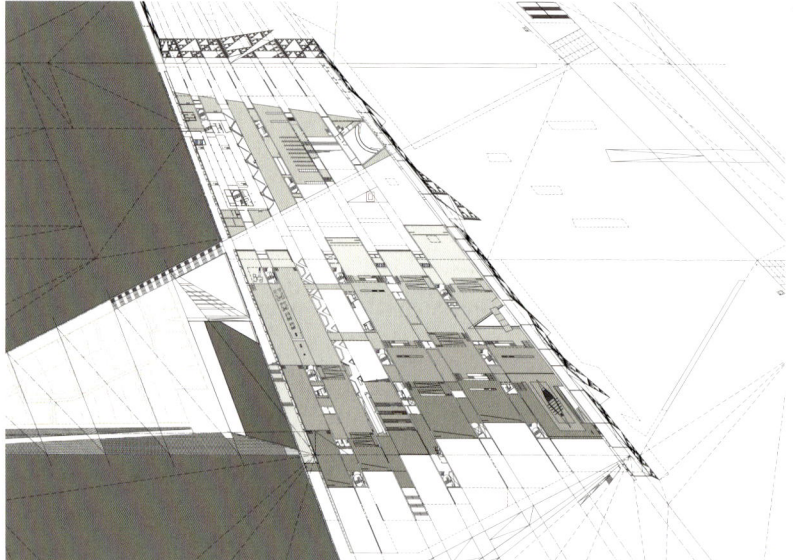

left: Museum as continuation of landscape_Translucent stone wall_Pyramid complex is the key artifact. right: Undulating roof as extension of desert plateau_Grand stair_Entrance courtyard.

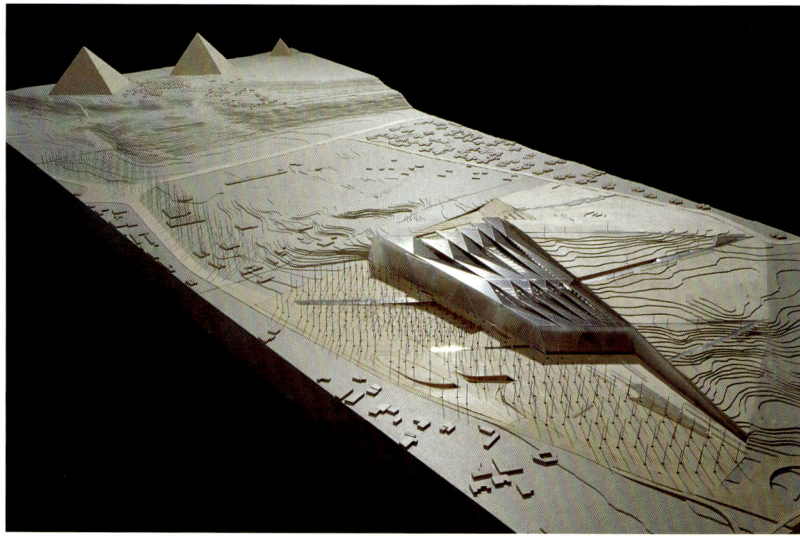

MOROCCO_VOLUBILIS **MUSÉE À VOLUBILIS**

ARCHITECTS: KILO_**COMPLETION:** 2009_**TYPE:** ARCHEOLOGY
MUSEUM_**GROSS FLOOR AREA:** 4,200 M²_**PHOTOS:** ELIO GERMANI

THE ARCHITECTURE

This site is a well-preserved example of an ancient Roman colonial town. The volume of the museum is embedded into the hillside so that visitors do not initially perceive its presence. The project is perceived as a narrow imprint on the perimeter of the ancient territory, eight meters wide by 200 meters long. The building consists of a succession of wooden volumes along an extended retaining wall, simultaneously buried and suspended in relationship to the rolling landscape. The project behaves much like the ruins it houses, with the tectonics of its construction and the lifespan of its materials inherently proposing a strategy for the building's eventual disappearance.

THE COLLECTION

The Musée à Volubilis in Morocco is the first of its kind in the country. Situated in a beautifully preserved Roman town, the visitor's center in the museum aims to educate visitors about the site's historic significance. Volubilis was an important Roman outpost in its time, and later became the home of Idris I, founder of the Idrisid dynasty. The entrance to Volubilis is through a gate in the actual Roman city walls, the museum buildings themselves feature a range of sculptural and altar remains from the site. To-date, less than half of the area has been excavated and archeologists continue to investigate the ancient area. In the middle of the site is the House of Orpheus, a large complex of rooms, which once belonged to one of the city's richest merchants. Conserved within this building is the mosaic that lends its name to the house, depicting the Orpheus myth. The site also contains the House of the Athlete, which contains an impressive mosaic showing an athlete being presented with a trophy for winning a race. One of the most impressive features of the site is the marble Triumphal arch. Built in honor of the Severian Emperor Caracalla and his mother, the arch is topped by a bronze chariot.

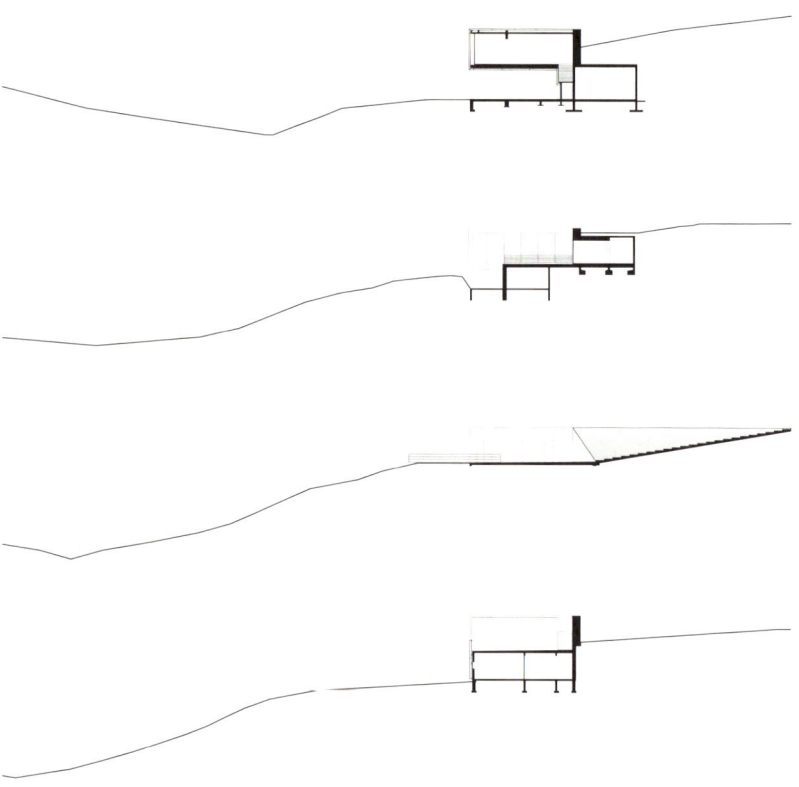

left: Sections_General view. right: Corridor_Between the buildings_Interior.

AUSTRALIA_CASULA (NSW) **CASULA POWERHOUSE**

ARCHITECTS: TONKIN ZULAIKHA GREER ARCHITECTS
COMPLETION: 2008_**ORIGINAL BUILDING:** NSW ELECTRICITY COM-
MISSION, 1951_**TYPE:** ART MUSEUM_**GROSS FLOOR AREA:** 2,000 M²
PHOTOS: BRETT BOARDMAN, NEWTOWN

THE ARCHITECTURE

The Casula Powerhouse combines a large regional gallery with art production and performance spaces, within a heritage-listed abandoned power station on the Georges River. The heritage fabric of the building was conserved, with new facilities fitted into its exciting large-scale spaces. The major volume, the Turbine Hall, is a multi-purpose space for large-scale activities and exhibitions, also providing a performance area with 750 seats. The Powerhouse is used by a range of regional professional and community groups as well as touring productions by professional companies, special exhibitions, and major one-off events. It has achieved a statewide reputation for innovation and excellence.

THE COLLECTION

Casula Powerhouse is a multi-disciplinary arts center, the museum aims to represent cultural diversity and to encourage visitors to reflect upon the world around them. The museum features seven galleries, and boasts a year round exhibition program of changing displays. In line with its aims of encouraging interest in cultural diversity, the museum's 326 seat theater hosts touring productions of some of the most widely renowned companies from across Australia. Live acts encompass everything from concerts to musicals to traveling theater company productions with a varied program that appeals to all ages and tastes. The museum's collection comprises of over 3,000 works of art and heritage objects reflecting the diversity of cultures that make up the city of Liverpool. The permanent collection focuses on the importance of si-multaneously entertaining and challenging visitors of all ages. The institution also promotes individual learning and self-discovery, offering a range of short courses and after school courses for children. Classes include life drawing and weaving as well as ceramics.

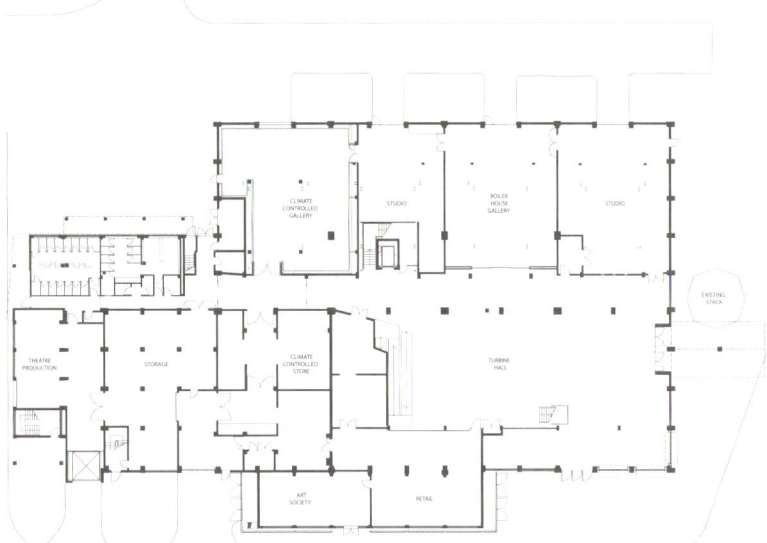

left: First floor plan_Exterior_Entry via the Turbine Hall_Original windows, inscribed beneath "Roll-call" by Nicole Ellis (recording the names of all the people who worked in the Powerhouse). right: Exhibition and performance space in the original Turbine Hall, with a floor piece by Judy Watson.

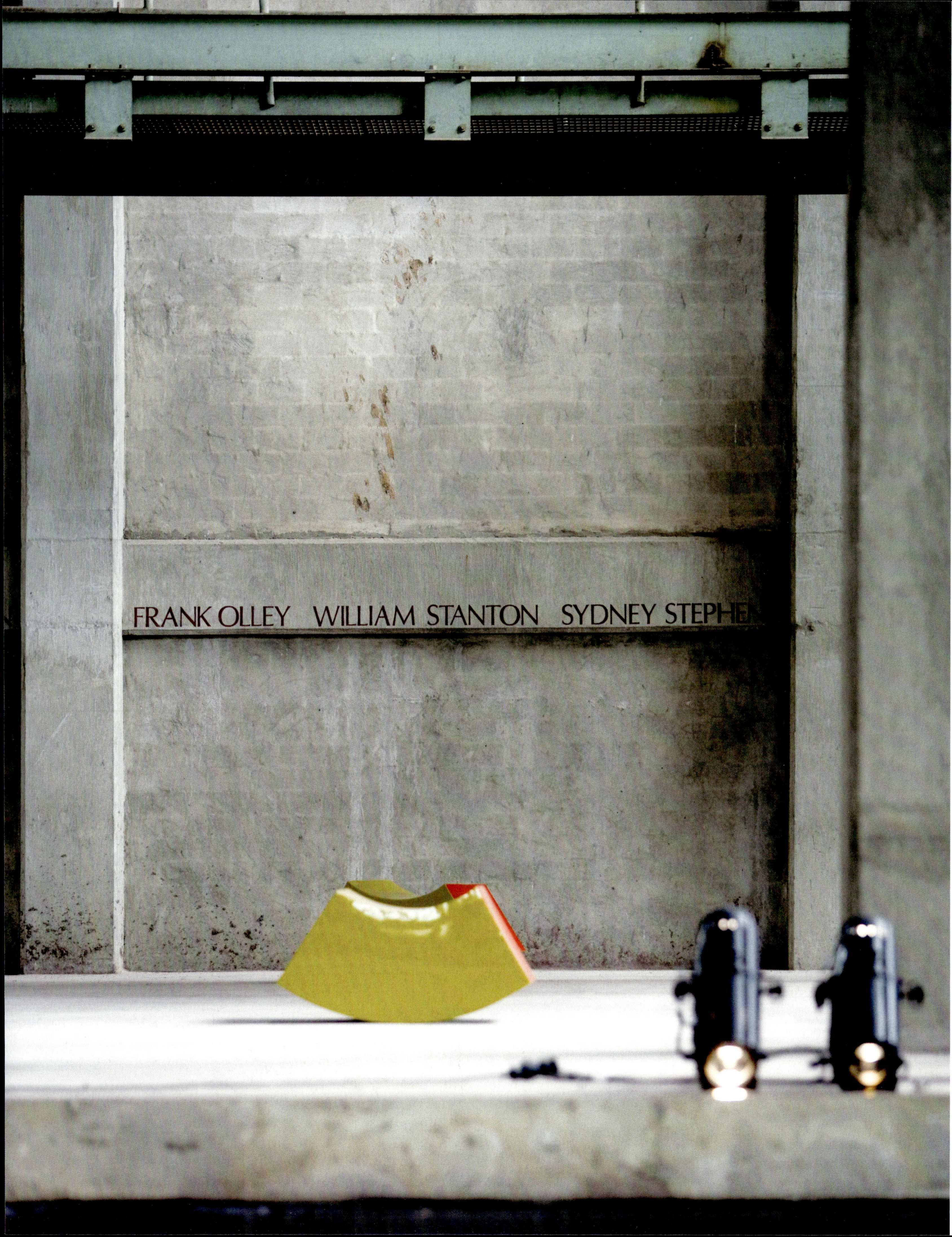
FRANK OLLEY WILLIAM STANTON SYDNEY STEPH

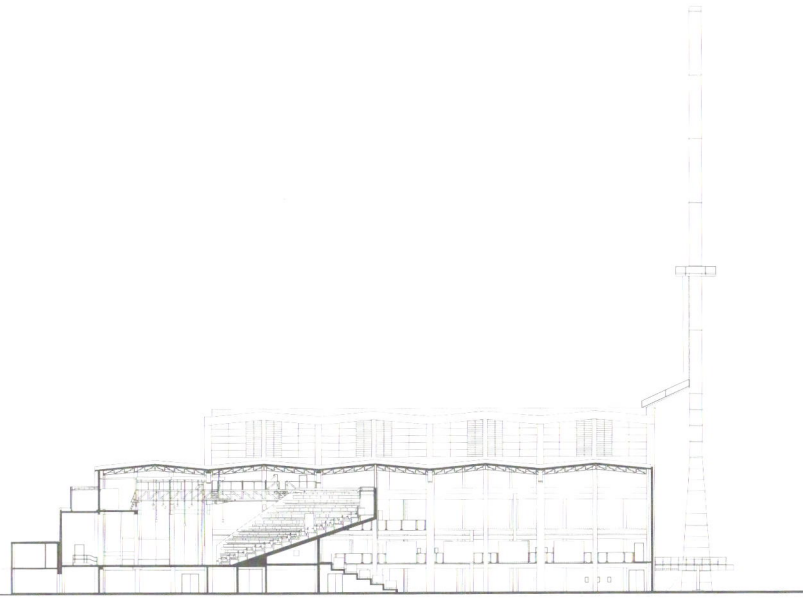

left: Detail of a temporary exhibition "Lap", 2000 by Wendy Paramor. right: Section_Exterior showing new cladding intertwined with restored industrial brick façade_Façade_Theater Interior.

asia

NE BOXES_CHINA_BEIJING_GUANGZHOU HUADU CULTURE & EXHIBI
ON CENTER_CHINA_GUANGZHOU CITY_XIXI WETLAND ART MUSEUM_CHI
A_HANGZHOU_ERDOS MUSEUM_CHINA_KANG BA SHI CITY_MARITIM MUS
UM_CHINA_LINGANG NEW CITY_SHANGHAI-PUDONG MUSEUM_CHINA_SH
NGHAI-PUDONG_EXHIBITION HALL OF NEW 4TH ARMY JIANGNAN HEAD
JARTER_CHINA_SHUIXI VILLAGE_DESIGN MUSEUM HOLON_ISRAEL_HOLON
ST CENTURY MUSEUM OF CONTEMPORARY ART KANAZAWA_JAPAN
HIKAWA_ECHIGO-MATSUNOYAMA MUSEUM OF NATURAL SCIENCE_JAP
N_MATSUNOYAMA TOMIHIRO ART MUSEUM_JAPAN_MIDORI NATIONAL ART
ENTER_JAPAN_MINATO-KU, TOKYO KANNO MUSEUM_JAPAN_SENDAI GEN
PAPER SCULPUTURE MUSEUM_JAPAN_TAMA-SHI, TOKYO_MATSUDAI CU
URAL VILLAGE MUSEUM_JAPAN_TOKAMACHI CITY_LEEUM SAMSUNG MUS
M OF ART_KOREA_SEOUL_SEOUL NATIONAL UNIVERSITY MUSEUM_KOREA S
UL LOUVRE ABU DHABI UAE SAADIYAT ISLAND NINE BOXES_CHINA_BEIJIN

CHINA_BEIJING **NINE BOXES**

ARCHITECTS: AI WEIWEI / FAKE DESIGN_**COMPLETION:** 2004
TYPE: ART MUSEUM_**GROSS FLOOR AREA:** 2,751 M²
PHOTOS: AI WEIWEI

THE ARCHITECTURE

The architect transformed nine houses, each with its own distinguished style, into art galleries and office spaces. The nine buildings were wrapped with light steel structures and a galvanized steel skin. The finished work sets these "steel houses" into a harmonic contrast with the gray brick structures of the other houses on the estate. The Nine Boxes are set in a grass and water landscape, which resembles a small garden city in contrast to the growing metropolis. The archetypical buildings reflect the surface of the lake as well as each other's steel walls. Small passageways between the boxes provide views of the surrounding landscape, integrating it into the architecture.

THE COLLECTION

The Nine Boxes museum was designed by Chinese artist, architectural designer and social commentator Ai Weiwei. He is known for the design of the Beijing National Stadium, the main stadium of the 2008 Olympic Games. Since the Sichuan earthquake in 2008, Ai is known for as one of China's most influential bloggers and social activists. He is known for his tongue-in-cheek humor and unabashed social commentary and has frequent run-ins with the Chinese authorities. He was also involved in exposing an alleged corruption scandal in connection with the construction of Sichuan schools that collapsed during the earthquake. On 15th December 2008, Ai began the investigation into the number of student casualties following the earthquake. The aim of the investigation was to compile a list of students killed in the earthquake by May 2009, the first anniversary of the disaster. The list contained 5,385 names, which were then published, along with numerous articles documenting the investigation, on his blog, which has since been shut down. Ai Weiwei was later taken to hospital for emergency brain surgery after suffering a beating by Chinese police, when he attempted to testify for a fellow comrade who also investigated the poor school construction and high casualty number following the earthquake.

left: Site plan_Exterior view with entrance gate. right: Between the boxes_Exterior view with fountains_Box entrance.

CHINA_GUANGZHOU CITY **GUANGZHOU HUADU CULTURE & EXHIBITION CENTER**

ARCHITECTS: ENDO SHUHEI ARCHITECT INSTITUTE_**COMPLETION:** 2011_**TYPE:** CULTURE MUSEUM_**GROSS FLOOR AREA:** 19,500 M²
PHOTOS: COURTESY OF THE ARCHITECTS

THE ARCHITECTURE
This site is located in the northern part of Guangzhou city, next to the district government of Huadu and Huadu Plaza. Its eastern, western and southern sides are bordered by roads. A cultural complex, the building incorporates three main functions: a cultural center with a theater seating up to 500, a convention center with digital cinemas and a large exhibition space and the Youth palace. The entrance to each function is placed underground, near the subway. Since the primary functions of the culture center, conference and exhibition space are located in the southern area, this becomes the main façade, with the volume of the building facing Quyingbin Ave.

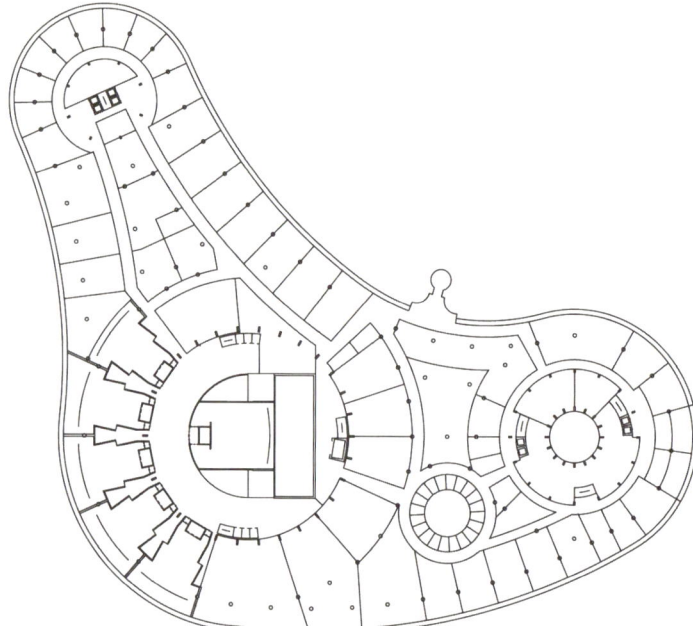

THE COLLECTION
The Guangzhou Huadu Culture & Exhibition Center is due to be completed in 2011 and highlights the economic growth of this area over the past few years. Due to its status as the cultural and economic hub of southern China and its unique Lingnan culture, dating back more than 2200 years, the city of Guangzho was one of the first cities to be listed as a Historical Town. The increasing attention being paid to the city's cultural identity has resulted in the municipal government vowing to promote and protect the areas highly respected cultural history. With the city's economy growing at such a pace, science, education and sports programs are also rapidly developing. Because of this, Guangzho has become one of the three most influential financial and economic centers in China. In 2003, archeological discoveries made during the construction of the city's University Town, have revealed many relics of great importance. Several large events have also been held in the city in recent years, such as the "Gold Bell Awards", which is a celebration of Chinese music, and an acrobatic contest called "The Golden Lion Award." Events such as these have established the city as a cultural hub of southern China. This new status made the creation of a new culture and exhibition center all the more important.

left: Third floor plan_Bird's eye view. right: General view_Entrance area_Façade.

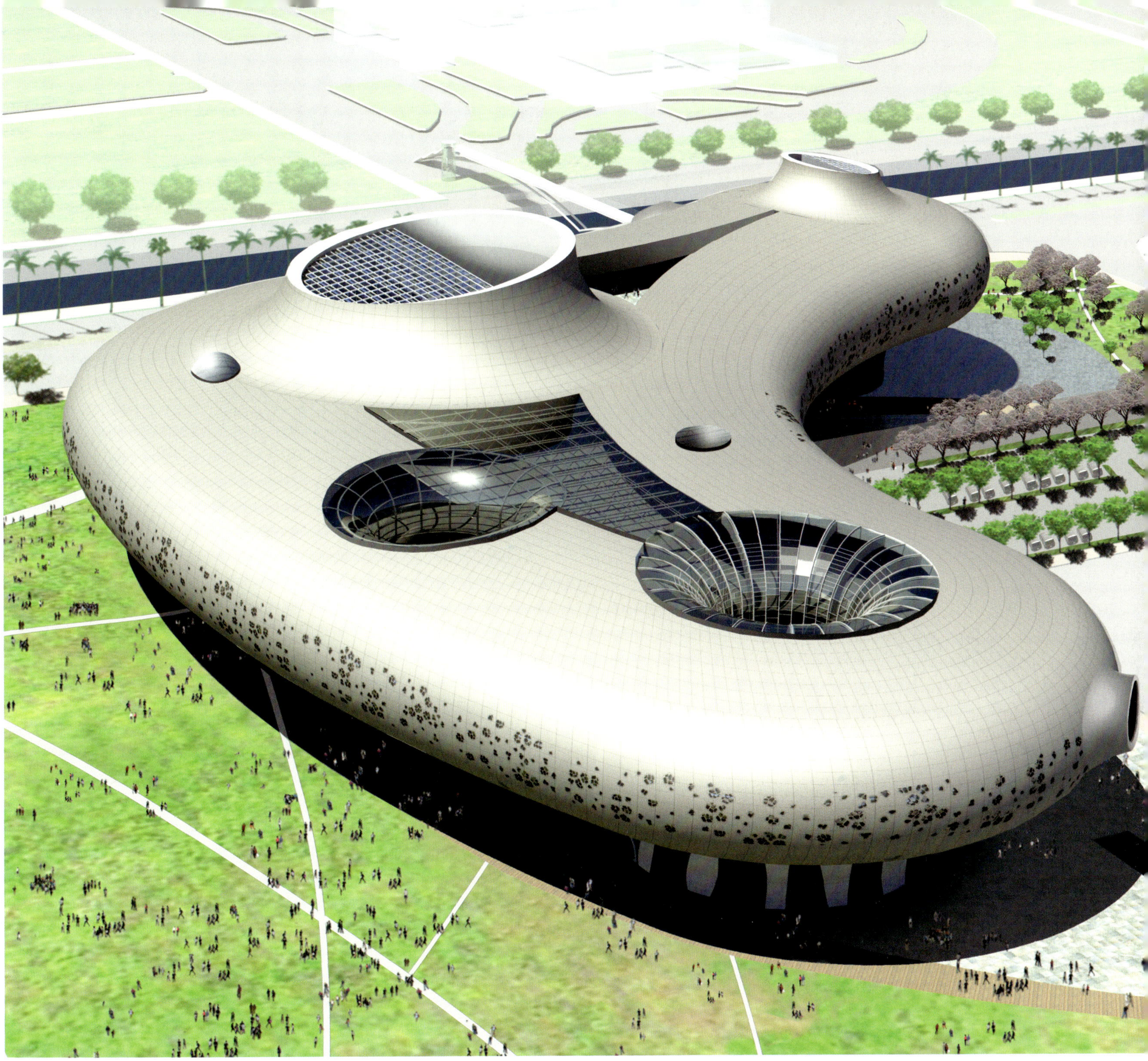

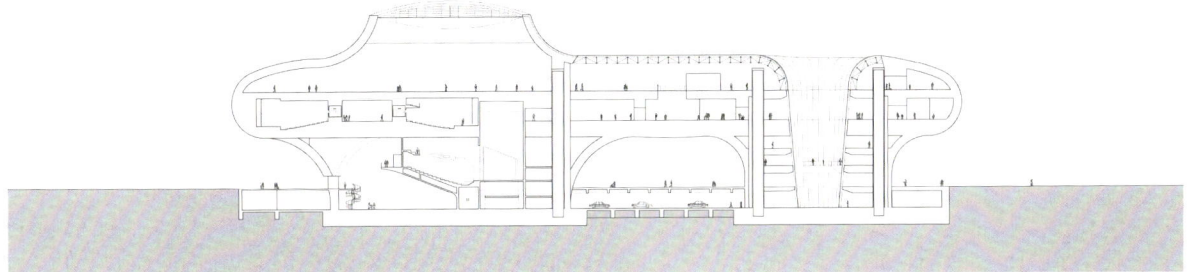

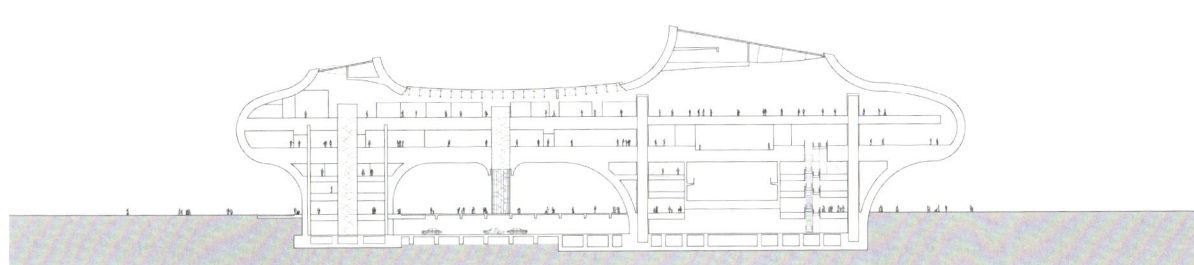

left: Courtyard. right: Sections_Skylight_Two Interior views.

CHINA_HANGZHOU **XIXI WETLAND ART MUSEUM**

ARCHITECTS: STUDIO PEI-ZHU_**COMPLETION:** 2010_**TYPE:**
ART MUSEUM_**GROSS FLOOR AREA:** 5,793 M² _**PHOTOS:**
COURTESY OF THE ARCHITECTS

THE ARCHITECTURE

The concept for this building stems from the interaction between building and nature. This design reproduces the genuine qualities of fallen leaves and shelter throughout the five buildings that are arranged like five leaves. When leaves fall from trees they arrive naturally on the ground and no two leaves on earth are identical, so each building also has a unique form. The buildings remain low to the ground but sections expand upward and outward toward the sky. Light colored, reflective zinc panels with a brushed finish cover each building. The windows and skylights are arranged according to a natural fractal that brings light into the building like soft filtered sunlight shining through the forest canopy.

THE COLLECTION

The Xixi Wetland Art Museum is located in the Xixi National Wetland Park. This park is the first wetland park in China and covers just 3.4 square kilometers of land. It is crisscrossed by six main watercourses as well as several ponds, lakes and swamps. Visitors can take a boat tour along the waterways for an opportunity to see much of the park's wildlife. The wetland area is more than 1800 years old and is, reportedly, the original birthplace of the Chinese South Opera and traditionally hosts an annual Dragon Boat contest. The museum is China's first professional wetland museum and uses multimedia technology for displays and exhibitions, to illustrate wetland ecology and the threats faced by wetlands both in China and worldwide. Designed as large "flying saucer" by noted Japanese architect Arata Isozaki, the 20,200 square meter museum is a landmark in the rural area. The museum contains four halls: Hall of Introduction, Hall of Wetlands and Mankind, Hall of China and Hall of Xixi Wetland. Exhibitions and displays within the museum "recreate" different types of wetlands, such as the West Siberian Peat Bog, the Lake Victoria Wetland in Africa and the Great Barrier Reef in Australia. To connect the museum with its natural surroundings, scale-down versions of trees soar to the ceiling and virtual birds fly on a screen behind the "forest."

left: Site plan_Exterior_Interior. right: Lobby_Exterior_Outdoor facility.

CHINA_KANG BA SHI CITY **ERDOS MUSEUM**

ARCHITECTS: MAD ARCHITECTS**_COMPLETION:** 2010**_TYPE:** CULTURE MUSEUM**_GROSS FLOOR AREA:** 41,227 M² **_PHOTOS:** MAD ARCHITECTS, BEIJING / FANG ZHENNING, BEIJING

THE ARCHITECTURE

This museum is located in the new city center, that is emerging dozens of kilometers away from the current city, driven by a booming economy. The urban master plan drew a symbolic but empty image of "the Ever Rising Sun on the Grassland" at the central plaza. The museum was conceived as a reaction to this plan. It takes the form of a natural, irregular nucleus in contrast with the strict geometry of the master plan. The structure is wrapped in polished metal louvers to reflect and dissolve the surroundings. The interior is defined by continuous curvilinear walls, all opening onto the shared public space that runs through the museum. The glazed roof and luminescent walls will introduce light into this environment.

THE COLLECTION

The History and Science Museum of Erdos, located in the central zone of Erdos' new city of Kang Ba Shi, acts as an external display window for the city of Erdos and the science and culture of inner Mongolia. It is the first of seven cultural buildings that form MAD Architecture's so-called "Master plan" of establishing a new contemporary international urban district within the central area of Kang Ba Shi city. Located several kilometers from the old city of Erdos there is nothing in the immediate area except the Gobi desert, and several hills in the background. The architects' design for this new building was apparently inspired by two different ideas, first by Buckminster Fuller's proposal for creating a glass dome, which would stretch across central Manhattan. Second, by a futuristic movie where, towards the end of the world, human beings are living enclosed by a large protective glass dome, outside of which are hostile conditions for humans. Representing the Mongolian environment, cultural characters, and the advancement of technology, these buildings form a brand new image for the whole region, an image that is both contemporary and dynamic.

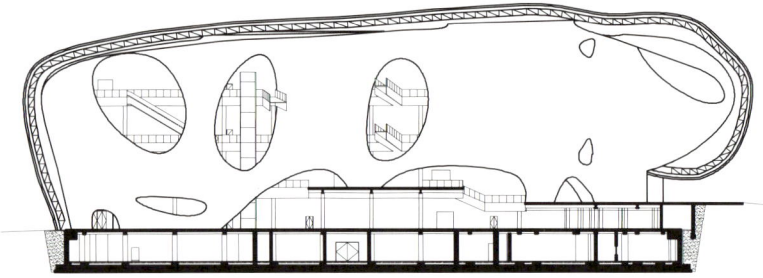

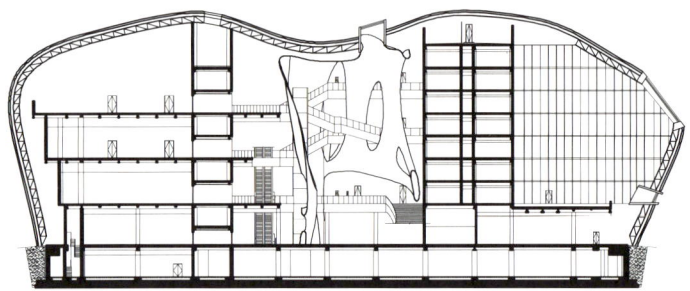

left: Section_Model photos. right: Interior_Metal louvers_Under construction.

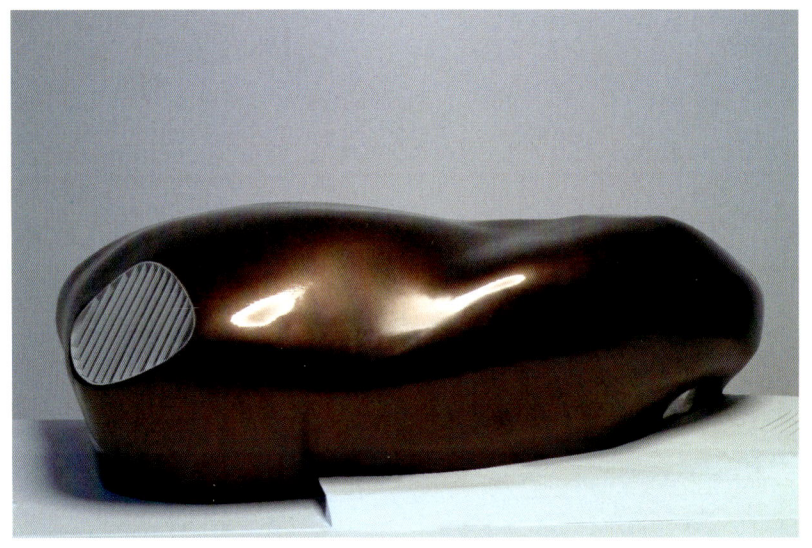

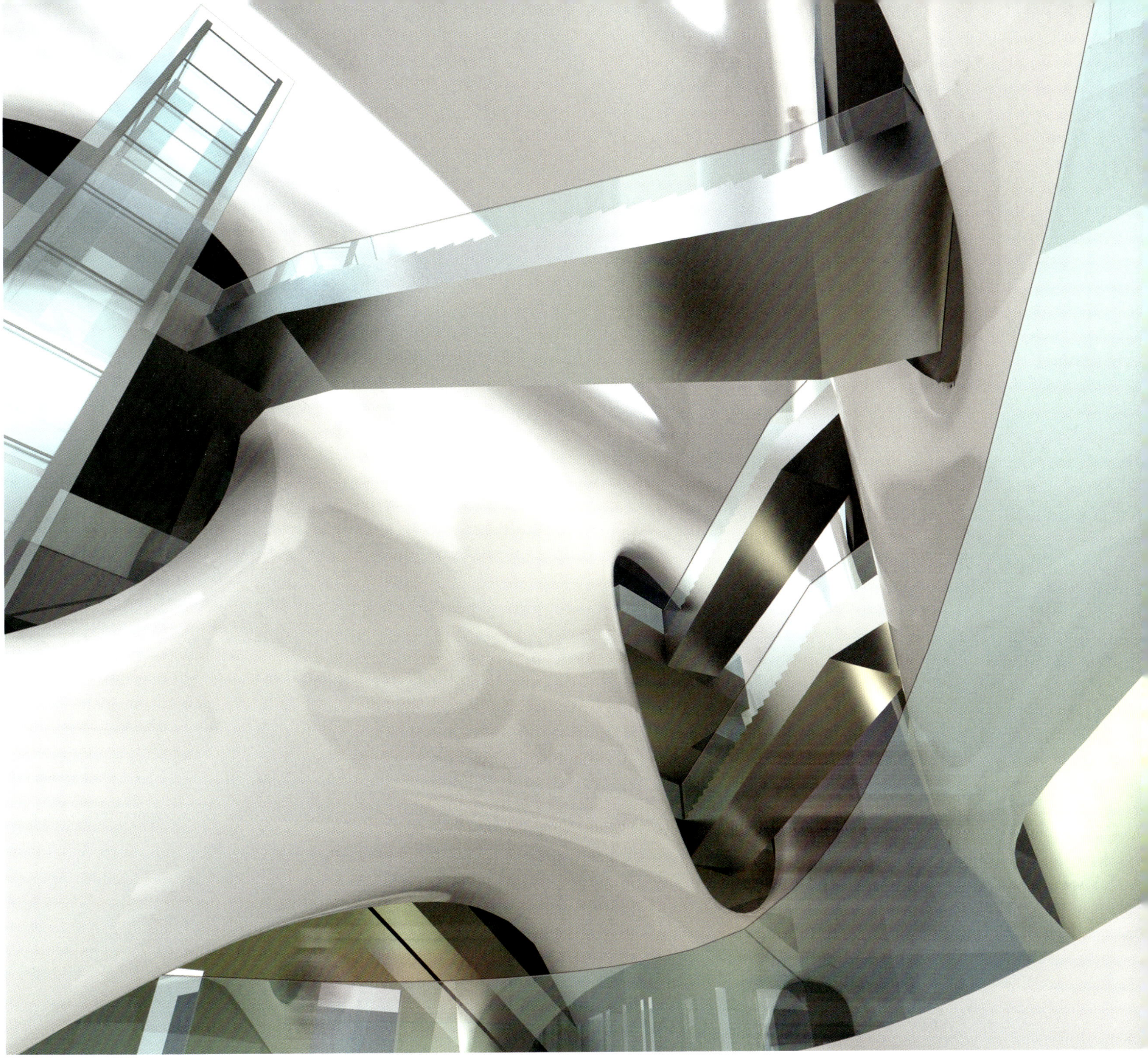

CHINA_LINGANG NEW CITY **MARITIM MUSEUM**

ARCHITECTS: GMP - ARCHITEKTEN VON GERKAN, MARG UND PARTNER_**STATICS:** WERNER SOBEK_**COMPLETION:** 2009_**TYPE:** MARITIME MUSEUM_**GROSS FLOOR AREA:** 46,400 M² _**PHOTOS:** HANS GEORG ESCH (470, 471 A., B. R.), JAN SIEFKE (471 B. L.)

THE ARCHITECTURE

This museum houses an exhibition of China's naval history and lies in the middle of Lingang New City, approximately 60 kilometers south of Shanghai. In perfect symmetry, two parallel four-floor wings define the rectilinear plan and the functional layout of the museum quarters. The museum is organized around a raised courtyard on a single-story pedestal, which accommodates all functions of the museum. The analogy of a ship in a port is developed further by the abstract symbolism of the two "sails" located almost at the center of the museum square. The 58 meter tall, concave grid shells lean against each other, touching only at one intersection point approximately 40 meters above the ground.

THE COLLECTION

The Maritime Museum in Lingang New City, China opened in 2010 and is the largest comprehensive maritime museum in the country. It is also the world's largest professional maritime museum. The project began in 2006 and was co-founded by the Ministry of Transport and the Shanghai Municipal Government. The museum showcases 20,000 items, including several thousand cultural relics, which are displayed in six exhibition halls. The six separate display spaces include the maritime history hall, the ships hall, the harbor hall, the marine and maritime safety hall, sailors' hall and military navigation hall. The museum has three floors for different exhibitions. The first floor showcases exhibits related to naval history in China and includes different types of ships, information about sailors, and China's fishing industry. The second hosts displays relating to sea ports, Chinese marines and recreational maritime sports and activities, while the third floor provides space for astrology and space exhibits. The most famous exhibit is a replica of a giant Ming dynasty boat that is displayed in the first floor hall. It is rebuilt at a 1:1 ratio in full accordance with the ship model, which was used by the famous Chinese Ming dynasty adventurer Zheng He. The replica boat can actually sail in the sea and visitors are invited to experience what it is like on board.

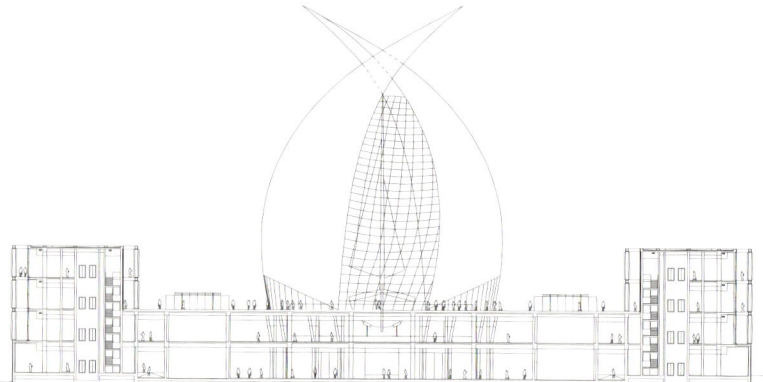

left: Building cross-section and view of steel/aluminum sails_Weight supporter of one of the sails Glazing between sails_Contact point between the two shells. right: Façade on river side_Façade on land side_Bird's eye view.

CHINA_SHANGHAI-PUDONG **SHANGHAI-PUDONG MUSEUM**

ARCHITECTS: GMP – ARCHITEKTEN VON GERKAN, MARG UND PARTNER WITH SIADR, SHANGHAI INSTITUTE OF ARCHITECTURAL DESIGN & RESEARCH CO., LTD._**COMPLETION:** 2005_**TYPE:** CULTURE MUSEUM_**GROSS FLOOR AREA:** 41,000 M² _**PHOTOS:** CHRISTIAN GAHL, BERLIN

THE ARCHITECTURE

The Shanghai-Pudong Museum is one of the most important urban projects in this new city district. It was created to comprehensively document and archive the district's history and development. At the same time, modern multifunctional and open exhibition spaces were created to inform the public, through a permanent exhibition and special exhibitions, on selected topics. Three elements form the building complex: the square-shaped horizontal glass body with exhibition halls, a much broader, four meter high base with surrounding stairs, which accommodates the archives, and a bar-shaped administration building on the eastern side.

THE COLLECTION

This museum in Shanghai-Pudong is one of the most important urban projects in this developing district. Opposite the city of Shanghai, a new "Manhattan" is being implemented on the other side of the river, with the developing area of Pudong already boasting the highest office and hotel building in China. The aim of the new museum is to document and archive the area's history and development, so that its culture and past are not lost as the city changes and modernizes. The exhibition spaces have been designed to house both permanent and temporary displays about the city's history and development. The base of the museum lifts the main building containing the exhibition halls above the level of the surrounding streets; this helps to emphasize the importance of the complex. Simplicity and reduction of the materials dominate the clear cube that is based on a square floor layout. The façade of the upper part of the structure serves as a medium between the museum and the public. The transparent, glass skin displays the content of the archive in small, patterned segments, which come together to form a complete picture when viewed from a distance. The glazed exterior connects the city and passersby to the museums exhibitions, generating a new interest in the displays.

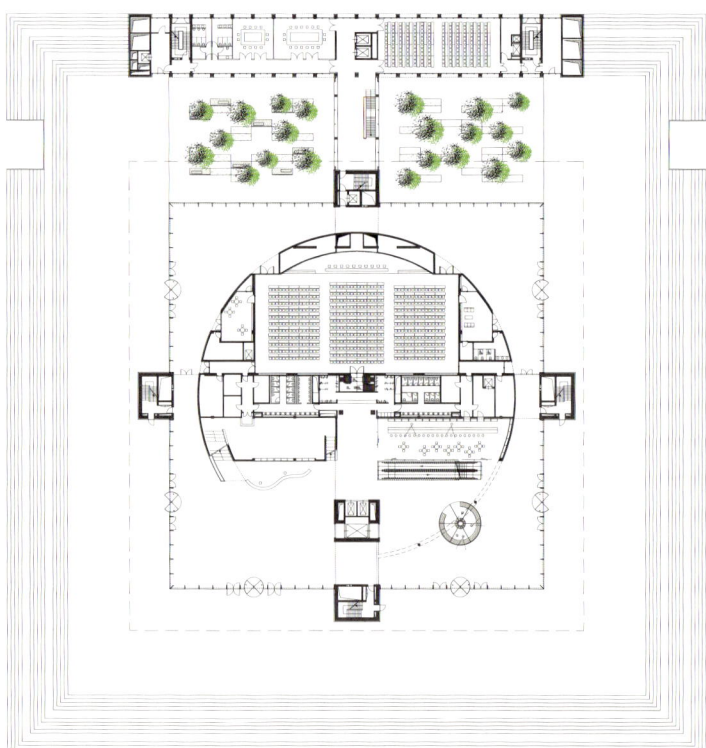

left: Entrance level_Composition of base, glass panneling, cube_View by night. right: Façade Interior.

CHINA_SHUIXI VILLAGE

EXHIBITION HALL OF NEW 4TH ARMY JIANGNAN HEADQUARTER

ARCHITECTS: ZHANG LEI / AZL ARCHITECTS **_COMPLETION:** 2007
TYPE: HISTORY MUSEUM **_GROSS FLOOR AREA:** 4,200 M²
PHOTOS: AZL ARCHITECTS / LV HENGZHONG (474, 475 A., 477),
AZL ARCHITECTS /JIA FANG (475 B., 476)

THE ARCHITECTURE

Situated in Liyang, located 70 kilometers southeast of Nanjing, the New 4th Army Jiangnan Headquarters Exhibition Hall was built to commemorate the history of the New 4th Army lead by the Communist party in the 1930s. Fragmental granite was used as the façade cladding of the strictly cubic volume, strongly expressing the monumental function of this project. The windows are tilted in line with the mosaic of the stone slabs. The courtyard was changed from an internal volume to an external façade, featuring dramatic red sections that indicate its revolutionary nature.

THE COLLECTION

This museum seeks to portray the complicated and eventful history of the New 4th Army. The army began as the 20th Army, a military formation of the People's Volunteer Army, during the Korean War. After the Japanese invasion, the 20th Army became incorporated into the New 4th Army. At this time it was first under the command of the Jiangnan Headquarters, with the nickname, "Jiangnan Anti-Japanese Righteous and Brave Army". After 1941, the army was reformed as 1st Division, New 4th Army. One of the most infamous incidents in the army's history is known as the Wannan Incident, which occurred in January 1941, during the second Sino-Japanese war. During this time, the Chinese Civil war was supposedly suspended to unite Communists and Nationalists against the Japanese. However, on January 5, Communist forces were surrounded in Maolin Township by an 80,000 strong Nationalist force, which then attacked. The Communist New 4th Army suffered a high number of losses. On 13th January, in an attempt to save his men, Ye Ting, the New 4th Army's political commissioner went to the opposition's headquarters to negotiate new terms. He was captured and killed. Only 2,000 people, led by Huang Huoxing and Fu Qiutao, managed to survive.

left: Ground floor plan_Southern façade. right: New building and old gate_North-east side.

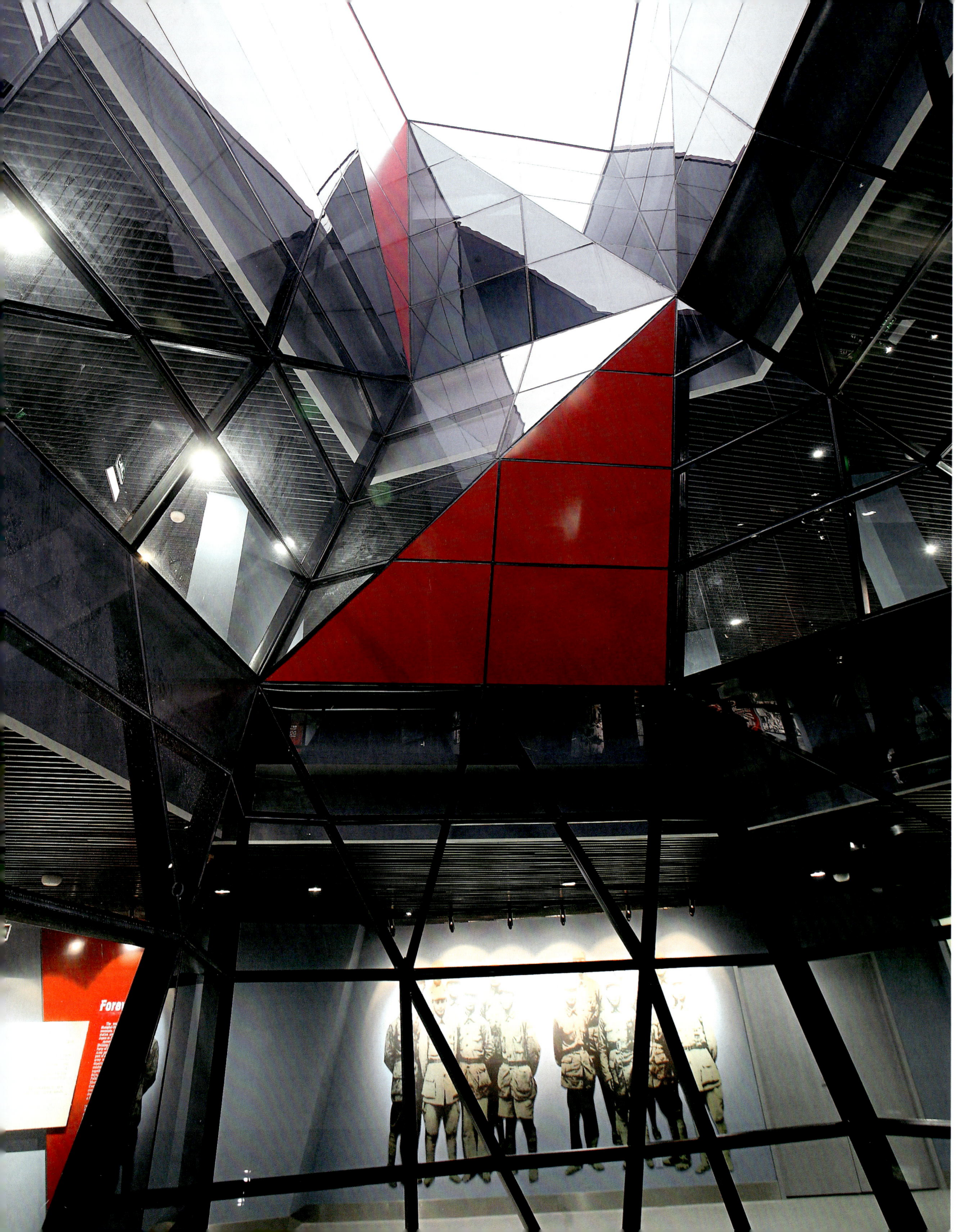

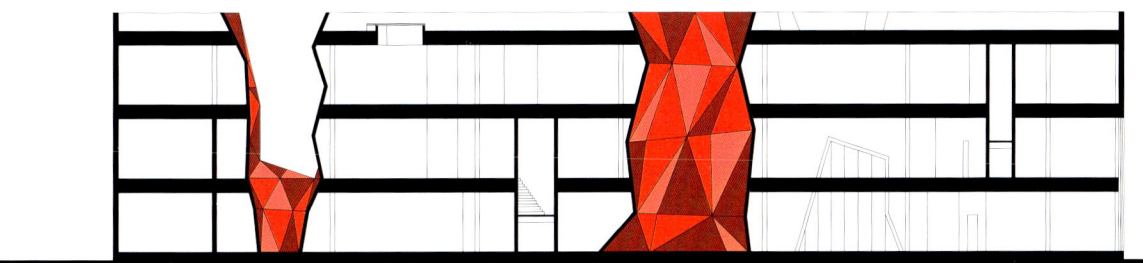

left: Courtyard in glass. right: Section_Entrance façade_East façade_Entrance, north-east side.

ISRAEL_HOLON **DESIGN MUSEUM HOLON**

ARCHITECTS: RON ARAD ARCHITECTS_**COMPLETION:** 2010
TYPE: DESIGN AND ARCHITECTURE MUSEUM_**GROSS FLOOR AREA:**
4,100 M² _**PHOTOS:** ASA BRUNO (479, 480, 481 L., B. R.), JAMES
FOSTER (478 B. L.), JESSICA LAWRENCE (478 B. R., 481 A. R.)

THE ARCHITECTURE

The DMH is the first national museum dedicated to design in Israel. The
publicly-funded building is situated in a self-proclaimed culture capital and
regional town south of Tel Aviv. It incorporates two primary galleries, an education wing, and several exterior spaces that capitalize on the local climatic
conditions which enable almost year-round utilization. The museum's distinc-
tive structural envelope is made of five weathering Corten steel curvilinear
bands — end-to-end over a kilometer long —, which provide it with an iconic
contextual presence and acrobatic structural support, and that serve as shading devices and visual threads through the museum.

THE COLLECTION

The Design Museum Holon in Israel is a new building which acts as a symbol
of the ongoing development of the city. Over the past ten years, the city has
introduced education programs, cultural festivals and opened museums as
part of its goal to introduce positive change and culture. The foremost aim of
the museum is to inspire and challenge design ideas and concepts, as well as
to question and develop the public's perception of design and the impact it has
upon an individual's life. USD $17million has been invested into this project,
which hosts a wide range of temporary exhibitions. A recent exhibition,
entitled "The State of Things" reflects the museum's ambitions to address issues of consumer culture, contemporary design and the impact of design. The
exhibition featured over 100 objects, concerning the practice, consumption
and usage of designs from ordinary household items to life-saving technologies. Each of the objects in the exhibition is representative of trends and
reflects our time and culture accurately, thus each object is a reference to the
current state of things. The museum's website also features a blog, offering
an in-depth look at the process of choosing and developing the institutions
various exhibitions and presentations.

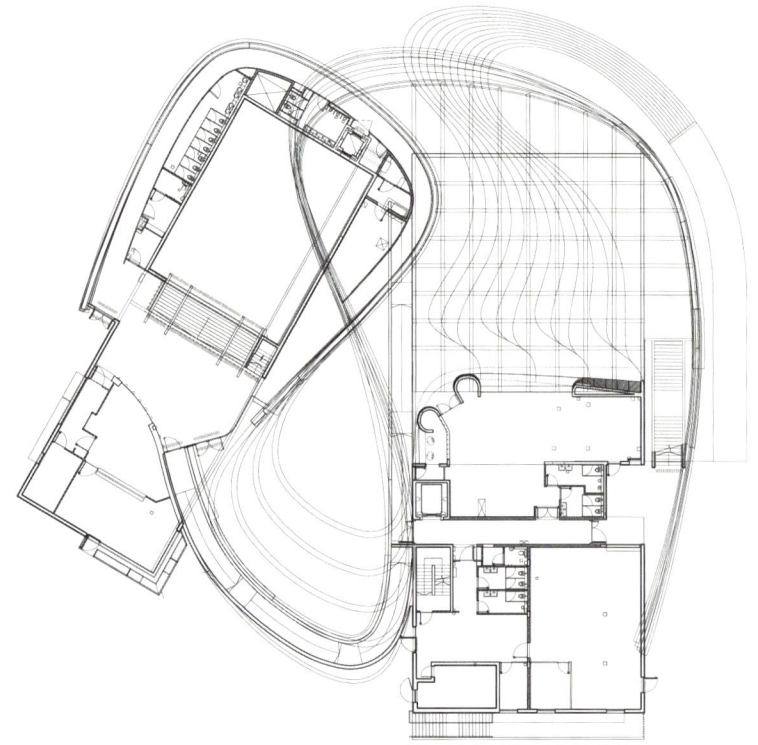

left: Ground floor_Entrance area_Stairs and ribbons. right: Airloop and façade.

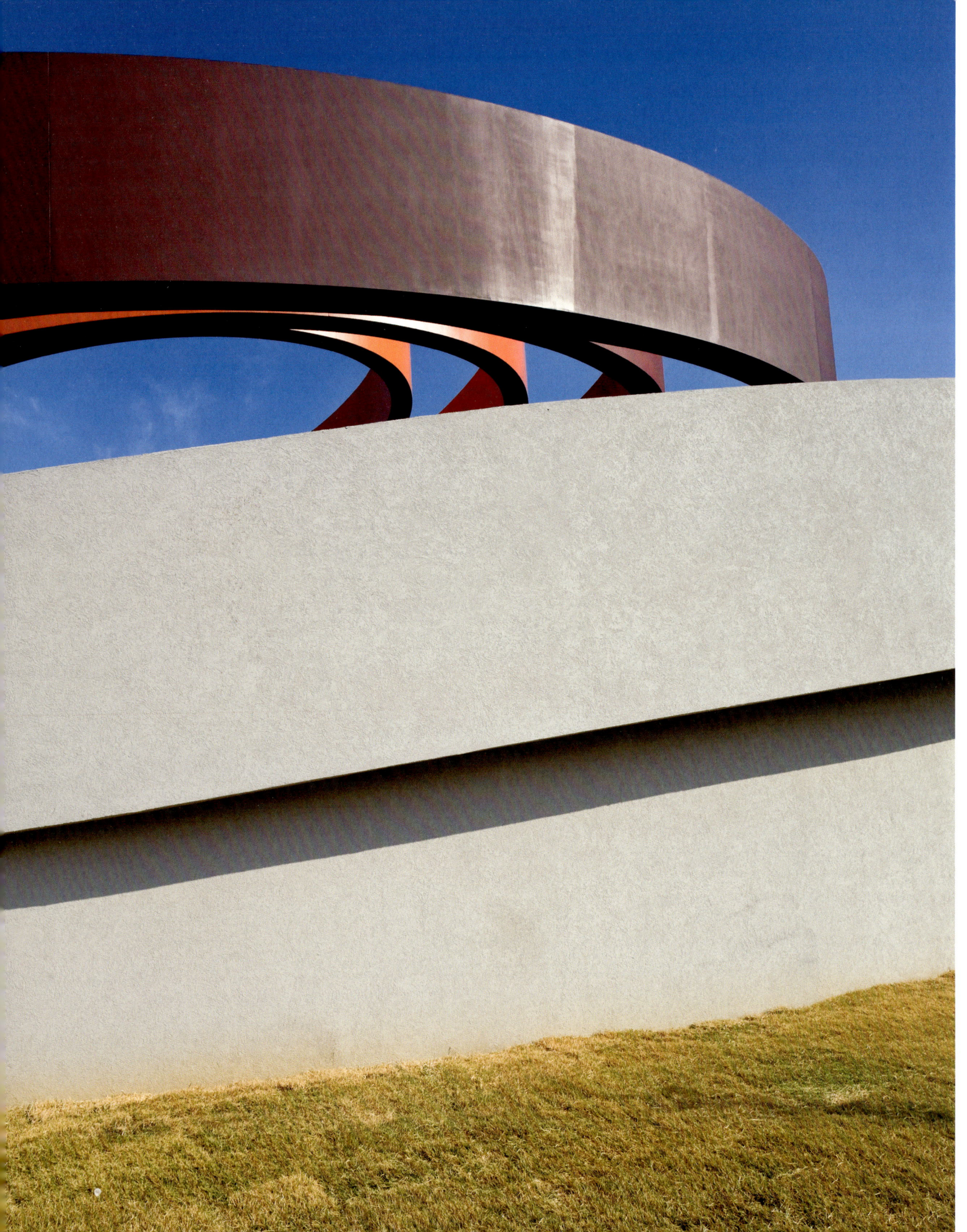

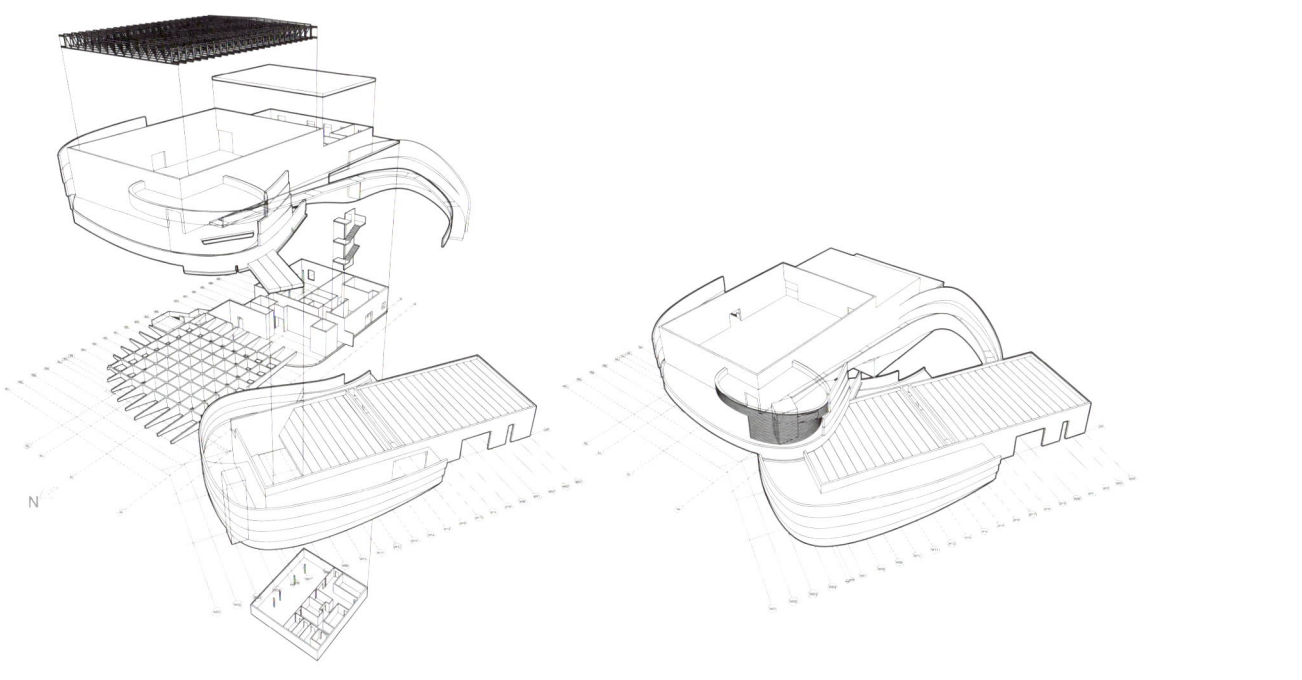

left: Loops above concrete. right: Structural diagram_Exhibition room_Loop above passage_Exterior.

JAPAN_MATSUNOYAMA

ECHIGO-MATSUNOYAMA MUSEUM OF NATURAL SCIENCE

ARCHITECTS: TAKAHARU & YUI TEZUKA ARCHITECTS / MIAS
COMPLETION: 2003_**TYPE:** SCIENCE MUSEUM
GROSS FLOOR AREA: 1,248 M²
PHOTOS: KATSUHISA KIDA

THE ARCHITECTURE

Great emphasis was put on incorporating the environment's natural and climatic settings into the concept of this facility. Located in the mountains of Matsunoyama, which are known for their heavy winter snowfalls, the surrounding Japanese beech trees get flattened each winter before they grow strong enough again in spring. The structure's pitched cross-sectional layout was inspired by the regional sheds that protect local roads from the snow. Shaped like a snake, the horizontal plan follows the pattern of the paths surrounding the site. The outer shell is entirely made of 6 millimeter thick welded Corten steel plates, which contract almost 20 centimeters in length during winter.

THE COLLECTION

The Echigo-Matsunoyama Museum of Natural Science is known for its unusual architecture, impressive butterfly collection, and the heavy snow that annually engulfs it. During the winter, the snow can reach a depth of seven meters, burying everything but the building's lookout tower. The building was designed with the intense weight of this huge amount of snow in mind, as the structure must bear winter after winter of deep snow. Inside the museum, large windows allow visitors to see the snow piled up outside, and occasionally, so it is said, the life forms that are suspended within it. To withstand the enormous pressure of the snow, the windows are made of seven centimeters thick composite acrylic, the same material used in aquariums. Nevertheless, the stress put on the structure is so great that the building can be heard "groaning" in the winter. While the tower serves as the only prominent landmark in winter's snow-filled landscape, it also offers sweeping views of the surrounding mountains and meadows. The museum hosts a large butterfly collection, and the so-called "Amusing Boxes." Contained in around 200 drawers, this display is a collection of "oddments from the nature and culture of Matsunoyama." Among the items to be found in the exhibit are snake skins, cicada shells, and objects made in the museum's workshops.

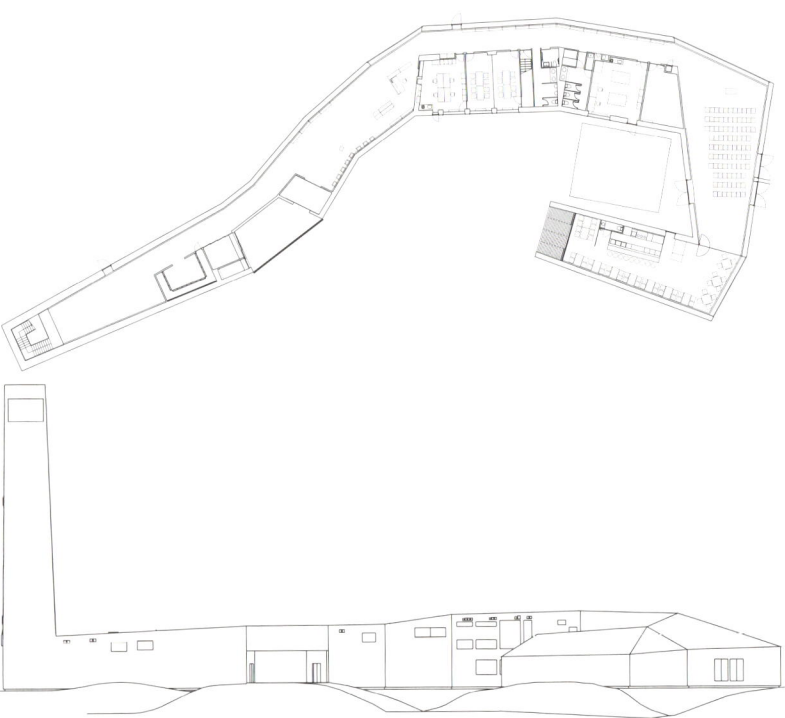

left: Ground floor plan and elevation_Exterior_Museum in the winter. right: Façade_Exhibition_View into the café.

ARCHITECTS: MAKOTO YOKOMIZO / AAT+MAKOTO YOKOMIZO ARCHITECTS, INC._**STRUCTURAL ENGINEERS:** ARUP, MITSUHIRO KANADA_**COMPLETION:** 2005_**TYPE:** ART MUSEUM_**GROSS FLOOR AREA:** 2,463.5 M²_**PHOTOS:** SHIGERU OHNO (486 B. L., 487 B.), CHRISTOFFER RUDQUIST (486 B. R.), CHRISTIAN RICHTERS (487 A.)

THE ARCHITECTURE

This museum layout consists of 33 circles. The size and location of each circle responds to the curators' requests. This circle planning process, like an arrangement of soap bubbles, resulted in a "self-optimized" design. The final layout of the museum is only one choice among many other possibilities. Each circle has a different function and a different finish, with the perfect continuity of the round space only interrupted by the passage from one cylinder to another. The museum interior offers many different experiences. The spaces between the circular rooms are used as gardens and contain various local plants. All pieces of the various cylinders were pre-fabricated in a steel factory and then assembled on site.

THE COLLECTION

Situated in the town in which he was born, the Tomihoro Hoshino Museum exhibits the poetry and artwork of Japanese artist Tomihoro Hoshino. Tomohiro Hoshino was completely paralyzed from the neck down in a horrific accident at the age of 24 and after this time spent nine years in hospital. It was during these years of rehabilitation therapy that he learnt to draw flowers and write poems, using just his mouth. At 33 he had his first exhibition in Gunma and went on to publish many books and essays. As his talent developed, his collection became world famous. The new Tomihiro Hoshino art museum was built to celebrate his life's work and opened in April 2005. Hoshino's written poetry is often compared to the Japanese form of Haiku, in which not what is said, but what is not said is of the greatest importance. Hoshino's poetry and art are always closely linked to nature and his surroundings. Though the original written material exhibited in the museum is in Japanese, the museum also provides a translation into English. Appropriately, the Tomihiro Hoshino museum is one of the few places in Japan with facilities for the disabled. Outside the museum is a small garden and views of the river below.

left: Plan_Museum in landscape_Exterior. right: Lounge facing lake Kusaki_Lobby_Exhibition rooms.

JAPAN_MINATO-KU, TOKYO **NATIONAL ART CENTER**

ARCHITECTS: KISHO KUROKAWA ARCHITECT & ASSOCIATES
DESIGN CONSORTIUM: NIHON SEKKEI, INC._**COMPLETION:** 2006
TYPE: ART MUSEUM_**GROSS FLOOR AREA:** 49,834 M²
PHOTOS: KOJI KOBAYASHI SPIRAL, TOKYO

THE ARCHITECTURE

This building is made up of seven enormous display rooms without columns. Each of 2,000 square meters, these spaces include a library, an auditorium, a restaurant, cafés and a museum shop. The floor area of the center totals approximately 50,000 square meters, making it Japan's largest art gallery. It will not be used as a space for archiving works of art, but as a space for exhibiting public open exhibits and traveling exhibits. The atrium façade, an enormous transparent undulation, was designed to rival the mechanical display space. As the trees surrounding the museum grow, they will enclose the atrium in a forested public space. The atrium space contains two inverted cones, the upper portion of each housing the restaurant and cafés.

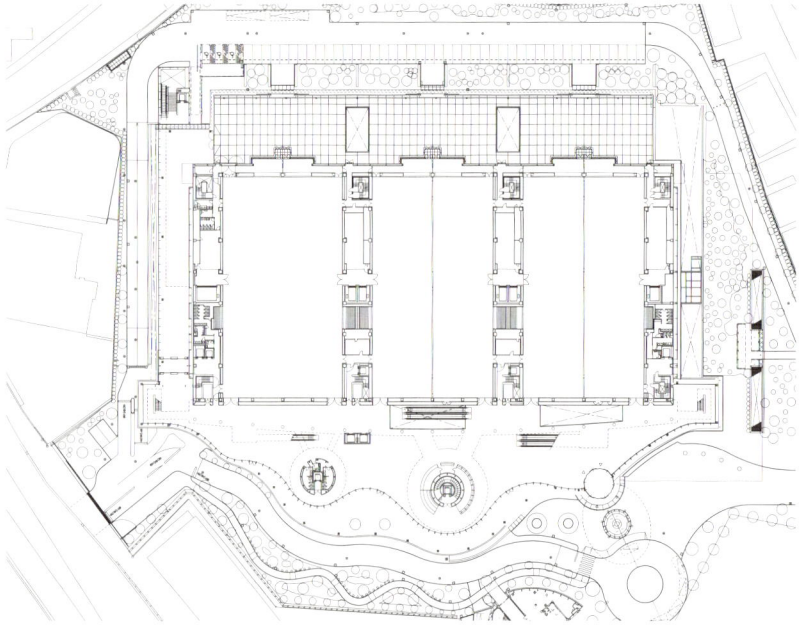

THE COLLECTION

Located in Tokyo, an international city that attracts people, products, and information from all over Japan and the rest of the world, the National Art Center Tokyo, is the fifth art institution to be realized under the umbrella of the Independent Administrative Institution National Museum of Art. The other four projects are The National Museum of Modern Art Tokyo, The National Museum of Modern Art Kyoto, The National Museum of Western Art, and The National Museum of Art Osaka. The National Art Center Tokyo is a unique and innovative art exhibition facility. The institution mainly serves as a venue for temporary exhibitions, which allows it to change according to new trends and ideas, keeping the museum current and interesting for its visitors. The center also provides educational opportunities through its outreach educational programs. Recent exhibitions include "Post Impressionism: 115 Masterpieces from the Musée d'Orsay". This exhibition featured nearly 100 masterpiece paintings from the legendary collections of the Musée d'Orsay and explored the various facets of painting from the late 19th century into the early 20th century, beginning with the roots in Impressionism, providing a fresh perspective on the bold challenges taken up by the Post-Impressionists, and the rich legacy of art that they created.

left: Second floor plan_General view_Perspective. right: Façade detail.

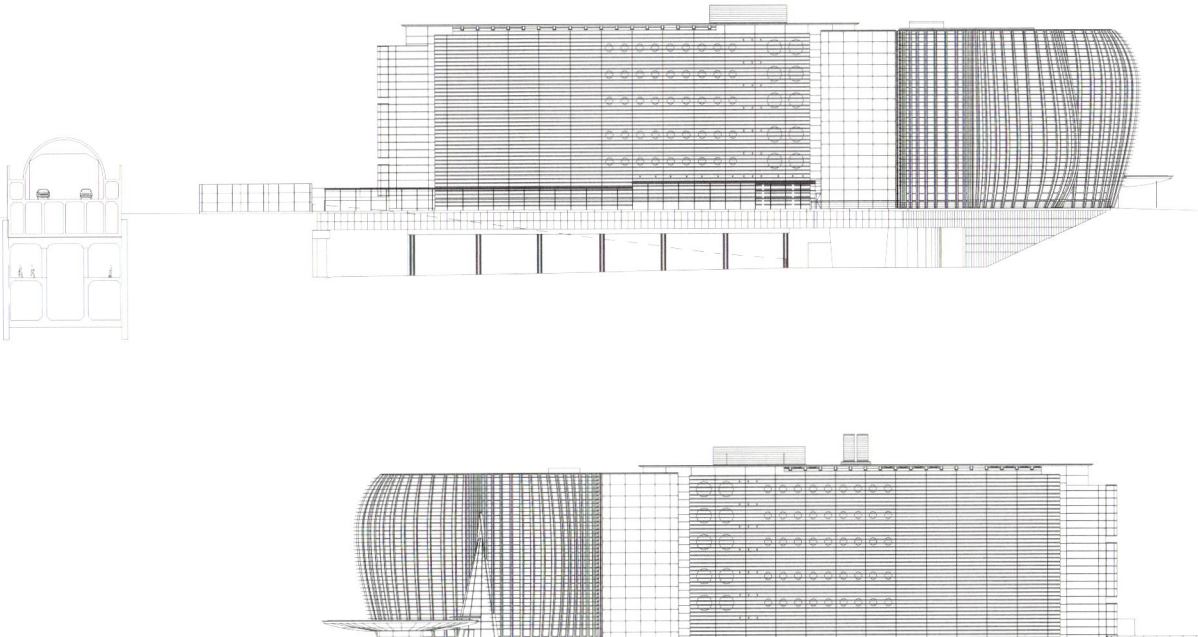

left: Atrium with restaurant. right: West and east elevation_Façade_Detail_Façade.

ARCHITECTS: ATELIER HITOSHI ABE_**COMPLETION:** 2005_**TYPE:** ART MUSEUM_**GROSS FLOOR AREA:** 220 M² _**PHOTOS:** DAICI ANO, SENDAI

The Architecture
Located in a small town on a hilly site with a view of the Pacific Ocean, this design for a private art gallery was created to permanently display eight sculptures owned by the client. Taking into account the situation of the town and the program of the building, it was decided that the space of the art gallery itself should be potent enough to stimulate local artistic activities. The building was not intended to be a "white cube" able to accommodate any type of exhibition, but a "cathedral" and an aggregation of specific settings for exhibiting each of the sculptures.

The Collection
Opened in 2006, the Kanno Museum in Sendai, Japan, is a small museum built in the hills overlooking the ocean. The museum houses a permanent collection of eight modern sculptures owned by a private collector, with a focus on Western works, such as Greco, Bourdelle and Fazzini. Each of the sculptures has a specifically created exhibition space within the museum, this organization makes it possible for visitors to walk around the sculptures and view each one from a different angle. Each space is made of embossed 3.2 millimeter steel plates. In addition to exhibiting the sculptures, the museum also hosts concerts and lectures, with the aim of sharing a vibrant culture with visitors and inhabitants of the region alike. The city of Sendai is also famous for other works of architectural interest, such as the Miyagi Stadium by Hitoshi Abe and the Sendai mediatheque by Toyo Ito. The city of Sendai is also famous for being Japan's greenest city, mainly because of its huge number of trees. These trees are decorated in the winter with thousands of lights, in an event called the Pageant of Starlight, which brings many visitors to the city.

left: Section_Exterior view from east_Exterior view from west. right: At the ground floor_At the mezzanine_Entrance gallery at the top floor_Embossed interior wall.

JAPAN_TAMA-SHI,TOKYO **GENJI PAPER SCULPTURE MUSEUM**

ARCHITECTS: CELL SPACE ARCHITECTS, MUTSUE HAYAKUSA
COMPLETION: 2003_**TYPE:** ART MUSEUM_**GROSS FLOOR AREA:** 1,410 M² _**PHOTOS:** SATOSHI ASAKAWA, TOKYO

THE ARCHITECTURE

Finer and more delicate materials than usual were used to achieve a balance with the artist's works. The architects experimented with many industrial woven materials that have a similar structure to Japanese paper which is made of plant fibers, ultimately a thin stainless mesh was selected. Laminated glass plates with lustrous stainless mesh achieve the desired effect for the partition of the hall and the façade. Thus, two opposite effects are superimposed, one is the reduced image visible through the stainless mesh and the other is the enlarged reflection on the glass surfaces.

THE COLLECTION

The Genji Paper Sculpture Museum exhibits Japanese paper carvings and sculptures created by Kiyoharu Uchiumi. The sculptures include interpretations of some scenes from the Tales of Genji, the masterpiece written by Murasaki Shikiby in the Heian period but the artist also recreates many figures from traditional Japanese tales and legends and is often asked to create figures for Japanese Television channel NHK. The museum not only displays these works, but also arranges them together with appropriate lighting, background and music, to give the exhibits a stronger presence and to help provide a context. The figures created by Uchiumi are left in their original paper color, while different colored background lights provide atmosphere and feeling to the display. Partitions within the museum are made of laminated glass, and inserted with a thin steel mesh. This design is thought to give a dream-like quality to the exhibits by dividing a visitor's view into different sections so that not only the whole object, but also its individual parts can be considered.

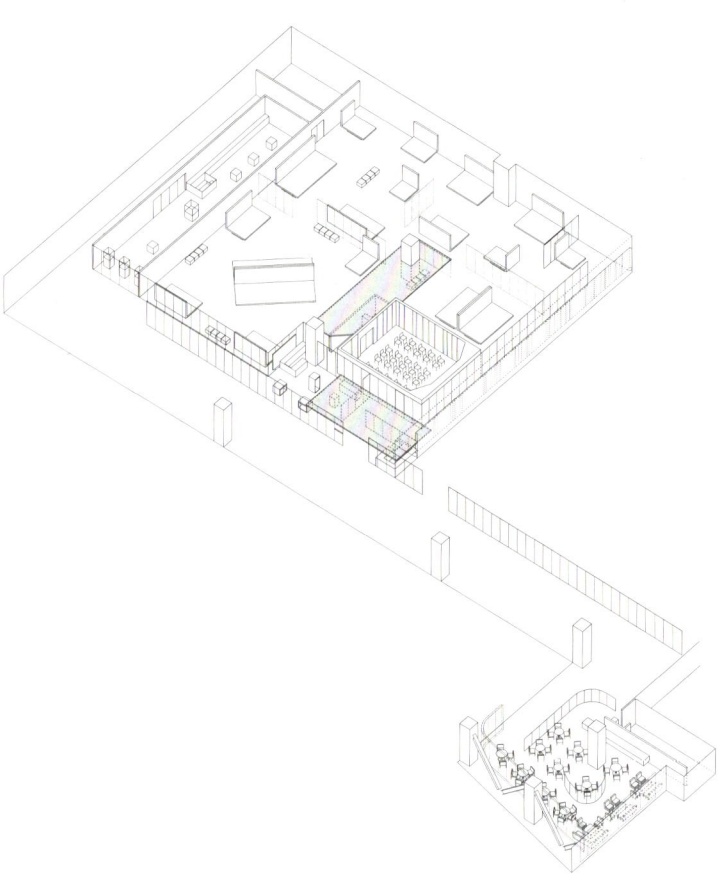

left: Axonometry_Entrance hall_Café. right: Time tunnel_Museum shop_Exhibition hall.

JAPAN_TOKAMACHI CITY **MATSUDAI CULTURAL VILLAGE MUSEUM**

ARCHITECTS: MVRDV_**COMPLETION:** 2003_**TYPE:** ART MUSEUM
GROSS FLOOR AREA: 2,770 M²_**PHOTOS:** ROB 'T HART

THE ARCHITECTURE

The village is located in the mountains of the Niigata prefecture. Once every three years, the "Niigata Art Triennial" is held in the region. During this festival, the building functions as the main stage of events and as an exhibition space. The building is raised on "legs", creating a public space underneath, that is snow-free in winter and dry and shaded during summer, where performances and concerts can be held. These "legs" form the physical structure, while at the same time providing access to the building. On the rooftop, a "rocky" landscape is formed by the structural demands of the leg-shaped bridges. The rooftop provides a platform for viewing the mountains and the artworks.

THE COLLECTION

The Matsudai Cultural Village Museum is located in the village of Matsudai. Due to the region's mountainous topography, the temperature of the region fluctuates greatly. The summers are hot and humid while the winters bring a thick layer of snow to the area. The Cultural Village Museum was built with the intention of using the center every three years as the main stage for the regional Echigo-Tsumari Art Festival. The building is raised on "legs," creating a snow-free zone in the winter and a shaded area in the summer. The architects of the building also collaborated with individual artists to create a series of unique exhibition spaces. Each artist was given a special space, painted a chosen color, in which to display their artwork. Fabrice Hybert's "Autour du Feu, Dans le Desert" is the most striking space. His work is situated in a cylindrical room that is painted dark green in color. On the wall of the room are 1,001 small holes with a light mounted in each one. A traditional Japanese hearth has also been placed in the center of the space, and seats are arranged against the wall, around the hearth, in an attempt to re-create a traditional Japanese gathering place.

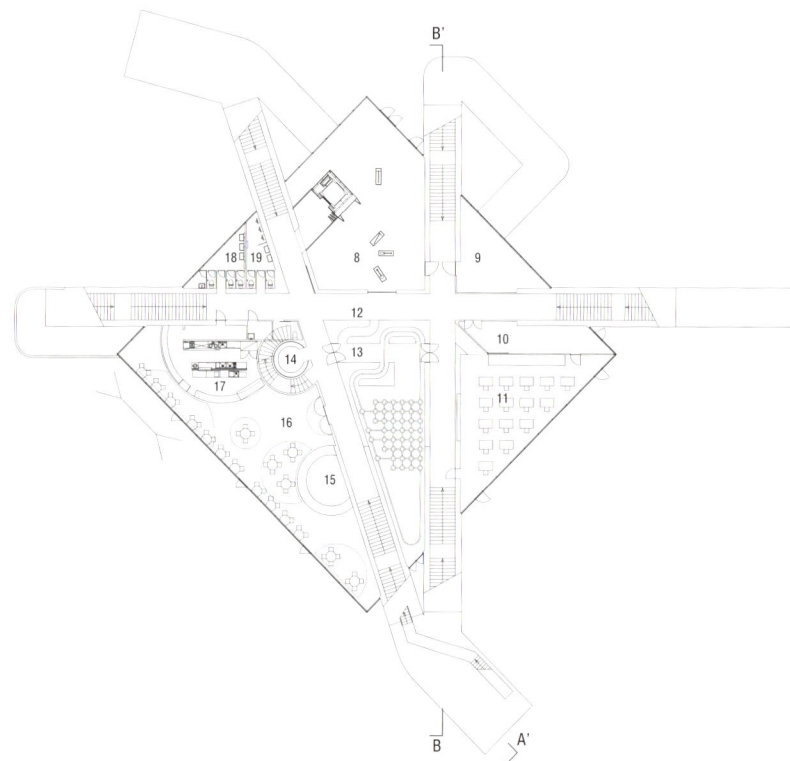

left: First floor plan_Exterior_Rooftop platform. right: Façade.

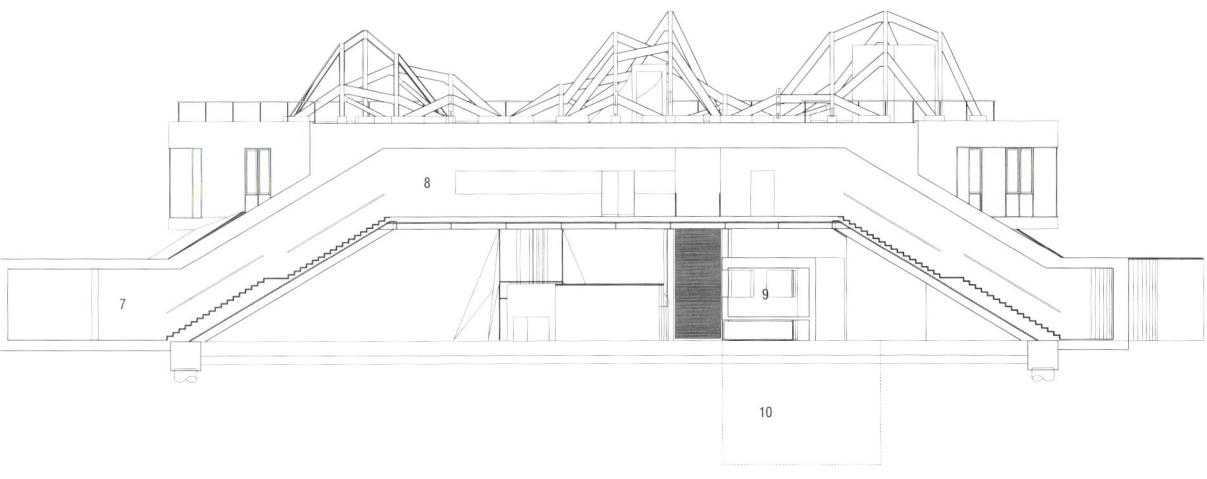

7　8　9　10

left: Café. right: Section_Public space underneath the building_Exhibition area_Exit to upper floor and restroom.

KOREA_SEOUL **LEEUM SAMSUNG MUSEUM OF ART**

ARCHITECTS: OFFICE FOR METROPOLITAN ARCHITECTURE (OMA)
LANDSCAPE ARCHITECTS: INSIDE OUTSIDE_**COMPLETION:** 2004
TYPE: ART MUSEUM_**GROSS FLOOR AREA:** 13,100 M² _**PHOTOS:**
OFFICE FOR METROPOLITAN ARCHITECTURE (OMA) (500),
PHILIPPE RUAULT (501)

THE ARCHITECTURE

This project, located in the residential district of Hannam-Dong near the city center, is comprised of three buildings by OMA, Mario Botta and Jean Nouvel. The three buildings converge into a central, multipurpose space that constitutes the lobby and information area. OMA's building covers a gross area of 13,100 square meters and houses temporary contemporary exhibitions, media, and office spaces. The dominant feature is a massive black concrete box. This box is suspended within a large excavation in the undulating topography, creating varying light conditions within the space. Visitor circulation is conceived around the idea of experiencing the black box by descending under it, into it and moving above it.

THE COLLECTION

The Leeum Samsung Museum of Art is a Korean institution dedicated to the preservation and representation of Korean art. The Samsung Foundation of Culture was established in 1965 and has committed itself to the preservation and exhibition of Korean cultural heritage. The foundation also operates the Ho-Am Art Gallery and Museum and the Rodin Gallery. The Leeum building is made up of three separate parts. One is devoted to the exhibition of traditional Korean artwork. The second showcases both modern and contemporary art by Korean and international artists and the third, the Child Education and Culture Center, offers educational programs aimed at students and children. The museum offers a comprehensive overview of Korean culture, with exhibits ranging from the prehistoric era to the Joseon Dynasty (1392-1910). The collection features 36 artifacts, which are designated as National Treasures and another 79 designated as Treasures. The huge scope of the institution's collections provides visitors with the opportunity to explore the art and culture of Korea as it evolved throughout history.

left: Elevations_Bird's eye view_Roof terrace. right: Interior_Exterior.

KOREA_SEOUL **SEOUL NATIONAL UNIVERSITY MUSEUM**

ARCHITECTS: OFFICE FOR METROPOLITAN ARCHITECTURE (OMA)
COMPLETION: 2005_**TYPE:** ART MUSEUM_**GROSS FLOOR AREA:**
4,478 M² _**PHOTOS:** PHILIPPE RUAULT

THE ARCHITECTURE
This museum is defined by its location on the side of a small hill, close to the entrance of the university. The building's shape was conceived as a basic rectangular box, theoretically sliced diagonally by the incline of the hill. This form is raised up on a small central core – the only point of contact with the ground — so the building is nearly fully cantilevered, extending up and down the hill. The museum's façade is translucent, revealing the structural steel truss work underneath. Outside and inside, free-flowing circulation was key to the thinking behind the building. The central core is an atrium with a square spiral staircase connecting the exhibition, education, library, and operations areas.

THE COLLECTION
The Seoul National University is a national research university in Seoul, Korea. It is ranked 24th in the world for its publications regarding data analysis from the Science Citation Index. Founded in 1946, the university was the first national university in South Korea and it has been recognized for its leading role in Korean Academia. The university has grown to such an extent that it is now comprised of 16 colleges and six professional schools, with a student body of around 30,000. The design for the Seoul National University Museum aims to emphasize the link between the university campus and the community. The building design and its situation create a pedestrian connection between the community and the campus. The museum features a collection of 237 registered works of art, collected by the Contemporary Art Department of the Seoul National University Museum, as well as 66 works of references and other related data. These collections are managed in rotation. The collections feature works from the Traditional Art Department of Seoul National University Museum as well as the collections from the College of Fine Arts, Seoul National University. Other works include endowments from the individual artists and private collectors.

exposed concrete   white concrete   plywood   white painted gypsum board   steel

left: Section_Façade_Staircase system. right: Exterior_Exhibition room_Exhibition under the roof.

UAE_SAADIYAT ISLAND **LOUVRE ABU DHABI**

ARCHITECTS: ATELIERS JEAN NOUVEL_**COMPLETION:** 2012
TYPE: ART MUSEUM_**GROSS FLOOR AREA:** 22,500 M²
PHOTOS: COURTESY OF THE ARCHITECTS

THE ARCHITECTURE
The Louvre aims to create a welcoming world that incorporates light and shadow as well as shimmering and calm places into a serene atmosphere. It is unusual to see a built archipelago in the sea, protected by a parasol flooded with a rain of light. Equally unusual is to access a museum by boat, or to find pontoons to reach it on foot from the coast. The project is based on the cupola, one of the major symbols of Arabic architecture. Here it is a modern proposal made evident by its obvious break with tradition. The dome is doubled and flat with a 180 meter diameter, offering a luminous geometry executed in a more random weaved material, which creates a shadow punctuated by sun bursts.

THE COLLECTION
The plans to establish a new Louvre museum in Abu Dhabi were announced by the Louvre in Paris in 2007. The project is part of a 30 year agreement between the city of Abu Dhabi and the French government. The museum will be located on the Saadiyat Island complex and will be approximately 24,000 square meters in size. This vast construction is expected to cost EUR 100 million to build. The building design features a web-patterned dome, which will allow the sunlight to filter through. Artwork from all over the world will be showcased by the museum, with a strong focus on the gap between Eastern and Western art. The aim of the agreement between the Louvre France and Abu Dhabi is not to create an "exact copy" of Paris' Louvre museum, but to transmit the values of this institution, namely, the desire to share France's culture and history with the Emirate of Abu Dhabi. However, the deal between the two museums has sparked much controversy, much of which has been led by art historian Didier Rykner. Protests led to 450 museums signing a petition against the deal between the Louvre and Abu Dhabi, arguing that "museums are not for sale." Rykner has also accused the Louvre of behaving like a corporation, putting profit maximization first.

left: Site plan_Flat double dome. right: Shadow punctuated with sun bursts_Exhibition area.

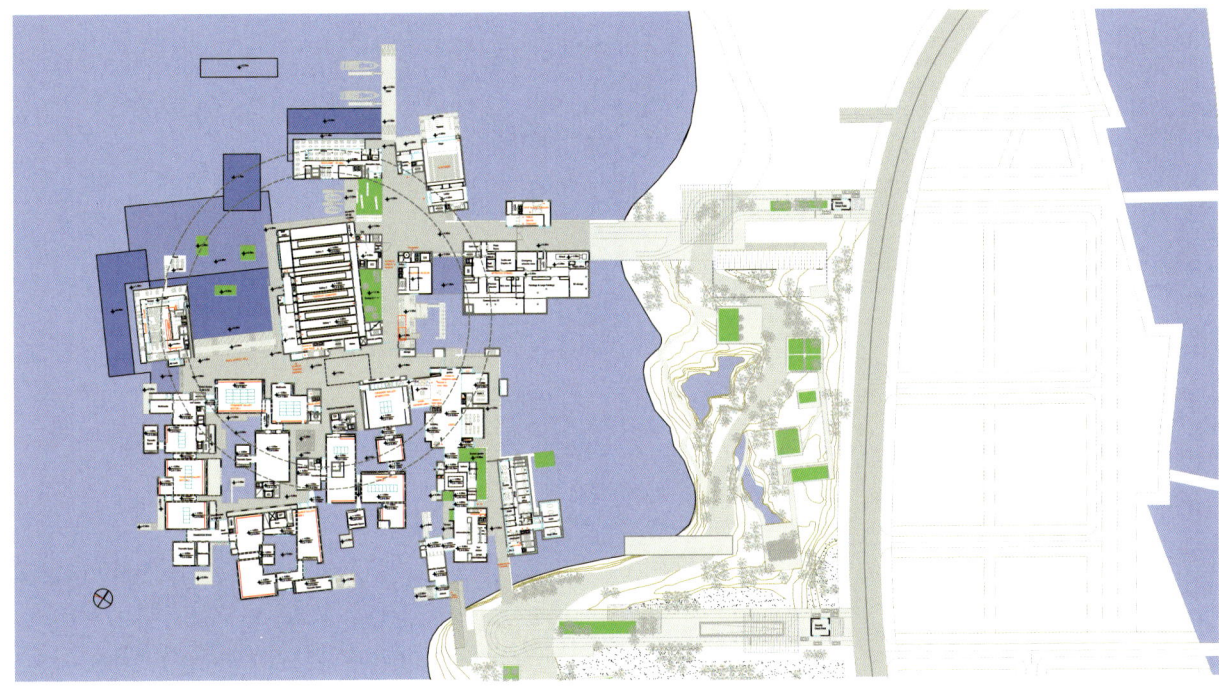

left: Interior. right: Ground floor plan_Exhibition area.

INDEX

ARCHITECTS

PROJECTS